D0712882

Law and Colonial Cultures

Law and Colonial Cultures advances a new perspective in world history, arguing that cultural practice and institutions – not just the global economy – shaped colonial rule and the international order. The book examines the shift from the multicentric law of early modern empires to the state-centered law of high colonialism. In the early modern world, the special legal status of cultural and religious minorities provided institutional continuity across empires. Colonial and post-colonial states developed in the nineteenth century in part as a response to conflicts over the legal status of indigenous subjects and cultural others. The book analyzes these processes by juxtaposing discussion of broad institutional change with microstudies of selected legal cases.

Lauren Benton is Professor of History at the New Jersey Institute of Technology and Rutgers University, Newark.

STUDIES IN COMPARATIVE WORLD HISTORY

Editors

Michael Adas, Rutgers University

Philip D. Curtin, The Johns Hopkins University

Other Books in the Series

Michael Adas, *Prophets of Rebellion: Millenarian Protest Movements Against the European Colonial Order* (1979)

Philip D. Curtin, *Cross-Cultural Trade in World History* (1984)

Leo Spitzer, *Lives in Between: Assimilation and Marginality in Austria, Brazil, West Africa, 1780–1945* (1989)

Philip D. Curtin, *The Rise and Fall of the Plantation Complex: Essays in Atlantic History* (1990)

John Thornton, *Africa and Africans in the Formation of the Atlantic World, 1400–1680* (1992)

Marshall G.S. Hodgson and Edmund Burke III (eds.), *Rethinking World History* (1993)

David Northrup, *Indentured Labor in the Age of Imperialism, 1834–1922* (1995)

Law and Colonial Cultures

Legal Regimes in World History, 1400–1900

LAUREN BENTON

NJIT and Rutgers University

CAMBRIDGE
UNIVERSITY PRESS

PUBLISHED BY THE PRESS SYNDICATE OF THE UNIVERSITY OF CAMBRIDGE
The Pitt Building, Trumpington Street, Cambridge, United Kingdom

CAMBRIDGE UNIVERSITY PRESS
The Edinburgh Building, Cambridge CB2 2RU, UK
40 West 20th Street, New York, NY 10011-4211, USA
10 Stamford Road, Oakleigh, VIC 3166, Australia
Ruiz de Alarcón 13, 28014 Madrid, Spain
Dock House, The Waterfront, Cape Town 8001, South Africa

http://www.cambridge.org

First published 2002

Printed in the United States of America

Typeface Palatino 10/13 pt.   *System* LATEX 2$_\varepsilon$ [TB]

A catalog record for this book is available from the British Library.

Library of Congress Cataloging in Publication Data
Benton, Lauren A.
Law and colonial cultures : legal regimes in world history, 1400–1900 / Lauren Benton.
    p.   cm. – (Studies in comparative world history)
Includes bibliographical references and index.
ISBN 0-521-80414-0 – ISBN 0-521-00926-x (pb.)
1. International law – History.   2. International relations and culture – History.   I. Title.
II. Series.

KZ1242 .B46   2001
341'.09 – dc21   2001035091

ISBN 0 521 80414 0 hardback
ISBN 0 521 00926 x paperback

For Eduardo,
Victoria, and Gabriela

Contents

ix

Acknowledgments

Some years ago I found myself in Philip Curtin's office at Johns Hopkins University asking if I could study comparative history with him. After I explained that I was interested in the history of the Iberian empires, he asked, "Why not world history?" I suggested broadening my studies to include West Africa. "World history would be better," he urged. I offered to label my interests Atlantic history and culture. "Study world history," he insisted. The training under Philip Curtin that followed – in world history – provided the foundation for this book, begun many years later and after many scholarly detours. I am grateful for his example, and for his unobtrusive mentoring over the years.

Many other scholars also provided inspiration and advice. Michael Adas encouraged the project from its earliest stages and offered sage guidance at critical points. I was able to spend a semester writing while a Samuel I. Golieb Fellow in Legal History at the NYU Law School, where William Nelson welcomed me into the Law and History Seminar. Many scholars read pieces of the work in progress and generously offered comments and encouragement. I want to thank especially Lawrence Rosen, Jane Collier, Bruce Kercher, James Muldoon, John Comaroff, Herman Bennett, Byron Cannon, Matthew Mirow, Davydd Greenwood, John Russell-Wood, Patricia Seed, Jack Greene, Richard Price, Richard Lariviere, Christopher Tomlins, Jerry Bentley, Yale Ferguson, and Peter Golden. My colleagues in the joint history department at NJIT and Rutgers University, Newark, responded patiently to queries about their diverse fields and offered uninvited but appreciated prodding. Over many good lunches, Cleo Kearns assured me that I was right – about everything.

I was lucky to find people willing to help me find my way in libraries and archives, too. David Hebb generously shared his expertise in using the India Office collections and the Public Record Office in London. John Charles Chasteen gave me pointers on using the judicial archives in Montevideo, and José Pedro Barrán kindly shared his own materials on law in Uruguay. Vince Harrison, Antonia Moon, and Jennifer Howes of the British Library and Nancy Brown of the University of New Mexico Library gave invaluable assistance in locating documents in their collections. I received excellent service from the interlibrary loan staffs at NJIT and Rutgers University, Newark, and Michael Byrnes at NJIT assisted in gathering bibliographic information.

Preliminary research was supported by a small grant from the Spencer Foundation on cross-cultural legal advocacy, and I was able to conduct research in Uruguay thanks to a Fulbright grant. Trips to London would not have been possible without the hospitality of Jane Waldfogel and David Hebb.

The best kind of help came from my family. The book would have taken much longer without Charlotte Benton's gentle, but frequent, queries about its progress. Eduardo, Victoria, and Gabriela Garcia managed to agree that I should keep working even when it took me away from them for too long. I will remember with sadness that the writing was punctuated by the illness and death of my father, George Benton, who taught me by example how to combine intellectual pursuits with the joy of family and friends.

I would like to thank several institutions and journals for allowing me to reprint material from the following articles: "'The Laws of This Country': Foreigners and the Legal Construction of Sovereignty in Uruguay, 1830–1875," *Law and History Review* 19 (3) 2001: 479–511; "The Legal Regime of the South Atlantic World: Jurisdictional Complexity As Institutional Order," *Journal of World History* 11 (1) 2000: 27–56; "Colonial Law and Cultural Difference: Jurisdictional Politics and the Formation of the Colonial State," *Comparative Studies in Society and History* 41 (3) 2000: 563–88, reprinted with the permission of Cambridge University Press; "Making Order out of Trouble: Jurisdictional Politics in the Spanish Colonial Borderlands," *Law and Social Inquiry* 26 (2) 2001: 373–401; L. Benton and J. Muth, "On Cultural Hybridity: Interpreting Colonial Authority and Performance," *Journal of Colonialism and Colonial History* 1 (1) 2000 (http://muse.jhu.edu/journals), © The Johns Hopkins

University Press, reprinted with permission of The Johns Hopkins University Press; and "From the World Systems Perspective to Institutional World History: Culture and Economy in Global Theory," *Journal of World History* 7 (2) 1996: 261–95.

ONE

Legal Regimes and Colonial Cultures

In the late fifteenth century, as Christians were extending their rule over the remaining pockets of Moorish dominion in the Iberian peninsula, a North African legal scholar named Al-Wansharishi issued a legal finding (*fatwa*) to address the situation of an influential Muslim advocate in Marbella. The man in Marbella wished to obey the edict directing good Muslims to abandon Christian jurisdictions in Spain, but he felt compelled to stay and continue to work as an advocate for Moors whose property and livelihood were being threatened under Christian rule. His appearances before Christian judges to represent Muslims seemed a worthy cause, one that he apparently thought would warrant an exception to the edict. The *mufti* disagreed. He ruled that it was the man's duty to flee Spain. Contact with Christians – particularly the close dealings with Christian judges that the advocate's role would require – was a form of contamination. The Moors staying behind were, in any case, hardly entitled to such care since they were already breaking with Muslim authority by staying in a Christian jurisdiction, the mufti explained. They should be left to their own devices.[1]

Al-Wansharishi made it clear that it was Christian authority, not Christians themselves, that made contamination inevitable. Christians with subject status posed no particular threat. But to live under Christian rule was "not allowable, not for so much as one hour a day, because of all the dirt and filth involved, and the religious and secular corruption which continues all the time."[2] The central rituals of Muslim religious

---

[1] L.P. Harvey, *Islamic Spain, 1250–1500*, pp. 56–58.
[2] Harvey, *Islamic Spain*, pp. 58–59.

life would be threatened – the collection of alms, the celebration of Ramadan, the daily prayers. Just as troubling to al-Wansharishi was the inevitable disappearance of distinctive forms of expression of Muslims: "their way of life, their language, their dress, their . . . habits."[3]

We do not know whether the Marbella advocate obeyed the fatwa. We know that some influential Moors chose to stay and fill the role of advocates for the conquered Moors. We also know that their actions, as agents seeking to reinforce one legal authority by representing cases before another, were remarkably common in territories of imperial or colonial conquest. We know, too, that al-Wansharishi's interpretation of the stakes of this decision was repeated throughout Muslim Spain and in other settings of conquest and colonization. Colonizing authorities understood just as readily that the structure of legal authority and the creation of cultural hierarchies were inextricably intertwined. Jurisdictional lines dividing legal authorities were the focus of struggle precisely because they signified other boundaries marking religious and cultural difference. As al-Wansharishi observed, the structural relation of one legal authority to another had the power to change both the location of boundaries and the very definition of difference.

Turning this statement around, we see that contests over cultural and religious boundaries and their representations in law become struggles over the nature and structure of political authority. Ways of defining and ordering difference are not just the cultural materials from which political institutions construct legitimacy and shape hegemony. They are institutional elements on their own, simultaneously focusing cultural practice and constituting structural representations of authority. Fine distinctions among groups attain an importance that appears exaggerated to observers outside a particular time and place but reflects participants' certain knowledge that they are struggling not just over symbolic markers but over the very structure of rule.

Colonialism shaped a framework for the politics of legal pluralism, though particular patterns and outcomes varied. Wherever a group imposed law on newly acquired territories and subordinate peoples, strategic decisions were made about the extent and nature of legal control. The strategies of rule included aggressive attempts to impose legal systems intact. More common, though, were conscious efforts to retain elements of existing institutions and limit legal change as a way of sustaining social order. Conquered and colonized groups sought, in turn,

---

[3] Harvey, *Islamic Spain*, p. 58.

to respond to the imposition of law in ways that included accommodation, advocacy within the system, subtle delegitimation, and outright rebellion. The legal conflicts of colonized and colonizers were further shaped by the tensions that divided the two sides. Jurisdictional jockeying by competing colonial authorities was a universal feature of the colonial order. It called up and altered cultural distinctions, as competing colonial authorities tied their jurisdictional claims to representations of their (special or superior) relationship to indigenous groups or sought to delegitimize other legal authorities by depicting them as tainted by indigenous cultures. Factions within colonized populations, too, entered into conflicts with one another because of different interests in and perceptions of the legal order.

These multisided legal contests were simultaneously central to the construction of colonial rule and key to the formation of larger patterns of global structuring. Precisely because imperial and colonial polities contained multiple legal systems, the location of political authority was not uniform across the international system. Yet international order depended upon the ability of different political authorities to recognize each other, even if that recognition fell short of formal diplomacy or treaty making. The law worked both to tie disparate parts of empires and to lay the basis for exchanges of all sorts between politically and culturally separate imperial or colonial powers.[4] Global legal regimes – defined for our purposes as *patterns of structuring multiple legal authorities* – provided a global institutional order even in the absence of cross-national authorities and before the formal recognition of international law. Their study reveals a global order that was far more complex and institutionally less stable than many approaches to world history, and to global economic change in particular, have suggested. Studying legal regimes leads along paths in two directions: toward an enhanced

---

[4] Given the importance of law in this regard, it is frustrating and surprising that its study has remained so resolutely within the boundaries of national political histories. Even some comparative legal scholars have exacerbated the problem by overemphasizing legal sources in categorizing legal systems. See, for example, Alan Watson, who argues forcefully that rulers and elites were mainly "indifferent to the nature of the legal rules in operation" and that this indifference gave legal sources their strength and resilience in diverse colonial settings (Alan Watson, *Slave Law in the Americas*). Regional historians are sometimes even criticized for placing their subject in a wider context; for example, Hoffer is taken to task for including a valuable chapter on European-Indian legal relations in his history of North American colonial law because attention to French and Spanish law is "misplaced in a volume that concentrates on British North America" (Gaspare Saladino, "Review of Peter Charles Hoffer, *Law and Peoples in Colonial America*).

understanding of world history and toward a more nuanced view of cultural interactions in particular colonial encounters.[5]

INSTITUTIONAL WORLD HISTORY

Global institutions broadly defined include widely recurring, patterned interactions (not limited to exchange relations or formal organizations) that emerge from cultural practice. This inclusive definition helps us to tackle persisting conceptual problems of global theory. Where gaps between local process and global structure, between agency and structure, and between culture and economy have been bridged by focusing on such objects of analysis as cultural intermediaries, transnational processes, and the discourse of colonialism, these analytical strategies can be expanded and combined, moving the analysis simultaneously out toward global (and structural) and in toward local (and cultural) phenomena. Rather than offering a technique for bridging these gaps (and thus salvaging established ways of representing the global order) this approach urges us to reimagine global structure as the institutional matrix constructed out of practice and shaped by conflict. These patterned sets of behavior do not exist at, or merely bridge, separate "levels," but themselves constitute elements of global order.[6]

---

[5] This project is designed to address several conceptual problems of world history, and in global theory more generally: capturing connections between local conflict and global structure; describing institutional change; and characterizing "culture," especially the relation between culture and economy. These problems have been addressed differently, but not successfully, in world systems theory, in institutional economic history, and in colonial cultural studies. I do not intend to review these approaches and their shortcomings here but will outline instead an approach to studying law as a global institution in an example of an alternative I call institutional world history. The approach, which I believe offers useful tools in response to the central problems of global theory, can potentially frame research on topics other than the law. See note 6 below and Lauren Benton, "From the World Systems Perspective to Institutional World History: Culture and Economy in Global Theory."

[6] As the reliance on work done on middle-ground phenomena, agents, and analytical categories suggests, institutional world history builds upon recent work across a range of disciplines. Economic institutionalists propose viewing global markets as culturally embedded; a particularly successful scholarly project has been the investigation of the links between political culture and postwar monetary regimes (e.g., John Odell, *U.S. International Monetary Policy*). But less obvious global structures and processes deserve attention and recall a somewhat expanded notion of Thomas's "colonial projects" – globally organized routines (or institutions) that form both through metropolitan policy and local colonial conflict (Nicholas Thomas, *Colonialism's Culture*). McNeill points to the structuring of communications as a source of global ordering (William McNeill, "Preface," in Andre Gunder Frank and Barry Gills, eds., *The World System: Five Hundred*

4

The example of international institutional ordering this book explores is the emergence, under varying historical conditions, of legal regimes in which actors immersed in different legal systems nevertheless constructed a shared understanding of legal power as a basis for exchanges of goods and information, even in the absence of an overlapping authority or a formal regulatory structure.[7] It is possible to speak of "order without law" as emerging at the international level just as it has been shown to do in small communities or in business agreements not based on contracts.[8] Legal regimes extended beyond the borders of particular legal systems and established repeatable routines for incorporating groups with separate legal identities in production and trade and for accommodating (or changing) culturally diverse ways of viewing the regulation and exchange of property.

Elements of such an international order can be found from the fourteenth to the seventeenth centuries in the replication of fluid,

---

Years or Five Thousand). Frank interprets this comment as an endorsement for his perspective, but I view it more as a challenge to push beyond the obvious ordering function of trade (Andre Gunder Frank, *ReOrient: Global Economy in the Asian Age*). Finally, the project I propose has a good deal in common with the "constructivist" perspective in international relations theory, which views international norms as emerging out of the social practice of states and other social actors. See, e.g., Frederich V. Kratochwil, *Rules, Norms, and Decisions*; and Vendulka Kubálková, Nicholas Onuf, and Paul Kowert (eds.), *International Relations in a Constructed World.*

7 It should by now be clear that my use of the term *regime* to describe an institutional field linking polities that were constituted in politically and culturally very different ways departs somewhat from the use of the term to describe areas for cooperation among states (see Stephen Krasner, "Structural Causes and Regime Consequences: Regimes As International Variables"). While explorations of the conditions under which state actors will enter into agreements is analytically relevant to my project, such an approach limits our focus to negotiations that are the outcome of international order rather than its building blocks. It is the *replication* of forms of political authority that after all makes interstate agreements possible. My interest, then, is not in the way interstate norms and agreements are shaped but in the ways that widely replicated "domestic" political processes and conflicts produce a framework for international norms. For another argument in favor of the conflation of "internal" and "external" processes, see James N. Rosenau, *Along the Domestic-Foreign Frontier.*

8 The classic works on these two phenomena are, respectively, Robert Ellickson, *Order Without Law*; and Stuart MacCaulay, "Non-Contractual Relations in Business." See also Lauren Benton, "Beyond Legal Pluralism." And, on the construction of rules in the international order, see Kratochwil, *Rules, Norms, and Decisions.* The study of customary international law also has some relevance here, though its focus on the emergence of law out of custom in the international arena is different from my approach to international order as a function of widespread patterns of organizing multiple legal authorities. See Michael Beyers, *Custom, Power, and the Power of Rules*; and Anthony D'Amato, *The Concept of Culture in International Law.*

multijurisdictional legal orders. We perceive this clearly in territories of colonial and imperial expansion, where culturally and religiously different peoples employed legal strategies that exploited (and further complicated) unresolved jurisdictional tensions, particularly those between secular and religious authorities. Such tensions provided the context for law in diaspora; where ethnically distinctive groups expanded without conquering significant territory, they exercised legal control over their own communities while fitting into preexisting plural legal orders. While the formation of legal institutions was thus open-ended (and determined neither the special dynamism of the West nor the cultural character of the East), the process itself also created a common institutional framework that extended from the Americas to the Indian Ocean and beyond.

From the late eighteenth century on, routines for subordinating the law of ethnic and religious communities to state law replaced more fluid forms of legal pluralism and began also to be widely replicated. By the mid-nineteenth century, state-centered legal pluralism was being promoted as a model of governance by European administrators. Just as important, though, was its emergence, simultaneously, as an institutional "fix" for the fluid jurisdictional politics of colonial settings. Diverse polities displayed similar processes urging this transition. Jurisdictional politics became symbolically important and politically charged. Attention focused in particular on debates about the legal status of indigenous peoples and, especially, the definition of roles for cultural and legal intermediaries. Legal actors played upon these tensions in crafting legal strategies that often involved appeals to state law, even before the colonial state had articulated claims to sovereignty. Paradoxically, such processes often meant sharpening artificial divisions between "modern" and "traditional" realms, and between state and nonstate legal authorities. And as political contests shaped a structure of state-centered legal pluralism and reproduced it (in some places as a fiction of governance rather than a political reality), this shift helped to form, in turn, the interstate order.

This account, and the approach favored here, suggests an important reorientation of world historical narratives. The perspective clearly challenges Eurocentric world histories that emphasize the unique, progressive character of European institutions or that view global change as emanating exclusively from the dynamics of Western development. Particularly for the early period, the approach challenges "world systems" frameworks that link the Americas to Europe but downplay connections to Asia and Africa in the early modern period. Even those world systems accounts that oppose Eurocentrism by claiming the primacy of an Islamic "world system" before the thirteenth century, or the centrality of Asian economies, miss institutional interconnections between East and West.[9] The reorientation allows us to identify international regimes in periods before the rise of an interstate system and as the products of both globalizing pressures *and* the internal dynamics of politics in particular places. The approach replaces searching for the roots of state formation and of a more connected globalism in Westernizing projects or in nationalist and anticolonial responses. At the same time, unlike critiques of Eurocentric world history that engage in a checklist of comparisons to establish that other world regions were as or more "advanced" than Europe, this perspective moves such measuring exercises to the margins of analysis.[10] Certainly social actors asserted claims about the more "civilized" or "modern" nature of "their" institutions. But the institutional order we are examining was not an exclusive cultural property but the product of an ordered and contested multiculturalism.

LEGAL PLURALISM

We do not begin the study of legal regimes without tools, but the tools need some refashioning. In legal studies, and in the anthropology of law in particular, the study of legal pluralism provides one starting place.[11] Throughout the book I use the term *legal pluralism*, and also some closely related terms, while also seeking to move beyond some

---

[9] Examples are Janet Abu-Lughod, *Before European Hegemony*; and, arguing that Islam constituted a cultural world system, John Voll, "Islam As a Special World-System."

[10] The claim by Frank (*ReOrient*) that the global economy was Asian-centered until around 1800 in this way reproduces the sorts of analytical biases that lead him to reject Eurocentered global history in the first place. See the last section of this chapter.

[11] Shaping a conceptual framework must take us outside colonial history. Though the multiplicity of law in colonial settings has long been recognized, comprehensive scholarly treatments are few. The works of M.B. Hooker are an exception, though it is fair to say that they had only marginal impact on colonial studies more generally (for example, his *Legal Pluralism: An Introduction to Colonial and Neo-Colonial Laws*). There are many case studies and monographs on law in colonial and postcolonial settings that frame their analysis in terms of *legal pluralism* (see note 14 below), but the dearth of comparative works has made it difficult to place such works in a larger context. In the study of law more narrowly defined, the fields of conflict of laws, and of comity of nations, also intersect with the approach to colonial law here. In contrast to these fields, though, I focus on formal legal issues as one part of a larger set of cultural and political tensions crystallized in jurisdictional disputes.

7

common assumptions about the relation of multiple systems of law and, in particular, the role of state law.

Plural legal orders have more often than not been represented as comprising sets of "stacked" legal systems or spheres. In part, this approach is implicit in prominent social theoretical takes on law. Unger, for example, describes customary law as patterns of interactions to which moral obligations attach. The law becomes more formal as layers of greater complexity adhere to this foundation. At the pinnacle of the legal order sits state law, a system with distinctive features, including the presence of specialized legal personnel.[12] The image of stacked or nested legal systems within or below an enveloping state law extends even to theoretical approaches to law that seek to place nonstate and state law in the same comparative context. The search to define universal features of legal systems, for example, has tended to render the plural legal order as a Hobbesian world: Each legal system coheres around a single coercive authority, and more powerful authorities subsume those that are weaker. State law caps the plural legal order through its ability to establish a monopoly on violence.[13]

Among the problems of these, or alternative, representations of the legal order as a set of stacked legal systems, two critiques have special relevance to the study of colonial law. One consists in the observation of rampant boundary crossing. Legal ideas and practices, legal protections of material interests, and the roles of legal personnel (specialized or not) fail to obey the lines separating one legal system or sphere from another. Legal actors, too, appeal regularly to multiple legal authorities and perceive themselves as members of more than one legal community. The image of ordered, nested legal systems clashes with wide-ranging legal practices and perceptions.[14] Mapping the plural legal order thus takes on the feel of early astronomy, with its attempts to plot heliocentric orbits on an imagined geocentric solar system – what is required, ultimately, is a return to faith to account for the inconsistencies.

---

[12] Roberto Mangabeira Unger, *Knowledge and Politics*.

[13] See, for example, Leopold Pospisil, *Anthropology of Law*, for an emphasis on coercive authority as the centerpiece of all legal systems.

[14] The anthropological literature on legal pluralism in particular highlights the fluidity and contingency of the relation of multiple legal authorities. See especially Sally Merry, "Legal Pluralism" and also the more recent *Colonizing Hawai'i*; June Starr and Jane F. Collier (eds.), *History and Power in the Study of Law*; Sandra B. Burman and Barbara E. Harrell-Bond (eds.), *Imposition of Law*.

A second problem is one of narrative. As in Unger's sociological framework, there is a common underlying assumption about the direction of legal change. State law descends – an imposition – though borrowing from and building upon existing custom. Even in accounts more attuned to the complexities of this process there is a sense of inevitability about the dominance of state law and about its independent origins.[15] But imagining the state as a fully formed entity with a coherent view of law and of its own place in the legal order may lead toward one of two, very different, mistakes, each producing a different flawed chronology in colonial history. The first is to take states' claims to legal sovereignty at face value. Early colonial authorities then appear as comprehensive political powers rather than internally fragmented entities that tended to insert themselves within local power structures even in places where there was a sharp imbalance of power. It is equally possible to err in a second, opposite direction, making statehood dependent upon specific institutional formations. In this view, the enactment of codification and other state-directed legal reforms in the late nineteenth century established the colonial state's claim to paramount legal authority, and nationalist movements everywhere came to identify the law as a crucial arena for the struggle for political control in the twentieth century. These narratives cannot, of course, both be right – that is, the interstate order cannot have appeared in the early colonial centuries and then again, de novo, in the twentieth.

A close analysis and comparison of legal politics in particular places allow us to identify transformative moments with greater precision. Subtle but important shifts in the definition of colonial state law and its relation to other law, it turns out, occurred at various moments in the long nineteenth century, in patterns replicated across a wide array of colonial and postcolonial settings. Colonies were not distinctive because they contained plural legal orders but because struggles within them made the structure of the plural legal order more explicit. The cultural significance of legal boundaries was central to colonial legal

---

[15] Sally Falk Moore, for example, in a careful study designed explicitly to understand "traditional" law as the product of colonial politics, repeatedly refers to local customary law in a colonial setting as the "residue" left over after the imposition of state law (Sally Falk Moore, *Social Facts and Fabrications*). In Chapter 7, I analyze E.P. Thompson's views of custom, and the descent of state law, as another variant of this tradition of legal pluralism. Like Moore's approach, Thompson's views move us beyond the constraints of a plural legal order conceptualized as stacked and separate legal systems, but significant problems remain.

politics. Designing, announcing, and fighting about rules ordering the interaction of various legal authorities fashioned a place for the state as an instrument and forum for the production of such rules. In short, what some approaches would represent as a natural condition of plural legal orders – the ascendance of state law – appears as the product of history, and of widely reproduced conflicts.

The comparative and interpretive study of these processes is at one level synonymous with the study of *jurisdictional politics*, a term that I define broadly to mean conflicts over the preservation, creation, nature, and extent of different legal forums and authorities. The opposition of "ruler" and "ruled" universally generated charged debates about jurisdictional politics. These debates were never two-sided, though, because multiple legal authorities on each side also asserted different sets of claims about the structure of legal authority (think of the divide between the North African mufti and peninsular Moors). The ways in which the politics of jurisdictional disputes played out were crucial to changing notions of cultural boundaries, in part because "jurisdiction" itself implied a certain sharing of identities and values among subjects. This association was not lost on social actors, who struggled purposefully to draw jurisdictional lines in ways that were consistent with their own images of group distinctions.

Many forces could bring jurisdictional disputes into sharper relief, but two stand out. One was the challenge posed by cultural intermediaries and the attendant conflicts about the place of such groups within the legal order. In jurisdictional politics, cultural intermediaries – and a particular group of them, indigenous legal personnel – aligned themselves in surprising ways, sometimes seeking to broaden jurisdictional claims of the colonizers in order to push for cultural inclusiveness, sometimes defending and reinventing "traditional" authorities as a way of protecting or creating special status. Their very presence tended to pose a challenge to colonizers' representations of cultural and legal boundaries. Intermediaries' place was redefined, further, in relation to shifting definitions of acts and groups placed outside the law – the illegalities of banditry, piracy, and criminality, and the presumed lawlessness of "savages."

A second force propelling jurisdictional politics into the foreground comprised contests over property. Conflicts over cultural difference in the law were intertwined with disputes focusing on the control of property and its legal definition. Culture and economy were not separate entities – one prior to, or determinant of, the other. Rather than developing

as a "framework" for the spread of capitalism in the period we are studying, legal institutions emerged *with* capitalist relations of production
through repetitive assertions of power and responses to power. Indeed,
transformations in the law of property (including definitions of rights
to land and labor) were sometimes perceived by social actors as primarily about changes in the ordering of legal authorities, rather than about
property rights per se.

Together, these areas of conflict shaped a body of "rules of engagement" in the law, or a set of shifting procedural and legal rules about
the relations among cultural (or religious) groups. We find these rules
distributed across the law and its institutions rather than residing in
one body, or one function, of the law. Colonial law had, in this sense, a
peculiar subtext of rules about rule – a regulating of the regulating system. Such rules had symbolic force, but they were not merely symbolic;
they constrained legal strategies and influenced perceptions of the law
and thus had an impact on choices of legal sources, their interpretation,
and legal practice in general. In short, the law's structuring of cultural
boundaries directly shaped its wider institutional profile.

In studying conflicts about the structure of the legal order, I rely on
a simple, broad typology. Multicentric legal orders – those in which
the state is one among many legal authorities – contrast with state-
centered legal orders in which the state has at least made, if not sustained, a claim to dominance over other legal authorities. Rather than
elaborating upon these models or arguing the degree to which various
historical examples constitute faithful representations, I use the typology to explore patterns in the historical shift from one legal regime to
another, the timing of this shift, and its intricacies. Other terms I employ
heuristically are *strong* and *weak* legal pluralism. The first denotes legal
orders in which politically prominent attempts have been made to fix
rules about the relation of various legal authorities and forums. Weak
legal pluralism occurs where there is an implicit (mutual) recognition of
"other" law but no formal model for the structure of the legal order, or
where the model is in formation. Colonial settings offer examples of both
strong and weak legal pluralism, as well as cases that fall between these
types.

The remainder of this introduction discusses in turn the three points
of entry I have chosen for studying global legal regimes – jurisdictional
politics, cultural and legal intermediaries, and changes in the law of
property. The choice of these entry points does not lead me to develop
a typology of plural legal orders based on patterned variations, in the

way that sociological theory building might proceed. Rather, the rubrics serve to illuminate processes shared across diverse colonial settings and to investigate the interrelation in particular historical contexts of cultural conflicts and institutional change.

JURISDICTIONAL AND CULTURAL BOUNDARIES

In his book *Marvelous Possessions*, Stephen Greenblatt explores the consequences of claims of legal authority in American colonial society. The mere act of extending a claim of possession over American Indians, he argues, changed Spaniards' representation of Indians' nature. The signs of civility and of shared humanity marveled at by Spaniards in their first encounters faded to insignificance after the formal act of possession – the extension of legal jurisdiction – turned the Indians into "outlaws and bandits . . . [living] outside of all just order, apart from the settled human community and hence from the very condition of the virtuous life."[16] The formal extension of legal jurisdiction in and of itself created a clear cultural boundary between the colonizers and the colonized by casting only one as the possessor of law, and of civility.

Greenblatt is examining a historical moment: the taking of possession. But, to corrupt a worn phrase, possession was not the law, or even nine-tenths of it. No sooner did the extension of jurisdiction formalize difference than the law also had to take up the task of structuring difference, that is, of making rules about cultural interactions within the law. For jurisdiction did not just mark new boundaries. It raised the possibility of shared identity as the colonizers and the colonized occupied the status of subjects before the law, and it opened the way for the colonizers and the colonized to act in similar functions within the law – as litigants, advocates, witnesses, judges. Not surprisingly, then, the act of extending formal jurisdiction was rarely simple. Colonizing groups in fact wished at times to restrict jurisdiction and thus to reinforce cultural divides (while at the same time limiting administrative costs of rule). Some indigenous groups struggled to be included on equal terms; others fought to maintain the legitimacy of alternative legal forums; still others pursued both strategies simultaneously. Odd coalitions formed across the divide between colonizer and colonized. In restricting his analysis to first contact, Greenblatt implicitly recognizes that in less than a generation after the formal ceremonies of possession marked

---

[16] Stephen Greenblatt, *Marvelous Possessions*, pp. 67–68.

stark boundaries between conquerors and subjects in the Americas, a much more complex map of differences emerged both in discourse and in institutional structures.[17]

Claims of legal jurisdiction uniformly set in motion a process of cultural distancing, but the process itself varied substantially. On the one side, the meaning of jurisdiction was conditioned by the nature and rhetoric of law in the colonizing society. Imperial powers possessed legal systems that were already formally plural. This background influenced the ways in which colonial jurisdictional claims were extended. The relation to subordinate, conquered peoples was crafted in the familiar terms of structured legal pluralism that the colonizers knew. Colonized subjects perceived the possibility of using these tensions to their advantage and devised legal strategies that explicitly exploited them. The tensions of jurisdictional politics at home thus extended, with new complications, to colonial settings. In the case that Greenblatt analyzed, this dynamic was very important. Though the rhetoric of conquest established possession by the Spanish crown, the ambiguities of jurisdiction were immediately present. A second legal authority, that of the church, was recognized by both conquistadors and the crown itself, and the resulting jurisdictional tensions came to influence profoundly the functioning of colonial law in Spanish America and, in particular, the legal status of American Indians.

Indeed, jurisdictional jockeying and disputes were pervasive, and they existed within state law itself. Administrative, civil, criminal, commercial law – there was no imperial handbook about which forms of the law were best to institute first in a colonial setting. Nor, for that matter, was it predictable which mattered most to colonizers (or to political factions among them) or which potentially created most political

---

[17] Seed improves upon Greenblatt's approach by giving more careful consideration to the differences among five "national" legal cultures and their ceremonies of possession (Patricia Seed, *Ceremonies of Possession*). Like Greenblatt, though, her book focuses narrowly on first contact and not the complexities of legal rule that follow. There is a danger that Seed's conclusion that different European powers could not "read" each other's symbolic statements of possession might be understood to mean that they could not read each other's legal orders. As I will argue in this book, I do not think this was at all the case, not only across European polities but also between many European and non-European polities. "Possession" and its manifestations might be an exception, but I tend to think that Seed has overstated her case, a result mainly of comparing symbolically different fields (for example, signs of legal possession in English colonies to astronomical markers of the Portuguese "known" world). I nevertheless consider the book a very valuable step in the direction of building a broader understanding of colonialism out of comparative study.

turmoil. While we find in practice that cultural boundary marking took place across the legal order, particular sorts of law emerged as focal points of tensions in particular historical circumstances. In eighteenth-century England, for example, the criminal law became an arena for public redefinitions of class boundaries. There are analogous cases in colonial settings where shifting definitions of criminality were also central to political strategies of domination by colonial powers. But mere administrative regulations – changing requirements to sit for civil service examinations, for example – could also emerge as focal points of controversy and in turn drive legal reforms in other areas. When we analyze colonial law, we must not restrict our view to particular kinds of law but must allow wide flexibility in order to identify critical moments. The danger of comparing apples to oranges is less troubling than the possibility of concluding that legal contests that were politically marginal in one place or time were marginal everywhere.

Conquered peoples showed themselves to be quite adept and sophisticated at interpreting the significance of claims to jurisdiction and strategically taking positions to undermine those claims. As in the case of the Muslim advocate in Marbella and the mufti ruling on his obligations, groups that appeared to be politically allied often adopted quite different approaches to jurisdictional issues. Undermining claims to jurisdiction might be approached by insisting on the legitimacy of alternative legal authorities, as the mufti was doing, or they might involve entering actively into an imposed legal system, as the Marbella man wanted, to protect particular interests and, in the process, preserve community status. Either approach – and also the dialogue about which was morally superior and tactically more promising – had an impact on changes in the ordering of legal authorities. In striking either of these positions (or in combining them in some way), groups used their knowledge of jurisdictional tensions present in the imposed legal order. For example, American Indians at times showed considerable sophistication in their appeals to religious as well as state legal authorities. Or, in a very different setting, Indian Ocean merchants carefully chose among religious, administrative, or customary forums when pursuing claims in the regions where they traded.

In different historical moments, the discourse of jurisdictional disputes focused on different divisions. One striking commonality of the Iberian overseas empires and the great Islamic empires was the focus of jurisdictional politics on the relationship between religious and state law, and the boundaries separating religious communities. In the extension of these empires, political jurisdiction did not necessarily produce religious jurisdiction, and vice versa. This relationship was a volatile one acted upon by local political contests, many of which focused explicitly on questions of religious identity and the limits of imperial authority.

Contrast this focus to debates in the late nineteenth century about the nature of citizenship in colonial contexts. The discourse of jurisdictional politics shifted decisively away from religion and toward membership in particular political communities. Groups seeking to undermine colonial law often found themselves arguing for broadening, rather than restricting, state jurisdictional claims so that rights recognized under state authority could be extended more widely. At the same time, those who wished to enhance state legal authority often sought to do so by drawing jurisdictional boundaries more sharply and closely. In nineteenth-century India, whole ethnic communities found themselves defined as being outside the law – as "criminal tribes" – while in many parts of Africa colonial administrators embraced efforts to shore up, and even re-create in quite distorted forms, "traditional" law.

We should not be surprised to find that people often perceived very clearly the close connections between jurisdictional claims and messages about cultural difference. Fights broke out about seemingly arcane changes in the extension or restriction of court authority. Even if his view was narrowly focused on the discourse of possession, Greenblatt was right to point to the utterances describing jurisdictional claims as being central to cultural self-definition, and to the discourse of colonialism (and to its institutions) more generally. We need to add to this dimension the impact of these debates on actual institutional structures, some of which endured and extended beyond the particular historical conditions that gave rise to them. Jurisdictional politics in this way shaped an institutional framework linking local cultural divisions to structures of governance and, in turn, to global ordering.

CULTURAL AND LEGAL INTERMEDIARIES

In Achebe's acclaimed novel of colonialism, *Things Fall Apart*, the protagonist, Okonkwo, is taken before a judge and jury, and convicted, without realizing what is happening. He is not awed by the event because he does not know it is a trial. He does not know that the presiding British official is a judge; he does not know that the twelve men brought in to listen to the exchanges in the room comprise a jury. Okonkwo's obliviousness may reflect Achebe's overstatement of Ibo isolation.[18] Still, the point is worth considering. Colonial powers sent some messages through legal institutions that were simply not received. Conquered peoples may also have ignored messages because they doubted the legitimacy of courts, or simply because they found the medium remote. Staging loud and impressive theatrical events was relatively easy for colonizers; making these displays mean what they were intended to mean was much more difficult.[19]

The burden of translating was present in the first moments of colonial encounter. Individuals and groups were identified right away to act as interlocutors or intermediaries. While culture change reverberated through interacting societies, it was concentrated in the cultural transformation of these individuals. Within a historically short space of time – certainly less than a generation – we observe cultural practices that are products of neither "dominant" nor "subordinate" culture, but of the interaction. Further, the interpretation of these new cultural forms is not easy and cannot be deduced from a simple algebra of domination and subordination. The variety of cultural representations on the two sides is the cause of some of this complexity. So, too, is the sophistication of cultural adaptation. As an example of this complexity, Bhabba points out that mimicry of colonial rulers (or colonial elites) may signal a recognition of cultural inferiority but may also reflect the hunger to usurp power, a capacity for parody, and a sense of security that external changes will leave one's own cultural core untainted.[20]

---

[18] Achebe's novel exaggerates the isolation of Ibo villagers, who lived in a region long incorporated in long-distance trade routes – including the slave trade – and exposed to cultural difference. Also, as Achebe shows us in another section of the novel, the Ibo had a court system of their own, and one wonders if Achebe is right to deprive Okonkwo of the power to form analogies. I do not mean to endorse Obeyesekere's presumption of universal practical rationalism (Gananath Obeyesekere, *The Apotheosis of Captain Cook;* and the response by Marshall Sahlins, *How "Natives" Think*), but instead to point out that Achebe's portrayal of Okonkwo's perceptions of British ceremony are a literary device.

[19] In *Ceremonies of Possession,* Seed emphasizes the disconnect between messages sent and received in legal rituals and suggests, too, that this failure sometimes favored European interpretations of Indian acceptance of their rule. Clendinnen, in her study of the colonial encounter on the Yucatan peninsula, suggests that miscommunication was perhaps inevitable and in fact exacerbated by factional politics on the part of the colonizers (Inga Clendinnen, *Ambivalent Conquests: Maya and Spaniard in Yucatan, 1517–1570*).

[20] This is a charitable reading of Bhabba, who stresses the less interesting point that Westernizing cultural change was not always functional to colonial rule. Homi Bhabba, "Of Mimicry and Man." For a critique of Bhabba that pushes further, see Nicholas Thomas, *Colonialism's Culture.*

In colonial law, similarly, it is tempting but wrong to view any participation in an imposed legal system as collaboration, on the one hand, and to represent any form of rejection of the law's authority as resistance. Groups emerged almost everywhere that simultaneously "collaborated" with an imposed legal order and "resisted" its effects. The Moorish "collaborator" discussed at the beginning of this introduction is a case in point. He is also, though, atypical in some ways. Whereas he made explicit his goal of protecting the Muslim community, many intermediary groups did not pursue a clear political agenda but crafted their strategies in terms of fairly narrow individual, family, or small-group interests. If they found the law a useful forum for forwarding those interests, they also maneuvered to strengthen legal mechanisms that improved their standing in the legal system. A most interesting tension emerged when intermediaries perceived that prevailing ways of marking cultural difference would continue the conditions that made their work as intermediaries indispensable but would also inhibit changes in the law that would benefit them in other ways.

As already noted, the mere act of claiming legal jurisdiction prompted a demand for rules about the sorts of people who would be permitted to serve as witnesses, advocates, and judges, and whether they would be treated the same way or differently from others in these roles. Cultural intermediaries who took part in legal proceedings – as litigants or legal practitioners – had an immediate and apparent interest in altering these rules. At times, they were aided by popular perceptions that cultural divisions within the law were symbolic and permissive of other inequalities; at times, their maneuvering favored narrower group interests. In either case, their actions influenced the standing of indigenous courts, procedures, and sources in the legal order and changed perceptions of the legitimacy of colonial rule.

The intermediaries' role was also both important and complex from the point of view of colonial or imperial administrators. Intermediaries were often viewed as essential to rule but at the same time dangerous and an affront to cultural divisions that ruling groups were struggling to uphold. Not surprisingly, questions about how to respond to challenges raised by these groups became the focus of political debates in many places. Debates about whether such intermediaries should be regarded as "foreign" subordinates with the power to undermine state authority or as colonial officials deserving of protection intersected with representations of cultural difference as a rationale for colonial rule.

As with jurisdictional issues, colonial agents faced with these problems relied in part on the blueprint of metropolitan law for distinguishing among categories of legal actors, and they looked for analogous distinctions in indigenous law. For example, the value of oath taking in both imposed and indigenous law depended on a witness's social standing and category. Colonial legal agents tried to create rough tables of equivalence of socially subordinate groups, which were in turn challenged in various ways in the courts. Roles and titles for legal advocates emerged out of a combined process of imposed order, established practice, and strategic responses of both colonial agents and indigenous litigants to opportunities for improvisation.

Perhaps most interesting about the shifting role of legal intermediaries is that their ambiguous status – as participants in the legal order who were not fully subjects of the law – prompted serious debate about the essential nature of law itself. What were the qualities that made imposed law supposedly out of reach for colonized practitioners? Answers to this question called forth generalizations about the nature of indigenous culture and sharpened colonial officials' claims about metropolitan law. In fact, the debates focused attention on the virtue of legal rules themselves, so that for nineteenth-century Europeans the defense of the colonial order became closely intertwined with representations of the rationality of the colonizers and their institutions. As with jurisdictional debates, such attention to the intricacies of the plural legal order ultimately reinforced the growing recognition that the colonial state *was* a state – an entity with the mission and authority to order and regulate all of society.

LAW AND PROPERTY, LAW AS PROPERTY

In Joseph Conrad's novel about the fictitious republic of Costaguana – a place that has much in common with the República Oriental del Uruguay visited by Conrad in his travels – the English-descended head of the local mining concession relies on familiar logic in explaining the benefits of reviving the mine. Charles Gould tells his wife:

> What is wanted here is law, good faith, order, security. Any one can declaim about these things, but I pin my faith to material interests. Only let the material interests once get a firm footing, and they are bound to impose the conditions on which alone they can continue to exist. That's how your money-making is justified here in the face of lawlessness and disorder. It is justified because the security which it

demands must be shared with an oppressed people. A better justice will come afterwards. That's your ray of hope.[21]

Gould's views would not seem strange to those historians who view state institutions in general, and the rule of law in particular, as instruments of informal empire and dependent capitalist development. Exchange and profit required stability, and a certain predictability for interactions; law followed investment to provide these conditions. Access to justice for Conrad's "oppressed peoples" was a rare and accidental byproduct of hard-to-come-by order.

For the period we are studying, there has been a marked tendency to describe global interconnectedness in terms of an increasing spread of capitalism outward from Europe and encompassing, by the end of the nineteenth century, all the regions of the world. What permitted this spread? In one version of the story, it is the diffusion of Western institutions – specifically, Western mechanisms for defining and establishing rights to property in ways that permit and stimulate the growth of markets. The rule of law emerged as part of a solution to the problem of high and volatile transaction costs. These transaction costs – the costs of "defining, protecting, and enforcing the property rights to the goods (the right to use, the right to derive income from the use of, the right to exclude, and the right to exchange)" – were minimized through institutional stability, in particular the ability of the state to enforce contracts.[22] In another version of the story, capitalist relations of production surged ahead, bringing supportive institutions in their wake, much in the way that Gould was predicting for the hapless Costaguana.

This narrative has been loudly criticized for, among other faults, its Eurocentrism.[23] It represents Western institutions as uniquely capable of facilitating economic growth. But the alternatives offered are saddled with their own problems. One possibility is to elaborate Marx's concept

---

[21] Joseph Conrad, *Nostromo*, p. 65.

[22] Douglass North, *Institutions, Institutional Change, and Economic Performance*, p. 91.

[23] Although this is surely the more usual complaint, I think that a deeper (and related) flaw of the approach is its inadequate treatment of culture, which is represented as either a sort of mystical substratum that occasionally and for inexplicable reasons acts to impede institutional transformations, or as an aftereffect, a mere dependent variable. These contradictory representations are never resolved. The odd result is that a perspective designed to center analysis around universal, rational-choice models, resides firmly on notions of deep cultural differences that are impervious to reason. For a wider discussion of this problem in the institutionalist literature, see Benton, "From the World Systems Perspective to Institutional World History."

of the mode of production. By defining a multiplicity of noncapitalist modes of production, one can, proponents argue, represent the complexity of regions that become in some senses (or sectors) capitalist while remaining noncapitalist in other senses (or sectors). This approach, articulated most clearly in world history by Eric Wolf, transcends the pure linearity of assumptions about the necessary link between Western institutions and capitalist growth.[24] But the end of the story – the "conquest" by capitalism of the global economy over the long nineteenth century – is surprisingly familiar. Further, the real puzzle in this perspective has proved to be the elaboration of "articulation," that is, the ways in which different modes of production are linked. They are linked – they *must* be linked – by patterned behaviors that have the regularity and standing of institutions, yet each mode of production is associated with a set of institutions that, in effect, constitutes and defines the mode of production. Are there specific institutional arrangements that then do the work of linking these other institutional practices? No one, to my knowledge, has succeeded in building a very convincing model of this nested institutional order, to say nothing of describing its changes.[25]

A different and in some senses opposite solution is simply to disregard institutions as secondary to economic forces and patterns – especially, in global narratives, to long-distance trade. Frank, for example, takes this view in arguing against a Western-centered account of capitalist institutions and their spread. Institutions, he argues, simply do not matter. They bend to economic forces.[26] This view accomplishes its goal of debunking Eurocentrism. Western institutions were hardly "needed" for a global economy to develop; that economy emerged well

---

[24] Eric Wolf, *Europe and the People Without History*.

[25] Indeed, the limitations of this perspective led Eric Wolf away from a focus on articulation and toward an effort to conceptualize power and conflicts over power more broadly. See Eric Wolf, *Envisioning Power: Ideologies of Dominance and Crisis*.

[26] Unfortunately, this point, which Frank describes as "a major thesis" of his book *ReOrient* (p. 206), is more an assertion supported by strings of quotes from other scholars than a developed argument in the book. It does appear, though, that in his eagerness to debunk the Eurocentrism of the institutionalists, Frank throws out the baby with the bathwater. He rejects any notion of "the social embedment of the economic process" (p. 206), based narrowly, it seems, on his rejection of Polanyi. This simply returns Frank to universal rationalism (p. 223). But for a strident reminder of the Western biases inherent in *this* assumption, see the introduction in Marshall Sahlins, *How "Natives" Think*; and J.M. Blaut, *The Colonizer's Model of the World: Geographical Diffusionism and Eurocentric History*. For a subtler discussion of economic social embeddedness, see Mark Granovetter, "Economic Action and Social Structure: The Problem of Social Embeddedness."

before the rise of what others call a capitalist global order; and where institutional environments conducive to global economic integration did not exist, they were forced into existence by integration itself. Yet, again, we are in a world of new puzzles and problems. In one direction, this path leads right into the den of the institutionalists, with their emphasis on necessary preconditions for capitalist growth. Frank finds himself arguing that the Chinese and others were just as rational as Europeans, and their institutions just as efficient and market friendly (though, if institutions do not matter, it is hard to see why we should care about this at all). In another direction, we find no tools for understanding the relation between institutional and economic change. The character of institutions is a response to economic trends, and to trade in particular; the world's economy was globally interconnected from an early stage; and it remained so, though its center shifted from China to Europe some time after 1800. In this nonnarrative narrative, the only relevant question posed about the state is whether "the state in China, Japan, India, Persia, and the Ottoman Empire" adopted, like European states, a range of policies to promote "national" economic growth (they did).[27] But how did "the state" become an entity for which such a question is even debatable? Did increases in the volume of trade and production at a global level stimulate the formation of such an institution everywhere? If so, how far are we really from the institutionalists' suggestion that expanding trade necessitated regulation? Excise the Eurocentric claim that the model for regulation was supplied by the West, and the two approaches converge rather neatly. State formation and the emergence of an interstate order are naturalized products of accelerated globalization.[28]

---

[27] Frank, *ReOrient*, p. 206.

[28] A somewhat different way of framing this critique is to point out that Frank's approach, in excising Eurocentrism, implicitly adopts the rather dubious view that colonialism had little influence on institutional or economic change outside Europe. Such a view might be true for parts of Asia before the late nineteenth century, but to borrow Frank's language, a "truly global" perspective that includes Spanish America and the territories under Ottoman rule, to name just two early modern examples, would show such a view to be ludicrous. I would not be fair to Frank if I did not acknowledge that at times he seems ready to admit the greater complexity of institutional-economic interactions (though he pulls away from this characterization ultimately). For example, he cites Perlin approvingly for arguing the need to view institutional similarities across diverse world regions as comprising "a framework of relevance" for the growth of international trade and the division of labor (the phrase is Perlin's, quoted on p. 210 of *ReOrient*). Frank also gestures at something he calls "interdependent institutional development" (p. 209). But he seems convinced that a perspective taking into account this global institutional framework must always view it as the product of global economic

The history of colonial and postcolonial state formation has hardly played along with this script. The process is historically messy and uneven. The state never constituted simply "more of the same," a larger and more elaborate institutional conduit for trade. It acted not just to regulate exchanges of property but also to enforce definitions of property and, as Foucault pointed out in somewhat different terms, to define a site for the accumulation of rules about property and social identities. And these functions of the state – the operation of which was itself the object of continual controversy – were not automatic and uncontested. The replication of state institutions was in fact shaped by the continual juxtaposition of alternatives.

Without making claims that the politics of legal pluralism *determined* shifts in political economy (a claim I do not want to make), we can grasp through its study the intersection between major reorganizations of the plural legal order and significant changes in the distribution and definition of property rights. The fluidity of jurisdictions in the plural legal order of the early modern world helped to structure the division of resources and constituted a framework for the "articulation" of different ways of organizing labor and property. This legal regime was fundamental to the expansion of long-distance trade, which was organized by communities of traders with distinctive legal identities. As colonial claims and the density and variety of economic interactions expanded, the outlines of this plural legal order also changed. Yet a formal attachment to pluralism persisted. Colonial legal policy relied on familiar categories in distinguishing between property disputes that were central to colonial interests and should therefore be handled in courts dominated by colonizers, and property transfers that could be properly viewed as familial, religious, or culturally specific and could safely be relegated to other forums. But the divisions of personal law were unwieldy for these purposes. Seemingly irrelevant cases of inheritance or marriage property could quickly become crucial to the production of labor, revenue collection, or the regulation of land markets. At the same time, local institutional practices sometimes offered opportunities for capital accumulation that colonial agents sought to preserve. Local (indigenous

interconnections. In this regard, I think he simply misreads the very quote from Perlin he provides, which seems to argue just the opposite, viz., that institutional similarities "formed part of the preconditions for the development of a system of international exchanges and dependencies" (p. 210). But I do not mean to argue causality. Focusing on this question leads us away from investigating interconnections and to the sort of grandstanding that so pervades Frank's efforts.

and settler) elites who stood to benefit from changes in the law of property often ran ahead of colonial administrators in advocating a greater role for the colonial state in regulating property transactions of all kinds. Others sought advantage in the preservation (and invention) of alternative, autonomous, or "indigenous" practices for organizing rights to land and labor. This jockeying over alternative visions of the plural legal order contributed to the formation of the colonial state as an arbiter of internal boundaries.

These transformative conflicts were sometimes perceived by social actors as primarily about broad questions of group rights, rather than more narrowly about access to, and definitions of, property.[29] This perception resulted not from some sort of false consciousness on the part of social actors unable to "see through" the shallowness of group distinctions to the "deeper" economic forces with which they should have concerned themselves. Precisely because group boundaries were marked by the institutional structuring of the legal order, they mattered very much in determining various groups' access to economic resources and opportunity. In addition, "public" positions, including most legal posts, were bought and sold according to the access they provided to "private" gains. It is unclear to me why we, as historians, should promote a stark division between identity and interests when contemporaries insisted on their congruence – and when the political/legal structure of multiple authorities and overlapping functions reinforced this understanding. Indeed, social actors often logically viewed legal status itself as a *form of property*, that could rise or fall in value and that could be inherited or usurped.[30]

This book addresses contests over property and its definition only as they intersected with the politics of legal pluralism. The intention is to avoid altogether the "chicken and egg" question about which came first, institutional change or the global economy. Instead, I propose the

---

[29] On the intersection of property conflicts and identity politics, or the social "embeddedness" of property, see C.M. Hann, "Introduction: The Embeddedness of Property," in C.M. Hann (ed.), *Property Relations: Renewing the Anthropological Tradition.*

[30] In a different context, critical race theorists have proposed that racial identity can itself be legally constituted as a form of property. See Richard Delgado, *Critical Race Theory.* Note that in *Plessy v. Ferguson*, the 1890s case in which the United States Supreme Court upheld the right of states to pass segregation legislation, the lead attorney for the plaintiff argued that "the reputation of being white" was a form of property "in the same sense that a right of action or of inheritance is *property.*" Whites would, he contended, be dispossessed if categorized as nonwhite (Albion Tourgée's *Plessy* brief, quoted in Mark Elliott, "Race, Color-Blindness, and the Democratic Public").

politics of legal ordering as the missing process of "articulation" that both structured long-distance trade across economically and culturally diverse polities and contributed to the replication of a hierarchy of specialized institutions regulating taxation, production, and trade. The approach moves us away from a narrative of the "spread" of institutions and toward the study of the conditions and conflicts producing the structurally similar institutional environments that constituted the global economy.

CULTURE / STRUCTURE

It should by now be evident that one of the central themes of the book is to contribute to the movement to resurrect "culture" as an element of global "structure."[31] This objective goes further than the demand that agency be reintroduced into structural theory, though the importance of this move should not be discounted. Assuming that the reader is by now convinced of the centrality of cultural identities to legal politics (an assertion to be supported, too, by the case studies of this book), let me be more specific about the ways in which legal politics has shaped global ordering.

Three elements of international order emerge out of contests over the shape of the legal order. The first, already alluded to, involves the location of political and legal authority. Institutional regimes (broadly defined as the repetition of structurally similar ways of organizing authority) make international regimes (narrowly defined as interstate agreements) possible by allowing political authorities to identify one another. Political authorities make assumptions about the similarities in the constitution of power inside other polities. These assumptions are rarely wholly wrong. They emerge out of long historical interactions in many cases. They also are the products of analogies based on a locally produced understanding of the structure of political conflict.

---

[31] Frank writes that the anthropologist Sidney Mintz has cautioned him for decades that "culture matters," and he has always replied that "structure matters" (Frank, *ReOrient*, p. xvi). Condensed in this way, my message would be that culture and structure both matter. This is by no means a lonely position. For other projects aiming at incorporating culture into global theory, see, in international relations, Yosef Lapid and Friedrich Kratochwil (eds.), *The Return of Culture and Identity in IR Theory*; in anthropology, Jonathan Friedman, *Cultural Identity and Global Process*; and in sociology, Manuel Castells, *The Power of Identity*.

24

Empires and emerging states recognized in each other similar strategies for dealing with cultural pluralism, captivity, religious differences, and frontier societies. The Iberian and Islamic empires constituted in this sense a single institutional framework, despite substantive differences in religious, economic, and political organization. It was not a framework that sustained peace, but it facilitated a long history of exchanges of ideas, personnel, and goods in the significant interludes of peace along the borders. In this way, too, the colonial state later emerged as part of an international state system not because it was created to do so but because colonial conflicts molded it into an overarching political authority with recognized claims to territorial sovereignty, however limited and fragile. In both phases of world history, the internal dynamics of challenges to legal authority and changing political schemes to craft a stable plural legal order were crucial in molding the character and reach of political authority and in making it intelligible to outsiders.

A second way that reproducing political and legal contests shaped an international order was by creating a framework in which culturally distinctive groups could maneuver across polities. Curtin has already demonstrated the vital role that trade diasporas of culturally distinctive peoples played in international interactions from the ancient through the early modern periods.[32] This protagonism was made possible in many cases by the ability of such groups to find a footing in "foreign" territories. By demanding legal recognition and protection wherever they operated, such groups themselves constituted a unifying force. The legal frameworks within which they operated established institutional routines for recognizing their "otherness" and permitting some scope for alternative political legal authority to operate. Such institutional patterns laid the groundwork for cross-regional ties that in many cases expanded into much more substantial economic and cultural connections. As states emerged everywhere as the imagined apex of political and legal authority, the protagonism of culturally different groups waned, though in time the space for limited alternative autonomy came to be claimed by other transnational groups and processes.

The third connection to international order exists in the ongoing process of interpreting cultural difference. Individuals and corporate groups crossing the borders of one legal sphere into another – from

---

[32] Philip Curtin, *Cross-Cultural Trade in World History.*

the lands of Christendom, for example, into Muslim territories, or into trading entrepôt cities of Africa and Asia – depended on their hosts' or enemies' abilities to understand and calculate the benefits of inter- action. Once begun, interactions produced routines that generated, if not trust, at least firm expectations about behavior. Missionary activi- ties, formal exchanges of prisoners, informal sponsorship of prohibited trade across religious borders, the migration and hiring of technical per- sonnel across borders – indeed, conversion itself, as a ritualized form of border crossing – these and other patterns formed the basis for an un- easy trust that permitted other more open forms of exchange, including expanded long-distance trade. Within limits, imbalances in exchanges could be regarded with a certain "studied ignorance."[33] The belief in the *possibility* of fairness undergirded order in the absence of an overarching political authority.[34]

But behind mutual tolerance always lay the possibility of conquest, the threat of rebellion, and the danger of mass conversion. Where they occurred, these forces recast both the distribution of power and its dis- course. Where they did not occur, they were ever-present possibilities of disorder and had to be anticipated without, at the same time, undermin- ing the framework for peaceful cross-border exchanges. This contradic- tion in the institutional order between flexibility and pluralism, on the one hand, and hierarchy and command, on the other, was itself another element of social life that created a certain continuity across borders. In practical terms, the contradiction amounted to a widely shared ability of polities to view other groups and political authorities as being "inside" their own political domain – as tolerated minorities with legal standing to be different, as subordinate entities with legally subordinate status, or even as unwelcomed conquerors whose superior force required adapta- tion and resistance. For the early empires, borders did not stand for the limits of the world but designated a category of people – those beyond the borders – as potential insiders rather than permanent outsiders. Put differently, the organizing force of centralized political authority acted much like the state in later periods in that existing patterns of

---

[33] See my discussion of Pierre Bourdieu's use of this phrase and its relevance to law in Chapter 7.

[34] This logic builds upon the analysis of E.P. Thompson in explaining the willingness of eighteenth-century plebeians to submit to the rule of law. E.P. Thompson, *Whigs and Hunters*. For a discussion of the connection of this argument to the structuralist critique of Bourdieu, see Benton, "From the World Systems Perspective to Institutional World History" and Chapter 7 below.

governance became the blueprint for governance even where authority was exercised weakly if at all.[35]

Further, the internal similarities of the constitution of power in many places meant that where conquest did occur, adjustments could be made by both conqueror and conquered without a sense of utter surrender to superior force or to the exigencies of rule. To recognize the prevalence of accommodation is not to suggest that conquest did not do fundamental violence, or that resistance was negligible. It does help us move beyond the dichotomies of collaboration and resistance, though, to see colonial struggles as connected to both indigenous patterns of conflict and the factionalism of colonizing powers. It was precisely the ability of participants to interpret the politics of the other in familiar terms that allowed them to alter their own behavior and institutions to accommodate differences. This process occurred even in places that had little historical opportunity to learn about one another. Lockhart, for example, points out that the Spaniards and the Nahuas of central Mexico had in many ways "more in common than either did with the other peoples of the hemisphere."[36]

The many ways in which political and legal similarities facilitated conquest and colonization in most places – not by producing order, exactly, but by generating a framework for conflict – become clearer when one compares them to places where there was no such fit. The British, for example, were notorious failures at making sense of the political structure of Iboland in eastern Nigeria. Consecutively disruptive policies were answered by continual revolt and, in response, the admission of failure in the form of government-sponsored anthropological expeditions sent to sniff out the "true" location of Ibo political authority. More famously, the response of Hawaiian islanders to Captain Cook's appearance was not to analogize to discover the nature of British political power but to fit British representatives into local cosmology as well as the circumstances permitted. Unfortunately for Cook, this meant killing him.[37]

Political homology, then, was neither inevitable nor universal. Where it did occur, it did not come out of "cultural understanding," or from

---

[35] Even where the state is not intrusive, social actors are aware of its existence and consider it at least a potential authority, so they tend to behave as if the state were in fact regulating their behavior. For an expansion of this argument in relation to the regulating functions of the modern state, see Benton, "Beyond Legal Pluralism."

[36] James Lockhart, *The Nahuas After the Conquest*, p. 5. Greenblatt, in *Marvelous Possessions*, makes the same point.

[37] Sahlins, *How "Natives" Think.*

universal techniques or tendencies of reason, but from similarities in the structural dynamics of conflicts that created certain shared expectations. And it came out of the determination of participants to view their social world as a single entity, with internal distinctions and borders but with no room for permanent outsiders. Hegemony was, in this sense, both a social force and a map of the world.

CONCLUSION

The contested historical movement from truly plural legal orders to state-dominated legal orders is the subject of this book. The analysis of disputes about jurisdiction and the rules of group interaction in law moves the focus from seemingly small conflicts – the difference of opinion, say, between a Marbella Muslim and a North African mufti – to legal cases that were widely regarded as defining the very nature of dominium. The aim of shifting the scale and scope of analysis from individual legal cases to broader patterns of colonial rule, and to international shifts, is to show the connection between particular legal conflicts over jurisdictional boundaries and larger (global) institutional shifts. The result is an intentional juxtaposition of microhistories and macrohistorical argument.

Each of the book's chapters pairs an overview of legal change in colonial contexts with analysis of specific legal cases. The approach risks offending regional specialists. Though I resist claims about the representativeness of the particular conflicts selected for study, the cases were chosen because they illustrate more pervasive tensions. I selected them by a process of narrowing: learning about larger legal and political trends and searching for records of cases that distilled widely diffused conflicts. World historians will, I hope, appreciate the importance of demonstrating the interconnections between small conflicts in particular historical settings and the revision of "master narratives" about global change, at the same time that they will recognize that a narrative produced by this method can hardly aspire to being comprehensive.

In addition to replicating a case study approach, each chapter focuses on a particular dynamic of legal politics and cultural change. Chapter 2 argues that jurisdictional fluidity was a consistent feature across diverse regions of the South Atlantic world. By forming a framework for the relation of communities in diaspora to host polities, the fragmented nature of the legal order supplied a known context for cross-cultural interactions. The next chapter shifts analysis to places where conquest brought more decisive claims of legal authority over culturally different subject populations. Rather than resolving tensions inside imposed legal orders, conquest and colonization often exacerbated those tensions, a point illustrated through discussions of the legal status of religious minorities in the Portuguese and Ottoman empires, and by the more detailed analysis of a particular case study of jurisdictional conflict in the Spanish colonial borderlands.

The fragmented legal order and the conflicts it generated tended to promote the institutional "fix" of rising colonial state power. This process was halting and only indirectly the result of planning. Chapter 4 analyzes cases from India and Africa to show the ways in which legal jockeying helped to create a space for the colonial state, even before such an entity formally existed. Policies promoting a structured legal pluralism brought challenges that in turn drew the state into a leading role in ordering multiple legal authorities, producing implicit and at times explicit claims for legal hegemony. Developing this theme further, Chapter 5 turns to cases in which only a weak pluralism was established. Here, too, we can identify a mid-nineteenth-century shift toward a state-centered legal order and more expansive claims of sovereignty. The shifting treatment of the Khoi in South Africa and the Aborigines in Australia shows that this change responded in no small part to the entanglement of seemingly separate issues, viz., the legal status of indigenous peoples and of subordinate factions of European settlers. Finally, Chapter 7 examines the impact of extraterritoriality on the legal construction of sovereignty in the nineteenth century in areas of informal empire. Paradoxically, foreigners' claims to immunity from national law tended to reinforce pressures for the creation of state-centered legal orders. In different ways, these three chapters support the argument that legal conflicts in the long nineteenth century contributed to the formation of a global interstate order.

A fortuitous, and not entirely accidental, byproduct of the book is to provide historical perspective for considering some of the disruptive forces of global politics in our own time. Cultural and religious factions have been neatly constrained by the nineteenth-century model of state-centered legal pluralism to choose among unsatisfying political alternatives: to press weak claims for sovereignty; pursue narrow, rights-based legal challenges; trade autonomous governance for civic- or status-based associations; or seek control over the state apparatus in an attempt to resurrect nonstate moral or religious authority. In response, the choices of supporting repression, on the one hand, or seeming to endorse a fragmenting parochialism, on the other, are deeply disturbing and limiting. By revealing modern state-centered legal pluralism as historically recent and contingent, we may perhaps help to make space for other frameworks that would allow for greater legitimacy for alternative political authorities without threatening the rule of law. Such an act of imagination may be forced upon us by challenges to traditionally defined states across the globe. But it may be helpful to begin by contemplating historical examples of "orderly disorder" as a way of preparing ourselves for the future.

TWO

Law in Diaspora

The Legal Regime of the Atlantic World

In the public bathhouses of Castilian towns established in the course of the Reconquest, simple attendance served as a reminder of legal identity. Women and men went to the baths on different days, and Jews and Muslims also had designated days. A bathhouse dispute or crime might come to the attention of one of four local legal authorities – the town magistrate, rabbi, qadi, or priest – depending on the gravity of the offense and the day it occurred. Conflicts among co-religionists would be handled by their communities' own judges; for Christians, these would be secular magistrates, unless the Christians had blasphemed or committed some other crime against the faith, in which case the clergy might step in. If a Muslim or Jew committed a serious crime, secular authorities were likely to assert a claim to jurisdiction. Most Castilians perhaps understood only in broad terms where to locate these jurisdictional boundaries, but they must have perceived clearly, even in the simple rituals of bathing, that they lived in a world of divided jurisdictions and that these divisions represented fundamental differences among them. Many Castilians knew, too, that neither the cultural and religious, nor the legal, boundaries were fixed. Crossing was not easy, but there were routines for doing so, from the weightier matter of conversion to the commonplace legal maneuvering that could be used to move a dispute to a more sympathetic forum.[1]

Historians' attention to the narrative of rising state power in Western Europe has tended to obscure the degree to which this fluidity of the

---

[1] On the schedules and rituals of bathhouses in towns of the Reconquest, see Heath Dillard, *Daughters of the Reconquest: Women in Castilian Town Society, 1100–1300*, p. 152.

legal order, and of social categories and identities, was for participants an expected, even naturalized, aspect of the social order. A compelling superiority over minority communities sometimes permitted dominant powers to suppress alternative legal authorities and forums. But power was not often so one-sided, and minority ethnic communities were often useful, particularly in their participation in long-distance trading diasporas. It was far more common for host polities to create or sustain a place in the legal order for "other" authorities, with rules in place about when jurisdiction would revert to ruling institutions.

This jurisdictional complexity was itself a source of continuity across widely different cultural and political entities. In this sense, a single legal regime spanned the interconnected regions of the Mediterranean, South Atlantic, and Indian Ocean worlds in the centuries of expanding long-distance trade. Indeed, structural similarities of different regional systems of law helped to make this expansion possible. Contact, settlement, and the forced migration of Africans to the New World had the effect of reinforcing these similarities. The main feature of this legal regime was a shared emphasis on legal distinctions between cultural and religious groups.

This chapter explores this interconnection by analyzing jurisdictional tensions and their influence in various legal arenas of the Atlantic world, with special emphasis on the South Atlantic. I examine, first, the origins of jurisdictional fluidity in the Iberian empires on the eve of overseas expansion. I then view legal practices in the African states drawn into trade with Europeans in the early centuries of maritime contact. Although Europeans often misinterpreted or denigrated African legal systems, they also responded to aspects of African law they found to be quite familiar – especially its jurisdictional complexity. The third section of the chapter shifts to an analysis of legal culture in the New World African diaspora and argues that an understanding of European and African models of legal pluralism sheds new light on treaty negotiations between planter regimes and maroon communities. I then examine the legal framework for other sorts of captivity and captive rescue in the Atlantic world, in particular the seizure of captives by Barbary pirates and the influence of this phenomenon on European expectations about New World captivity. Across these disparate regions and sets of interactions, and in legal systems reliant on different legal sources, the law structured polities in which the existence of multiple legal authorities gave institutional space to culturally and ethnically different groups. The project of structuring this plural legal order itself created a certain institutional consistency that also allowed various kinds of "strangers" to recognize and learn to manipulate the legal processes of foreign, or host, polities.

Jurisdictional complexity was an inherent part of the legal order of Iberian society on the eve of conquest. The legal order contained overlapping authorities and forums, and the scope and precise nature of claims to legal control were continually in dispute. One set of tensions focused on the boundary between secular and religious legal authority. Another contested boundary was that between local and centralized law. These jurisdictional debates sometimes intersected, and the dynamics and language of one arena of conflict tended to influence the other. Patterns of jurisdictional jockeying established both an institutional framework and a rhetorical resource for colonial legal disputants, who imported into Latin America the association of legal authority with cultural and religious group boundaries.

The divide between canon and state law in medieval Europe more generally was important in setting the terms of jurisdictional conflicts of all sorts. The early history of the Catholic Church established canon law as an independent judicial system with jurisdiction over significant areas of social life. The transformation from a relatively unimportant force in the rule of a minority of Roman society to a central element of imperial administration occurred mainly in the fourth century. During this period, the nature and structure of church authority were transformed. The period marked the development of a church hierarchy – largely in response to and in emulation of the hierarchy of Roman imperial administration – and church synods and councils began to function as courts and legislative bodies. Unsurprisingly, the change in the position of the church went hand in hand with new jurisdictional complexities. On one side, church authority had to be separated from imperial authority; on the other, the increasing power of canon law sharpened distinctions between Christians and non-Christians.

The church secured recognition of its authority over matters related to belief and practice, and this jurisdictional scope was interpreted widely by church leaders to include purview over marriage and family law, slavery, some types of economic and commercial behavior, and military service. In addition, church leaders became preoccupied with regulating interactions between Christians and non-Christians, using law to accentuate the borders separating religious communities. Non-Christians were further broken down into the categories of heretics, apostates, and unbelievers. In addition to being barred from participating in shared religious celebrations with other groups, Christians were forbidden to engage in an array of social interactions with non-Christians. Such restrictions extended naturally to the law. Whereas the canon law has been described as historically novel for its application to all Christians, regardless of gender or class, the law distinguished sharply between the legal status of Christians and non-Christians. The latter were not permitted under ecclesiastical law to sit as judges or magistrates in cases involving Christians. Jews could not serve as witnesses in suits involving Christians. Church leaders reserved the greatest wrath and restrictions for lapsed Christians or those who had deviated from Christian teaching.

Thus two sorts of jurisdictional distinctions were being made early: one that established authority by reference to particular activities and another that awarded jurisdiction by asserting authority over particular classes of persons. The definition of law as personal law was reinforced under the Germanic rulers. One effect of this emphasis was to reduce the authority of canon law in the early medieval period. The decline in imperial authority, of course, also weakened the centralizing power of the church. Canon law developed along local lines and responded increasingly to the directives of local rulers. The exception to this trend came under the Carolingian empire, when eighth- and ninth-century reforms tightened the relation between secular and religious law. While enhancing the legitimacy of church institutions, including canon law, the reforms aimed at bringing the church into the service of imperial order. Their force did not outlast the fragmentation of Carolingian control. Into the tenth century, the prominent pattern everywhere was, as Brundage puts it, "subordination of ecclesiastical institutions and religious values to the whims and drives of soldiers, adventurers, and thugs."[2]

This balance began to shift again in the eleventh century. Papal strategies to assert church independence, protect church property, and discipline recalcitrant rulers were closely intertwined with the reform of church law. The refashioning of canon law included an attempt at a thorough systematization of legal doctrine, through compilations of existing law and additions to it and the writing of new law. Just as

---

[2] James Brundage, *Medieval Canon Law*, p. 34. I have drawn extensively on Brundage's excellent summary of medieval canon law in my account.

important, though, was a procedural overhaul to establish an orderly court system and prosecute offenders. These objectives overlapped as eleventh-century canonists sought to reinforce the jurisdictional hierarchy within the church by weighting decisions of superior authorities more than those of local, now subordinate councils and synods. Procedural reforms happened more slowly, and by trial (literally) and error. Papal legates sent out to resolve local disputes were used extensively, though sometimes ineffectually, to reinforce papal authority. Gaining control over monasteries and parishes that sought exemptions under the protection of local rulers proved particularly difficult. A smoothly functioning system of ecclesiastical courts would prove elusive until well after other institutional and political shifts in the twelfth century.

Berman has labeled the period from the middle of the eleventh century to the middle of twelfth century, a period encompassing the Gregorian Reformation and Investiture Struggle, as revolutionary.[3] The events of this period, he has argued, laid the basis for a distinctive Western legal tradition, and the origins of an orderly legal pluralism in the West are to be found precisely in the tensions between secular and religious law that I have begun to outline. That is, the legacy of tensions between secular and religious law came to be imprinted on the state and the institutional ways of resolving these tensions constituted an important source of regional order. Further, Berman argues, the similarity of jurisdictional tensions across polities *inside* the West were a fundamental element of the creation of a *transnational* legal order. This argument is consistent with the main themes of this book. But Berman goes further in claiming that the jurisdictional complexity of the West was historically unique – he cites it as "the most distinguishing characteristic" of the Western legal tradition.[4] This claim is one I will challenge in this chapter and the next. One does not have to accept it in order to agree that the period from 1050 to 1150 marked a fundamental reorganization of legal authority in the West and that jurisdictional tensions defined this shift.

In 1075, Pope Gregory VII declared that the papacy had complete authority within the church and should not be subject anywhere to secular authority. The conflicts between the papacy and secular rulers that followed this declaration ranged from diplomatic sparring to open warfare and cannot be surveyed here. Essential for our purposes (and for

---

[3] See Harold J. Berman, *Law and Revolution: The Formation of the Western Legal Tradition.*
[4] Berman, *Law and Revolution*, "Introduction," and especially p. 9.

Berman's) is the observation that establishing papal authority depended upon a more rigorous separation of ecclesiastical law from secular law. This separation created, in turn, irresistible pressures for the emergence of a class of legal professionals and a separate court hierarchy, and for a clearer definition of the jurisdictional boundaries of the two legal systems. Paradoxically, this drive for systematization also led to more pervasive borrowing of legal practices and principles across canon and civil law systems; to prevalent cross-training among legal professionals; and, by the end of the thirteenth century, to the conceptual unification of Romano-canonical law into the *ius commune,* or the body of law that was common to Christian territories and that could supersede customary law everywhere.

The interdependence yet separateness of the two legal systems are illustrated well in the career paths of legal professionals. At Bologna, which emerged as the undisputed center of legal studies in Europe, and at other universities, it was possible to specialize in canon law and, by the early decades of the thirteenth century, to receive a degree that designated specialization. By the middle of the century or so, canonists comprised a distinctive occupational group that sought to regulate admissions to its ranks and establish norms of professional conduct.[5] In practice, however, canonists included in their ranks those with broader legal training who were prudently preparing to represent any sort of clientele in any kind of forum. And law-trained personnel of all varieties were assuming positions of prominence in civil affairs. The interplay between secular and ecclesiastical law was more than doctrinal and procedural; it was embodied in the personnel staffing both legal systems.

Not surprisingly, jurisdictional boundaries shifted often and tended to form a focus for legal politics. Claims establishing church authority continued to have a dual rationale asserting church control over particular classes of actions and beliefs and over particular classes of persons. Canonists claimed jurisdiction, for example, over clerics in all matters, no matter how serious the alleged infractions. But the claims extended, too, to broad categories of persons who were seen by the church as requiring its protection. These groups included crusaders, "wretched persons" (poor people, widows, orphans), and travelers (for example, merchants, students, and sailors), who moved from one local jurisdiction to another. For all these classes of persons, secular jurisdiction might apply in particular times and places – this was true even for the clergy,

---

[5] See Brundage, *Medieval Canon Law,* pp. 64–65.

though technically they and members of their households fell narrowly under the purview of ecclesiastical courts. The jurisdictional rules established the right of the church to intervene only where secular authorities were not protecting the interests of a member of these groups.

Ecclesiastical courts also claimed jurisdiction over certain classes of activities. The realm of ecclesiastical authority was in general considered to cover activities related to spiritual concerns. But this was broadly defined. It included the traditional preserve of canonists, namely, marriage, inheritance, and in general the constitution of families, intrafamilial relations, and sexual relations. It extended, too, to commercial and financial actions of various sorts: usury, benefices, the collection of tithes, and the administration of church property.[6] As they had in the past, canonists on the eve of conquest claimed a special authority to define and punish heresy. The formation of the Inquisition relaxed the stringent proofs required to establish guilt under canon law and allowed judges wide latitude in interrogating the accused. The Inquisition was in this sense a special type of court and court procedure in a plural legal order. It was an institution specializing in defining and enforcing the boundary between Christians and the legally distinctive categories of heretic, apostate, and unbeliever.

Alongside these guidelines establishing church authority existed mechanisms for virtually anyone to submit voluntarily to the jurisdiction of ecclesiastical courts. Litigants could do so at the time a dispute arose or even in advance, as an element of a contractual agreement. More broadly still, any litigant could take a dispute to an ecclesiastical court if he thought that it was impossible to obtain justice in a secular court. The church thus recognized the existence and legitimacy of secular courts while at the same time asserting a theoretically higher authority that justified an informal appellate role.

In Iberia, these jurisdictional tensions were pervasive in Christian territories. With the exception of the persecution of crimes of heresy, church claims were often contested by secular authorities. There was also cooperation, though, as when ecclesiastical judges released criminals to secular authorities for much harsher punishments than the church could inflict, or where political enemies sought to discredit each other by exhorting ecclesiastical courts to punish sinful behavior.

---

[6] Canonists' broad definition of church authority also brought ecclesiastical courts more frequently into the prosecution of criminal complaints, especially in matters involving clergy, where church claims were clearest. See Brundage, *Medieval Canon Law.*

Beyond corporate struggle and cooperation, individual litigants encountered a legal landscape in which choices of forums (in turn loosely
linked to different sources of law) defined legal strategies. Church law
was well regarded for its more orderly and uniform doctrine and procedure, and (notwithstanding the reputation of the Inquisition) its generally more lenient punishments. Secular law was more permissive in
certain areas and stringent in its requirements for establishing the validity of local custom. This possibility of recurring to different jurisdictions
not only contributed to legal sophistication but also focused the attention of jurists themselves on the boundaries of legal systems.[7]

A particular source of disruption to the distribution of authority was
the encounter of Europeans with increasing numbers of non-Christians.
Canon law had, in its early formulations, asserted only limited authority over unbelievers. Jews, for example, though subject to ecclesiastical court jurisdiction in disputes with Christians, were free to disobey
church law regarding marriage. They were also not required to pay
tithes, even when they lived in Christian-ruled territories. These rules
came increasingly under scrutiny as the Reconquest of the Iberian peninsula brought larger numbers of Muslims under Christian rule. Both the
practical tensions and theological debates prompted by this trend urged
a shift in the dynamics of legal pluralism and set the terms for struggle
and debate about the legal claims of conquerors and the rights of the
conquered. Although many historical accounts emphasize the crown's
break with tolerance – the expulsion and forced conversion of Jews and
Muslims – these events followed a long period of accommodation in
which complex and locally varied arrangements allowed for the coexistence of multiple legal authorities, including those of religious "others"
in conquered territories.

Such accommodations were based closely on the model of shared and
mutually limited jurisdictions of church and state. Before the thirteenth
century, canonists had shown relatively little interest in defining the
relation between Christians and infidels outside Europe. In the middle
decades of the thirteenth century, Pope Innocent IV addressed Christian-
infidel relations and in a commentary on the seizure of infidels' lands
held that infidels had the right to hold property. Yet Innocent IV also

---

[7] As Berman puts it, "the limitations placed upon the jurisdiction of each of the polities
of Western Christendom, including the ecclesiastical polity . . . made it both necessary
and possible for each to develop not only laws but also a *system* of laws, and more
than that, a system of *law*" (Berman, *Law and Revolution*, p. 223).

anticipated circumstances under which the church would have the authority to intervene in infidel society. His reasoning exactly paralleled, and in fact built upon, the logic of arguments that the church could intervene in secular affairs if needed to preserve or obtain justice. Innocent IV thus concluded that the pope had "jurisdiction over infidels *de jure* but not *de facto*."[8] The church could assert its authority in cases where the actions of infidels violated divine law. Going further still, Innocent IV argued that the pope could intervene in cases where unbelievers violated *their own* law. Again, the logic was parallel to that which had been used to establish church legal authority when secular courts had failed to administer justice. In subsequent commentary, canonists were both carefully limiting the jurisdiction of the church and establishing a special responsibility of the church to intervene and protect natural law.

In the Iberian peninsula, where interdependence drove Christians, Jews, and Muslims together, all three groups sought to reinforce the idea of an orderly pluralism in which communities followed their own laws. There were obvious incentives to make such a system work. Christians on the frontier often found themselves dependent on non-Christians. Muslims who did not follow the edicts of religious leaders to leave Christian-controlled territories were crucial to the agricultural economy. In some regions, especially in Valencia, they also made up the majority of skilled workers in craft occupations. Jews served Christian elites in advisory roles in matters of finance and statecraft, and they were prominent in medicine and commerce. Though church leaders feared "contamination" for Christians living among unbelievers, Christian residents in the newly conquered regions sought to contain conflict. For Muslims, practical considerations also often outweighed pressures for religious conformity. Although Islamic teaching had long recognized the rights of Christians and Jews to live under their own law, Muslim scholars had not anticipated a situation in which one of these groups, rather than Muslims, would be in power. Religious leaders found no support in Islamic scholarship for living as a subjugate population. Large numbers of refugees did leave for North Africa or for Granada, where an Islamic state held out against Christian incursions until 1492. But many also

[8] Quoted in James Muldoon, *Popes, Lawyers, and Infidels: The Church and the Non-Christian World, 1250–1550*, p. 10. Muldoon's work remains the best study of debates about the legal incorporation of non-Christians. See also Robert A. Williams, *The American Indian in Western Legal Thought: The Discourses of Conquest*.

stayed behind and sought a quiet accommodation with Christian rule. Religious leaders on both sides advocated separation – social distance and residential segregation. Particularly given the pressures in favor of conversion, on the Christian side, and flight, on the part of Muslims, it is not surprising that the architecture of this plural legal order was difficult both to design and to sustain. Jurisdictional tensions (though somewhat difficult to study in detail because of the nature of sources) recurred and probably contributed to the growing sophistication of legal culture on the peninsula and the rising importance of legal training among elites.

We thus find examples of legal arrangements that would have surely been rejected by religious doctrine on both sides receiving tacit acceptance. Merely by remaining in Christian lands, Muslims (*mudejars*, the common term for subject Muslims in Christian territories) were already disobeying religious teaching. It seems to be the case, too, that they reinforced Christian authority in some places as a protection against the abuses of local lords. In the kingdom of Aragon, for example, where mudejars generally occupied a low level in the socioeconomic order as sharecroppers, Muslims also benefited from a measure of royal protection. The Aragonese crown claimed special jurisdiction over mudejars in the region. This device was probably an adaptation of the legal status of Jews throughout Europe. Although mudejars' special legal status reflected their exclusion from the rights of "citizenship," individual Muslims undoubtedly used the status of protected outsider in appeals to royal justice to remedy local abuse. Harvey suggests that some Christians would have preferred the ambiguity of Muslim legal status.[9] At the same time, legal offices were still needed in the Muslim community for the adjudication of disputes not involving Christians. In Aragon, as in other regions, Christian authorities made appointments to these posts (which were sometimes lucrative) on the basis of patronage ties, political considerations, and financial interests. It was not uncommon in the later centuries of the Reconquest to find *Christian qadis* – an abomination by Islamic legal standards, but a practice that would not have been inconsistent with developing canonist ideas about the obligation and ability of Christians to administer law other than their own. Even where the qadis were Muslim, their close ties to royal authority made their independence highly doubtful.

---

9 Harvey, *Islamic Spain*, p. 102. The summary of jurisdictional complexities in Spain around the time of the Reconquest draws especially on Harvey's work. See also Richard Kagan, *Lawsuits and Litigants in Castile, 1500–1700*.

Muslim litigants in Aragon also blurred the separation of the two legal systems. It was possible for Muslims to take their disputes to a Christian forum, and it is not unlikely that some chose to do so to avoid harsh penalties they might have incurred under Muslim law. There is certainly evidence that Muslims chose on occasion prominent Christians as arbitrators. Choosing arbitration was a well-established Islamic legal practice and, though Islamic jurists would have been appalled by the designation of non-Muslim arbitrators, this strategy made sense when litigants believed that judgments by Christian elites would have greater legitimacy and possibility of enforcement. Finally, though Muslims presided over their own courts, royal jurisdiction offered a final level of appeal, thus drawing the separate systems together. We do not know how often Muslims took cases to the king, but even though he was theoretically bound to judge cases according to the shari'a, the formal role for a non-Muslim in cases involving Muslims was historically new and, from the perspective of Islamic jurists, inevitably contaminating.

It was in the region of Valencia where the contradictions and tensions of the plural legal order were most apparent. Whereas in other newly conquered regions, Muslims became a minority in a generation, in Valencia they remained in the majority and the Christian settler populations stayed small for centuries. The Christians found that by paying a salary to qadis and other Muslim officials they would ensure order and support the peaceful collection of taxes and tribute. Thus qadis had the contradictory role of preserving Islamic law and submitting to Christian authority. In Valencia as in Aragon, the king exercised the function of a judge in cases on appeal. Rule on appeal by nonreligious authorities did not in and of itself go against Islamic legal tradition; as we will see in a later chapter, there was considerable support among Islamic jurists for obedience to secular authority. The situation was historically novel, however, since the authority in this case was not even Muslim. There is little evidence, too, that the shari'a was seriously referred to by the king, who instead used appeals cases to demonstrate the power of Christian mercy.

Consider a case described by both Burns and Harvey, in which James I pardoned a slave who had been found guilty in a qadi court for killing another slave.[10] The first slave had tossed a javelin, not aiming for the

---

[10] Robert Burns, *Islam Under the Crusaders: Colonial Survival in the Thirteenth-Century Kingdom of Valencia*, p. 252; Harvey, *Islamic Spain*, pp. 131–32.

second slave, who had tried to catch it and was struck in the throat and killed. The different expected outcomes in Islamic and Christian forums might seem to reflect different traditional treatments of intentionality.[11] But Harvey believes that the problem is not the accidental nature of the killing, for which the Quran lays down explicit punishments in the case of slaves, but the fact that both slaves were the property of a Christian. No laws or precedents applied to such a case in Islamic law. It was the anomaly created by the complex social order, and not the clash of legal cultures, that led the case to the king. In situations such as this one, where power determined who would decide unprecedented cases falling between one system of law and the other, the legal outcome was a gradual undermining of the force of the shari'a, even while the structure of the system still protected its authority. That this gradual erosion was apparent even in Valencia suggests that the Islamic jurists were in fact right to warn that by accepting a subject status in a Christian-ruled polity, Muslims would find the moral authority of their leaders inevitably undermined.

Over time, a gradual weakening of Muslim (and Jewish) authority did occur through restrictions on non-Christian law. Cases involving Christians and Jews were tried only in royal courts, the crown reserved the right to bring criminal cases, and even civil suits among co-religionists could be appealed to a royal court. By 1476, Jews and Muslims involved in disputes with co-religionists could bring suit before a Christian judge. Even where Jewish and Muslim courts continued to operate, then, they did so with significant direct and indirect influence of Christian and crown law.

These sources of gradual change gave way to a much more aggressive assault in the wake of the conquest of Granada. At first, Christian rule was established in the pattern that had been followed in other regions: Muslims were to retain their right to practice their own religion and obey their own laws. The Capitulations of Granada specified, "The Moors shall be judged in their laws and law suits according to the code of the shari'a, which it is their custom to respect, under the jurisdiction of their judges and qadis."[12] Suits between Christians and Muslims were to be judged by both a Christian judge and a qadi. Muslim inheritance law

---

[11] On intentionality in various cultural contexts, see Lawrence Rosen, ed., *Other Intentions: Cultural Contexts and the Attribution of Inner States.*

[12] Harvey, *Islamic Spain*, p. 318.

was also explicitly protected. Yet this attempt to re-create mudejar status for Muslims in Granada was short-lived. Forced conversion of elite Muslims, some after being tortured and publicly humiliated, together with the open persecution of *elches*, or Christians who had converted to Islam, helped to spur the revolt in 1500. After this date, forced conversion became widespread. Its acceptance was clearly linked to the formal shift in the legal position of Jews, who were required in 1492 to convert or emigrate. Thus the completion of the conquest of Iberian territories coincided neatly with the official end of a policy of protected legal status and the separation of legal authorities.

Still, we should not mistake this shift for a full claim of sovereignty by the state. Forced conversion sought to eliminate the tensions of religious pluralism by removing the subjects of non-Christian religious communities – not by emphasizing or defining more precisely their subordination to secular authority. It was the inability of the crown to control and order diversity that led to the extreme measures of expulsion and forced conversion. The possibilities of pluralism remained a part of the legal order in the continuing coexistence of Christian and state law, the dualism that had served as a model for the legal pluralism of the various religious communities in conquered territories.

Complexities in the legal order stemmed only in part from the coexistence of religious groups with separate legal authorities. An even more pervasive tension was found in the relationship of local custom to royal legal authority. As the Christian conquest edged across the peninsula, each major settlement adopted its *fuero*, a written or unwritten body of customary law. The fueros drew on Roman law and were substantially alike. They regulated everything from criminal procedure and punishment, to sexual conduct, to the selection and qualifications of local magistrates. The crown's formal efforts to establish royal authority as superior to the fueros had begun in the mid-thirteenth century with the Fuero Royal and the Siete Partidas. Royal claims had been more forcefully asserted in 1348, when the Ordenamiento del Alcalá established an order of precedence for sources of law that noted the superiority of royal law to fueros. But the force of custom continued to guide most judicial decisions. As in its relation to the law of religious minorities, at the same time, the crown asserted its right to act as a court of appeal and in this way began to influence procedures and actions in local forums. As Christian territory expanded, moreover, Castilian law was applied to conquered territories, a practice that was continued in the Americas, in contrast to the legislative independence awarded colonists in North America.[13]

In addition to this indirect influence, the crown established the right in the Siete Partidas to intervene directly – to oversee the court of first instance – in cases involving widows, orphans, the aged, crippled, sick, poor, or "wretched." This claim set up a parallel relationship between royal and local authority, on the one hand, and ecclesiastical and secular authority, on the other, with the subtle but important difference that the crown's jurisdiction over the various classes of disadvantaged persons rested not on any claim to divine authority but on the obligation to provide summary judgment for these subjects and release them from the burdens of protracted litigation. The costs of litigation and the long delays involved in most suits were already a well-known part of the legal culture of the peninsula. Later, the crown's obligation to provide summary judgment and legal representation to widows, orphans, and *miserables* would provide a model for the legal status and treatment of American Indians.

In Portugal, as in Spain, the Reconquest produced a patchwork legal order. In the south of Portugal, Muslim offices and administrative boundaries were adapted to Portuguese use. The local unit of judicial administration was the township (*conselho*), which contained various officials involved in the administration of justice, the most important of whom was the *juiz ordinário*, municipal magistrate. Gradually, the crown enacted legal reforms to improve its control over local administration of justice. The crown created the office of *juizes da fora* ("judges from outside") in 1352, to oversee local magistrates, and strengthened royal courts of appeal. By the fourteenth century, justice "was firmly monopolized by the crown."[14] Further centralization took place in the early sixteenth century, when the crown issued the Ordenaçoes Manuelinas, greatly increased the number of juizes da fora, and extended the authority of *corregedores*, superior crown magistrates who occupied a next level of royal judicial overview.

Yet, the Portuguese legal order had the same forces operating within it as in Spain to create a certain jurisdictional looseness. Limited legal autonomy continued to be extended to non-Christian religious

---

[13] A particularly good overview of the similarities and differences of the fueros (and their relation, too, to the law of different religious communities) can be found in Dillard, *Daughters of the Reconquest*. See also Kagan, *Lawsuits and Litigants in Castille*.

[14] A.H. de Oliveira Marques, *History of Portugal, Vol. I,* p. 99.

communities, and Jews were segregated in designated, self-regulating quarters of the larger cities. Military-religious orders continued to function under a separate legal bureaucracy, with officials called *ouvidores*, appointed by the military order, rather than crown-appointed corregedores. As in Spain, ecclesiastics enjoyed immunity from secular courts, and they sought jurisdiction over special classes of people and crimes against the faith.

In summary, the legal order of Iberia on the eve of overseas conquest was one that is best characterized as "essentially a patchwork of customs and law . . . and of judicial jurisdictions."[15] Spain, in particular, was a relatively litigious society, in which legal strategies and expertise were widely used to defend group, family, and individual interests. As Borah has noted, overseas conquest and colonization seemed to offer the crown an irresistible opportunity to simplify and solidify the jurisdictional patchwork.[16] Simplicity was not, however, what colonial conditions would produce. Chapter 3 will explore the new jurisdictional tensions of Spanish America. Here we will turn to the legal complexities of the Portuguese Atlantic diaspora, with its roots in both the European legal pluralism we have already described and the multicentric legal orders of the Atlantic world beyond Europe.

LAW IN THE PORTUGUESE TRADING-POST EMPIRE

The complex legal landscape inside Portugal before the fifteenth century helps to explain the crown's willingness to follow ad hoc arrangements for the administration of justice as the Portuguese moved into the Atlantic. In administering military outposts on the coast of North Africa, Atlantic island settlements in the Azores and Madeira, the islands off the coast of Guinea, the islands of São Tomé and Cabo Verde, and the West African coastal trading factories, the Portuguese combined a strategy of delegating legal authority to captains and privateers with sporadic attempts to assert royal supervision. The laws of Portugal were

---

[15] Borah makes this point about Spain. It would also apply to Portugal, though the earlier completion of the Reconquest also shifted to an earlier century the prominence of debates about the legal incorporation of non-Christians. See Woodrow Borah, *Justice by Insurance: The General Indian Court of Colonial Mexico and the Legal Aides of the Half-Real*, p. 8; Kagan reports that Castile was a "hodgedpodge of confused laws and competing jurisdictions that crafty litigants exploited to their own advantage" (Kagan, *Lawsuits and Litigants in Castille*, p. 5).

[16] Borah, *Justice by Insurance*, p. 16.

to be applied in the overseas territories. In many outposts, captains were awarded summary judicial powers and had ultimate jurisdiction except in the most serious cases. Some captains were permitted to appoint ouvidores, as in the Azores and on Madeira. In Angola and Brazil, *donatários,* nobles who had been awarded control over extended tracts of territory, also had judicial authority but could appoint ouvidores. The crown periodically expressed its dissatisfaction with this system and sent corregedores to investigate ouvidores appointed by captains and privateers.[17] This occurred in the Azores and, in 1516, on the islands of São Tomé, Cabo Verde, and the islands off the Guinea coast. The crown showed its readiness to intervene when judicial powers were seriously abused. At Mina, on the West African coast, judges from Lisbon were sent in 1562 to investigate the activities of an outpost commander who, when accused of involvement in illicit trade, had sent the local bailiff to the galleys.[18]

Consistent across the Portuguese territories and trading posts, from Brazil to Malacca, was an official reluctance to assert jurisdictional claims outside the Portuguese community of settlers, soldiers, privateers, and crown officials. This did not mean that the line dividing this population from indigenous communities was easily defined. In many of the Atlantic islands, Angola, Goa, and certainly Brazil, the Portuguese administered law to a heterogeneous population of Portuguese-born settlers, indigenous inhabitants who had not been enslaved, non-Portuguese slaves, Portuguese convicts, and a growing population of mulatto and mestizo residents who spoke Portuguese and considered themselves Christians. Where jurisdictional claims extended outside these groups, it was usually in an attempt to supervise the behavior of Christians who lived outside the bounds of Portuguese towns or posts.[19] In Mina, a fortified outpost devoted to trade, the vicar arrested a baptized former slave named Grace in 1540, who had gone to live in the nearby African

---

[17] The crown also had a standing interest in trying to control the conduct of illicit trade. A royal official called the Judge of Guinea and India had authority to take depositions from returning ships' crews and to order arrests or fines for any deviations from sailing orders. John Vogt, *Portuguese Rule on the Gold Coast, 1469–1682*, pp. 38–39.

[18] See Vogt (*Portuguese Rule on the Gold Coast*) for a discussion of this case of 1563.

[19] Outside the Atlantic, the pattern of Portuguese legal administration was similar, though in Goa, the administrative center of the trading post empire, a larger local subject population and the creation of a sizable community of nominal Christians through intermarriage produced new legal challenges. A tribunal of the Inquisition was established in 1560 in Goa, further complicating legal politics. See Chapter 3 for an analysis of Portuguese policies and local responses in Goa.

village and, by her own admission, had forgotten her Christian teaching. The Portuguese went to the village and searched her house, where they found fetishes. The vicar had her sent to Lisbon, where she was tried before the Inquisition and sentenced to perpetual imprisonment.[20] Such attempts to extend authority outside the factories occurred, though, very rarely. In Angola, where the royal family and members of the court converted, the Portuguese left judicial affairs of Africans entirely in their hands. Members of the elite traveled to Portugal, where their education would have included canon law, but they were not made part of the Portuguese legal administration on their return, and we have little knowledge of the impact of their training on local administration of justice. The overall pattern remained one of restricted rather than expansionist claims about the boundaries of judicial authority.[21]

Even in Brazil, where the Portuguese were not able to operate under the same trading post system but, from the 1530s on, pursued a policy of settlement and plantation agriculture, Portuguese law was applied narrowly to Europeans. Indians were either condemned as living outside the law or treated to virtually unregulated disciplinary excesses if they lived within Portuguese-controlled territory. Private justice, and severe, ad hoc punishments were administered to Indians suspected of crimes against Portuguese. Sixteenth-century Jesuit writings complained that the Portuguese administered this rough justice to Indians while treating infractions against Indians by Portuguese with great leniency. One Jesuit father wrote that Indians were regularly "hanged, hewn in pieces, quartered, their hands cut, nipped with hot pinchers, and set in the mouth of pieces, and shot away."[22]

---

[20] John Vogt, *Portuguese Rule on the Gold Coast*, p. 56.

[21] The only territory over which the Portuguese attempted to extend tighter control was in the seas. Here claims of sovereignty were understood to justify all manner of interventions, from seizures of ships' cargoes to blockades. The Portuguese relied on papal bulls recognizing their control of ocean trade in asserting this claim. But the Portuguese were painfully aware of its limitations. Africans, Asians, and other Europeans plied "Portuguese" waters with persistent regularity, and Portuguese renegades themselves skirted crown controls over trade. Although Patricia Seed makes much of the Portuguese tendency to claim possession of sea lanes delineated by navigational markers, this claim of sovereignty was, much like land ownership in coastal enclaves, a useful fiction (Patricia Seed, *Ceremonies of Possession*). More important to the world of the Portuguese was their sense that legal authority extended over people who in one sense or another belonged to the community of the Portuguese, as Christians, subordinates, or slaves.

[22] Stuart B. Schwartz, *Sovereignty and Society in Colonial Brazil: The High Court of Bahia and Its Judges, 1609–1751*, p. 31.

The Jesuits, of course, were engaged in a long struggle with secular officials and settlers over control of the Indian population. Schwartz describes the legal dimensions of this struggle as involving "constant jurisdictional dispute" in the decades leading up to the ascension of Spanish sovereignty over Portugal in 1580.[23] The Jesuits aligned themselves on a number of occasions with the *ouvidor geral* against governors, and governors in turn were known to seize the estates of crown judges and send them back to Portugal. Hapsburg reforms after 1580 sought to move Brazil toward a more tightly centralized system, but these efforts were not always effective. In 1609, a new High Court of Brazil, the *Relação*, arrived in Bahia and soon after published a new law issued in Madrid making it illegal to employ Indians without paying them a wage and declaring that all Indians captured illegally should be freed. Measures for enforcement included provisions that the governor and High Court chancellor would appoint a special magistrate for each village to adjudicate disputes between whites and Indians. But this new regime was never successfully put in place. Instead, the law was replaced in 1611 with a decree permitting slavery under certain conditions and awarding full judicial powers over Indians to Portuguese captains in each settlement. The law included provisions for appeals to the local ouvidor or to an official specially designated as a magistrate of Indian affairs. But this retreat reestablished the status quo of the legal marginalization – and effective exclusion – of Indians in Brazil as legal actors.

The limited legal authority of the crown in Brazil was reproduced in outlying regions. Here the crown's attempts to provide for the administration of justice were desultory. The interior region of the *sertão* had a reputation as a place of lawlessness – a refuge, in fact, for fugitives. In the south, slave raiding against Indians in the interior was difficult to control, and royal officials found that "intentional disregard" served their own interests better.[24]

It is important to note that despite the difference in settlement patterns in Brazil and Africa, Portuguese officials treated the regions as part of the same legal realm. Portuguese *degregados*, or convicts, were exiled from Brazil to Angola; even African slaves were sometimes punished in this way. In the mid-sixteenth century, the crown even officially extended Brazilian legal jurisdiction to include parts of West Africa. Although Angola was never formally placed under the authority of the

---

[23] Schwartz, *Sovereignty and Society in Colonial Brazil*, p. 39.
[24] Schwartz, *Sovereignty and Society in Colonial Brazil*, p. 166.

High Court of Bahia, this measure was suggested, and some judicial oversight, mainly in the form of supervision of reviews of royal officials in Africa, was instituted.[25] This perception on the part of Portuguese officials that they were operating in a single judicial field is significant in and of itself. The limits placed by Portuguese policy makers in Brazil on the expansion of the judicial bureaucracy and on its authority must be understood in this wider Atlantic context, in which the Portuguese were accustomed to operating as one of many competing judicial authorities with relatively narrow purview.

This is not to say that the Portuguese did not view law as crucial to overseas empire.[26] As in Spanish America, though, colonial conditions exacerbated sources of jurisdictional tension between the crown and the church, and institutional controls dissipated on the frontier. In addition to these forces, the Portuguese were influenced by their insertion into a legal universe in Africa that was itself structured around the coexistence of multiple legal authorities. This homology – rather than any striking difference with African legal institutions – reinforced practical adaptations made by the Portuguese in restricting legal jurisdictional claims. In a narrow sense, surely, the Iberian empires were imposing state law; in a broader sense, they were formulating state law as an extension of personal law.

LEGAL PLURALISM IN AFRICA

The continuing jurisdictional complexity and fluidity of the Iberian legal orders must be kept in mind when evaluating the tendency of some scholars to emphasize fundamental differences in the nature of legal authority in Europe and Africa in the early centuries of maritime trade. Thornton, for example, has argued that the distinctiveness (and unity) of

---

[25] Schwartz, *Sovereignty and Society in Colonial Brazil*, p. 254. Schwartz points out that some Portuguese officials who were sent to Africa in judicial posts were given titles as officials of the High Court of Bahia, though they never set foot in Brazil. In 1744, he reports, leaders of a São Tomé slave rebellion were sent to Bahia where the High Court was expected to sentence them. The court refused, claiming it had no jurisdiction over Africa.

[26] Boxer reports that "maladministration of justice (*a falta de justiça*) was the theme of continued complaints in both official and unofficial correspondence" from all corners of the Portuguese overseas world over the span of several centuries. Portuguese chroniclers observed the corrosive effects of the widespread flaunting of judicial procedure on perceptions of Portuguese rule among non-Europeans. See C.R. Boxer, *The Portuguese Seaborne Empire, 1415–1825*, p. 144.

African legal traditions is key to an understanding of European-African relations between 1400 and 1680. In particular, the expansion of the maritime slave trade had only a controlled effect on Africa because slavery not only already existed but was fundamental in African economic and legal systems. Thornton writes that slavery "was widespread in Atlantic Africa because slaves were the only form of private, revenue-producing property recognized in African law. By contrast, in European legal systems, land was the primary form of private, revenue-producing property, and slavery was relatively minor."[27] Thornton concludes that Africa was not "backward or egalitarian," only "legally divergent."[28] Europeans were so conditioned by the experience of their own, very different legal institutions that they failed to understand this fundamental difference and behaved, at times, as if Africans also had a market in land and measured both wealth and sovereignty in terms of control over land.[29]

While a substantial improvement on approaches that would ignore African institutions or represent them as irrevocably damaged by contact with Europeans, such a view exaggerates the differences in European and African institutions and overlooks substantial similarities and even some direct connections. In drawing the distinction between African and European systems of law, Thornton makes much of the central place of landholding in European legal traditions, even calling "the concept of landownership ... the fundamental starting point of law."[30] He notes that the Siete Partidas states clearly that all land should have an owner, either private persons or the state. Yet, as we have seen in outlining legal tensions in early modern Spain, such a statement was not incompatible with the continued influence of forms of personal law. Indeed, even where the definition of property was concerned, it is not clear that the concept of ownership was radically different in Iberia from what it appears to have been in many African kingdoms. Thornton notes that conquest in precolonial Africa generated income in tribute and taxes, not rights to landed property, per se. African "nobles" thus "ultimately derived their rights from their position in the state and

---

[27] John Thornton, *Africa and Africans in the Making of the Atlantic World, 1400–1680*, p. 74. Thornton does note in regard to slavery in Europe and Africa that "legally the institutions were indistinguishable" (p. 86, note 58), but he insists that the different treatment of land made the institutions function in strikingly different ways.

[28] Thornton, *Africa and Africans*, p. 76.

[29] Thornton, *Africa and Africans*, pp. 76–77. See also pp. 95 and 105.

[30] Thornton, *Africa and Africans*, p. 76.

not as landowners in the European sense."[31] But this statement would also describe both Portuguese who were awarded captaincies in the Atlantic islands or in Brazil and Spaniard *encomenderos* in the Americas. In the latter case, the crown's reluctance to approve a legal equation of *encomienda* rights with rights to land was at the heart of colonial political conflicts for much of the sixteenth century. The creation of both institutions grew out of practices in place in the Iberian Reconquest, and they could hardly be considered as inconsistent with the European legal order.[32]

The historical experience of the Reconquest also shaped Iberian notions of sovereignty in ways that suggested a certain homology with the African legal system's emphasis on the protection of "rights to people." To begin with, it is important to note that raiding was a very familiar modus operandi for Iberians. Raiding was, indeed, the central activity of the Reconquest, with actual conquest and settlement following protracted rounds of raiding and retreat. Seizures of people as slaves in raids was an "ordinary" feature of the Mediterranean world from antiquity through the nineteenth century.[33] Although, as Thornton notes, raiding gradually gave way to regulated trade by Europeans in Africa, this does not mean that the raiding Thornton views as so central to African understandings of conquest was in any sense foreign to Iberians. Raiding continued as a prominent activity of entrepreneurial Spanish and Portuguese settler-merchants through the eighteenth century in the Americas, particularly in frontier regions in contact with un-Christianized and seminomadic indigenous peoples. Because raids were less practical in the African context did not make them institutionally anomalous.[34]

---

[31] Thornton, *Africa and Africans*, p. 80.

[32] In an interesting parallel argument, Subrahmanyam asserts that differences between the legal order of agricultural empires in Asia in the same period (most notably the Ottoman state) and small-scale, coastal Asian states are also often overstated. The latter are typically described as trade based and the former as supported by revenue collection from landed estates. But, he argues, it is difficult and perhaps impossible to distinguish between revenues from "land" and those from "trade." Land "was a convenient category for purposes of assignment, since it concealed the fact that what was being parceled out was the right to use coercive force" (Sanjay Subrahmanyam, *The Portuguese Empire in Asia, 1500–1700: A Political and Economic History*, p. 12).

[33] James William Brodman, *Ransoming Captives in Crusader Spain: The Order of Merced on the Christian-Islamic Frontier*, p. 1.

[34] The Portuguese, in fact, transported an emphasis on raiding to African shores in early encounters. As one historian notes, "north Africa had always been associated politically and culturally with Hispanic Islam," and early chronicles of voyages to Africa feature descriptions of raids on the villages of "Moors" to seize captives (Brodman,

There are other reasons to suggest a homology between European and African legal practices, too, that relied on either substantive or structural similarities. To begin with, the mutual influence in Iberia and Africa of Islamic law has undoubtedly been underestimated. The usual assumption of Western legal historians is that the influence of Roman legal sources was so profound as to overshadow any significant direct influence by Islamic law. Patricia Seed has found, however, that the Spanish *Requerimiento*, the statement of rights to conquest that was read by conquistadors to uncomprehending Indians in the Americas, was drafted for the crown by jurists informed by Islamic legal proscriptions on the announcement of *jihad*.[35] Historians of North and West Africa, for their part, have commented on the substantial similarities in some aspects of legal practice in Europe and Islamic Africa. Most prominently, the legal status and treatment of slaves were similar in many respects, despite the difference in legal sources for slave law.[36] No doubt such connections between European and Islamic law deserve greater scrutiny; it would be surprising, given what we know about the dynamics of legal change elsewhere, if centuries of coexisting adjudication in Iberia and cross-cultural contact in the Mediterranean did not produce significant mutual influence.[37]

Ransoming Captives in Crusader Spain, p. 3). For an example of these detailed accounts of raids in North Africa, see the excerpt from the Portuguese history by Gomes Eannes de Azurara, reproduced in Robert Edgar Conrad (ed.), *Children of God's Fire: A Documentary History of Black Slavery in Brazil*, pp. 5–11.

[35] Seed, *Ceremonies of Possession*, Chapter 3.

[36] Fisher and Fisher, for example, note that both Iberians and North African Muslims had come to associate slaving with the conquest of religiously different peoples. In Islamic North Africa, as in Iberia, slaves were rarely co-religionists (at the moment they were enslaved); their capture was justified as an outcome of religious war; and similar restrictions limited recognition of slaves as legal actors. Allan B. Fisher and Humphrey J. Fisher, *Slavery and Muslim Society in Africa: The Institution in Saharan and Sudanic Africa and the Trans-Sahrara Trade*, pp. 6, 17, 39. Paul Lovejoy also argues that Islamic links were important in structuring early Portuguese slave trading in West Africa. Paul Lovejoy, *Transformations in Slavery: A History of Slavery in Africa*. It should be noted that asserting institutional continuities between Muslim and European slave trading should not be mistaken for a "cultural" or "noneconomic" explanation of the expansion of the African slave trade. The institutional connection helped establish a framework for trade but did not create demand or set prices. Manning overstates criticism of institutional approaches to slavery on these grounds. See Patrick Manning, *Slavery and African Life*.

[37] One quite plausible possibility of overlap that would have been directly transmitted to colonial settings is in the area of adjudication of water rights; the Moorish origins of irrigation systems in Iberia, and the continued presence of *mudejar* cultivators, would have created the perfect conditions for the transmission of both legal concepts and

One does not, though, have to rely on conjectures about undis-covered Islamic influences; Islam was a unifying influence in another way. The long history of contact with and incorporation of Muslims in Iberian territories accentuated the dualism that was already implicit in the overlapping jurisdictional claims of church and state. This same force was also at work in African territories where Muslim traders had established communities in diaspora. These communities were self-regulating. Qadis judged disputes within merchant communities even where local sovereigns remained non-Muslim.[38] The situation created in some settings a form of governance that was openly divided, as, for example, in the medieval kingdom of Ghana, where Muslim travelers noted, as early as the eleventh century, the parallel existence of Muslim and non-Muslim legal functionaries. The Muslim geographer al-Bakri describes the physical and administrative separation of two towns, one inhabited by Muslims "with their *imams*, their *muezzins*, their readers (of the Coran)," and their scholars and jurists.[39] In the king's town, Muslims were readily received and could presumably bring disputes before the king, who personally oversaw the settlement of legal disputes involving his co-religionists. The two populations signaled their subservience to the king in different ways:

> [The king] holds an audience to repair injustices. . . . The beginning of the audience is announced by beating on a drum, called a *daba*, which is a long piece of wood (evidee). The people begin to assemble right away. His co-religionists, when they approach, throw themselves on their knees and touch the ground with their heads: this is their way of saluting the king. As for Muslims, they are content to clap their hands.[40]

procedures. (Thomas Glick has found such influence in the regulation of water rights and irrigation in Valencia; I am indebted to Lawrence Rosen for mentioning the appar-ent similarities between some aspects of adjudication of water rights in Morocco and in the southwestern United States.) Even if such Islamic influences were muted over time, this sort of intermingling of legal traditions would have influenced legal defi-nitions of property and would have created another, more direct connection between Iberian and African legal practices.

[38] Curtin notes, "Throughout the Western Sudan, Muslim clerics were often found with their own ward in a town, sometimes with a separate town alongside the secular town, or simply with the right to apply Muslim law to Muslims with the non-Muslims following their own customs" (Philip Curtin, *Economic Change in Precolonial Africa: Senegambia in the Era of the Slave Trade*, p. 44).

[39] Joseph M. Cuoq, ed., *Recueil des sources Arabes concernant l'Afrique occidentale du VIIIe au XVIe siècle*, p. 99; my translation.

[40] Cuoq, *Recueil des sources Arabes*, p. 100; my translation.

This recognized existence of multiple legal authorities was common even outside areas of Muslim influence. African cities and towns were structured to admit the settlement of outsiders. The accommodation was a practical one; long-distance trade was mainly in the hands of diasporic communities held together by ethnic and kinship ties. It was expected that these communities would obey local laws in interacting with local residents but that they would also provide their own legal controls. The system fit well with the institutions of rule of local populations, in which wards were typically the site of judicial control in the first instance, with appeals possible to higher authorities. Special wards set aside for outsiders coincided with an existing level of legal supervision.[41]

In some cases, merchant diasporas extended their jurisdiction beyond their own community borders. This was not always the result of conscious policy but was nevertheless consistent with both religious goals and commercial interests. Muslim merchants who brought Islam into non-Muslim parts of Africa benefited when rulers converted. As in other areas of Islamic expansion, Muslim justice undoubtedly also appealed to some litigants on nonreligious grounds, for the relative certainty and authority of judgments.[42] This possibility of transforming the law of a diaspora into a central institution was not, however, limited to Muslim communities. The Aro, a trading diaspora of Iboland in what is now southeastern Nigeria, benefited commercially and politically from the religious status among non-Aro groups of the Aro's oracle at Arochukwu, in Aro territory. Non-Aro peoples increasingly sought out the oracle as a means for settling disputes, sometimes making long trips to Arochukwu. This gave the Aro the curious status in many regions as a community of outsiders with religious prestige and, as a result, considerable practical legal authority.[43]

[41] This physical and legal separation was also applied to communities of "white" Muslims, that is, light-skinned North Africans and Egyptians, in the capital of Mali in the fourteenth century and in the Niger River city of Gao. See Richard W. Hull, *African Cities and Towns Before the European Conquest*, p. 82. Subrahmanyam (*The Portuguese Empire in Asia*, p. 46) notes that jurisdictional subdivisions for culturally different groups were common to medieval cities of Europe and Asia; with numerous resident foreigners, the cities "tended to develop systems of internal regulation for these foreign communities, which at times gave them considerable social and judicial autonomy."

[42] On the influence of Muslim legal institutions, see Hull, *African Cities and Towns*, pp. 84–85. Chapter 3 contains further discussion of Islamic law.

[43] For a brief discussion of the Aro (and a broader discussion of the importance of institutions in tying together communities in diaspora), see Philip Curtin, *Cross-Cultural Trade in World History*, pp. 46–49.

Separate legal authorities for different corporate groups existed not just for trade diasporas but also for subordinate or conquered corporate groups within loosely confederated African states. As Thornton points out, smaller conquered states typically continued to exercise local authority, including legal authority, and could effectively check the power of larger states in some circumstances.[44] Curtin notes that this fragmented legal authority was also a feature of a Senegambian political structure in which corporate groups defined by lineage retained authority despite formal subordinate status in relation to larger state structures.[45] Related to the recognition of the (limited) sovereignty of outsiders and constituent polities, African states also operated in an established system of international relations. The recognition of immunity for ambassadors was fairly widespread in precolonial West Africa, as were regulations for the conduct of warfare.[46] It was the existence of this system that allowed the Portuguese and, later, other European powers to set up trading relations and factories along the African coast. The Portuguese sent regular embassies to local rulers before establishing trading posts.[47] Although it is possible that Africans and Europeans misunderstood the meaning of Portuguese tenure on these relatively small holdings, different interpretations of landholding were hardly significant at this stage. More important was the understanding on both sides that the factories did not establish Portuguese sovereignty over Africans themselves. This limited jurisdiction was familiar to both sides; on the one hand, it fit with existing patterns of merchant diasporas and, on the other side, it was part of a repertoire of practices used in interactions with non-Christian populations on the frontier.[48]

The existence of a precolonial system of international relations was linked, too, to broad patterns of customary procedures and law that cut

---

[44] Thornton, *Africa and Africans*, p. 91.

[45] Curtin, *Economic Change in Precolonial Africa*, and see note 48 below.

[46] Robert Smith, *Warfare and Diplomacy in Precolonial West Africa*, pp. 3–4.

[47] See A.J.R. Russell-Wood, *A World on the Move: The Portuguese in Africa, Asia, and America, 1415–1808*, p. 21. Russell-Wood notes that the Portuguese in Africa used force "usually only as a measure of last resort" and relied instead on negotiations with local rulers.

[48] Curtin notes, for example, that Senegambian leaders dealt with European traders as if they were simply another corporate group. "If the Europeans asked permission to build a factory or set up a town of their own, Senegambian practice had plenty of precedents with dealing with aliens through their own chiefs. From the African point of view, a European trading post was not ceded territory, merely another religious minority, more easily dealt with by letting it live under its own laws" (Curtin, *Economic Change in Precolonial Africa*, p. 45).

across cultural and political boundaries. Despite the emphasis among Europeans on written sources in European law, Portuguese traders learned that Africans recognized unwritten contracts, sanctified by oaths or other unwritten practices, and these lent a certain stability to early coastal trading relations.[49] However, Europeans also misinterpreted African political and legal structures, and they consistently portrayed them as inferior to European law. Thus European chroniclers often mistakenly interpreted the sovereignty of African kings as rule "above the law." Though longer contact revealed community acceptance of rule and cooperation in the enforcement of law – familiar limitations of sovereignty for European powers – as unifying features of West African polities, it was also commonplace for Europeans to characterize African legal practices as uncivilized and inferior. This attitude was consistent with the Africans' status as non-Christians. It contributed, too, to formal policies of exclusion of Africans or Afro-Portuguese from positions of legal administration.[50]

Yet these representations did not disturb the fundamental perception among European chroniclers that African polities were indeed sites of legal administration, however autocratic or arbitrary. Jurisdictional disputes arose from time to time involving crimes committed across the borders of fortified European posts. In a 1577 case in Mina, a Portuguese captain killed two sons of the Efutu ruler after a dispute. The Efutu demanded the Portuguese punish the captain, and the conflict escalated to a costly battle. The reverse situation occurred when the Portuguese

---

[49] See Smith, *Warfare and Diplomacy*, on these understandings as an aspect of African international law.

[50] Two scholars comment that Europeans "were content to believe that African rulers were more autocratic than contemporary rulers in Europe, whereas they were most probably often a good deal less autocratic" (A. Teixeira da Mota and P.E.H. Hair, *East of Mina: Afro-European Relations on the Gold Coast in the 1550s and 1560s: An Essay with Supporting Documents*, p. 21). Officially, "purity of blood" was necessary for appointment to judicial posts in the empire, though in practice this requirement had to be relaxed in some places. For example, at São Tomé in 1528 the governor was instructed by the king not to oppose the election of mulattos to the town council (Boxer, *The Portuguese Seaborne Empire*, p. 280). Relaxing this requirement did not seem to affect views about the unsuitability of non-Portuguese-born residents for legal posts. An anonymous report from Mina written in 1572 suggests that settlers should be encouraged from the Azores and São Tomé but should not be entrusted with the administration of justice "unless they are home-born Portuguese ... [because] the older folk do not, as a rule, speak highly of their worth and honesty." Document translated in Mota and Hair, *East of Mina*, p. 82.

sought to have "rebels" from the nearby town of Caia "handed over to [Portuguese] justice" and threatened to punish the whole town.[51] These sorts of jurisdictional disputes were familiar elements of frontier politics for both sides.

Another unifying feature of African legal systems existed in the institution of slavery. Enslavement of Africans by Africans, though not universal on the continent, was a widespread and well-established practice before European demand for slaves to transport to the Americas prompted a radical shift in scale of this activity. Despite regional variations in the economic importance of slavery and in the specific terms and conditions of bondage, institutional similarities extended to quite different regions. The mechanisms for enslavement – economic (the purchase of slaves), political (taking slaves as war captives), and judicial (the awarding of slaves as part of legal judgments) – formed a familiar repertoire with widespread legitimacy, if different frequency. In a more fundamental sense, as Miers and Kopytoff have argued, slavery existed as an institutional category in which, independently of different terms and conditions of bondage, slaves were marginalized from the status of community insider. Thus, even though some African slaves were incorporated into kinship groups and households, these steps moved them toward a status of "belonging" (more meaningful in the African context than the status of "freedom") but did not remove their stigma as outsiders.[52]

Distinctions between economic enslavement and military or political enslavement that resulted from warfare increasingly became blurred as decisions to go to war were influenced by economic interests. Judicial mechanisms for enslavement declined in relative importance, though they also intensified in response to the rising demand. Nevertheless, it is significant that the rise in slave raiding did not lead African states to abandon a legal basis for slavery. Enslaving war captives was itself recognized as legitimate, and justifications for war could always be produced. An advisory letter to the then-united Spanish-Portuguese crown in 1612 reported that African traders were aware of papal restrictions on slavery and would "falsely assert that the persons whom they

---

[51] The first incident is described by Vogt (*Portuguese Rule on the Gold Coast*); the second is described by the anonymous report from Mina reproduced and translated in Mota and Hair, *East of Mina*, p. 87.

[52] Suzanne Miers and Igor Kopytoff, "Introduction" in *Slavery in Africa: Historical and Anthropological Perspectives*.

bring to be sold are captured in a just war."[53] In at least some cases, captives or their former patrons themselves challenged the legality of their enslavement by questioning the legitimacy of acts of aggression. In sixteenth-century Kongo, legal institutions were strengthened in an effort by the king to continue to control distributive wealth as slave raiding and trading expanded and threatened that authority. Kongalese elites found they could use the courts simultaneously to improve their own access to slaves and to challenge the legality of ownership of slaves by others. While increasingly seeking slaves as legal remedies, elites also forwarded their own interests by taking charge of slaves they had induced to "free" themselves from less powerful masters. The latter challenged these actions in court but with little success. In the early sixteenth century, the Kongolese ruler Afonso had used the courts to challenge Portuguese trading that bypassed his control. Afonso appointed three judges to rule on whether slaves purchased by the Portuguese had been captured in legitimate wars or were merely being kidnapped.[54]

Europeans, for their part, responded to shortages of labor in West African outposts by increasing forms of judicial enslavement using quite similar mechanisms. Suggesting responses to the dire need for galley slaves so that the Portuguese could effectively patrol the Mina coast, for example, a sixteenth-century report proposes condemning criminals in São Tomé and the Island of Fogo to service in the galleys "either for a limited period or for life." It warns that cases should be removed from the hands of African judges as much as possible because they were too lenient.[55] The exile of criminals from Portugal and Brazil to Angola became a central feature of the imperial penal system. And in Brazil, as we have already commented, the possibility of declaring Indians slaves through declaration of just war outlived Spanish reforms. It hardly matters for our purposes whether African and Portuguese mechanisms of judicial enslavement were precisely the same; they coexisted, with substantial similarities, through the first three centuries of Atlantic contact and commerce, and constituted another element of mutual recognition.

In summary, the legal features of precolonial Africa we have surveyed briefly – limited legal autonomy of religious communities, established norms for interstate relations, and a separate legal status for captives

---

[53] "Proposta a Sua Magestade sobre a Escravaría das Terras da Conquista de Portugal," pp. 11–15 in Conrad, *Children of God's Fire*, p. 12.

[54] Anne Hilton, *The Kingdom of Kongo*, pp. 85, 122–25.

[55] Anonymous report from Mina in Mota and Hair, *East of Mina*, p. 74.

and slaves – were hardly foreign to European powers trading along the African coast from the fifteenth century on. Indeed, the familiarity of the legal order permitted Europeans to pursue the only possible expansionist strategy, given the high costs of military protection and the obstacle of Africa's hostile disease environment. On the one hand, the trading post networks minimized internal jurisdictional complexities. These emerged forcefully only in places where significant groups of European settlers and descendants, or of Christian converts, challenged the neat designation of Europeans as yet another community living in Africa in diaspora, with limited legal autonomy and authority. On the other hand, jurisdictional complexity was implicit in the patchwork of African polities and small European outposts. The legal status of slaves, who were outsiders under the complete authority of culturally different societies and masters, must be understood as the negation of the rights of outsiders to membership in corporate communities with their own legal authorities. These shared features of plural legal orders were to continue to influence legal politics in the Americas.

MARRONAGE AS A LEGAL STATUS

Keeping in focus the structural similarities of Iberian and African legal orders provides us with another perspective on the legal relationship of Africans and Iberians in the New World. In emphasizing the continuity of legal categories from one side of the Atlantic to the other, we need not fall into the pattern either of tracing African cultural "survivals" or of asserting the transformative influence of the experience of slavery. Certainly the historical conditions of slavery in the New World were unique. But it is significant that Africans who became slaves both possessed political theory, based on prior understandings of captivity as a legal category, and developed a reading of Portuguese (and Spanish) legal orders that would have shifted but not dramatically altered these ideas.

From the narrow perspective of sources of law, the law of slavery of the South Atlantic is uncomplicated. Both Portuguese and Spaniards adopted legal statutes that were derived with relatively minor change from Roman law. Slaves did not have legal personality – they could not be parties to lawsuits and could appear as witnesses only under very limited circumstances. As in Roman law, masters were awarded nearly complete control over their slaves, with restrictions added that only moderate punishment would be permitted and that slaves would be remitted to government officials for more serious punishment. These restrictions resulted, however, in few interventions in masters' treatment of slaves and in relatively little local legislation until the first decades of the nineteenth century.[56] In one sense, slavery itself fortified jurisdictional divisions in the plural legal order by awarding considerable judicial power to slave masters and limiting circumstances for intervention by, or appeal to, state courts.

Yet, we should take care not to view the legal context of slavery as overdetermined by Roman legal sources or isolated from change because of the severe limitations on slaves as legal actors. The background of legal pluralism in Africa and Europe informed both masters and slaves about the fit of slavery within a larger array of legal possibilities, and these continued to exert an influence on slave strategies and planter responses. Indeed, the perspective gained by this exercise helps to shed light on the "problem" posed for historians by slaves who embraced "comparatively moderate ambitions" or who "visualized freedom" in ways that seemed oddly incomplete.[57] The approach helps to explain, too, the puzzle of maroon communities that seemed to relinquish too much, too easily, in treaties with plantocratic polities, while undermining their separatism in other ways by staying "curiously close" to settled plantations.[58] Rather than viewing attempts to define a political space for semiautonomous communities as politically naïve or necessarily doomed, an understanding of models for plural political and legal authority shared in a broad sense by both Africans and Europeans suggests that such strategies were logical and viewed as workable, even if potentially unstable, over the long term.

Consider the legal response to *marronage*. Under the slave law shaped in the Americas largely out of Roman law sources, slaves who were

---

[56] Watson argues that this heavy reliance on Roman law extended to the English colonies and was imported through common references to civil law sources. Further, he questions the distinction made by Klein and others between legal views of slaves as chattel in the English colonies and the extension of legal personality to slaves in Spanish and Portuguese America. In the Iberian colonies, he argues, close adherence to Roman law meant the adoption, with only minor variation, of the view that slaves did *not* possess legal personality, though they could be treated as "thinking property" in ways that distinguished them from inanimate objects. I could draw on Watson's arguments to buttress my case for an interrelated legal order in the Atlantic world, but to do so would be to rely too narrowly on the importance of legal sources. As Watson himself points out, his analysis shows "how difficult it is to deduce much about a society from an examination of its legal rules." See Alan Watson, *Slave Law in the Americas*, especially pp. 121–22, and quote on p. 129.

[57] Michael Craton, *Empire, Enslavement, and Freedom in the Caribbean*, pp. 277–78.

[58] Craton, *Empire, Enslavement, and Freedom*, p. 64.

fugitives were simply criminals, and actions to help slaves escape or to hide fugitives were also criminalized. Various provisions in slave laws thus permitted harsh punishments for fugitives and in many places made assisting escape a capital offense. Living in settlements where Europeans were heavily outnumbered by enslaved Africans, sugar planters considered harsh penalties for runaways and rebellious slaves essential to their safety. They feared the influence of maroon communities and everywhere sought first to destroy these settlements and recapture the fugitives. In Jamaica, maroon communities in the mountainous interior were targets of repeated military campaigns. In Brazil, where an extensive network of villages, or *mocambos*, was linked in the largest maroon polity of the Americas, Palmares, the first response was also a series of military campaigns to burn villages and recapture slaves. In an expedition against Palmares in 1676, the commander told a force of 185 whites, mestizos, and Indians that "the blacks fought as fugitives" and the troops were "hunting them down as lords and masters . . . it being a disgrace for every Pernambucan to be whipped by those whom they had themselves so many times whipped."[59]

The undisputed label of fugitive slaves as criminals did not prevent colonial authorities from also imagining the existence of a tight political structure within runaway slave communities. In many places, chroniclers reported that maroons lived under the control of powerful kings, or chiefs. In Palmares, for example, the political order was described as comprising a network of "rulers and powerful chiefs" in dispersed mocambos, who were in turn under the authority of a king, Ganga Zumba.[60] Maroon leaders elsewhere were described in similar terms.[61] As in European representations of African polities, this portrayal coexisted with descriptions of maroons as uncivilized or lawless.[62] Historians, too, have sometimes reproduced these contradictory images of maroon life. In characterizing maroon communities as re-creations of African polities in the Americas, some historians have emphasized the monarchial

---

[59] From a manuscript written in the late seventeenth century by an anonymous chronicler of the war against Palmares, translated in Conrad, *Children of God's Fire*, p. 372.

[60] Phrase quoted in manuscript in Conrad, *Children of God's Fire*, p. 369.

[61] I refer in my account to a few examples; for comparative cases that bear out these generalizations, see Richard Price, *Maroon Societies: Rebel Slave Communities in the Americas*; for Brazil, João José Reis and Flávio dos Santos Gomes, *Liberdade por um fio: História dos quilombos no Brasil*; and for the Caribbean, Michael Craton, *Testing the Chains: Resistance to Slavery in the British West Indies*.

[62] See, for example, my discussion of local officials' portrayal of palenques in New Spain at the end of this section.

character of rule in these communities while also representing marronage as part of a "restorationist project" intended to rekindle egalitarian impulses of a romanticized African past.[63]

Yet, as Richard Price has pointed out, political centralization in maroon communities was exaggerated both by European observers and strategically by maroons themselves. Price notes that Europeans found representations of monarchial rule understandable in terms of European political models; our discussion in the previous section shows that such representations had already become standard (and equally misleading) in descriptions of states in Africa, and this precedent was probably influential. More importantly, Price tells us that at least in the case of the Saramaka of Surinam, political centralization was never as strong as it appeared and that the maroons themselves played an important part in misrepresenting the nature of political authority to Europeans.[64] Price suggests that a similar combination of purposeful misrepresentation and misreading probably took place in Portuguese dealings with Palmares.[65] Certainly there is evidence from here and elsewhere that political authority was quite dispersed, giving rise in times of crisis to intense rivalries that were capable of splitting the groups apart. Lines of division included ethnic boundaries of groups from different regions (and different areas from within the same regions) of Africa and rifts between creole and African-born slaves. Such divisions remind us, as Price puts it, that the communities were necessarily in the midst of shaping a new culture out of a confluence of African and American influences, a process he calls "creolization-while-in-a-state-of-war."[66]

It is possible, then, to understand the influence of African political and cultural practice without devoting ourselves to a search for African cultural "survivals" or ignoring the impact of American realities. Extending this approach to an understanding of representations of legal order leads to the observation that the continuing homology between African and European representations of plural political and legal orders – and not just failed separatist strategies – underlay the political negotiations of

---

[63] The trend is discussed in João José Reis and Flávio dos Santos Gomes, "Introdução – Uma história da liberdade," p. 11. For an early and prominent example of this argument, see R.K. Kent, "Palmares: An African State in Brazil."

[64] See Richard Price, *First Time: The Historical Vision of an Afro-American People;* and Richard Price, *Alabi's World.*

[65] Richard Price, "Palmares come poderia ter sido."

[66] Price, "Palmares," p. 57.

maroons and planters. That is, both sides had recent and working models of limited sovereignty in mind. Maroon communities could be redefined as having both independent political authority and recognized subordination to European power. In legal terms, this meant jurisdiction over all matters except the most serious capital cases, which were to be referred to colonial courts. This relation reproduced, on the one hand, familiar African political arrangements whereby communities in diaspora controlled their own internal affairs while at the same time referring specific sets of disputes and criminal prosecutions for specific types of offenses to resident rulers. At the same time, the relationship reproduced for planters the jurisdictional arrangements under which they themselves held local legal authority. Nearly complete legal authority was limited by specific guidelines for referrals to both crown and church. Viewed in this context, the treaties signed by maroons appear as neither purely compromising documents nor restorationist projects; they built on widely shared understandings of the structure of political authority and responded to the exacerbated jurisdictional fragmentation of colonial legal administration.

In Jamaica, colonial authorities authorized a fifteen-article peace treaty with the maroons in 1739. It contained the usual provision that the maroons agree to return runaways, including those who had joined the community within the previous two years.[67] Legally, the treaty awarded Cudjoe, the maroon leader, judicial authority within the maroon community except in capital cases, which would be referred to the colonial judiciary.[68] Maroons in such cases would be tried by "proceedings...equal to those of other free negroes." Other jurisdictional guidelines were also familiar, and limited maroons' authority.

---

[67] They were to be returned to their former masters, though, only if they were willing to go; otherwise they were to "remain in subjection to Captain Cudjoe," the maroon leader, and thus required to abide by the peace. Craton, *Testing the Chains*, p. 89. Price points out that these familiar clauses in maroon treaties were probably much less effective than one might assume. Saramakan maroons harbored a significant "illegal" population of recently freed slaves while also finding other ways around the requirement that they not assist fugitives. Such strategies would have been available to other maroons, too. Price, "Palmares."

[68] This pattern had already been applied in dealing with maroons on the island. When the English took Jamaica from the Spaniards, one of the first English governors offered an alliance with a palenque leader, Lubolo, proposing that he be made "colonel of the black regiment of militia, and he and others appointed magistrates over the negroes to decide all cases except those of life and death." Quoted in Richard Hart, *Slaves Who Abolished Slavery, Vol. 2: Blacks in Rebellion*, p. 6.

Whites committing offenses against maroons would not be subject to their courts but would respond to complaints brought before "any commanding officer or magistrate in the neighborhood," while maroons who injured whites could be brought before colonial courts.[69]

In Palmares, European chronicles describe the signing of the treaty of 1678 as an act of submission. The men coming from the *quilombo* to negotiate the treaty with the governor, Don Pedro de Almeida, "prostrated themselves at D. Pedro's feet, striking their palms together as a sign of surrender and to acknowledge his victory."[70] The governor, advised by the members of the city council, the high judge, the royal treasury officer, and two military commanders, agreed to a treaty requiring cooperation in the capture of fugitives and relinquishment of recent arrivals, in exchange for a place of settlement and freedom for all those born in Palmares. The treaty included two clauses that would seem contradictory: that the residents of Palmares "would remain obedient to the orders of the government" and "that their king would continue as commander of all his people."[71] As in Jamaica, the arrangement was clearly a familiar one of limited autonomy, the division of authority over internal and external affairs, and over routine versus exceptional cases.

Such treaties have often been blamed for the subsequent weakness of maroon communities. Craton argues, for example, that the treaties enabled colonial agents "to argue that the establishment of physical boundaries, the definition of maroon autonomy, and the right to send in liaison officers implied that ultimate suzerainty resided with the colonial regime."[72] Yet, though the treaties did in fact implicitly recognize colonial sovereignty, the relation must be understood in the context of a concept of the state as less than completely dominant. Certainly sixteenth- and seventeenth-century maroons, like the Europeans they negotiated with, were accustomed to a world in which fragmented authority was a normal part of the political order, easily understood

---

[69] Craton, *Testing the Chains*, p. 90.

[70] Anonymous chronicle of Palmares war, Conrad, *Children of God's Fire*, p. 375. Note the similarity of this gesture with the actions of Muslim traders coming before the Ghana king as vassals who maintained a separate polity-within-the-polity (described in the previous section). The actions described by the Portuguese could have signified a recognition of limited sovereignty, but not surrender.

[71] Treaty as described by anonymous seventeenth-century chronicler, quoted in Conrad, *Children of God's Fire*, p. 376.

[72] Craton, *Testing the Chains*, p. 65

and not necessarily unstable. Neither side would have confidently predicted either the gradual erosion of maroon autonomy that took place in Jamaica or the return to hostilities that occurred in the case of Palmares. But both sides would have understood these as possible outcomes of arrangements of divided authority.

Under some circumstances, planters also reproduced the logic of jurisdictional claims made for the express purpose of "civilizing" non-Christians. In colonial Mexico, runaway slaves formed *palenques* in the mountains of Veracruz from the earliest beginnings of plantation agriculture in the region. A series of especially violent rebellions, in 1725, 1735, 1741, 1749, and 1768, led to the creation of a string of new settlements; the 1735 revolt alone gave rise to the formation of six new mountain strongholds. In 1769, the residents of one palenque petitioned the royal audiencia for freedom. Negotiations and a series of depositions taken in connection with the case revealed that the ex-slaves had an intricate web of relationships with the surrounding communities, including serving as intermediaries between the district magistrate and local Indians. The *alcalde*, in turn, aided the rebels by helping to draft their petitions to the audiencia and by arguing, in an extraofficial capacity, the merits of their case for freedom.[73] The reasons given by local officials in support of a pardon included their desire to bring the maroons under state legal authority. The "unfortunates" had been living "abandoned to vice . . . and in a word, without Christian or political governance." After being given liberty, it would be possible for them to "elect an alcalde, *or* alcaldes, and other officials, however many the law entitles them to according to the number of families," and the mountain communities would be reconstituted as officially recognized towns.[74] This argument reproduced in a different context the logic of thirteenth-century canonists describing a rationale for extending crown jurisdiction into heathen lands. The perspective continued to provide background to the accommodation of maroons in the colonial order.

Although treaties with maroons were frequently broken, and a return to a state of war was a constant threat, a surprising number of settlements did make the transition to legally constituted communities that were

---

[73] See Patrick Carrol, "Mandinga: The Evolution of a Mexican Runaway Slave Community, 1735–1827."

[74] Archivo de la Nación, México, Tierras tomo 3543, exp. 1, 1769. My translation. I am grateful to Herman Bennett for drawing my attention to the Veracruz palenques and for allowing me to study his copy of this document.

either partially or completely incorporated in the colonial legal order.[75] This was not an impossible outcome and, given the available models of jurisdictional complexity available to participants, neither was it an irrational goal. Had the demographic and political conditions of slavery in the New World been different, the threat posed by marronage would have been greatly lessened and the possibilities greatly increased for multiplying a model that treated maroon settlements as one of a series of corporate communities within a fragmented colonial order.

BARBAROUS RAIDS, CIVILIZED RANSOM

We can find further evidence of a widely shared legal framework in attitudes and routines surrounding captive redemption. The seizure of captives was a phenomenon that encompassed the trans-Atlantic slave trade but also extended chronologically and geographically beyond it. Captive taking was commonplace across the Atlantic world, from the sea lanes of northern Europe, to eastern Mediterranean lands oriented toward the Atlantic, and to all parts of the New World. Though Europeans in captivity were proportionately a small part of those who were held for ransom or enslaved, the threat of captivity and accounts of its conditions were symbolically central to Europeans' understandings of the Atlantic world and their own relations with cultural and religious others.

Scholars have long taken note of the consistency of themes of captivity narratives, and of their popularity. These accounts constituted their own genre in European letters from the sixteenth century on. The narratives focused attention especially on the fear that captivity would result in cultural or religious conversion. Dreaded "incorporation" into captor societies took a literal form when cannibalism figured among the horrors reported by freed captives.

Accentuating the fear of captives' becoming "lost" – and the promise of their temporal and spiritual salvation – involved emphasizing the differences between "civilized" captives and "barbarous" captors. But the subtext of captivity accounts was quite different and drew quiet attention to shared understandings and established routines that made responses to captivity – in particular, redemption – possible. Just as the

---

75 Caroll, in "Mandinga," notes that twelve such cases have been well documented in the South Atlantic. It is probable that other examples exist but have not received scholarly attention because of the small numbers of runaways involved or the unofficial routes taken to achieve legal integration, such as settlement in established communities.

cultural categories employed to define captors were transposed from one group to another – from Barbary pirates to New World Indians, for example – expectations about negotiations and redemption were also reproduced across a wide interregional sphere. Encounters with captor groups created and reinforced different kinds of knowledge: new findings about the legal practices of others; affirmation of ideas about the multicentric character of law; and a necessary tolerance for the contradiction of treating "outlawed" groups of criminals, brigands, and "savages" as legally constituted polities.

The activities of the Barbary pirates formed a particularly important background to captive taking elsewhere in the Atlantic world. What had been largely a Mediterranean threat became also an Atlantic one in the early seventeenth century. Following the expulsion of Moriscos from Spain in 1610, corsair raids against Spanish ports and ships accelerated, with the numbers of captives seized reaching a peak between 1610 to 1639.[76] The raids reached all the Spanish coasts; in 1667, Basque officials pleaded with the crown to be excused from meeting the quota for the levy on seamen because North African pirates had taken so many local men.[77] French and British ports were also targets, as were ships from these countries traveling in both the Mediterranean and the Atlantic. Hebb estimates that between 1622 and 1642, the English had more than three hundred ships and seven thousand captives seized by Barbary pirates, losses that fell disproportionately on London and southwest ports.[78] Several estimates place more than twenty thousand Christian captives in Algiers alone in the 1620s and 1630s.[79]

Corsair activity endangered cross-Atlantic voyages. Iberian ships sailing both to and from the West Indies and Brazil faced the threat of lost cargoes and the captivity of their crews. English and North Atlantic ships and routes were also affected. In 1625, William Bradford complained that a ship on its way to England with beaver skins was seized "almost within sight of Plimouth."[80] The American merchant Joshua Gee set sail from Boston on a trading voyage in 1680 and was

---

[76] Ellen G. Friedman, *Spanish Captives in North Africa in the Early Modern Age*, p. 13. Friedman calls the raiding an "undeclared war" of North African Muslims against Spain in the seventeenth century (p. 23).

[77] Friedman, *Spanish Captives in North Africa*, p. 19.

[78] David Hebb, *Piracy and the English Government, 1616–1642*, p. 139. Expanding the estimate to include the decades prior to 1622, Hebb arrives at the estimate of four hundred ships and eight thousand captives.

[79] Paul Baepler, "Introduction," *White Slaves, African Masters*, p. 3.

[80] Nabil Matar, *Turks, Moors, and Englishmen in the Age of Discovery*, p. 94.

captured by corsairs from Algiers. For these merchants and other traders and travelers, North African captivity was a real threat, one that was made more ominous by the religion of the captors and the supposition – more imagined than real – that captivity in the North African city states inevitably meant forced conversion and sexual slavery.[81]

Corsair activities also extended their reach across the Atlantic because for some they represented rival opportunities. Privateering was hardly unique to North Africans; Drake and other English privateers called in North African ports, and substantial, if uncounted, numbers of English seamen joined Mediterranean pirates. John Smith was not exaggerating when he commented that his countrymen were more interested in joining the ranks of the corsairs than in settling the New World.[82] Indeed, many men sailing to the New World had already had Mediterranean experience and knew of or had taken part in corsair raiding. The German privateer Hans Staden, for example, sought prizes along the Barbary Coast before being drawn across the Atlantic to assist the Portuguese at Pernambuco, where he fell captive to Tupinamba Indians.[83]

The backdrop of Barbary piracy and captive taking no doubt helped to shape Europeans' perceptions of captivity in the New World. Timing perhaps made this transposition inevitable. In South America, Portuguese encounters with the Tupinamba in the sixteenth century overlapped with routine captive taking across religious lines in the Mediterranean. In North America, the seventeenth-century threat by corsairs to cross-Atlantic shipping reached its peak just as the phenomenon of settlers in Indian captivity was transfixing public attention. Joshua Gee, the Boston merchant seized and held in Algiers, had set sail for Europe only three years after Mary Rowlandson was released by her Indian captors.[84] Cotton Mather shared the pulpit of North Church with Gee's son and preached on the spiritual plight of Christian captives

---

[81] Matar traces the European fixation on sodomy among Muslims in Chapter 4 of Matar, *Turks, Moors, and Englishmen*.

[82] Matar, *Turks, Moors, and Englishmen*, p. 58.

[83] Hans Staden, "The True History of His Captivity," p. 19.

[84] Baepler ("Introduction," *White Slaves, African Masters*) observes the proximity of these events and suggests that Gee, a resident of Boston at the time of Rowlandson's release, would certainly have known about her captivity. Rowlandson and several of her children had been seized by Indians during King Philip's War. Her captivity account, *The Sovereignty and Goodness of God*, was published in England and Massachusetts in 1682, received a wide readership, and became a classic in the genre of American Indian captivity.

among both Indians and North Africans; both groups faced the challenge of maintaining faith in the face of what Mather supposed to be constant pressure to recant Christian beliefs and civilized habits.[85]

Both converting to Islam and adopting Indian ways signified an abandonment of Christianity. Narratives of captivity tended to celebrate the resilience of devout Christians, while also noting the fall of weaker captives. This was Mather's theme, for example, when in a 1703 sermon he told of North Africans threatening to kill two captives, a Frenchman and an Englishman, if they refused to convert; the Frenchman gave in, while the Englishman died resisting. This theme carried through to – and was in turn borrowed from – narratives of Indian captivity. Rowlandson confessed her own moments of weakness and attributed her survival and return to her private devotion. Such examples were set against other illustrations of degradation. Jean de Léry, in his account of sixteenth-century Brazil, reported with horror that some "Norman interpreters" who had lived eight or nine years among the Tupinamba had not only abandoned Christianity and "polluted themselves by all sorts of base behavior among the women and girls . . . but . . . even boasted in my hearing of having killed and eaten prisoners."[86] Many Spanish captivity narratives in the New World told of women who were abducted and never returned after marrying Indian captors.[87] On the other side of the Atlantic, travelers repeated stories of Christian captives who had voluntarily converted and then joined in corsair raids. The commonality of representations of captives as "fallen" united discourse about Indian and North African captivity. As Matar observes, the term *renegadoe* itself originated as a label for someone who had converted to

---

[85] Baepler notes the representations in similar spiritual terms of North African and American Indian captivity ("Introduction," *White Slaves, African Masters*, p. 6).

[86] Jean de Léry, *History of a Voyage to the Land of Brazil*, p. 128.

[87] Bonnie Frederick suggests that the gender of captives in Hispanic narratives shifted from one side of the Atlantic to the other. New World captivity narratives tended to feature women and to portray them as helpless, and the accounts dropped the heroic rescue theme that was common in male-centered captivity narratives in the Mediterranean. Frederick's main examples are from nineteenth-century Uruguay and Argentina, and earlier narratives might not support the point as well. Matar observes, too, that the danger of rape was also implicit in representations of male captivity in North Africa (Matar, *Turks, Moors, and Englishmen*). While conceding the point that captivity accounts were important in the shifting social construction of gender and that this discourse was in many ways specific to time and place, we still observe continuities in the themes of sexual and spiritual danger on both sides of the Atlantic. See Bonnie Frederick, "Fatal Journeys, Fatal Legends: The Journey of the Captive Woman in Argentina and Uruguay."

Islam and was later used for settlers who joined native communities in the Americas.[88]

Such parallels made for a certain easy transposition of cultural categories. Muldoon writes, in a different context, of the "Indian as Irishman" in English settler eyes; captivity narratives show us the "Indian as Muslim."[89] Matar argues, though, that Britons inverted this superimposition by representing the far more numerous captive seizures by Barbary pirates in terms familiar from the less numerous and more containable instances of Indian captivity. In this way, the much more powerful Barbary pirates could be portrayed as culturally primitive, the equivalent of New World "savages." Indeed, both "enemies" were frequently portrayed as lawless. No European settler would have faulted Hannah Dustan for hacking ten of her New England Indian captors to death with a hatchet and escaping. As Mather noted in his sermon on the event, Dustan "had not her own Life secured by any Law unto her" and so "thought she was not forbidden by any Law to take away the Life of the Murderers, by whom her Child had been Butchered."[90]

Despite the common representation of captors as lawless, and the widespread fear that captivity meant a descent from civility, these themes coexisted with other, less prominent representations of captivity as forming part of an array of regulated and in this sense "lawful" exchanges and practices. Captive taking was after all usually motivated by an interest in collecting ransom.[91] Though Europeans feared forced conversion at the hands of Muslim pirates, North African leaders systematically discouraged conversion since only Christian captives would be redeemed.[92] This explicit interest in captive taking as a source of revenue was not consistent everywhere across the Atlantic world, and even where it was most organized, redemption did not free the majority of

---

[88] Matar, *Turks, Moors, and Englishmen*, p. 96.

[89] See James Muldoon, "The Indian As Irishman."

[90] Cotton Mather, "A Notable Exploit; Wherein, Dux Faemina Facti," in Equiano, et al., *American Captivity Narratives*, p. 185.

[91] There were exceptions. North woods Indians in North America sent out raiding parties to seize captives to replace members of their own groups who had died; the captives were expected to take on the identities of the deceased and their place in the kinship order.

[92] Friedman reports that in 1718 the governor of Algiers ordered that any slaves attempting to convert should be flogged. Conversions by prominent captives were especially discouraged, since they could potentially bring higher prices. Friedman, *Spanish Captives in North Africa*, p. 89.

captives.[93] But the possibility of buying freedom from captivity generated institutional arrangements, expectations about captivity and captor societies, and routines for exchanging prisoners for ransom that had a certain cross-regional continuity.

Some aspects of captivity fit the broader Atlantic pattern of subordinate groups' controlling their own internal affairs within host polities. Captives in North Africa were housed in crowded quarters called *baños* and had officials who both adjudicated internal disputes and reported to the ruling sultans. The captives were organized by nationality into groups that controlled their own areas of the baños and had their own officials. From the thirteenth century on, Trinitarian and Mercedarian friars from Spain were permitted to enter the North African principalities to minister to the religious needs of Christian captives, a function that was not only tolerated but encouraged since the mendicant orders themselves came to play a central role in redemption. Of course, the legal status of these captive populations was not strictly similar to that of ethnic or merchant communities that regulated their own affairs. Conditions in the baños were notoriously horrid, and captives were forced to work hard and had only limited contact with their home communities. But some institutional similarities were striking. Captives who came to occupy high posts had considerable liberty and sometimes acted themselves as go-betweens in negotiations for redemption. The majordomo, the elected official, of each national group of captives, in addition to distributing alms sent from abroad, had the power to adjudicate internal disputes and administer punishments.[94] Mather pointed to these aspects of captives' self-governance as evidence of the spiritual resilience and enduring civility of Christians in captivity. The English captives in the Barbary states, he preached: "formed themselves into a SOCIETY, and in their *Slavery* enjoyed the *Liberty* to meet on the Lords Day Evening, every Week & annually chuse a *Master* and *Assistents*, and form a *Body of Laws*, to prevent and suppress Disorders among themselves."[95]

---

[93] Some captives passed into private hands and were difficult to retrieve; others indeed converted, while still others died in captivity. About nine years after a group of 302 men, women, and children from Iceland were seized and taken to Algiers, a delegation sent to redeem them were able to locate only 37. Hebb estimates that only around a third of English captives in the Barbary states were ever ransomed and returned (Hebb, *Piracy and the English Government*, p. 163).

[94] Friedman, *Spanish Captives in North Africa*, p. 62.

[95] Cotton Mather, "The Glory of Goodness," pp. 63–64.

Further, slaves had some, if limited, legal protections. The American John Foss's account of his captivity in Algiers between 1793 and 1797 gave a detailed report of the punishments inflicted for various crimes committed by both "Turks" and slaves. The practice of asylum for locals in Marabout mosques, he reported, extended to slaves. If they had committed a crime, they could seek asylum and eventual pardon in a mosque, or they could hold onto a special chain attached to the gates of the Dey's palace. A slave could also come to the chain and request justice if he had "been cheated by any Turk, Cologlie, Moor, Arab, Renegado, or Jew" and could expect an investigation by an officer of the Dey and punishment of the accused if his claim was proven.[96]

The self-regulation of captive communities could not be reproduced in the New World, where European captive numbers were far smaller. But Europeans did transpose the expectation that captives shared interests and identities that should lead them to cooperate in efforts at redemption. Though in North Africa captives had quarters and leaders organized by nationality, Christians from different national groups often helped one another and could be substituted for each other in redemption negotiations – sometimes purposefully by Barbary negotiators to frustrate redeemers and inflate the price for their compatriots. In the New World, Christians' failure to stick together in confronting captivity occasioned outrage. In North America, French collusion with Indian captive taking among English settlers prompted colonists to compare papists to Muslims.[97] In Brazil, the German Hans Staden, in captivity among the Tupinamba and awaiting his turn to be ritually eaten, looked forward to intercession by a fellow Christian, a Frenchman, who instead told the Tupinamba, "Kill him and eat him, the good-for-nothing, for he is indeed a Portuguese, your enemy and mine."[98]

When redemption did occur, customary practices, and in some cases well-established institutions, formed to regulate it. In negotiations with the Barbary states, redemption became increasingly a state-controlled affair. Religious and also sometimes legal ceremonies marked the

---

[96] John Foss, "A Journal of the Captivity and Sufferings of John Foss." p. 84.

[97] The comparison may have reflected, too, the French practice of soliciting ransom for English captives taken by client Indian groups. For various examples of redemption along the border of English- and French-controlled areas of eastern North America, see Colin G. Calloway, *North Country Captives: Selected Narratives of Indian Captivity from Vermont and New Hampshire*.

[98] Staden, "The True History of His Captivity," p. 32.

transition from captive to free person. Redemption was too frequently successful to be portrayed as an aberration, and it was, in any case, a cause that organized the efforts and resources of captives, their families, and whole communities throughout the seventeenth century. Despite representations of captors as barbarous, redemption implied that they had the capacity to follow behavioral norms – in a word, it implied civility.

The level of institutionalization of redemption was highest in European dealings with the Barbary states. In Spain, Mercedarian and Trinitarian friars organized collections of funds and official redemption voyages with the blessing and participation of the Spanish state. Spanish officials in North Africa and travelers from North Africa to Spain also sometimes participated in negotiations. Travelers engaged in redemption efforts received papers granting them free passage, and the records indicate that they were in fact remarkably safe when in "enemy" territory. Efforts to redeem English captives were more often private affairs, though the government also dispatched redemptionists directly and sent embassies to Constantinople (and from there to North Africa) to threaten naval attacks and the suspension of trade if English captives were not freed. Among Spanish, French, and English captives, organized and private redemption efforts existed side by side. The family and friends of captives enrolled merchants to carry letters back and forth. Individual captives in the Barbary states were sometimes successful in obtaining loans from local merchants to secure their own release.

One result of all this activity was that information circulated widely about the Barbary polities and how to succeed at redemption. In most accounts, the behavior of Barbary sultans was represented as wildly unreliable and capricious. Negotiators who believed they had arrived at a price found that the price had changed when they arrived in port. Redemptionists sent to free specific individuals were encouraged to pay ransom for other, less desirable captives first. One Mercedarian wrote in the late seventeenth century that the state in Algiers was "not governed by law or reason, nor do they keep their word if it conflicts with their interests."[99] Rulers changed often and had singular power. Yet, despite these complaints, redemption voyages continued unabated, and many were successful. Along with the representation of Barbary sultans as impossibly shifty, understandings

[99] Friedman, *Spanish Captives in North Africa*, p. 131.

emerged about routines of the negotiation process. The seemingly erratic price shifts came to have a recognizable pattern, so that redemptionists understood that the first price would rarely stand and could prepare to pay a second, higher price.[100] And because negotiations passed through the sultans, redemption had a certain legal framework within the Barbary states themselves. On arrival in Algiers, captives were taken directly to the Dey's palace. The Dey selected some captives for his own service and might publicly declare the rationale of the capture (in John Foss's case, the Dey railed against the American government's reluctance to negotiate a treaty). On their release, captives also went to the Dey and received passports required to leave the port legally. While in captivity, as we have seen, slaves had precise, if extremely limited, legal rights, and punishments were harsh but not arbitrary.[101]

The sensationalism of accounts of captivity in the Barbary states tended to overshadow the many details about its political and legal regulation. Such information did not, after all, legitimize Barbary captive taking or make it seem less ominous. It is clear, though, that captives themselves concentrated on learning and reporting about the legal framework of Barbary slavery as knowledge both crucial to their quest for liberty and important to the fates of other travelers. The captivity narrative of the American James Cathcart offers many examples of the easy mix of pedagogy and suspense. Cathcart was taken captive by Algerians in 1785 and rose to become the private secretary to the Dey before his ransom and release. He offers close portraits of the structure of authority while preserving his own image as an outsider. For example, when a Muslim notable had a learned discussion with Cathcart about the Quran in a local tavern, Cathcart reports that the qadi was summoned to declare him a convert. The qadi was not at home, and Cathcart was able to bribe several witnesses to affirm that he had shown only his knowledge of Islam, not his faith. His summary of the incident points out both his understanding of the legal probabilities

---

[100] Hebb suggests that the first price came to be understood as a formal offer to be followed by further negotiations and agreement on a second price. Hebb, *Piracy and the English Government*, p. 152.

[101] When Maria Martin, an American captive in Algiers in 1800, failed in an escape attempt, she and her accomplice were taken before the bashaw's court. The accomplice was sentenced to be executed, and Martin condemned to close confinement and meager rations. Maria Martin, "History of the Captivity and Sufferings of Mrs. Maria Martin," p. 155.

and his desire to turn this knowledge into a lesson:

> The escape . . . ought to serve as a warning to all who read this journal and travel in those countries; for in fact had the Cadhi been at home he was in duty bound to have demanded my admission among the true believers, the Dey himself dare not have opposed it; and had I refused after having recited the symbol of their faith I would have been put to death as an apostate from it.[102]

Here, as in other captivity accounts, the celebration of a narrow escape mixes easily with lessons about legal process.

Just as becoming a captive and securing freedom followed regular and regulated patterns, rituals in Europe framed captives' return to public life. In Spain and France, the mendicant orders involved in redemption organized public celebrations and displays, used in part to raise more money for further efforts at redemption. Returning to England, former captives were required to present a deposition to authorities. The objective was in part to gather information about other captives and corsair activities; the depositions were an opportunity, too, for captives to offer testimony about their individual resistance to cultural and religious corruption.[103] For captives who admitted to or were suspected of conversion, the church devised its own legal procedure. Former captives were brought before a bishop's court and convicted of apostasy, then required to perform penance.[104]

Redemption was less highly regulated and institutionalized in the New World, but European expectations were perhaps not very different. Mary Rowlandson's narrative is similar to those of North African captives not only in presenting captivity as a metaphor for spiritual struggle and salvation but also in its prosaic details about redemption. Rowlandson's ransom of twenty pounds "was raised by some Boston gentlemen," her son was redeemed for seven pounds, paid by "the good people" around Portsmouth, and a nephew was freed after the Council paid four pounds. The Indians were clearly quick to set prices and to negotiate for additional goods to be provided with the ransom. For all its emphasis on the wild nature of the Indians and the risks of being among them, Rowlandson's narrative mainly underscores the willingness of both the Indians and the settlers to

---

[102] James Leander Cathcart, "The Captives, Eleven Years a Prisoner in Algiers," pp. 144–145.

[103] Matar, *Turks, Moors, and Englishmen*, p. 75.

[104] See Hebb, *Piracy and the English Government*, p. 167.

negotiate.[105] After their "General Court" met and seemed to affirm her release, Rowlandson found that the Indians – "those roaring lions, and savage bears" – had no difficulty recognizing and even celebrating her release: "[T]hey assented to it, and seemed much to rejoice in it; some asked me to send them some bread, others some tobacco, others shaking me by the hand, offering me a hood and scarf to ride in; not one moving hand or tongue against it."[106]

Redemption was both dependent upon mutual understanding and an opportunity for learning. Negotiations revealed, certainly, details of material culture and the structure of power. In showing captives and their rescuers the rituals of release, it conveyed the meaning of captivity itself. In Hans Staden's account of captivity among the Tupinamba, he explains that he arranged his release by carefully instructing the crew and captain of a French trading ship to offer chests of merchandise to his master as a "reward" for his good care and to promise to return Staden after a short stay on the ship: "Meanwhile we had arranged between us that some ten of the crew, who were not unlike me, should gather round and say that they were my brothers and wanted to take me home . . . saying that I must return with them, as my father longed to see me once more before he died."[107] After his stay among the Tupinamba, Staden knew that only an appeal involving ties of kinship would work peacefully – plus the payment of additional goods, "some five ducats' worth in knives, aces, looking-glasses, and combs."[108]

Even if negotiations for redemption fell short of creating an atmosphere of trust or predictability, they produced knowledge – about the legal standing of captives in captor societies, and, also, about the internal legal practices of captor groups. The narratives were a source of information, and many are organized much like early ethnographies,

---

[105] When Rowlandson's band receives a visit from John Hoar and two Christianized Indians, sent by the Council to try to secure her release, she learns that her master has promised to let her go home if Hoar provides him with a pint of liquor: "Then Mr. Hoar called his own Indians, Tom and Peter, and bid them go and see whether he would promise before them three: if he would, he should have it; which he did, and he had it. Then [the Indian leader] Philip smelling the business called me to him, and asked me what I would give him, to tell me some good news, and speak a good word for me, I told him, I could not tell what to give him, I would [give] anything I had, and asked him what he would have? He said, two coats and twenty shillings in money, and half a bushel of seed corn, and some tobacco" (Mary Rowlandson, "The Sovereignty and Goodness of God," p. 168).

[106] Rowlandson, "The Sovereignty and Goodness of God," p. 171.

[107] Staden, "The True History of His Captivity," p. 58.

[108] Staden, "The True History of His Captivity," p. 58.

with a cataloguing of customs in various areas of social life. One of the categories of description was legal affairs. In this respect, travelers' and captives' narratives were similar in structure, and even the tone was not greatly different.[109] Both sensationalized the strangeness and primitiveness of the groups they observed while also systematically conveying the orderliness of custom.

This built-in ambiguity of knowledge produced through stories about captivity itself provided a certain continuity for the practice of redemption, and for other, more violent responses to captive taking. Expectations of lawlessness *and* lawfulness coexisted. The cultural lessons of captivity and redemption were multilayered. Europeans learned in some settings that even the most alien-seeming captors would settle into patterns of exchange that included the semiautonomy of captives and, ultimately, their release. Europeans learned, too, that this process required a certain flexibility and willingness to play by foreign rules, as both captives and redemptionists. This knowledge implied, then, that there *were* rules to play by and that they included familiar rule making about the legal standing of cultural and religious outsiders. As much as chroniclers wanted to emphasize representations of captors as capricious and cruel, they had an inescapable interest in producing knowledge about specific kinds of ordered behavior.

Redemption was, in this sense, a window both on certain legal practices – the embeddedness of captives in a plural legal order, rituals surrounding changes in legal status – and on a much larger and systemic orderliness of these "wild" peoples. Through redemption, "savages" and "pirates" took on the unmistakable marks of legal authority, political order, and diplomacy. These lessons were too valuable to lose, though through the emphatic insistence on Europeans' unique civility and spiritual righteousness, they could be well hidden – even, if we are not careful, from our own more probing gaze.

AN INTERNATIONAL LEGAL REGIME

This survey of legal complexity in the Atlantic world has ranged from the relation between ecclesiastic and state law in the Iberian peninsula,

---

[109] Thus, for example, Jean de Léry's description of the Tupinamba in his travels to Brazil (*History of a Voyage to the Land of Brazil*) nearly parallels Staden's account ("The True History of His Captivity"); both insert descriptions of captive taking in a catalogue of observations about Tupinamba social life, though the anxiety and suspense of Staden's description of cannibalism are missing from Léry's account.

to European interactions with Africans in the early centuries of maritime trade, to pacts between maroon communities and colonial authorities in the Americas, and to the legal framework for captivity and redemption. The connecting thread is that these disparate sets of relations were shaped out of the same legal matrix: a structuring of multiple legal authorities that permitted both parallel and independent adjudication and, under specific and clearly defined circumstances, an appellate or controlling authority for state's law. Europeans, we have shown, relied closely on the model of jurisdictional arrangements between church and state, and between crown and nobility, in crafting legal relations with non-Christians. Africans, for their part, had long experience with plural legal orders, especially where trade diasporas established a pattern of dual legal authority. Africans in the New World were in effect responding to opportunities of jurisdictional complexity in widespread attempts to create communities that were simultaneously subordinate to, and independent from, colonial government. Rather than representing self-defeating compromises, such strategies were a logical response to a familiar institutional landscape. Similarly, European captives and redemptionists learned that captivity and release fit into a larger legal framework that assigned a special and permanently separate legal status to captives, regulated the payment of ransom, and ritually marked both incorporation into captor societies and reinsertion into home polities after captives' return. Even the most "barbarous" inhabitants of the Atlantic world, it was understood, possessed both law and legal routines recognizing and regulating subordinate others.

Asserting this *institutional* continuity in the Atlantic world does not require finding *cultural* continuity. There is, though, a cultural connection. One of the impulses for the perpetuation of jurisdictionally complex legal orders – and one of its outcomes – was that legal boundaries were closely associated with the production of cultural boundaries. In the Iberian peninsula, and in Europe more generally, religious distinctions both created legal boundaries marking religious and cultural differences and generated patterns for accommodating difference. As Europeans encountered new types of non-Christians, legal boundaries did not precisely parallel ethnic boundaries, but they existed as an important constraint and rhetorical resource used in shaping ethnic identities. In the South Atlantic, conceptualizing other polities as possessing a legal status that could, under some circumstances, be continued within the territory of another polity placed cultural difference at the center of political theory and practice. In Africa and the New World, slavery represented the negation of this legal status, the complete subordination of an outsider to the control of a culturally different society and master. The theoretical possibility of reversing this shift – not just for individuals through manumission, but for whole communities through negotiated settlements – was important both to the strategies of Africans in the New World and to Europeans' responses to marronage. Jurisdictional autonomy of a limited kind for communities of runaway slaves created a legal boundary around a space of cultural production; where the boundary remained in place, it came to define not just a political but also an ethnic community. European captivity similarly heightened both awareness of European religious singularity and attention to the divergent interests and identities of various nationalities. Despite the rhetoric in captivity narratives damning captor societies as lawless, redemption depended on institutional regularities that permitted captives to retain their "otherness" and framed cross-cultural negotiations.

This view of legal models and arrangements in the fifteenth century through the end of the eighteenth century in the Atlantic world suggests a different shape and meaning of global interconnectedness in this period. Rather than mapping long-distance trade, modeling core-periphery relations, or tracing civilizational or regional evolutions, a comparative institutional analysis suggests that the world stretching from the Iberian Americas, to Christian Europe, coastal and Islamic Africa, and into the vast Indian Ocean world formed part of a single international legal regime. Broad structural similarities in the ways that power and identity were defined in the institutional order made these culturally diverse regions mutually intelligible for travelers and traders, thereby undergirding (rather than merely following) global economic interconnections. By reproducing this jurisdictional legal complexity, continued contests over cultural and ethnic identities themselves constituted a feature of international order.

THREE

Order out of Trouble

Jurisdictional Tensions in Catholic and Islamic Empires

An Augustinian friar traveling through Bengal in 1640 found himself in the uncomfortable middle of a criminal case. One of his Muslim attendants had killed a peacock while the traveling party was stranded overnight in a Hindu village. After making a meal of the bird, the party had been unsuccessful in hiding the deed from the villagers, who were predictably scandalized at the killing of a sacred bird. The group reached the safety of a nearby town, but there the Hindu guides denounced the killing to local Mughal authorities, and all the travelers were immediately thrown in jail. Later, the *shiqdar*, a revenue collector responsible for the local administration of justice, decided to punish just the man who had killed the bird. The Augustinian argued the defense; surely the man had "committed no fault against God or against His precepts or those of your Alcoran [Qura'n]." But the shiqdar was adamant. Bengalis were to "live under their own laws and customs." Muslims in a Hindu district had to follow the laws and practices of Hindus.[1]

The principles guiding the Mughal official certainly would have been less foreign to the friar than he let on. As the last chapter shows, it was more common than not for both colonizing and colonized in early modern polities to recognize the existence of multiple legal authorities. Bowing to local customs and law, and even taking on the task of administering local law in some form as this Mughal official was doing, were familiar practices of expanding empires. This is not to say that the results were institutionally uniform. In practice, conquest and colonization produced varying patterns of legal accommodation and administration.

---

[1] Richard M. Eaton, *The Rise of Islam and the Bengal Froniter, 1204–1760*, p. 181.

The commonalities were more broadly structural. Conquest and colonization created conditions that pulled at the boundaries of the legal order and often enhanced jurisdictional fluidity. Conquered people had to be incorporated in the imposed legal order; as we saw in the previous chapter, colonizing powers already possessed a blueprint for recognizing alternative legal authorities, and they relied on existing models in designing the legal status of newly conquered groups. But conquered peoples did not passively accept the roles assigned to them. They became litigants and legal advocates, and quickly discerned ways to find opportunity in the jurisdictional tensions of the imposed legal order. At the same time, jurisdictional divides within conquering forces became battlegrounds for ruling factions. Far from the control of centralized institutions, political factions reopened "settled" questions of legal boundaries. In doing so, they defined their positions in relation to their authority over conquered territories and populations. Contests over legal prerogatives became arenas for discourse about cultural difference. At the same time, central institutions sought ways to respond to jurisdictional looseness and in fact saw, in imperial expansion, an opportunity for legal administrative streamlining.

This chapter explores the interrelation between conquest and jurisdictional tensions by considering a particular example of jurisdictional politics in the Spanish American borderlands. I then place this case in a wider comparative context by discussing the complexities of the legal rule of non-Muslims in the Ottoman empire, and of non-Christians in the Portuguese settlement of Goa. The juxtaposition of Catholic and Islamic empires is designed to show not substantive legal parallels but a similar multicentric character to law. Across religiously different spheres that some historians too blithely categorize as different "civilizations," legal complexities provided continuity. Specifically, jurisdictional disorder emerged as an element of interregional order.

NEW JURISDICTIONAL PUZZLES FOR SPANIARDS

Quite early in the process of conquest, the Spanish crown insisted on complete authority over ecclesiastical matters in the New World. In the early colonial period, the crown based these claims rather narrowly on papal bulls of 1493, conceding dominion of the Indies to the Catholic kings and awarding them exclusive rights to Christianize the indigenous population; of 1501, granting the crown control over church tithes from the Indies; and of 1508, awarding the crown rights of universal patronage over the Catholic Church in the Indies. While clearly establishing the supremacy of the crown in the New World, the *real patronato de las Indias*, as the arrangement established by these bulls came to be called, left intact the clergy's right to trial in ecclesiastical courts, the *fuero eclesiástico*. But ecclesiastic appeals to the papal court were eliminated in a papal bull of 1578, which provided that all ecclesiastical cases should be decided in the New World. This bull was not published by Philip II; royal orders called for its enforcement only in 1606, when the balance of power in the New World had shifted more clearly in favor of the crown. Together, these measures seemed to simplify considerably the complexities of the legal order in Spain, and to strengthen royal control. The Council of the Indies had ultimate jurisdiction over most legal matters in the New World, and viceroys were to sort out any jurisdictional disputes that would arise between church and state authorities.[2]

The great exception to this arrangement was, of course, the Inquisition. This institution had authority over the investigation and trial of matters involving conformity to church beliefs and rituals. Before the first tribunals were established in the New World in 1571, bishops and their delegates could represent the Inquisition. Pope Adrian VI's bull of 1522 provided that prelates of the missionary orders could exercise legal authorities corresponding to secular clergy and bishops, and this is precisely what occurred before the arrival of the first bishop in New Spain in 1528 and thereafter in remote areas of the empire. Although the Inquisition had long since been brought under the control of the crown in Spain, it still operated with considerable independence of royal or ecclesiastic control. No secular authority in the Americas could overrule its judgments. Appeals went to the Consejo de la Suprema y General Inquisición in Spain, a body that was responsible to the crown but independent of the papacy and distinct from the Council of the

---

[2] Mecham provides a clear summary of the origins of the *real patronato* and notes the crown's strenuous defense of its authority over the church. He describes, for example, a case in Charcas in the mid-seventeenth century, in which a lawyer of the Audiencia of Charcas argued that the crown did not have a right to hear ecclesiastical cases. Royal officials had him fined one hundred ducats and banned from practicing for four years, a penalty the king later approved. J. Lloyd Mecham, *Church and State in Latin America: A History of Politico-Ecclesiastical Relations*. On the *fuero eclesiástico* and efforts to dismantle ecclesiastic immunity at the end of the eighteenth century, see Nancy Farriss, *Crown and Clergy in Colonial Mexico, 1759–1821: The Crisis of Ecclesiastical Privilege*.

Indies, which handled all other legal matters and appeals from the New World.

Until 1571, the Inquisition had jurisdiction over transgressions of faith by Indians as well as Spaniards. The Franciscan friar Martin de Valencia prosecuted newly baptized Indians under the Inquisition in 1524 in New Spain. Zumárraga, as the first bishop and as commissary of the Inquisition, conducted some nineteen trials involving at least seventy-five Indians between 1536 and 1543.[3] In the 1560s, a challenge to Diego de Landa's authority as a Franciscan prelate to conduct trials in the Yucatan under the Inquisition reached Spain. Though Landa was exonerated, reports of the use of torture on Indians to get them to confess to idolatry helped to call attention to a debate about the fairness of including Indians – new converts inadequately schooled in Catholic rites – in the jurisdiction of the Inquisition. When it was formally introduced into New Spain in 1571, the Holy Office was instructed to exempt Indians.[4] All other residents of the colonies, including *mulatos* and *mestizos*, fell under its purview.[5]

In general, the crown did not arrive at any sort of coherent legal policy regarding indigenous inhabitants of the Americas for at least half a century. Initial approaches actually left considerable room for Indians to continue to exercise their own local legal authority. Though they received official appointments as local judges (alcaldes) in the Spanish hierarchy, Indian leaders continued to administer customary law based on preconquest practices. Spanish judges were also encouraged to use

---

[3] Richard Greenleaf, "The Inquisition and the Indians of New Spain: A Study in Jurisdictional Confusion," p. 139. See also Richard Greenleaf, "Historiography of the Spanish Inquisition: Evolution of Interpretations and Methodologies."

[4] Klor de Alva has argued that the humanitarian reasons given by contemporaries, including Zumárraga, for curtailing the authority of the Inquisition are misleading, and that this move only signaled the greater efficacy of a disciplinary regime based on close control of Indians' lives rather than a regime supported through punishment. Jorge Klor de Alva, "Colonizing Souls: The Failure of the Indian Inquisition and the Rise of Penitential Discipline."

[5] The Inquisition could continue to investigate crimes against the faith by Indians. Empowered to try Indians in cases of heresy or apostasy, the ordinary ecclesiastical courts in some places mimicked the Inquisition in procedures and appearance, on occasion giving rise to complaints by the Holy Office. Residents themselves seem to have been confused about the differences between the two institutions. The directives to exempt Indians in some ways made the jurisdictional muddle more complete. See Richard Greenleaf, "The Inquisition and the Indians of New Spain: A Study in Jurisdictional Confusion." See also Roberto Moreno de los Arcos, "New Spain's Inquisition for Indians from the Sixteenth to the Nineteenth Century."

indigenous traditions as the basis for legal decisions.[6] Gradually, and in the same way that conquest on the peninsula had led slowly to a weakening of the legal authority of religious minorities, the availability of appeals to courts applying Spanish law produced a shift in legal rhetoric and procedure toward Spanish influences. At the same time, of course, the persisting differences of courts presided over by indigenous and Spanish officials offered opportunities for indigenous litigants, who could, and often did, take disputes from one forum to another, changing legal arguments and advocates as appropriate.[7]

Indians in Central Mexico perceived almost immediately the potential benefits of litigation in Spanish courts. Suits begun by Indians multiplied rapidly and became a factor in an ongoing debate about the legal status of Indians.[8] Disputes over land and inheritance, as well as complaints against individual Spaniards, drew Indians into protracted litigation and prompted calls for simplified procedures and relief for Indians from high legal fees. Clerics had established themselves early in the colonial period in the role of defenders (*protectores*) of the Indians, but the crown was eager to reestablish authority in this area. In the middle

---

[6] See "Introduction" in Susan Kellogg, *Law and the Transformation of Aztec Culture*. Borah (*Justice by Insurance*, p. 57) describes the practice of one Spanish delegate of the audiencia of summoning native judges to ask them about local customs. Though it was unusual to use Indians as legal assessors in this way, the practice would not have been out of keeping with the generalized recognition of the validity of custom that was not in conflict with Spanish and Christian law. This recognition was, in turn, consistent with legal policies under the Reconquest.

[7] Kellogg, in *Law and the Transformation of Aztec Culture*, provides substantial evidence of the shift, including its significance for how Indians were represented, and portrayed themselves, as litigants. A 1593 inheritance case provides a good example of the kinds of strategies employed by Indian litigants to take advantage of the complex legal order. Gaspar Lopez died in 1588, leaving a house site and several garden plots. His son Diego sought restitution in the Real Audiencia when an illegitimate half-brother Felipe sold several rooms in the house to another Indian. In the same month, Felipe took the case to the Indian alcalde and argued, based on the testimony of Indian witnesses and preconquest inheritance patterns, that the sale should be upheld. It was. A month later, Diego went before the native governor of Tenochtitlán and succeeded in having the property placed in the possession of one of his relatives. Later in the year Felipe had hired a lawyer to argue the case to the audiencia. It is not clear how the case was resolved, but the strategy of appeal to different forums, together with a flexible use of Nahua and Spanish legal arguments, appears fairly typical.

[8] I am concerned here narrowly with the jurisdictional implications of the way this legal status came to be defined. For a more general treatment of the important theological debates about the rationality of Indians, see Colin M. MacLachlan, *Spain's Empire in the New World: The Role of Ideas in Institutional and Social Change*; and Robert A. Williams, *The American Indian in Western Legal Thought*.

decades of the sixteenth century, administrative and judicial hierarchies fought over control of Indian litigation; Indians in New Spain could not be certain whether to take complaints to the viceroy or the audiencia, the regional high court, and often took them to both.[9] The crown resolved, finally, to create a special forum, the General Indian Court, and to create a separate bureaucracy with paid *protectores de Indios* financed by a special tax on Indians. The rationale was borrowed from familiar legal precedent, one that the crown had in turn borrowed from the canonists: Indians were the equivalent of Old World *miserables* and were entitled as such to summary judgments and legal representation by crown-appointed officials.[10]

These trends together – exemption of Indians under the Inquisition and the creation of a special court and system of representation for them – marked Indians with a clearly separate legal status in the colonial order. This separation coincided with the blurring of cultural and biological differences between Indians and others. Not surprisingly, the legal distinction quickly came to be used strategically. Indian identity in some circumstances – and certainly in the face of Inquisitorial interest and in many civil actions – was a valuable commodity, something to be produced, if possible, even when it had been denied in other contexts. Greenleaf claims, for example, that "soon after the 1570s, many bigamists, blasphemers, and sorcerers *claimed* to be Indians in order to escape the Holy Office's jurisdiction and remain subject to the ordinaries."[11] He documents a number of cases in which charges were dropped after officials traced family ties to find that individuals accused by the Inquisition (and who were clearly Hispanicized in many ways) were indeed Indians. This flexibility in legal identities mirrored the fluidity of the *sistema de castas*. Douglas Cope has shown, for example, that plebeian residents of Mexico City often represented themselves (or were represented) as Indians in some records and mestizos in others.[12] The shift in status encouraged Indian communities, too, to plead cases based on corporate rights and to draw boundaries closely to exclude mestizo

[9] Borah, *Justice by Insurance*, p. 77.

[10] Borah's *Justice by Insurance* is a history of the General Indian Court in colonial Mexico. For a study of the institution of the Protector de Indios outside central Mexico, see Charles R. Cutter, *The Protector de Indios in Colonial New Mexico, 1659–1821*.

[11] Greenleaf, "The Inquisition and the Indians of New Spain," p. 149.

[12] See R. Douglas Cope, *The Limits of Racial Domination: Plebeian Society in Colonial Mexico City, 1660–1720*.

"outsiders" from community prerogatives or interests.[13] Yet, protected Indian legal status also had the effect of reinforcing ideas about Indians as uncontrollably litigious people who nevertheless had little respect for and knowledge of the moral imperatives underlying legal procedure. They were branded as unreliable witnesses or, worse, habitual perjurers.[14] By the end of the sixteenth century, respect for Indian custom as a source of law had essentially disappeared.

CHURCH, CROWN, AND INDIANS IN NORTHERN NEW SPAIN

The legal isolation of Indians took place against the background of continuing, sometimes strident jurisdictional disputes between ecclesiastical and secular authorities. These disputes carried over some of the modalities of struggle between royal and ecclesiastical authorities in Spain, but they now centered pointedly around the relation of these groups to Indians. Disputes over ecclesiastical immunity, conflicts over rights to impose sanctions on Indians and settlers for heresy, and struggles over the flow of information to appeals courts – these sorts of contests were a constant feature of colonial political culture in the New World. They were, on one level, symptoms of the struggle over Indian resources and Indians-as-resources. Yet the complexity of the legal order, the existence of a legal culture attentive to jurisdictional divides, and the clear association of legal distinctions with cultural and ethnic boundaries also gave these conflicts an independent, at times more urgent, meaning.

These processes are most visible in frontier regions of the Spanish empire, where distance from the centers of power allowed for creative interpretations of institutional constraints, and where sometimes meager resources and rewards intensified contests over seemingly small prerogatives. It is this *visibility* of jurisdictional fights that calls our attention to the frontier, rather than some fundamental difference in the way that jurisdictional tensions were played out there. As Parry notes in his study of politics in New Galicia, frontier jurisdictional disputes sometimes

---

[13] Kellogg, *Law and the Transformation of Aztec Culture*. Pueblo Indians, for example, established claims over land by appealing to protected Indian interests and specifically excluded mestizo neighbors from these benefits. See Charles Cutter, "Community and the Law in Northern New Spain "; and my discussion below.

[14] Kellogg, *Law and the Transformation of Aztec Culture*, pp. 66, 77; Borah, *Justice by Insurance*, p. 57.

offered an excuse for simple disobedience of crown directives.[15] Yet the choice of jurisdictional fighting was based on more than mere convenience. Law was central to marking boundaries around colonial constituencies and defining their relation to one another. Making such connections was almost effortless for colonial cultures immersed in the language and ceremony of legal distinctions.

Jurisdictional conflicts in the borderlands on occasion intersected with and even directed larger, jurisdictional debates within the Spanish empire. An example of such interaction would be the case already mentioned of Landa's insistence on Franciscan legal prerogatives in Yucatan, and the push it gave for the crown's clarification of the structure and scope of church legal authority in the New World. Debates over the jurisdiction of the Inquisition in Peru provide another example of conflicts on the edge of empire that reached back to its center.[16] Rather than focusing on this interaction, though, I want to examine the discourse of jurisdictional disputes in one frontier setting, northern New Spain in the seventeenth century, in an effort to show the intersection of disputes about institutional structure and efforts to shape cultural boundaries. It is an advantage that the region has been the subject of considerable scrutiny by other historians, who provide both materials and alternative interpretations to frame this exercise. Early scholarship tended to regard the pervasive jurisdictional tensions in New Mexico as the logical outcome of the contest over power between church and state; in effect, legal disputes were simply the most prominent of an array of vehicles for the pursuit of political advantage. More recent studies have suggested that attention to jurisdictional boundaries disguised other tensions – the fight over resources or the clash of hegemonic and subaltern worldviews. I will attempt to show that the region's preoccupation with the law was more than a way of channeling political strategy or refashioning legitimacy. Legal understandings permeated daily struggles. Colonists, missionaries, and Indians responded to the complexities of

---

[15] J.H. Parry, *The Audiencia of New Galicia in the Sixteenth Century: A Study in Spanish Colonial Government*, pp. 168–69.

[16] See Greenleaf on the generalized "jurisdictional confusion" surrounding the question of Indian idolatry in Mexico and its repercussions (Greenleaf, "The Inquisition and the Indians of New Spain"). On the Inquisition in Lima, see Paulino Castañeda Delgado and Pilar Hernández Aparicio, *La Inquisición de Lima, Vol. 1*; and, more generally, on the suppression of idolatry in the Andes and its larger imprint on Spanish policies, see Kenneth Mills, *Idolatry and Its Enemies: Colonial Andean Religion and Extirpation, 1640–1750*.

the imposed legal order while creating, through their own maneuvering, new sources of cultural and jurisdictional tension.

New Mexico was a poor outpost of the larger political unit of New Spain. Our knowledge of legal disputes comes from the necessarily biased accounts sent to the viceroy of New Spain; to the regional *audiencia*, the high court to which unresolved legal disputes were referred; and, later, to the Holy Office of the Inquisition, in Mexico City. As was the case elsewhere in Spanish America, secular legal authority in the settlement was formally in the hands of the appointed provincial governor. The church laid claim to its own jurisdiction, as we have outlined for Spanish America more broadly, and, in the absence of a secular clergy, this authority resided in the head of the Franciscan missions throughout the period of early settlement.

Let us begin with one episode that shows the tiny group of ruling Spaniards, their soldier-settler charges, and the New Mexican Indians struggling over symbols of legal privilege. In 1639, the town council, or *cabildo*, of Santa Fe, wrote to the viceroy of New Spain complaining that the Franciscans were refusing to minister to the religious needs of the Spanish settlers. Church officials had refused to hear confession during Lent, "in contempt of the royal jurisdiction."[17] As in the bitter disputes of the past, this one had begun over a claim of ecclesiastical immunity by the friars.[18] Also as in conflicts in the past, other complaints surfaced

---

[17] My analysis in this section relies on documents translated by Adolph and Fanny Bandelier and published under the editorship of Charles Hackett (Charles Wilson Hackett, ed. *Historical Documents Relating to New Mexico, Nueva Vizcaya, and Approaches Thereto, Vol. III*). This quote is from "Report to the Viceroy by the Cabildo of Santa Fe, New Mexico, February 21, 1639," in Hackett, *Historical Documents*, p. 66.

[18] A treasurer of the Santa Cruzada had been arrested for financial improprieties, and the Franciscans invoked immunity to have him freed. The Santa Cruzada was a special tribunal similar in its relative independence to the Inquisition. It collected funds through the sale of bulls. It is interesting to note that secular officials responded to the claim of ecclesiastical immunity with jurisdictional issues of their own. They complained that the Franciscan commissary of the Santa Cruzada had never formally presented his appointment to the town council. They also argued that he had interfered with civil jurisdiction by meddling in the affairs of the province in various ways, including confiscating property (France Scholes, *Church and State in New Mexico, 1610–1650*, pp. 122–24). Decades later, Don Bernardo López de Mendizábal, when brought on trial before the Inquisition, would defend his own questioning of ordinary ecclesiastical jurisdiction by claiming that it had been customary in the province for local officials to challenge ecclesiastical judicial prerogatives. Although his agrument was weak legally, López may have drawn from local stories about the dispute over the Santa Cruzada officials in fashioning a legal precedent for his own actions. "Auto of Mendizábal, June 12, 1660" (Hackett, *Historical Documents*, p. 168).

quickly. Town officials and friars accused each other of monopolizing Indian labor. They turned their attention, too, to more symbolic markers of disputed authority.

Of particular concern to town officials was their perception that the exercise of church authority had the effect of placing them in the role of outsiders. The friars lived outside Santa Fe, in the missions, and seemed to care more about the religious needs of the Indians than those of the soldier-settlers. In order to see the Franciscans in charge of all the province's missions, town councillors had to travel to the pueblo of Santo Domingo. When they had gone to try to resolve the current crisis, an earlier letter reported, the custodian had "said that he did not recognize the cabildo" and he had ordered them housed "in an Indian *estufa* [kiva] – a most indecent thing."[19] The officials seemed to understand that they were implicitly being equated with Indians as a group subordinate to clerical authority. The letter moves without transition to complain of the "grave and atrocious crime" committed by the Franciscans when they imprisoned the provincial governor Don Pedro de Peralta, and a description of his treatment:

> The said governor and captain-general, having escaped from his prison in the rigor of winter, went on foot and half naked, covered with a buffalo robe like an Indian, to a farm which is two leagues from the said pueblo. Learning where he was, his jailer, Father Fray Estevan de Perea, went with a large number of Indians, armed with bows and arrows, and surrounded the said farm.[20]

The association of the two cases would seem unremarkable, except that Peralta's imprisonment had taken place twenty-five years before, in the context of another, different jurisdictional dispute (though one that had begun, like the conflict now raging, over a disputed claim of

---

[19] This is from a communication one week earlier, "Opinion of the Cabildo of the Villa of Santa Fe in New Mexico in Regard to the Affairs of the Religious, February 14, 1639" (Hackett, *Historical Documents*, p. 63). The choice of the kiva probably added to the affront; these buildings were used to house Indian religious artifacts and rituals, and the Franciscans had ordered them dismantled in many of the missions. According to Gutierrez, the Franciscans had purposely established a spatial relation of insiders and outsiders because they understood Indian distinctions between Inside Chiefs, who had political authority, and Outside Chiefs, who were responsible for military protection. The association had been useful in establishing Spanish authority in the region. See Ramon Gutierrez, *When Jesus Came, the Corn Mothers Went Away: Marriage, Sexuality, and Power in New Mexico, 1500–1846.*

[20] "Opinion of the Cabildo of the Villa of Santa Fe in New Mexico in Regard to the Affairs of the Religious, February 14, 1639" (Hackett, *Historical Documents*, p. 64).

ecclesiastical immunity). The only earlier account we have of Peralta's imprisonment and escape contradicts every aspect of the cabildo's recollection twenty-five years later, except for one detail: the image of Peralta seated on a horse "and covered with a skin like an Indian."[21]

In this account and many others, complaints focused in detail on the visible symbols of authority and their manipulation, and legal distinctions between Spaniards were made by asserting or denying cultural closeness to Indians. In the dispute involving Peralta, a key point of contention had been the terms of his absolution following his ordered excommunication. The Franciscans had insisted that Peralta be absolved at the church door before entering and hearing mass "barefoot and a candle in his hand, in the presence of all the people." Peralta and his allies stubbornly (and successfully) held out for a more private ritual. But continued feuding with the Franciscans led to a worse public affront: The governor's chair was thrown out of the church before Sunday mass, and Peralta had to pick it up and place it just inside the church door, "among the Indians," instead of at the high altar. Indians were arguably the intended audience of this event. They were later summoned by the friars to watch Peralta being led to jail and to witness an execution (of an Indian) ordered by the Franciscan prelate to demonstrate his power over the secular authorities who carried it out.

Such contests between secular and church authority dominated all aspects of provincial politics in New Mexico between 1610, when the crown committed to preserving the settlement despite its poverty, and 1680, when the Pueblo Revolt forced the Spaniards out of the region for more than a decade. The disruptions to order in the province were hardly negligible. The first governor, Juan de Oñate, was forced from power; Peralta, the second governor, was imprisoned and sent back to Mexico; the third, like Peralta, was excommunicated; and successors were intimidated by investigations under the Inquisition, including one, López de Mendizábal, who was arrested and sent back to face trial by the Office of the Holy Order in Mexico City. He died in jail, though the Holy Office exonerated him posthumously. France Scholes surveyed these events and found in them a pattern of jurisdictional jockeying that continued up until the Revolt of 1680. Cutter has pointed out that Scholes was relying on biased documents – appeals to the audiencia and Inquisition records. One would expect disputants to present

---

[21] See Scholes, *Church and State in New Mexico*, p. 36.

their complaints in terms of legal prerogatives in such documents. What the friars and settler-soldiers were really fighting about, Cutter tells us, was control of Indian resources and labor; the struggle for legal control was "a sidelight."[22] Gutierrez sees the struggle differently. He views Indian acquiescence as dependent upon the perception that the two authorities, though divided, worked together, much like the Inside and Outside Chiefs of the Pueblo political order who were responsible for internal authority and external military protection. Secular objections to Franciscan control only became more strident and more visible to Indians in the middle decades of the century and coincided with the spread of disease and the escalation of demands on Indian resources. As Franciscans' ability to protect Indians came into question, a resurgence of Indian religious rituals occurred. "The relationship between the sacred and secular force enshrined in the structure of authority since the conquest had crumbled before its Indian audience."[23]

How do we reconcile the contention that these conflicts were really about economic interests with the view that they were important mainly as elements of hegemony? Neither view deserves to be dismissed. It is abundantly clear that the Franciscans and civil authorities were engaged in an ongoing struggle over control of Indian resources. Both missionaries and settlers depended almost exclusively on Indian labor for local production, personal service, and even for carrying on trade with the seminomadic, un-Christianized Indians beyond the borders of the missions. Indian labor built and maintained the churches. Franciscans' role as missionaries entitled them to Indian labor, but its distribution and control flowed through secular authorities. The latter could, and often did, use their responsibility for protection of the settlement as a rationale to remove Indians from Franciscan control. And as the small population of soldier-settlers increased, the Hispanicized community began to covet Indian land for ranching and agriculture and came into conflict

---

[22] I do not want to be accused of misrepresenting Cutter's position, so I reproduce this quote in full: "While the central divisive issue in the seventeenth century involved control of Indian resources and labor, an important sidelight was the struggle for judicial supremacy between the civil and clerical arms of government" (Charles Cutter, *The Legal Culture of Northern New Spain, 1700–1810*, p. 32).

[23] Gutierrez writes this in describing Indian reaction to an anticlerical outburst in church by Governor Rosas in the 1630s. But it applies to his representation of the decline of Spanish authority later in the century; in fact, he sees Rosas's governorship as a turning point (Gutierrez, *When Jesus Came*, p. 116).

with the friars over efforts to displace or use Indian (and mission) herds, gardens, and water.

The symbolic force of jurisdictional conflicts is also very clear. As in the examples I have already cited, Spaniards were acutely aware of the effect on Indians of symbolic statements about relations of power. Where officials sat in church, whether words were spoken loudly or in anger, when Indians might see Spaniards engaged in physical labor or subjected to punishment – these particulars consumed the attention of witnesses. As Gutierrez shows us, the Indians, though rarely present as legal actors in the seventeenth-century records, are there as audience. The Spaniards had in fact cultivated them as an audience through rituals and performances at the outset of the conquest intended to communicate Spaniards' power and the inevitability of Indian subjection.[24]

But is it fair to say that Spaniards who insistently fought for seven decades (and beyond, too, into the early decades of the eighteenth century) about jurisdictional matters were "really" fighting about something else? The conflicts did center around narrow and repetitive legal issues. Many of the participants were trained, too, to focus on such issues. López de Mendizábal, the governor who was tried before the Inquisition in 1661, was trained in canon law, first in Jesuit schools and then in the Royal University of Mexico. Certainly many of the Franciscans and probably some other governors shared considerable legal sophistication.[25] Disputants seemed to understand, too, that these legal issues determined the distribution of resources, not the reverse. Careful attention to jurisdictional infringements would have also heightened awareness of the meaning of public displays of authority, as the example of the town council's letter suggests. Scholes perhaps had the right starting place after all: Jurisdictional arguments were the true center of political conflict in the seventeenth century. And we can push his

---

[24] On the rituals, performances, and plays of the Spaniards before the Pueblo Indians, see especially Gutierrez, *When Jesus Came*, pp. 83–87.

[25] Clendinnen's account of one jurisdictional dispute in Yucatan offers an example of the legal sophistication of both Franciscans and settlers. When one settler, Francisco Hernández, was arrested by ecclesiastic authorities for blasphemy, he appealed multiple times to secular and ecclesiastical authorities outside the province. Landa, too, played one jurisdiction off against the other, probably as a tactic for wearing Hernández down through delay. After five years of conflict, Hernández grew ill, confessed, and died a few days after his release from jail. Although it is apparent that Landa was in many ways exceptional, in this case his tenacity, not his legal acumen, was more unusual. Even the simpler Hernández knew to use jurisdictional tensions to his advantage. See Inga Clendinnen, *Ambivalent Conquests*, pp. 60–63.

analysis further. Seemingly narrow jurisdictional issues commanded passionate struggle precisely because they both organized economic rights and gave institutional embodiment to cultural hierarchy. Spaniards understood these connections, and so, perhaps, did the Indians.

The centrality of jurisdictional conflicts emerges clearly in the well-documented Inquisition trial of Don Bernardo López de Mendizábal, who served as governor of New Mexico between 1659 and 1662, when he was arrested by the Franciscan commissary of the Holy Office in New Mexico. When López died in prison in Mexico City in 1664, he had spent the last two years of his life defending himself against charges lodged by the friars.[26] The Franciscans reported (and, indeed, López later admitted) that he had made statements soon after arriving in New Mexico denying the jurisdiction of the custodians as ordinary ecclesiastical judges.[27] The friars complained that López had even instructed the Indian captains of the pueblos not to punish the Indians for any infractions, including concubinage. In the pueblos of Salinas, he had appointed a hostile *alcalde mayor* (local magistrate), Nicolás de Aguilar, who was heard stating that by the governor's orders, "no governor, alcalde, or judge shall punish any sin that may be committed, nor shall they consent that the ministers punish them."[28] The formal accusation, after the doubtful but commonplace charge that López had been "performing and using Jewish ceremonies," reports his "scandalous spirit opposed to religion."[29] A key piece of evidence was his permission to the Indians to dance the *katsinas*, rituals the Franciscans had tried to suppress. López was accused, too, of violating ecclesiastical immunity

---

[26] Scholes provides a detailed summary of López's trial and of the other trials of the Inquisition in this period in France Scholes, *Troublous Times in New Mexico*. The Inquisition played a relatively minor role in New Mexican affairs until the second half of the century, when it became the most effective instrument used by the church to oppose civil authority, particularly in the period from 1659 to 1664. The tribunal of the Holy Office in Mexico City tried two governors, a former custodian of the missions, and two soldier-settlers who were aligned with the governors (and had served as *protectores de indios*). See also Cutter, *The Protector de Indios*.

[27] Trouble seems to have started even before, when López was en route to New Mexico and taunted Franciscans with him saying that he was the "universal" head of the settlement. "Testimony of Fray Nicolás de Freitas" (Hackett, *Historical Documents*, p. 157).

[28] "Deposition of Fray Garcia de San Francisco. Senecú, May, 1661" (Hackett, *Historical Documents*, p. 184).

[29] "Case of the Fiscal of the Holy Office against Bernardo López de Mendizábal, Governor of New Mexico, for Heretical Statements and for Being Suspected of the Crime of Judaism" (Hackett, *Historical Documents*, p. 176).

on a number of occasions and of speaking out against it. He was heard to say that "the friars of that kingdom ought not to reply to him, for he was their judge, and that he had the right to bring suits against them."[30] At one point López gathered depositions from several supporters reporting that the friars had improperly assumed ordinary ecclesiastical jurisdiction in giving special dispensation to marriages between close kin.[31]

The jurisdictional issues raised by López's case fell into two overlapping categories. Franciscans' complaints about López's interference in their disciplining of mission Indians show that the Franciscans were accustomed to meting out punishments for transgressions of all kinds. Of particular concern to the Franciscans from the beginning of the missions in New Mexico was the "lascivious" conduct of the Indians.[32] The continued performance of Indian religious rites was of course also viewed as a threat to the missionary enterprise. If the Franciscans had become accustomed to punishing such behavior freely, both they and López were aware that their legal right to do so was closely proscribed. The Inquisition had no jurisdiction over Indians. As ecclesiastical judges ordinary, the friars could investigate Indians and order them to be disciplined, but punishment had to be performed by the secular arm, usually by Indians appointed to official posts in each mission. There was a direct link between López's denial of ordinary ecclesiastical jurisdiction and his orders (passed through delegates) to Indians that they should "live under whatever law they pleased."[33] Without the cooperation of the secular arm, there *was* effectively no ecclesiastical jurisdiction. The most visible symbol of the Franciscans' resulting lack of legal authority was the dancing of the katsinas permitted by the governor. The Franciscans had no legal means of stopping the dances on their own. On one occasion, a friar was able to stop them only by flagellating himself violently

---

[30] "Letter of Bernardo López de Mendizábal to the Tribunal of the Inquisition, Santa Fe, December 12, 1661" (Hackett, *Historical Documents*, p. 174).

[31] AGN 587, Pt. 2, Inquisition, transcription, from France V. Scholes Collection, MSS 360, Center for Southwest Research, General Library, University of New Mexico, Albuquerque. AGN 587, transcription in F. V. Scholes, UNM 972 M 57i.

[32] See Gutierrez (*When Jesus Came*) for a discussion of preconquest Pueblo Indian views of sexual liaisons and marriage, and their clash with Franciscan ideals. Both groups associated certain patterns of sexual conduct with spiritual values.

[33] "Hearing of June 16, 1663, Requested by López" (Hackett, *Historical Documents*, p. 210). Friars did sometimes administer harsh punishments themselves – one friar publicly whipped an Indian and then set him on fire at the church door. But these acts were reported to the custodian; outrage alone might have led him to discipline friars in such cases, but the custodian was pressured, too, by the need to demonstrate the legitimacy of ecclesiastical justice.

on the plaza. The display worked – probably by reinforcing the friar's image as a holy man – but at the expense of his image as a judge who might have had the lashes administered to the Indians instead.[34]

For his part, López could also argue that he was operating within an accepted legal tradition in allowing the Indians to live according to "whatever law they pleased" so long as their behavior did not offend Spanish law. In his defense, he claimed that the katsinas had nothing in them that was objectionable – he had watched them to make sure of this. In making this claim, López was equating Indian rituals with custom and arguing for a form of legal pluralism that allowed nonoffensive custom to continue as law. The Franciscans, by insisting on the religious content of the dances, were categorizing the practice as apostasy, clearly punishable under the law. Consider López's description of his judgment in a case of illicit sexual relations in the pueblo of Alamillo:

> Among the men and women who came forward to tell him their troubles and molestations, or to make whatever complaint they had against any person, was an old Indian woman, who stood up, saying that an Indian captain had used her carnally and had not paid her the price, which they had agreed upon long years since. [López], having chided her for her sin, caused the Indian to appear and compelled him to pay the price.[35]

The friars cited this case as one of many examples of López's refusal to punish sexual liaisons or to order his delegates to do so. López (and Aguilar) in turn accused the friars of excessive cruelty in disciplining the Indians. Beneath the controversy over punishments was a more fundamental conflict over judicial authority and its rationale. While the friars could claim that López was usurping their role as enforcers of church law in the missions, López emphasized Indians' cultural difference and represented their offenses as harmless customary practices that should be tolerated.

Placed in this context of struggles over legal authority, the reports regarding the katsinas may have a somewhat different meaning than the one presented by Gutierrez. He views the resurgence of "idolatry" as a probable response to the increasingly fragile hold of the friars on the mission Indians and a reaction to the various disruptions of

---

[34] Gutierrez (*When Jesus Came*) analyzes this event and suggests the friar's actions quiet the Indians because they share a view of flagellation as a spiritual act.
[35] "Reply of Mendizábal" (Hackett, *Historical Documents*, p. 216).

the previous decades, including severe epidemics and increasing economic pressures. But as Clendinnen points out eloquently in her analysis of idolatry in Yucatan, exaggerating idolatrous activity among the Indians had the effect of enhancing Franciscan jurisdictional claims. In Yucatan, the Franciscan prelate Diego de Landa seems to have done this as a response to the encroachment of episcopal authority.[36] In New Mexico, the emphasis on idolatry underscored the urgency of Franciscans' complaints about the intervention of secular officials in the judicial administration of the missions. There is little reason to believe that the Indians had ever significantly curtailed their practice of the katsinas after conquest, though informal sponsorship by the governor gave them a greater openness. But the rituals took on new meaning in the context of heightened church-state tensions in the 1660s – not just for Indians, who may have redefined them as opposition to Spanish authority, but also for the Spanish participants in struggles over institutions of rule.

The dispute over ecclesiastical immunity is an even more prominent part of the cases against López, and against Nicolás de Aguilar, the alcalde mayor who was also brought before the Inquisition. The Franciscans complained that López's visitations to the pueblos were not inspections but judicial proceedings, designed to elicit accusations against the friars. The friars reported that López "seated himself in his chair, with paper and ink, in the form of a court" and even commanded Indians to come before him to make accusations.[37] In one instance, the governor sent Aguilar to investigate the complaints of an Indian that a friar in the pueblo of Taxique had "taken his wife from him and . . . maintained illicit relations with a large number of Indian women."[38] The friars charged that Aguilar behaved in the pueblo as if running an inquest. He gathered the resident Indians together, took testimony from Indian women, and separated witnesses who had complaints about the sexual conduct of the friar. The custodian excommunicated Aguilar, and he was later brought to trial before the Inquisition. His defense was rather feeble but suggested a clear understanding of the protections of the *fuero eclesiástico*. Aguilar reported that he had acted extrajudicially and only to identify

---

[36] See Clendinnen, *Ambivalent Conquests*.

[37] "Hearing of June 16, 1663, Requested by Mendizábal" (Hackett, *Historical Documents*, p. 201).

[38] This is from López's own testimony, in which he tries to show that he was not usurping ecclesiastic authority. "Hearing of June 16, 1663, Requested by Mendizábal" (Hackett, *Historical Documents*, p. 202).

witnesses, not to record testimony or pass judgment. It was apparently especially galling to the friars that Aguilar was "a mestizo, a man of evil life and customs," who had been appointed by López in place of a man of higher social standing.[39]

Ecclesiastical immunity was seen by the friars as the most vital privilege they had since it protected them not only from trial but also from imprisonment or physical punishment by civil authorities. The symbolic force of being brought before secular officials as if before judges was also not lost on the friars. In the same visitation conducted by López in Alamillo at which he ordered restitution rather than punishment for an Indian, the governor heard a complaint by another Indian that she had been raped by the aged *doctrinero* of the pueblo. López's response was to send a soldier to ask the accused friar to send a piece of cloth for the Indian woman. The messenger came back with an antelope skin, which the woman rejected as insufficient payment.[40] The audience of soldiers and Indians of "all the pueblo . . . gave many shouts of laughter, seeing what took place."[41]

This action, admitted to by López as a routine part of his visitation, was for the Franciscans a clear violation of their immunity. Application of a roughly understood form of Indian justice to the actions of a friar was an affront. And the friars were well aware – as was the governor – that the Indians stood as witnesses to this displacement of Franciscans as judges of Indians, and of the friars themselves. If in Aguilar's actions the Franciscans saw the threat of being judged by a mestizo and accused by Indian witnesses, in López's actions they saw the horror of being judged as Indians, before Indians.

I have said little so far of the complaints of economic abuses by the governor and his delegates. There is evidence that these were substantially worse than those of some of his predecessors. López used Indian labor to collect and transport piñones, manufacture leather goods and textiles for export, and build wagons, all for operations for his own profit; many Indians complained that they were not paid. López also sponsored frequent raids on surrounding Apache and Navajo Indians in order to take captives for sale. The friars complained, too, of their own worsening poverty as a direct result of the governor's actions. López and his delegates were said to have ordered mission Indians not to serve the

---

[39] "Ratification by Miguel de Noriega" (Hackett, *Historical Documents*, p. 185).
[40] "Reply of Mendizábal" (Hackett, *Historical Documents*, p. 216).
[41] Scholes, *Troublous Times in New Mexico*, p. 71.

Franciscans.[42] López and Aguilar claimed, in turn, that the Franciscans routinely compelled Indians to work for them in ways hardly necessary to the functioning of the missions. One of López's first acts as governor had been to raise the wage that settlers were required to pay Indians and to impose the same requirement on the Franciscans. Such actions brought him not only the enmity of the friars but also the hostility of many powerful local families.

Accusations on both sides about the use and abuse of Indian labor were routinely presented in the context of larger concerns about legal authority. Rather than mere posturing, the strategy reflected the widely held view that economic rights were defined by legal entitlements. The friars, in particular, would have had no special standing without their exempt legal status, and their economic claims would have been reduced to the level of those of the increasingly mestizo settler population that was trying to encroach on Indian land and water rights. Indeed, the friars often absorbed economic attacks by the secular officials, merely mentioning past abuses as part of complaints filed later. They would never have conceded even minor violations of ecclesiastical immunity without an immediate fight; to imperil their legal standing would have been to lose everything. For their part, secular officials accused the friars of using ecclesiastical jurisdiction for economic gain by levying fines on their opponents in exchange for reversing decrees of excommunication. In a deposition solicited by López, one captain complained that the friars had "always tried to use ordinary ecclesiastical jurisdiction against the secular residents," absolving them only when they paid fines, as he had been forced to do when he was excommunicated and forced to pay "several bars of *membrillo*" and a fine of thirty cotton blankets, which he arranged to be paid by Indians of his encomienda.[43]

And what do we learn about the Indians' actions in privileging the purely legalistic nature of these conflicts? Gutierrez might be right in

---

[42] In a complaint that recalls the accusations of the town council's letter of 1639, the Franciscans reported that one friar had been forced "to go to the forest for wood, and though a priest, to bring it back on his shoulders. Fray Diego de Parraga was obliged to cook their food, which he did, though poorly, not knowing how to do it, because the governor would not give them an Indian to serve them" ("Hearing of February 21, 1661, Mexico. Fray Nicolás de Freitas," Hackett, *Historical Documents*, p. 136).

[43] AGN 587, Pt. 2, Inquisition, transcription, from France V. Scholes Collection, MSS 360, Center for Southwest Research, General Library, University of New Mexico, Albuquerque.

suggesting that the Indians watched the repeated performance of the split in Spanish authority and concluded that the old gods must be brought back. But there is another possibility. The Indians were hardly surprised by a division they had perceived in the earliest days of the conquest and were, as legal actors, exploiting the jurisdictional tensions. Although few records showing Indians as litigants survived the 1680 revolt, certainly some evidence suggests that the Indians were active in using and even exacerbating the disputes over legal authority. One sort of evidence is produced only after the rebellion and the return of the Spaniards, when, as Cutter reports, the Indians emerged very quickly as astute legal strategists. They rapidly established a legal right to keep non-Indian settlers at least one league away from their pueblos, for example; this standard, the so-called Pueblo league, was better than that attained by most Indians in New Spain.[44] Could the legal acumen of the early 1700s have been entirely new? The reverse seems more likely. The few surviving records of actions brought by Indians before the revolt shows that they readily filed suit. In doing so, they appear also to have taken advantage of the legal and political conflicts. Individual plaintiffs and even entire villages came forward during López's *residencia* (the routine investigation of an outgoing governor by his replacement) to complain that he had not paid them for various goods and services; this would have been while López was under investigation by the commissary for the Inquisition, and at a time when Indians would have been right to believe their complaints would receive a sympathetic hearing.[45]

The Indians were clearly responsive, too, to the opportunity to appeal to secular authorities about the abuses of the friars. López was able to say in his defense that he did not intend the visitations to resemble judicial proceedings but merely responded to "the Indian men and women who came forward to tell him their troubles and molestations, or to make whatever complaint they had against any person."[46]

---

[44] See Cutter, *The Legal Culture of Northern New Spain*; Jenkins outlines the cases of suits against mestizos brought by Tewa Indians in Taos in the eighteenth century. The strategy in these cases involved representing a sharp divide, too, between Indians and mestizos, even where the families involved were closely related or even lived inside the pueblos. Myra Ellen Jenkins, "Taos Pueblo and Her Neighbors."

[45] For a summary of these accusations, see Scholes, *Troublous Times in New Mexico*; see also Cutter (*The Protector de Indios*, pp. 34–35). We do not know the outcome of any of these cases, which were presented for the Indians by the protector de indios.

[46] "Reply of Mendizábal" (Hackett, *Historical Documents*, p. 216).

The Indians often seized this opportunity to urge the secular officials to challenge Franciscan judicial authority. Tewa Indians in Taos pueblo had complained in the 1630s of the immorality of their friar; when the governor referred the case to the custodian but no disciplinary action was taken, the Indians complained again, leading the governor to forward their sworn testimony to the Holy Office.[47] Even in open rebellion, there was an apparent sense of legalism. At Jémez in 1680, Indians hauled a friar from his bed and took him to the cemetery, where they paraded him naked on a pig and beat him before killing him. Such public whippings were standard instruments of discipline of the Franciscans. (In the one trial of an Indian that has survived from before the revolt, a Hopi man was found guilty first of impersonating a friar and leading some Indians in mock worship, then twice of stealing; he was paraded through the streets on pack animals and given 200 lashes before being sold into slavery.)[48] As Serulnikov has argued in analyzing the rebellions of Andean peasants in the late eighteenth century, the Indians may have viewed legal maneuvering and rebellion as closely related strategies.[49] The Indians held, as Stern has noted in another context, an "understanding of rights and obligations, of justice and vengeance" that was resilient to the imposition of Spanish rule and also compatible with a range of old and new protective strategies.[50]

While historians of the Spanish colonial bureaucracy in the early colonial period have documented and probed jurisdictional tensions, their study has largely remained within a functionalist framework in which the fragmentation of colonial constituencies is viewed as a purposeful and largely successful attempt to create order through

---

[47] Scholes, *Church and State in New Mexico*, p. 145, n. 16.

[48] As Cutter (*The Protector de Indios*) points out, Scholes's assumption that such a punishment was "typical" is probably wrong; the Hopi man was viewed as incorrigible. Nevertheless, it would not have taken many such public displays to have impressed upon Indians an understanding of the possibilities of punishment, and lesser offenses frequently brought public whippings.

[49] Sergio Serulnikov, "Disputed Images of Colonialism: Spanish Rule and Indian Subversion in Northern Potosí, 1777–1780." This view is consistent with E.P. Thompson's argument that eighteenth-century plebeians often understood food riots as punitive. See E.P. Thompson, "The Moral Economy of the English Crown in the Eighteenth Century." See also E.P. Thompson, *Whigs and Hunters: The Origin of the Black Act*, for a parallel argument about eighteenth-century foresters engaged in a ritualistic form of poaching.

[50] Steve Stern, *Peru's Indian Peoples and the Challenge of Spanish Conquest: Huamanga to 1640*, p. 8.

flexibility, institutional balance, and consensus.[51] In this perspective, as Clendinnen points out, the colonial borderlands appear as places where the usual functionality of institutional divisions simply did not reach. Like Yucatan, New Mexico could be characterized as "a frontier society where institutionalized authority was too weak or too remote for its interventions to be decisive, and where power would lie with those most relentless in pursuit, most ruthless in its exercise, and most jealous in its possession."[52]

Yes and no. Clearly the borderlands were different. Traveling to appeal to the royal audiencias was difficult and costly. In New Mexico as in the early decades of colonization in Yucatan, the power of the Franciscans was unchecked by episcopal control. Frontier conditions, including the real threat of warfare with un-Christianized Indians, created new elements of uncertainty and altered the nature of civil authority. And *mestizaje* was an even more salient presence, changing representations of cultural and political hierarchy.

Yet it is also true that jurisdictional uncertainties on the borderlands were present throughout the colonial order. Being on the fringes of empire was just one of a number of circumstances in which political and legal practice had the effect of exacerbating endemic jurisdictional divisions. Such confusion occurred throughout the legal order in the first two centuries of rule – in the prosecution of Indian crimes against the faith, in the jockeying of audiencias and viceroys, and in the administration of the Inquisition.[53] In this sense, the indeterminacy of power on the borderlands reflected a larger structural condition. The border itself – the line between imperial control populated by Christian subjects of the crown and the hazardous lands of the "wild" Indians – was simply a more visible example of the many "borders" separating groups with different legal and cultural status within the empire.

Such a view does not conflict with representations of Spanish colonial institutions as flexible, but it does deemphasize their functionality.

---

[51] John Leddy Phelan, "Authority and Flexibility in the Spanish Imperial Bureaucracy." Lynch calls for a refining of Phelan's views, but his characterization of the early colonial order as based on "consensus" amounts to little more than a change in emphasis. John Lynch,"The Institutional Framework of Colonial Spanish America."

[52] Clendinnen, *Ambivalent Conquests*, p. 63.

[53] See Parry's discussion of jurisdictional complexities in New Galicia, where the audiencia "could always find some excuse for turning its disobedience into a conflict of jurisdiction." Parry, *The Audiencia of New Galicia*, pp. 168–69.

Jurisdictional confusion was often a source of *disorder*. To the extent that it promoted order, it did so not by consistently producing consensus or even a mechanism for institutional adjustment, but by structuring similar conflicts across culturally and economically diverse regions. Participants understood the contests to be simultaneously about definitions of cultural and racial distance and about control over resources. These interconnections gave jurisdictional issues their special, central place in the political order of sixteenth- and seventeenth-century Spanish America. They also provided institutional continuity to the rest of the empire – and to other empires, where the multicentric character of law, and the centrality of jurisdictional politics, were also pervasive and persistent characteristics of the legal order.

ISLAMIC JUSTICE, OTTOMAN STRATEGIES

In labeling non-European, nonrational law "kadi justice," Weber was constructing an ideal type rather than describing Islamic justice. Nevertheless, his approach reinforced a tendency to view Islamic law as institutionally and culturally unique. Weber pointed to the wide discretion of qadis in rendering judgments, in contrast to their Western counterparts, more closely restrained by legal sources and precedent. This view fit with once-standard interpretations of Islamic jurisprudence as having reached an end in its development in the early tenth century, with the closing of the doors of *ijtihad* (the gate of interpretation), a declared end to further elaboration of Islamic legal principles and sources. The unique nature of Islamic law and administration is signaled, too, by the peculiar role that qadis played as both judges and administrators in Islamic empires from the time of the Umayyads and on. With no clerical hierarchy paralleling that of the Catholic Church, qadis had simultaneously wider latitude in administering local law and less opportunity to challenge or subvert the legal authority of sovereigns when it was asserted. Even if divine law, the shari'a, was not always applied, in theory at least it subsumed state legal authority; the twelfth-century "revolution" of the jurisdictional split between canon and royal law in the West did not occur.[54]

Such a view has its problems, however, and they are hardly trivial. There is, to begin with, much evidence of overlap and borrowing of legal

---

[54] Thus Berman argues that "the existence and competition within the same community of diverse jurisdictions and diverse legal systems" is unique to the Western legal tradition (Berman, *Law and Revolution*, p. 10).

conventions between Islam and Christendom, and between Islamic and Jewish law.[55] The idea of the stagnation of Islamic jurisprudence after the tenth century has also been largely discredited.[56] The common representation of qadi legal judgments as arbitrary and disconnected from rational legal reasoning is contradicted by studies of the functioning of qadi courts. Even when qadis adhered to modified understandings of shari'a, they made consistent and rational judgments more often than not.[57] Finally, new interpretations of Islamic empires have questioned whether even at the height of their power, Ottoman and Mughal states should be viewed as early models of absolutism. They acted more often to order the relation of fragmented and semiautonomous political and cultural fields.[58] In short, the similarities between early modern Western and Islamic legal politics and state structure are in many ways more striking than the differences.

To these arguments I wish to add the observation that certain structural similarities in legal politics brought Islamic empires within an

[55] Observations about the mutual influence of Islamic and Western (Roman and canon) law are not new, though they have received new scholarly attention recently. Coulson noted that throughout the Umayyad period, elements of foreign law, including Roman law, "gradually infiltrated into legal practice, so that Muslim jurisprudence in the mid-eighth century could take them for granted when conscious knowledge of their origin had been lost" (N.J. Coulson, *A History of Islamic Law*, p. 28). Bernard Lewis points out some of the ways in which Jewish and Islamic law exerted mutual influence. See Bernard Lewis, *The Jews of Islam*. On the more general nature of Muslim and Jewish symbiosis, see Steve Wasserstrom, *Between Muslim and Jew: The Problem of Symbiosis Under Early Islam*. For a recent discovery of the influence of Islamic legal formulations regarding jihad on Spanish policies toward Indians in the Americas, see Seed, *Ceremonies of Possession*. And see below, for the influence of Byzantine legislation on religious minorities on the Ottoman formulation of the *dhimmi* contract.

[56] See Wael Hallaq, "Was the Gate of Ijtihad Closed?" and Sir Hamilton Gibb and Harold Bowen, *Islamic Society and the West: A Study of the Impact of Western Civilization on Moslem Culture in the Near East*, p. 24.

[57] See Gerber for an expanded discussion of this aspect of a critique of Weber. I do not think Gerber is quite correct to link Rosen's interpretations of Islamic law with Weber's. Rosen has argued that the qadi courts of Morocco view the return to sociability of litigants as the main goal of adjudication and will adjust their adherence to shari'a accordingly. But this is not the same as arguing that they fail to adhere to consistent standards. See Haim Gerber, *State, Society, and Law in Islam: Ottoman Law in Comparative Perspective*; and Lawrence Rosen, *The Anthropology of Justice : Law As Culture in Islamic Society*.

[58] Thus power in the Ottoman Empire has come to be viewed by revisionist historians as much more fragmented and as "one of a group of 'early modern states'" (Suraiya Faroque and Cornell Fleischer, "Preface," Rifa'at 'Ali Abou-El-Haj, *Formation of the Modern State: The Ottoman Empire, Sixteenth to Eighteenth Centuries*). And see below on the political and legal administration of the Ottomans in the sixteenth century.

international legal regime in the early modern world. The last chapter noted some similarities that permitted Christian and Islamic traders to hold mutually recognizable views of the legal place of merchant diasporas. In addition, Islamic law and practice had qualities that produced structurally similar tensions in areas of conquest and colonization of Islamic empires. In particular, these qualities comprise tensions between shari'a and administrative law (*kanun* under the Ottomans), the relation of Islamic to customary law, and the legal treatment of non-Muslims in conquered territories. In the Ottoman empire, on the one hand, territorial expansion and the conquest of non-Muslim populations produced a strengthening of state legal authority and administration; on the other hand, the same conditions preserved jurisdictional complexity and ambiguity in the state's claims to legal authority.

The relation of kanun to shari'a law has been an issue of some controversy among Islamicists; the various positions may not be so far apart as some historians suggest, though. An early, common view was that because the shari'a addressed only a fixed range of legal issues, its application was inevitably partial. Sovereigns issued law that was independent of the shari'a, though it was not intended to challenge or conflict with divine law. Thus Islamic legal scholars identify a "gap" between theory and practice – a disconnect between claims for the authority of the shari'a and the reality of its limited and selective application. This opposition would seem, at first blush, to parallel the tensions between canon and secular law in Christian Europe. But one must be careful in proposing such a parallel. The absence of an ecclesiastical hierarchy, the conflation of religious and administrative law in the role of the qadi, and the universally accepted understanding that divine law subsumes state law – these factors made the tension between secular and religious law different, though still visible. As Gerber argues, too, the shari'a did in some places increasingly overshadow other sources of law, as it did, he suggests, in Bursa and other core areas of the Ottoman empire in the sixteenth century.[59] We should resist turning this observation into an overcorrection, though. Rosen points out that customary law was widely accepted *as* Islamic law so long as it did not contradict the

---

[59] Gerber (*State, Society, and Law in Islam*, p. 69) argues that separate jurisdictions diminished significantly in importance under the Ottomans. Separate courts such as the *mazalim* or state courts of Mamluk Egypt did not exist under the Ottomans, and lesser administrative officials played only minor roles in adjudication. Nevertheless, Gerber notes that kanun itself hardly disappeared and, in fact, appeared in "a kind of symbiosis of compromise" with shari'a (p. 72).

propositions in the Quran.[60] In many ways, Gibb and Bowen's general statement about the place of shari'a law remains accurate:

> It is true that the only tribunals whose competence and theoretical authority were unrestricted and universally accepted were the shari'a courts administered by the [qadis] and their substitutes, and equally that the only written law was the shari'a.... But the most casual student cannot fail to be struck by the fact that the shari'a courts were not called upon to adjudicate in large areas of what we should regard as the field of law. The organization of society in innumerable small self-contained groups created an equal number of local jurisdictions for the handling of disputes between members of the same group.[61]

Tensions between secular and shari'a law extended to, and in part derived from, differences in procedural and evidentiary practices. In shari'a courts, plaintiffs had to produce two adult male Muslims to testify direct knowledge of the truth of a claim. Written or circumstantial evidence could not serve as substitutes. The same standard of proof applied to criminal cases. In practice, such requirements could occasionally be overlooked. But the potential clearly existed for "considerable injustice" to result, and the possibility led officials under the Abassids to create a separate *mazalim* jurisdiction under state officials to administer criminal, fiscal, and land law.[62] Also largely reserved for oversight by lower-level state officials was an array of minor administrative matters

---

[60] Lawrence Rosen, *The Justice of Islam: Comparative Perspectives on Islamic Law and Society.*

[61] Gibb and Bowen, *Islamic Society and the West*, p. 12. Schacht's assessment of the comparison between Islamic and canon law could be regarded as a classic statement of the "gap between theory and practice" in Islamic law, except that he is careful to note that the "gap" opened or closed in different historical settings: "Canon and Islamic law ... are dominated by the dualism of religion and state, where the state is not, in contrast with Judaism, an alien power but the political expression of the same religion. But their antagonism took on different forms; in Christianity it was the struggle for political power on the part of a tightly organized ecclesiastical hierarchy, and Canon law was one of its political weapons. Islam, on the other hand, was never a 'Church', Islamic law was never supported by an organized power, consequently there never developed a real trial of strength; there merely existed discordance between the sacred Law and the reality of actual practice of which the regulations framed by the state formed part, a gap more or less wide according to place and time, now and then on the point of being closed but continually reasserting itself" (Joseph Schacht, *An Introduction to Islamic Law*, p. 2). One could certainly read this as a statement supporting a view of Islamic legal institutions as fundamentally different from those in the West, but the opposite reading is also possible: Tensions between secular and religious law characterized the legal order of Islamic empires despite the striking differences in organizational frameworks.

[62] N.J. Coulson, *A History of Islamic Law*, p. 127.

considered beneath the dignity of qadis. The precise relation of administrative, military, and criminal law to shari'a law varied across Muslim
polities. The understanding was widely shared, though, that qadis
served at the behest of sovereigns and that their jurisdictions could be
limited.

A further feature lending jurisdictional complexity to early Islamic
empires was the absence of a formal appellate structure.[63] Litigants who
were dissatisfied with rulings in one forum could take them to another,
where they would be tried de novo. In fact, Muslim sovereigns considered this function key to their legitimacy and an important curb on the
power of local officials. In the Mughal empire, for example, the emperor
typically set aside a day each week to hear cases and complaints, including accusations against qadis for abuse of power.[64] The existence
of this forum created an incentive for disputes to be settled in "lower"
courts. But it also created the possibility for litigants to engage in "forum
shopping" and to extend disputes by shifting cases from one forum to
another. A related strategy here and in other regions involved seeking
legal opinions from prominent legal scholars and presenting these to
provincial qadis, who often felt obligated to accept the rulings.[65] Both
strategies gave the legal order a certain openness and rewarded strategies that played upon jurisdictional ambiguities.

These aspects of built-in jurisdictional complexity of Islamic legal
orders were further complicated by Islam's continual expansion. The
issue of how to administer law to conquered non-Muslim populations,
and to newly converted populations with non-Muslim customary law,
emerged under the Umayyads and remained a central problem of
Muslim state administration. In part, the solution involved the absorption of foreign legal concepts and practices, in particular the acceptance
of customary law and its continuity in conquered areas. As a matter

---

[63] See David S. Powers, "On Judicial Review in Islamic Law."

[64] On legal administration in the Mughal empire, see K.M. Yusuf, "The Judiciary in India
Under the Sultans of Delhi and the Mughal Emperors."

[65] See Muhammad Khalid Masud, Brinkley Messick, and David S. Powers, *Islamic Legal
Interpretation: Muftis and Their Fatwas*. Gerber (*State, Society, and Law in Islam*, Chapter
3, especially pp. 84–85) argues that only a ruling by the sultan could reverse a qadi's
ruling in the core areas of the Ottoman Empire, but Baber Johansen has found evidence
that strategies for annulling qadi judgments that had existed under classical Hanafite
law were expanded during the Ottoman period by the muftis, who considered their
rulings more authoritative. Appealing judgments to the mufits was a further strategy
in some settings, then, for dragging out litigation (Johansen, *Contingency in a Sacred
Law*, pp. 444–45).

of practice, the legal systems emerging out of this arrangement were quite variable both over time and across regions of Muslim conquest. In general, particularly in places where the ruling Muslim population remained a minority – the Mughal empire in parts of India, for example, or the western Balkans under the Ottomans – strategies of conquest featured some protections for indigenous institutions, including customary law.[66] Though they served both as judges and imperial administrators, qadis also had to recognize non-Muslim law.[67] Where customary law did not clash overtly with the shari'a, it was often accepted and incorporated in practice. Indeed, as Rosen argues, it could be accepted as Islamic law, a tendency that had the effect of pushing litigation down to the local level.[68] Mass conversion to Islam, where it occurred, changed the dynamics of rule over time and permitted increasing Islamicization of legal institutions, but customary legal practices could outlive even this shift. An example is the persistence of Berber customary law in parts of North Africa; another is the preservation of customary or *adat* law in Indonesia.

A second mechanism that lent fluidity and jurisdictional complexity to the legal order was the practical accommodation and recognition of non-Muslim legal authority. Islamic doctrine divided the world into two parts: the predominantly Muslim *Dar al-Islam* (the abode of Islam) and the regions beyond, the *Dar al-Harb* (the abode of war). Non-Muslim groups in the Dar al-Islam were awarded formal recognition by the contract of *dhimma*, under which non-Muslims paid a poll tax in exchange for the right to preserve their own religious tribunals and administer their own personal law. It is important to note that this

---

[66] For this general argument in regard to the Ottoman Empire, see Esin Orucu, "The Impact of European Law on the Ottoman Empire and Turkey." Anderson makes a similar point about Mughal legal administration, pointing out that "the social impact of Mughal legal institutions remained limited to particular groups, especially the Islamic gentry and the urban merchants based in the *qasbah* towns. Many communities jealously guarded their autonomy, operating under the umbrella of imperial tolerance to retain localized institutions, practices, and norms which operated in derogation of a strict application of the *shari'a*" (Michael R. Anderson, "Islamic Law and the Colonial Encounter in British India," p. 171). See also K.I. Ewing, ed., *Shari'at and Ambiguity in South Asian Islam.*

[67] An example showing the porousness of Islamic institutions in the early centuries of conquest and conversion in Bengal is the case outlined at the beginning of this chapter in which Mughal officials punished a transgression against local Hindu law. See Eaton on this case and on administrative policies in Bengal more generally. Eaton, *The Rise of Islam and the Bengal Frontier.*

[68] Rosen, *The Justice of Islam.*

right constituted a concession made by Muslim sovereigns. Dhimma status could be revoked at any time, and non-Muslims remained at all times obligated to conform to government laws regarding taxation and other matters of central interest to the state, for example, criminal law.[69]

Members of dhimmi communities chose strategically when to use qadi courts and when to bring cases to their own religious forums. Without a system for appeals, all subjects also retained a right to shift cases from one local forum to another, or even directly to the sovereign's court. Multiple forums meant multiple sources of law. In some settings, shari'a law was applied in both civil and criminal cases in the vast majority of cases, including those involving both Muslim and dhimmi subjects.[70] In other settings, communal legal forums persisted and actively resisted loss of jurisdiction to qadi courts. These and other sources of complexity created a legal landscape across much of the Middle East, Central Asia, India, and parts of Southeast Asia that would have been structurally quite familiar to travelers from the Atlantic world, even if the substance of the law was different.

Indeed, a final source of jurisdictional complexity came from the claims of travelers for immunity from local law. In the Ottoman empire, foreign merchants were awarded the right to take legal disputes to consular courts where the law of their own countries was applied. Individual dhimmis employed by foreign nationals also actively sought consular protection. The logic for granting these concessions was similar to that for tolerating dhimmi semiautonomy; the so-called Capitulations

---

[69] Not only was this status different from that of non-Muslim residents of the Dar al-Harb, but the boundary could not be casually crossed. Cohen recounts the case of a 1560 petition in Jerusalem presented by a non-Muslim, a Venetian Christian, who was applying to the local authority to change his status from that of a *musta'min*, a non-Muslim inhabitant of Dar al-Harb, to that of a resident alien responsible for paying the poll tax. Ammon Cohen, *Jewish Life Under Islam: Jerusalem in the Sixteenth Century*, p. 1.

[70] Jennings found that the Christians of Cyprus between 1571 (the date of Ottoman conquest) and 1640 used qadi courts there for virtually all legal matters, both in "mixed" cases involving Christians and Muslims and in cases concerning members of just the Christian community. "Although the masses of the island's Greek Orthodox Christians may have had the legal right to apply to their own clergy in certain internal matters of a communal nature involving fellow believers, no records of any such courts survive, and indeed few references even suggest their very existence" (Ronald C. Jennings, *Christians and Muslims in Ottoman Cyprus and the Mediterranean World, 1571–1640*, p. 69).

were understood as a concession by the state and "by no means regarded as a derogation of sovereignty."[71]

Against these built-in sources of jurisdictional complexity, imperial expansion, as in the Spanish overseas empire, offered an opportunity for legal administrative streamlining and a strengthening of state legal superiority. This is precisely what occurred in the early Ottoman Empire. Until the second half of the fifteenth century, the empire contained a Christian majority under the rule of a Muslim minority.[72] Ottoman institutions, particularly law, were designed to permit the integration of culturally and religiously different groups while also encouraging assimilation. At the same time, exceptions to state legal jurisdiction remained a recognized and constant feature of the legal order, as we shall see in discussing the legal treatment and strategies of Jewish communities.

Legal administration in the Ottoman Empire fit into a larger schema for balancing central and local authority. Ottoman power revolved crucially around the administration of rights to land. Under the *timar* system diffused through much of the empire by the sixteenth century, all land was considered state-owned while appointed landholders acted as imperial representatives for revenue collection.[73] On the one hand, local institutions in a conquered region had to be somewhat "Ottomanized" in order for the timar system to be established; its imposition required a careful survey of population and resources in the area. On the other hand, the timar system preserved much of the indigenous social order and "was in fact a conservative reconciliation of local conditions and classes with Ottoman institutions."[74] The system carried

---

[71] Orucu, "The Impact of European Law," p. 42. The French were the first to be granted Capitulations in 1537. Other foreign national communities later received the same recognition. See Chapter 6.

[72] Benjamin Braude and Bernard Lewis, "Introduction," p. 10, in Benjamin Braude and Bernard Lewis, eds., *Christians and Jews in the Ottoman Empire: The Functioning of a Plural Society, Vol I.*

[73] The timar system was not established in Egypt, Baghdad, Abyssinia, Basra, and Lahsa, and was somewhat different in its operation in Anatolia. There were also autonomous provinces such as the Christian vassal principalities of Moldavia, Wallachia, Transylvania, and Dubrovnik, as well as Muslim principalities such as the knanate of Crimea. Provinces where the timar system was in force were more typical. Halil Inalcik, *The Ottoman Empire: The Classical Age 1300–1600*, pp. 105–09.

[74] Halil Inalcik, *The Ottoman Empire: Conquest, Organization, and Economy*, p. 103. Reconciling the timar system with local customs was prudent, too, because it ensured continuity in the collection of tax revenues. Inalcik, *The Ottoman Empire: The Classical Age*, p. 71.

an implicit threat to centralized control if the interests of landholders became too entrenched and too much separated from those of the state. In particular, Ottoman officials considered it crucial to protect tax-paying Muslim subjects, the *reʾaya*, from abuse by timar holders. Measures enacted over the course of the sixteenth century, most notably a system for the rotation of timar holders, were designed to ensure state control while also preventing "any permanent legal relation between the land holder and the land."[75]

The imposition of Ottoman law was closely and directly related to this effort. Each official land registry, or *deftar*, included a listing of kanun laws and exceptions or innovations to such laws that were to be applied in the province. Inalcik has traced the origins of these law books (*kanun-name*) and notes that although Suleiman I (1520–1566) is often credited with the creation of a law code for the empire, he was in fact building on a tradition of authorship of kanun-names both by past sultans and in provincial deftars, and was drawing directly on the text of existing kanun-names. These early kanun-names fused Ottoman laws with preconquest practices so long as the latter did not clash with imposed law.[76] This syncretism was especially evident in Western Anatolia and in the early conquests in the Balkans. Efforts to curtail customary practices aimed mainly at protecting reʾaya from more exacting tribute traditionally paid to local elites while at the same time maximizing payments to the state. In each newly conquered area, military personnel (*askeri*) were distinguished from reʾaya, and each group carried a formally different legal status. This boundary could be crossed; in the Balkans, for example, large numbers of Christians were incorporated in the askeri class and made timar holders in the fifteenth century. The Ottomans also developed *devsirme*, the practice of taking unmarried Christian males into the service of the state as slaves (for which there was no basis in shariʿa law). As Ottoman subjects converted to Islam, the process paralleled the gradual replacement of customary law by Ottoman law.[77]

---

[75] Karen Barkey, "In Different Times: Scheduling and Social Control in the Ottoman Empire, 1550–1650," p. 467.

[76] Inalcik, *The Ottoman Empire: Conquest, Organization, and Economy*, p. 129.

[77] Inalcik, *The Ottoman Empire: Conquest, Organization, and Economy*, p. 119. Inalcik generalizes that the Ottomans tended to preserve local laws after conquest before 1540 and replace them with Ottoman regulations after this date, with some prominent examples remaining of places where local tax practices were preserved or adapted, as in Hungary. Inalcik, *The Ottoman Empire: The Classical Age 1300–1600*, p. 71.

The system of legal administration depended crucially on the role of qadis, who were to enforce both shari'a and kanun law. Each Ottoman province, or *sanjak*, was assigned a military official, or *bey*, and a qadi. The bey was not to inflict punishment without the qadi's judgment, and the qadi could not carry out any punishments. Because their religious authority gave qadis greater moral authority than military administrators, they had at least the potential for greater political autonomy. Rotation was used to prevent their establishing local interest groups and loyalties. The effects on the administration of justice were no doubt negative since qadis had greater incentive to seek to enrich themselves by accepting bribes during their appointments. The qadis' power continued to grow as Ottomanization and Islamicization curtailed customary law and reined in the power of minor officials.[78] Gerber argues that the transition from a legal order with "a multiplicity of conflicting judicial bodies and enforcement authorities" to one increasingly dominated by qadi courts should be understood as a process of fusion, or symbiosis, of kanun, shari'a, and customary law.[79] Barkey cautions, though, that qadi power was balanced (and even necessitated) by the preservation of institutional fragmentation, itself a reflection of a fractured social structure in which military officials, merchants, men of learning, leaders of religious minorities and others preserved institutional protections, including semiautonomy in the field of law.[80]

Certainly important legal distinctions persisted. As Braude and Lewis point out, the fundamental distinctions between masters and slaves, men and women, and believers and unbelievers were fundamental to Ottoman society and enshrined in Islamic law and identity. Each of these distinctions had a legal dimension, but only the boundary between believers and unbelievers was one that not only could be crossed but also was purposely made porous.[81] While dhimmis retained special legal status under the Ottomans, they were viewed as inferior and marked

---

[78] Recourse to the imperial council, which functioned somewhat like a high court, continued to exist, and all subjects could present complaints by sending delegations to Istanbul, a practice that was, not surprisingly, more common in the regions closest to the imperial capital.

[79] Gerber, *State, Society, and Law in Islam*, p. 78.

[80] Barkey, "In Different Times," p. 480. Barkey is relying in part on Kasaba here. See Resat Kasaba, "A Time and a Place for the Nonstate: Social Changes in the Ottoman Empire During the Long Nineteenth Century." See also Abou-El-Haj, *Formation of the Modern State*.

[81] Braude and Lewis, "Introduction," p. 4.

by special limitations on dress, property, and worship.[82] Dhimmi status was not automatically assigned to non-Muslims but depended on an individual's tax status; various local non-Muslim community leaders who assisted with tax collection and other official duties were made exempt from the poll tax because they were considered servants of the state.[83]

Under this system, Jews throughout the empire retained the formal right to oversee their own courts and apply their own religious law.[84] In practice, the vitality of these courts depended greatly on local politics and on the strategies of both ruling elites and Jewish litigants. The latter had the right to take cases to qadi courts, and the motivations for doing so varied. Jewish leaders in diverse parts of the empire in the sixteenth century harshly condemned Jews who took disputes to non-Jewish courts. In sixteenth-century Jerusalem, Jews preserved their own courts and maintained relative autonomy.[85] In Turkey, the respected rabbi Samuel De Medina and other prominent rabbis repeatedly warned co-religionists that it was forbidden to bring cases to government courts and that doing so undermined Jewish legal authority, which could be superseded only "in matters that pertained to taxation, commercial transactions, and contracts."[86]

---

[82] There is some controversy about to what, if any, degree Ottoman practices were an adaptation of Byzantine regulations. Jewish autonomy had been curtailed under the Byzantines; any similarities would appear to be to Roman regulations embedded in Byzantine practice. In contrast, the Islamic roots of Ottoman policies toward non-Muslims are clear, and one need not accept the argument that they are syncretic in order to view them as homologous with policies of the Christian empires. For an argument in favor of syncretism, see Bat Ye'or, *The Dhimmis: Jews and Christians Under Islam*, p. 49 and especially p. 87.

[83] Kemal H. Karpat, "*Millets* and Nationality: The Roots of the Incongruity of Nation and State in the Post-Ottoman Era."

[84] The term *millet* has often been used to describe the Ottoman system for the rule of non-Muslim religious communities. The term implies that the communities had designated individuals who served as administrative leaders for the communities. Cohen (*Jewish Life Under Islam*) argues that millet – the system of autonomous organization for Christians and Jews in the Ottoman Empire – did not exist formally in sixteenth-century Jerusalem, except as a description for the organization of the Muslim community. It did, however, exist in practice since Jewish leaders were recognized and deferred to on relevant matters as communal heads. There is some doubt in general whether the much-used term *millet* has applicability anywhere in the empire before the nineteenth century, except in reference to Muslims. On the origins of the term, see Benjamin Braude, "Foundation Myths of the *Millet* System."

[85] Cohen, *Jewish Life Under Islam*.

[86] Morris S. Goodblatt, *Jewish Life in Turkey in the XVIth Century As Reflected in the Legal Writings of Samuel de Medina*, p. 122.

Nevertheless, Jews could and did strategically appeal to government courts. In Jerusalem, Jewish leaders sometimes asked the qadi to intercede to control or sanction unruly members of the Jewish community. In 1593, for example, Jerusalem Jews appealed to the qadi for help in expelling a disruptive Jew from Safed.[87] Throughout the century, Jewish litigants and witnesses participated in Muslim court proceedings when it was expedient, or when cited to do so. Jews who wanted to bring cases against Muslims had to do so in qadi courts, where they found a surprising objectivity.[88] Jews also sued other Jews in Muslim courts. Cohen suggests that the motivations to do so probably included a search for greater impartiality (when, for example, Jewish litigants had unequal social standing), the need to establish a government record of transactions or to ensure enforcement, and the possibility of influencing the outcome of cases through bribes. But the different legal status of Jews and Muslims was preserved. Jewish testimony was weighed differently when the testimony was prejudicial to Jews or Muslims.

The legal opinion of Samuel De Medina in sixteenth-century Turkey in a lawsuit between two Jews, a homeowner and his tenant, illustrates both the hostility of Jewish leaders to the tactic of taking other Jews to qadi courts and the plausibility of this tactic in even minor disputes. In this case, the landlord, Simon, had been engaged in a long-running dispute with his tenant, Reuben, who rented the bottom floor of Simon's house. Simon waited until Reuben had returned from synagogue one Sabbath, then drilled a hole in the floor and poured water on Reuben while he slept. Retaliating, Reuben broke the vessels in the house. Simon first had Reuben arrested by the officers of a government court. He also took the case to the Jewish court, where Reuben was fined for desecrating the Sabbath by breaking the vessels. De Medina's opinion harshly criticized this ruling, arguing that Simon should be penalized for causing Reuben to desecrate the Sabbath and for "the greater guilt" of reporting him to a non-Jewish court:[89]

> [I]t was entirely wrong on the part of Simon to report him to a non-Jewish court...since it is well known that non-Jewish judges are greedy and unscrupulous, dealing mercilessly with Jewish litigants. It is a wrong policy to expose our inner affairs to non-Jews. It is, therefore,

---

[87] Cohen, *Jewish Life Under Islam*, p. 10.
[88] Cohen, *Jewish Life Under Islam*, p. 113.
[89] Goodblatt, *Jewish Life in Turkey*, p. 133.

my opinion that it was wrong to put Reuben under the jurisdiction of a non-Jewish court and then punish him in a Jewish court, especially since there were no witnesses to testify that they had seen him perform the act.[90]

De Medina's harsh condemnation of the appeal to government courts is revealing, but so is the fact that the landlord denounced his tenant to state officials first, before reporting him to the Jewish court. It must have been tempting to make his tenant suffer at the hands of government court officials – De Medina notes that the man had incurred some cost in freeing himself – and it is possible that the landlord even anticipated that his action would serve to swing the Jewish court to his side because it would be known that he could get a ruling in his favor in another forum. This case and others show us the fluidity of jurisdictional boundaries. As in sixteenth-century Iberia, the complexity of the legal order no doubt contributed to growing legal sophistication as a part of daily life.

In summary, legal complexities that were built into the system of administration carried over and were enhanced by the conditions of frontier expansion. In particular, the Islamic empires adapted legal devices to deal with the existence of large populations of non-Muslims, a persistent feature of empire despite incentives for conversion and in part because of institutional protections for communal legal forums. These aspects of the Islamic legal order would have been quite familiar to travelers from other parts of the world. Indeed, Jewish, Armenian, and Christian traders found institutional continuity across Islamic and Western regions, negotiating for and adopting strategies to enhance this resemblance.

HINDUS AS LEGAL SUBJECTS IN GOA

One further example is necessary to establish the shared complexities of imperial legal politics across a wide geographical and cultural plane. At Goa, the administrative capital of the Portuguese trading post empire in Asia, the Portuguese were drawn into an attempt to establish more extensive legal controls over the local population. They encountered, in doing so, a web of difficulties, including enhanced jurisdictional tensions within their own law and new problems of assigning legal rights

---

[90] Goodblatt, *Jewish Life in Turkey*, p. 132.

to culturally diverse groups with different political standing. The Portuguese were met, at the same time, with the combination of pragmatic acceptance and strategically sophisticated resistance that we would expect from a population accustomed to maneuvering through similarly complex legal systems.

As in other small settlements in Portuguese trading posts, judicial administration was required in Goa and was intended, initially, to apply to Portuguese residents and their dependents. Soon after taking Goa in 1511, Albuquerque created a handful of judicial posts, including local magistrates. Any appeals were to be handled by the *capitão-mor*, who thus had the same judicial powers as captains of the fortified trading posts of the African coast.

But Goa was unusual in many respects, too. It soon became the center for the Portuguese trading post empire in Asia, and its administrative structure was the structure of the empire. Further, as Portuguese settled in Goa, and the population of Portuguese descendants and nominal Christians grew, it became increasingly important for judicial administration to be extended and better defined in its relation to the local population. As in Spanish America, this process excited internal disputes and intensified jurisdictional tensions.

A bitter dispute in Goa over who would succeed the governor and capitão in 1526 was resolved by an ad hoc procedure drafting local dignitaries to serve as judges. The decision, which went against the crown's appointee, was later overturned by the High Court of Lisbon. The incident called attention to the need for a strengthened judicial hierarchy in Goa. In 1530, the crown sent a new *ouvidor geral* who had complete authority in civil matters; the governor was to retain authority in all criminal cases.

A dispute between the ouvidor geral and the governor broke out almost immediately. The governor, Nuno da Cunha, asked the new ouvidor geral, Antónia de Macedo, to march in his procession at the head, carrying a staff of justice. Macedo viewed this request as an affront and refused. No doubt Macedo understood that he would appear in the procession as an underling of the governor, a mere functionary, whereas he understood his authority to be at least partly independent. It was not long before the two men found themselves involved in a heated jurisdictional dispute.

The conflict began when a criminal being taken into custody called out for help from the servants of a nobleman (*fidalgo*) who had close ties to the governor. The servants pulled the man through the door of the fidalgo's house to rescue him. When he found out what had happened, the ouvidor Macedo demanded that the prisoner be released into his custody, and finally took him by force. The owner of the house, Diogo da Silveira, arrived at the house and began to rant against both the ouvidor and the king. The governor had no choice but to imprison Silveira in his house while he investigated the accusations against him; and, when witnesses testified that he had indeed insulted the king, the governor was forced to authorize Silveira's arrest. The governor did recommend, though, that the ouvidor refer the case to his office rather than proceed against Silveira. Macedo argued that the governor did not have jurisdiction to try this sort of crime, and that the case ought to be sent to Lisbon. Instead, the governor freed Silveira and even appointed him to a sea captainship. Macedo continued to insist that the case, and Silveira, be sent to Lisbon. The governor replied that he was in charge and could kill "100 Ouvidores, if they disobey me." It was not long until the governor found a pretext for seizing Macedo and imprisoning him for insubordination.[91]

This episode was just one in a series of conflicts between governors and judges that led, in 1544, to the creation of the Relação (High Court) of Goa, an act designed by the crown to end the intervention of governors in judicial decisions. The Relação was to have jurisdiction not just at Goa but also over judicial personnel and decisions in posts from East Africa to Macau. Rather than ending conflict with royal officials, the existence of the Relação became a favorite complaint of viceroys in Goa, who viewed the court as the cause of growing litigiousness and portrayed the magistrates as corrupt and self-serving. Only three years after it was established, the viceroy João de Castro wrote to the king that the High Court was "the most unnecessary thing" and that "these lettered men who act the part of magistrates, come here starving to death" and ready to use their influence to make their fortunes.[92] The crown remained unconvinced by these complaints and continued to staff the Relação, even expanding the number of magistrates as the volume of cases increased and, in 1550, elevating the Relação to the category of Corte, a body that could hear and resolve cases without the presence of the governor.

[91] Carlos Reinato Gonçalves Pereira, *Historia da administractraçao da justiça no Estado da Índia, século XVI, Vol I*, p. 53.

[92] Pereira, *Historia da administractraçao da justiça*, p. 93. My translation.

The tensions between judicial and administrative officials were no doubt heightened by the distance from Lisbon and the prominent role of force in creating and maintaining Portuguese interests in Asian trade. The "hegemony" that the Portuguese sought in the Indian Ocean was not based on claims of sovereignty or the ability to create a framework for peaceful trade. Revenues depended on forcing non-Portuguese traders to call at Portuguese ports, under the threat that sailing without a Portuguese *cartaz*, or pass, might result in ships' being seized. Some Portuguese recognized that persistent brutality, and the "maladministration of justice," signified missed opportunities to create hegemony of a different kind – one based on allegiance to Portuguese rule.[93] Judicial officials and governors did work together on occasion to respond to abuses of the local population. The first case on record was a complaint against a fleet captain for raping a *moura*, a local Muslim woman, who was taken onto his ship. He was condemned by Albuquerque and hanged. A similar case was brought in 1514, this time against a friend of Albuquerque; after he was executed, the pieces of his quartered body were hung from palm trees along the beach.[94] Portuguese leaders no doubt viewed such cases as crucial to maintaining discipline among sailors and soldiers; it is less clear whether they were intended as a performance for local communities where the Portuguese had already acquired a reputation for brutality.

Judicial institutions responded, too, to the complex problem of ordering relations with indigenous inhabitants in the few areas of territorial control. This issue, less salient in the trading forts of the South Atlantic, surfaced with special force at Goa, both because it was the centerpiece of Portuguese administration and because it had within it a substantial population of non-Christians. The Portuguese had taken one brutal measure to address the problem of religious diversity. After retaking Goa in 1511, Afonso de Albuquerque had ordered the entire Muslim population slaughtered. Albuquerque envisaged mass conversions among the remaining Hindu population, but these were slow in

---

[93] Boxer reports that "maladministration of justice (*a falta de justiçia*) was the theme of continued complaints in both official and unofficial correspondence" from all corners of the Portuguese overseas world over the span of several centuries. Portuguese chroniclers observed the corrosive effects of the widespread flaunting of judicial procedure on perceptions of Portuguese rule among non-Europeans. See C.R. Boxer, *The Portuguese Seaborne Empire*, p. 144.

[94] Pereira, *Historia da adminisctraçao da justiça*, p. 14, 28.

coming. In the 1540s a more vigorous anti-Hindu policy was adopted. The Portuguese destroyed Hindu temples on Goa and its adjacent islands and took other measures against Hindu practices. Some incentives were also held out for conversion, most notably changing inheritance laws so that Indian daughters would be permitted to inherit estates from deceased Hindu fathers if no male heirs existed, provided they first became Christians. Pressures but also complications involving this "policy of systematic religious persecution" increased after Portugal also took over two districts on the mainland in 1543. Bardes to the north and Salcete in the south were much bigger and more populous than Goa and its adjacent islands.[95] The Portuguese also took measures against Hindu rituals in these districts, though the size of the districts and the reluctance of most Hindus to convert prevented these efforts from being effective. Hindus and even converted Christians were permitted to continue Hindu practices that "appeared to be merely civil and political in nature."[96]

The coexistence of a sizable Hindu population, groups of converted (in many cases nominal) Indian Christians, a large community of so-called Thomas Christians who were in the area before the arrival of the Portuguese, and a population of Portuguese residents who were themselves divided into status groups (depending on where they were born and their parentage) placed a burden on legal institutions to define the boundaries among these groups. The Portuguese believed the local population to be especially litigious, and special judges were appointed to try cases quickly, with limited right to appeal. These forums were open only to Christians, and Hindus were to continue to use their own legal forums. This solution, however, did not eliminate the need for legislation applying to Hindus, and such actions opened the way for direct appeals by Hindus to the Portuguese king for justice. Further, the introduction of the Inquisition created an element of

---

[95] A.K. Priolkar, *The Goa Inquisition*, p. 52.

[96] The phrase is from an edict published in Goa in 1736, which complained that the deleterious effects on converts of these practices had not been fully understood and outlined a detailed series of new infractions regarding weddings, marriages, childbirth, housework, and a variety of other practices. As Lariviere has pointed out in discussing British legal policy in India, the Portuguese were clearly confused about the status of Hinduism; having treated it as a "religion" separable from other social spheres, they came increasingly to understand that its practice comprised much more than narrowly defined religious rites. Richard Lariviere, "Justices and *Panditas*: Some Ironies in Contemporary Readings of the Hindu Past." And see Chapter 4 below on law in British India.

uncertainty in jurisdictional matters that affected legal actors in all these categories.

The Portuguese intended to leave indigenous legal forums and administrative structures in place. Yet various pressures, including divided views among Portuguese officials, changed this order. The Portuguese found that village community administration, in the hands of village members called ganvkars (*gancares*), inhibited revenue collection. In 1526, Afonso Mexia, the overseer of the revenue, compiled a *foral* (the term used for local legal codes in Portugal) covering indigenous customs, which he hoped to use to regulate Hindu property transactions and, in particular, the affairs of the ganvkars. He consulted with members of the local elite and produced the *Foral dos uzos e costumes os gancares e lavradores desta ilha de Goa e outros annexos nela* (Charter of uses and customs of ganvkars and peasants of the island of Goa and other territories annexed to it). Although the foral was represented as a faithful compendium of existing norms, it in fact established revenue rights for the Portuguese, regulated land transactions by ganvkars, and omitted aspects of inheritance that the Portuguese must have wished to eliminate, namely the distribution of equal shares of an estate to the off-spring from multiple unions. The guidelines on inheritance were challenged soon after the foral was published, in an action brought before the ouvidor geral by two Hindu Brahmins from a family with close connections to the Portuguese.[97] The litigants were the sons of two women who were married to the same man. They claimed that the foral prepared by Mexia did not agree with custom in divisions of property among children of a deceased man's multiple wives. The ouvidor geral called together the litigants and some prominent locals and asked about the discrepancy. The Hindus explained that although sometimes parents wished for an unequal distribution of the estate, it was also common to distribute the estate equally when there was no dispute. The ouvidor geral wrote a modification to the foral to allow for both kinds of inheritance, and the change was endorsed by the governor. As a result of the Hindu litigants' actions, the Portuguese had formally recognized inheritance rights in marriages with multiple wives. They had also demonstrated a responsiveness to Hindu legal actions that was to be a consistent feature of the plural legal order.[98]

---

[97] A son of one of the litigants had served as a diplomatic agent of the Portuguese to several kings in the region.

[98] Pereira, *Historia da administcraçao da justiça*, pp. 63–65.

In the middle decades of the sixteenth century, the Portuguese established various posts and procedures for hearing cases brought by indigenous litigants. In 1537, the position of *pai dos cristãos*, father of Christians, was established to represent and protect converted Hindus. In 1548, the king appointed two more magistrates to the High Court and also established that the ouvidor geral would hear cases brought by indigenous litigants other than those in several categories of elites, and their cases could not be appealed. Although we do not have records of the cases brought, we do know that by the middle of the century, the Relação was overwhelmed with work, fueling a complaint by the Municipal Council of Goa that the magistrates were slowing the course of justice. Problems surfaced, too, with the father of Christians, who was supposed to settle all petty cases arising among converts. Converts from outlying villages had to travel to Goa to bring minor cases. In 1563, the viceroy approved a plan of the Relação to allow friars or churchwardens to hear the cases, if the parties all agreed.

Measures designed to provide summary justice to non-Portuguese litigants coincided in mid-century with an escalation of actions against non-Christians. In addition to forbidding proselytizing, multiple marriages, and non-Christian religious rites, the Portuguese in 1567 ordered all qadis out of Portuguese territory and banned infidels from holding public offices of any kind. Temples in Salcete were destroyed. In 1573, the governor ordered restrictions on the rights of Hindu members of village communities. In villages where Christians outnumbered Hindus, the latter were not to be allowed to attend village assemblies. Hindus who migrated out of Portuguese territory to escape restrictions could also not return to claim a portion of revenues owed them as village members.

These restrictions came on the heels of a 1559 royal order that was a source of particular hardship in the Hindu community. The decree ordered that orphaned Hindu children would be handed over to the Society of Jesus to be baptized and instructed in Catholicism. Over a century later, Hindus were petitioning the king for relief from abuses under this measure. In 1677, the king wrote to the viceroy to report on a petition by Brahmins, high officials, and artisans of Goa and neighboring villages complaining that Hindu children who were not orphans but whose mothers were still living were being taken away and the estates seized. The Hindus complained of attempts to extort money for the return of the "orphans." In a letter to the viceroy in 1709, the king reported Hindu complaints about the "excess of zeal" of the father of Christians. The Hindu petitioners

> represent that when they seek to demonstrate that some of the children who are taken away have fathers, they are faced with the difficulty that the official concerned does not admit Hindus as witnesses and those who are Christians fear to come and declare the truth owing to the fear and respect which they entertain for the father of Christians.[99]

The harsh treatment of Hindus, and their use of the courts and even appeals to the king in response, were elements of the legal order that were further complicated by the introduction in 1560 of the Inquisition in Goa. As in Spanish America, the Inquisition in Goa had a special jurisdictional status. Only the highest Portuguese officials were exempt from its actions, and even they could be brought under its umbrella if the Inquisitors received permission from Lisbon. The original motive for establishing the Inquisition was to find and punish backsliding new Christians. But converts could also be charged, and non-Christians could be brought before the Inquisition for proselytizing. Between 1561 and 1623, some thirty-eight hundred cases were brought, a large number considering that the population of Goa was about sixty thousand in the 1580s, with perhaps twenty thousand of these being Hindus.[100] Among Portuguese residents, the Inquisition had a well-deserved reputation for harshness. Prisoners had no one to intercede as advocates or friendly witnesses, since it was well-known that coming to the defense of an accused heretic might easily lead to imprisonment in the Inquisition's jails alongside him. A Catholic French surgeon named Dellon who was arrested for making disparaging comments about "superstitious" practices among the Portuguese described a harrowing two-year imprisonment during which he was driven by the deplorable conditions and the psychological torture of the uncertainty of his fate to try to commit suicide. There is evidence, too, that the Inquisition was used against Indian Christians and Hindus as a tool of repression and a simple means for enrichment.

Both Christians and non-Christians used the threat of denunciation to the Inquisition against each other. In 1702, six recent Indian converts

---

[99] Quoted in Priolkar, *Goa Inquisition*, p. 130.

[100] Pearson, *The Portuguese in India, The New Cambridge History of India,* I, p. 93. There were even more cases in the next century, or a total of 16,172 cases between 1561 and 1774, when the Inquisition was halted by Pombal (though reinstated three years later, through 1820). See Pearson, *The Portuguese in India,* and Priolkar, *Goa Inquisition,* p. 49.

were charged with extorting money from Hindu residents under threat that they would be denounced. Hindus petitioned the king to instruct the Holy Office not to lend credence to accusations of Hindus against other Hindus. In complaining about the seizure of orphans and their property, Hindus complained that when they appealed for help to the judge of orphans in cases where the "orphans" had living parents, the accusers were being "dragged before the tribunal of the Holy Office"; the king wrote to the viceroy objecting to such actions as a clear infringement on royal jurisdiction.[101]

The so-called Thomas Christians posed a special problem. Between eighty thousand and two hundred thousand of these Christians were living in the area around Goa when the Portuguese arrived, according to Pearson. The Portuguese were appalled by their practices, which they found tainted by Hinduism. But the Christians resided in the small principalities surrounding Portuguese territories, where they had the status of a protected minority. There was little the Portuguese could do to meddle directly in their affairs. The Thomas Christians were under the authority of the Syrian patriarch, who was recognized by Rome. The Portuguese pleaded successfully to have them reassigned to the *padroado* in 1599, but this resulted in a schism among the Thomas Christians, many of whom simply refused to recognize this change and resided, in any case, outside Portuguese territorial control.

The activities of the Inquisition fit, here as in Spanish America, into a larger pattern of conflict between church and state. The Jesuits worked hard to gain converts, and in outlying areas the activities of ecclesiastics went unchecked by civil administration.[102] The tensions, present from Albuquerque's time, are illustrated in a case in Cannanore, near Cochin, in which a Christian who had killed a Hindu sought refuge with the local priest. Albuquerque ordered the man released to the rajah, and the local captain obeyed. But when Albuquerque left the port, the priest fined the captain for obeying the governor and violating church sanctuary. Such disputes were common throughout the period, but the Inquisition supplied ecclesiastics with a much stronger weapon. Even the governor from 1588 to 1591 was investigated for consulting Hindu mystics about the arrival of ships. Wealthy Portuguese traders

---

[101] See Priolkar, *Goa Inquisition*, pp. 108–10, and for the letter from the king in 1704, p. 133.
[102] For a detailed account of the Jesuits' activities in the region, see Dauril Alden, *The Making of an Enterprise: The Society of Jesus in Portugal, Its Empire, and Beyond 1540–1750*, Chapter 3.

became a favorite target – the French surgeon Dellon claimed in his eighteenth-century chronicle that men without influence or property were rarely prosecuted.

The powerful Inquisition, though, was also constrained by the limited political control of the Portuguese. There was a massive out-migration of Hindus to territories outside Portuguese control.[103] In at least one instance, outsiders reached inside the Portuguese realm to intervene in the Inquisition. When local clergy became jealous of a French priest at Madras who was drawing Portuguese residents from nearby St. Thomé, they conspired to draw him to Portuguese territory and had him arrested and sent to the Inquisition in Goa. He was saved not by the intercession of powerful Europeans but by the actions of the army of the rajah of a province of Carnatica, who laid siege to St. Thomé and demanded that the father be freed.

The administration of justice in Portuguese India conformed in many ways to the larger pattern of law in diaspora. The Portuguese, having inserted themselves by a combination of force and diplomacy to rule coastal enclaves, at first established a pattern of rule that conformed to existing political patterns of the surrounding patchwork of small principalities. Portuguese fell under the jurisdiction of Portuguese captains and governors and, later, judicial personnel; existing forums were left intact. In contrast to the forts of coastal Africa, however, the Portuguese came to control an area inhabited by a sizable population of non-Christians, mainly (though not exclusively) Hindu. This difference generated a greater degree of jurisdictional complexity and confusion. Of greatest significance was the active role of the Hindu residents of Portuguese territories – and even of Hindu rulers in surrounding principalities – in challenging the structure and function of Portuguese law. This challenge consisted partly in boundary crossing: the opportunistic conversion to Christianity automatically brought a change in legal status and no doubt contributed to the flood of litigation in Portuguese courts. But Hindu litigants also petitioned courts, and the king, to alter both legislation and the structure and function of courts when Hindu interests were adversely affected. Despite the open persecution of Hindus and Muslims, they retained some legal protections and had an economic value to the Portuguese that also provided some incentive

---

[103] P.P. Shirodkar, "Socio-Cultural Life in Goa during the 16th Century," p. 35. There was also a wave of new baptisms, as residents sought the relative safety of the status of converts.

for controlling abuses against them. When such defensive actions failed, the limits of Portuguese territorial control permitted escape to adjacent territories, a move that had the effect of creating and strengthening the diasporic character of local communities, despite Portuguese attempts to limit cross-border contacts.

The actions of Hindus and Christian converts in direct response to Portuguese legal policies underscores their familiarity with a multilayered legal order in which legal and cultural boundaries were linked but also fluid. The legal regime in the Indian Ocean world, which we have only sampled in discussing Portuguese Goa, had in this sense a recognizable institutional continuity with the interconnected world of the South Atlantic and the legal culture of Islamic territories. The Portuguese diaspora reached across these regions but did not unify them, either politically or economically. Their unity consisted instead in the political and legal conditions that both helped give the Portuguese an entrée and shaped their strategies once they had established a presence. The religious militancy of the Portuguese, their inspired adaptation of light canon on small ships, and their strategy of profiting from the control of sea lanes – these features of their enterprise introduced new but not transformative political and economic forces into the region. The structures of rule in India were familiar constraints to which the Portuguese largely conformed and that were, in any case, consistent with the experience of fragmented political and legal authority at home, in Africa, and, as we have seen, on the other side of the Atlantic.

"CIVILIZATIONS" AND CONFLICTS IN COMMON

Tensions built into the legal order of European and Islamic colonizing powers were reproduced in the institutional order of colonies. Here distance from metropolitan centers, the existence of large numbers of culturally different subjects, and the pursuit of legal strategies to take advantage of the complexities of the legal order acted to make a relatively fluid legal order more fluid still. As in the example of jurisdictional disputes on the Spanish American frontier, conflicts over the legal order structured economic contests and at the same time shaped cultural boundaries separating colonial constituents.

This dynamic appears to have been shared throughout a surprisingly wide region of the early modern world. In the Iberian overseas empires, in the Ottoman and Mughal empires, and in much of Africa, jurisdictional politics focused on the unstable relationship between religious and state law. Even in a period of strengthening state bureaucracies and authority, law was widely, if selectively, understood as personal law. The relationship between state and religious law was a volatile one acted upon by local political contests, many of which centered explicitly around questions of membership in, and prerogatives of, religious communities.

The similarities in the structuring of legal authority and in the tensions created through imperial expansion add to doubts about characterizations of the Islamic and Christian worlds as different "civilizations." Such portrayals live on in standard histories and continue to define the boundaries of research fields. Their persistence, years after Braudel argued for the cultural unity of the Mediterranean world and Hodgson drew attention to the cultural continuities of a much larger Afro-Eurasia encompassing Islam, suggests that findings of legal continuities will not succeed in altering this representation of separateness.[104] But the parallels need pointing out nonetheless. Despite the differences in strategy between the Portuguese in the east and the Spaniards across the Atlantic, the two empires responded in similar ways when faced with the challenge of legal administration over a large population that was culturally and religiously different. And both Catholic empires resembled the Islamic powers in the fundamental tensions of imposed law. The Iberian and Ottoman empires made parallel efforts to streamline legal authority, only to see this impulse disturbed by a combination of indigenous legal response and jurisdictional disputes among colonial and imperial factions. In all these settings, law was not a casual arena for conflict but one that focused the strategic efforts of administrators, local elites, cultural intermediaries, and perhaps others whose actions are more difficult to read in the historical record. All these social actors fought for particular outcomes but also perceived clearly the importance of the law for marking community boundaries and structuring access to property, and the congruence of these functions.

This multilayered significance of law and the multisided disputes perpetuated under conditions of imperial expansion together provided the basis for a certain institutional continuity both within and across empires. In this way, the orderly disorder of jurisdictional fluidity in the long sixteenth century made political authority across a wide range of culturally different territories intelligible to outsiders. The intelligibility

---

[104] Marshall G.S. Hodgson, *Rethinking World History: Essays on Europe, Islam, and World History.*

derived both from the pervasiveness of an open-ended jurisdictional politics – even, as we have seen, in regions where centralized political authorities were making aggressive attempts to consolidate legal control – and from the universal importance of questions of cultural and religious difference as structuring elements in the law.

Such a perspective is helpful not only to reimagining the boundaries of the early modern world but also in understanding the later historical movement from truly plural legal orders to state-dominated legal orders. This shift, as we shall see, involved complex adjustments to both political ideology and cultural representation. It responded, also, to the sheer accumulation of appeals to state authority that began in the earlier period and are noticeable in the legal maneuvering of Spanish American Indians and settlers, the legal appeals of Hindus to both Mughal and Portuguese authorities, and the maneuvering of foreign traders and dhimmi in the Ottoman Empire. Indeed, the later, widespread replication of patterns of colonial state formation must be understood in the context of an existing interregional legal culture.

Such a perspective – and the admittedly ambitious claims about its significance for world history – places seemingly local colonial legal conflicts squarely at the center of global institutional formation. At the same time, the approach plucks "old-fashioned" colonial institutional history from its dusty corner and places it alongside more prominent narratives of cultural and economic change. Colonial legal actors fought passionately about jurisdictional boundaries because they understood, perhaps better than we have, their fundamental importance in shaping the structure and meaning of imperial and colonial rule.

FOUR

A Place for the State

Legal Pluralism As a Colonial Project in Bengal and West Africa

The imposition of a hierarchical system of rule in which foreign-derived law topped a pyramid of "other" legal sources and systems was not the first or only possible strategy of European colonizing powers. It was not, even, an obvious strategy. European polities were themselves only beginning to shape a hierarchy of legal authorities which super-imposed state law on alternative legal systems, including customary, canon, and merchant law. The agents of colonial expansion were them-selves in many cases given judicial authority that was understood to be independent from the state. The complexity of jurisdictional politics at home was such that multiple jurisdictions in colonial settings seemed unexceptional to administrators. Further, cost considerations played a large role in colonial legal policy. There was little interest on the part of governments, charter companies, or private agents in absorbing the costs of erecting an elaborate judicial administration. Well before "indi-rect rule" was articulated as a political strategy, colonial administrators understood and expressed the need to sustain indigenous legal forums as a means of promoting order.

Nevertheless, colonial rule still carried with it the imperative of *some* judicial involvement. Europeans did not want to be judged by or liti-gate in indigenous courts – nor, in some cases, did indigenous social actors who were tied by interest, culture, or blood to the colonizers. Depending on the nature of the colonial economy, certain types of con-tracts, transactions, and disputes might come to be regarded as so vital to European interests that they could not be regulated or resolved ex-cept in European-dominated forums. Finally, the temptation to regulate and change indigenous practices through legislation was powerful for colonizers; in many places, jurisdictional claims of colonial powers were extended expressly to support movements begun outside the colonial administration – often by missionaries – to eradicate a local practice represented as morally repugnant or to defend an indigenous group from abuses by European settlers.

These and other pressures to extend judicial control combined with interests in limiting legal administration to create policies supporting formal legal pluralism. That is, colonial powers sought simultaneously to establish limited jurisdiction and to reinforce – and in some cases create – indigenous legal forums. As with indirect rule, legal pluralism as a colonial project often required the creation of "traditional" authority and the reification of legal practices and sources of law that had existed formerly only as fluid elements of a flexible legal process.

Establishing legal pluralism was hardly a straightforward colonial project. The elaborate rules required to establish procedural links, jurisdictional boundaries, and the roles of legal personnel in the articulated legal order were forced to change as quickly as they were promulgated. Indigenous actors used the rules to manipulate strategically through the legal order, and their successful maneuvers revealed to colonial administrators the flaws in the architecture of the plural legal order. Colonizers themselves found jurisdictional politics irresistible, as various factions sought changes to the system in support of their own interests. Meanwhile, cultural intermediaries of various types – including emerging groups of indigenous legal personnel – played an active role in advocating changes in procedural rules. For all these social actors, disputes over the rules articulating the connections of this complex legal order were not merely procedural conveniences or tactical weapons but were important, even vital, symbolic markers of the boundaries separating colonial constituencies. The boundaries, in turn, signified judgments about the character of these groups and the qualities that separated them from one another. Far from being arcane, the rules of courtroom behavior and the "rules of engagement" linking increasingly interrelated legal realms enjoined quick and passionate debate.

Given the inherent instability of this carefully crafted legal pluralism, it may seem obvious that the institutional "fix" would be a gradual movement toward greater control by the state and a more hierarchical order in which appellate procedures directed disputes ultimately to colonial state courts (and to metropolitan courts beyond them). But the inevitability of this outcome was hardly apparent to most participants. This chapter explores the intricacies, and the many contingencies, of the transition from a more fluid legal pluralism to the more planned pluralism of "high" colonialism in British India and French colonial Africa. Jurisdictional tensions in both places were exploited by local litigants whose appeals tweaked at the structure of legal institutions. In British India, Indian litigants helped to create a space for the colonial state before it was formally called into existence. In West French Africa, jurisdictional challenges in early colonial enclaves convinced colonial administrators to sharpen the boundaries between state and nonstate legal authorities. In both places, the construction of a colonial state empowered in law proceeded haltingly, and in response to myriad conflicts over the definitions of difference, property, and moral authority.

LEGAL POLICY AND JURISDICTIONAL COMPLEXITY IN BRITISH INDIA

In E.M. Forster's *A Passage to India*, Adela accuses Dr. Aziz of molesting her on a trip to the Marabar Caves. Aziz is arrested at once, and the European community at Chandrapore unquestionably believes Adela's confused account of the events at the caves. For the British community, the upcoming trial is about protecting an Englishwoman from the contaminating and "evil" contact with an Indian – and so is about marking and protecting the lines separating the British and Indian communities. The Indians also view the case as part of a much larger political cause. The Indian *vakils* (legal advisors) and barristers perceive that their best strategy is to politicize the trial and bring in a well-known nationalist barrister who is a Hindu and so has a wider following. Once in the courtroom, the two sides loyally play their parts. They are attentive to the details of public symbolism in the courtroom, arguing over the positioning of chairs in the courtroom and waging a battle for the soul of the Indian judge, who represents for one side the decay of British power and to the other, the dangers (and the promise) of collaboration.

Then, in a telling passage for an ostensibly anticolonial novel, the courtroom casts a spell on the star witness. Adela, who has had doubts about her own attack, rises to take the stand and realizes, in one quick moment, that she is going to hide nothing from the court – not even her most intimate thoughts about her engagement. She feels protected by a "new and unknown sensation."[1] Prompted by the superintendent,

---

[1] E.M. Forster, *A Passage to India*, p. 227.

she begins to relive her excursion to the caves, until at last she arrives at the vision – or the absence of the vision – of the attack. She recants and then, after being reminded by the Indian judge that she is under oath, recants again. After a brief moment of celebration of victory and stunned contemplation of defeat, Forster tells us, "the flimsy framework of the court" breaks up, and life returns "to its complexities."[2]

The novel returns to its complexities, too. For a few pages, we have been asked to accept what we are told to deride in the rest of the book – the legitimacy of a British colonial institution. Whether we like it or not, the truth has been revealed *in the courtroom*. Though Adela's return to clarity is understood by Fielding as a "nervous breakdown," the fact remains that she was *under oath* when she fully perceived, and uttered, the truth. She was kept from the truth when she was surrounded by other Englishmen and women who "disbelieved in Indians." But the courtroom stands for something else; it is almost sacred ground. The Indians participating in the courtroom ritual understand that the rules of the court have made this outcome possible. The nationalist barrister calls for calm at a key moment, and the Indian judge moves swiftly to dismiss the case when the opening arrives. Procedural justice has produced real justice. The court has plucked the truth out of the muddle of everyday sexual and cultural politics. The rule of law survives in the novel as Britain's one true gift to India.[3]

This is not to suggest, of course, that the novel is therefore tragically flawed. It was written in 1924. By then, Indian nationalism was indeed focused on wresting the colonial state from British hands rather than creating an alternative authority. By then, too, the colonial state *was* a state. It was an entity that laid claim to a monopoly on violence and to ultimate authority within its jurisdiction. Law was not just a casual support for these claims, it was central to them. The colonial state had a juridical existence which, as Young has observed, was in many

---

[2] Forster, *A Passage to India*, p. 231.
[3] Another subtext, too, is that the Englishwoman Adela has the inner qualities that make her susceptible to this force in the courtroom. The value of her sworn testimony is less than that of an English*man*, but still greater than that of an Indian. (Thus Forster gives us the contrast to the Brahmin witness. Forster salvages his submerged anticolonial message by implying the existence of a higher truth of which only the Brahmin is aware. But, again, this truth hardly matters because it is presented in antirational musings by the Brahmin that appear to the English observers as mere shiftiness.) The English view of their special cultural relationship to the truth is highlighted even more in the film version of the story, in which Adela, pressed to recant her revised version by the prosecutor, insists, "I was raised to tell the truth."

ways quite different from its empirical existence.[4] The legal authority of the state was singular; it existed not alongside other legal and political authorities but above them, at the top of a hierarchy in which multiple communities, cultures, religions, and moral orders might still reside, but in which they were now clearly subject to the overarching authority of state's law. The British-controlled courtroom where Aziz was tried was not just *a* courtroom, it was the *only* court with jurisdiction in the case. It was, in some sense, recognized by British and many Indians alike as the arbiter of truth – even if all the participants knew that politics and prejudices distorted the truth more often than not. For Europeans, the rule of law depended on the twin themes raised in Forster's treatment of colonial law: the view that English law possessed a singular, rule-bound neutrality, and the idea that the strengths of the legal system grew out of English subjects' special relationship to the truth.

The English had traveled very slowly to this position. They had at first followed closely the precedents of other European powers in the region and had narrowly restricted jurisdiction by British-controlled courts.[5] But the British East India Company (BEIC) began gradually to exercise political control over larger territories, and larger indigenous populations, than any of its European predecessors had done. One is hardpressed to identify a moment of "possession" by the British in India. British control on the subcontinent was extended slowly, in piecemeal fashion, from the establishment of the first British trading colonies in the late seventeenth century to the formal usurpation of British government control of the British East India Company, and the quasi-state functions it had assumed, in 1858. Not just at first but for nearly two hundred years of involvement in India, the British tried to craft a legal system that was formally plural and that allowed Muslim and Hindu courts to

---

[4] Crawford Young, *The African Colonial State in Comparative Perspective*, p. 5. Young cites Carl Rosberg and Robert Jackson on this contrast, discussed mainly in connection with the analysis of postcolonialism but relevant, too, to the colonial state itself.

[5] See Chapter 3 on Portuguese policies in Goa. Dutch strategies in their South Asian enclaves were similar and recognized VOC legal authority over mainly VOC employees, while local rulers continued to preside over their own legal forums. French policy differed at first only slightly. Hindus were permitted to litigate in French courts if they chose to, and the French occasionally intervened to resolve disputes in indigenous courts. But closer involvement and a concerted effort to create an ordered relationship between French and indigenous legal forums, and between French and customary law, did not emerge until the early nineteenth century. See J.D.M. Derrett, "The Ministration of Hindu Law by the British," for more on shifts in French legal policy in India.

operate independently from Company or state courts. At several critical junctures, the architecture of this legal order was modified in ways that participants believed were fundamental to defining the character of British rule.

Questions about how and to what degree to administer British law, and to whom, surfaced almost from the beginning. The Mughal system of law the British encountered was complex and locally varied in its operation. The British faced the challenges of, first, understanding the existing legal system and, then, designing changes to it that would promote order, protect British economic interests, and create a space for British jurisdiction over British subjects. In the early years when the British were confined to their trading colonies, these tasks were simpler, though they gave way quickly to complexity and ambiguity. Indigenous forums continued to operate. Petty cases were overseen in Madras by the hereditary village headman, the *adigar,* in the local "choultry" courts; there were also caste tribunals. Gradually, though, as Leue notes, "the original lack of interest in the life of the non-European communities turned into a deliberate legal dualism."[6] The early experiments in dualism featured some interesting hybrid forms. In 1654, the "choultry" judges were made Company servants. When the Charter of 1661 established the authority of the governor and Council of the settlements over criminal and civil matters, their jurisdiction included Company servants and nonofficial Europeans. The Madras Mayor's Court, a municipal court established in 1688, was initially staffed by both European and indigenous judges. One rationale for this arrangement was to curtail administrative costs. In 1692, the Company asked that the number of English aldermen on the Mayor's Court be reduced and local elites used to replace them. The report came back that there was a shortage of suitable locals to serve; "the Armenians refused to accept the office, the Jews qualified for it had left Madras, the Portuguese were unwilling to officiate for fear of their countrymen settled in St. Thomé, and it was not safe to confide in the Musselman."[7] Some forty years later, after mayors' courts were established for the three English Presidency towns of Madras, Bombay, and Calcutta, the practice of mixing English legal

[6] J.J. Leue, "Legal Expansion in the Age of the Companies: Aspects of the Administration of Justice in the English and Dutch Settlements of Maritime Asia, c. 1600–1750," p. 134. The rest of this paragraph draws on Leue's description of early legal policy by the British in India.

[7] C. Fawcett, *The First Century of British Justice in India,* quoted in Leue, "Legal Expansion in the Age of the Companies," p. 136.

personnel – the poorly qualified "merchant-judges" of the Company – with non-English officials disappeared.[8] Leue attributes this shift in the 1720s to the desire of English Company servants to have access to courts whose judgments on property transfers would be recognized and upheld in England, where the mayors' courts were awarded the status of king's courts. A perusal of the case logs of the mayors' courts shows that non-English residents of the settlements came before it in much greater numbers than did English litigants. This "popularity" of English justice is difficult to interpret, however.[9] Some Indians certainly used English courts as alternatives to other forums, and they may have done so for similar reasons – the desire for enforceable judgments, for example. They acted, though, in what was still a very fluid legal order. The status of Indian legal subjects had yet to be spelled out, Indian legal sources had an ambiguous standing in the mayors' courts, where English law was applied but local custom sometimes taken into consideration, and the relationship of English law courts to the various indigenous forums remained uncertain.

Resolving the ambiguity of such questions gained a new urgency when, continuing the British strategy of inserting themselves in the Mughal governance and revenue system, the BEIC assumed the official Mughal post of Diwani for the regions of Bengal, Bihar, and Orissa in 1765. This move made the BEIC responsible for the administration of justice in a large and populous area. Some Company officials were sufficiently outraged by what they characterized as the corruption of Mughal justice, particularly the injustices produced by the concentration of revenue and judicial functions in the hands of the *zamindars* (Mughal revenue collectors), that they advocated imposing closer British control of all courts. But the BEIC was reluctant to assume the burden of direct

---

[8] The label "merchant-judges" is from Fawcett, *The First Century of British Justice in India*, quoted by Leue in "Legal Expansion in the Age of the Companies." The term is useful in that it reminds us that the foremost priority of the Company officials who served as judges was to profit in trade and return, fortunes made, to England.

[9] Many of these were criminal cases. The courts were so overwhelmed by litigation that both caste leaders and Company officials advocated limiting access for indigenous litigants. In 1753, the jurisdiction of the courts over cases involving indigenous litigants was restricted, requiring unanimous acceptance by all parties of the court's authority. The measure did not satisfy caste leaders, who noted that litigants continued to find ways to use the courts. See A.F.T. Reyes, "English and French Approaches to Personal Laws in South India, 1700–1850." See also Leue, "Legal Expansion in the Age of the Companies," pp. 140–41. For a critical discussion of the view that English courts were "popular" with Indians, see Pamela Price, "The 'Popularity' of the Imperial Courts of Law: Three Views of the Anglo-Indian Encounter."

administration and hesitant to pose such an explicit challenge to Mughal rule. Beginning with Hastings's important judicial reforms in 1772 and lasting, with some changes, until 1860, legal policy was consistent with the broader British strategy in India of overlaying British authority on existing, or re-created, Mughal structures of governance.

The relationship of indigenous and British forums, and indigenous and British legal practitioners, was specified in the 1772 reforms. A plan drawn up by Warren Hastings created two courts for each of the districts. One court, the Diwani Adalat, was to handle civil cases, while a second court, the Foujdari Adalat, was to oversee trials for crimes and misdemeanors. The revenue collectors of each district were to preside over the civil courts, thus consolidating in British hands control over revenue and property disputes. The civil courts would apply Muslim law to Muslims, and Hindu law to Hindus. The criminal courts would apply Muslim law universally. An appellate structure was also created, with one of two courts at Calcutta to hear appeals from inferior civil courts.

Though British (Company) officials would preside in civil courts, the system built in formal and informal roles for Mughal officials. In a move that was purely pragmatic, zamindars were allowed to maintain jurisdiction over local, petty disputes. They had no formal rights to such jurisdiction, but the system simply would not function effectively without their playing a role they had assumed in the Mughal system. The criminal country courts continued to be operated entirely by Mughal officers, and in the civil courts, Muslim and Hindu legal experts were given monthly salaries as Company employees for their work in advising on local and religious law.

This system was unstable from the outset. One set of disruptive pressures was economic. Because revenue collection and legal administration were so closely intertwined, it became necessary to adjust jurisdictional boundaries continually to maximize British profits and protect client elites. Hastings's initial plan already formally distinguished zamindars and *talukaris* – both types of rent farmers in the Mughal system – from other Indians. Disputes involving successions of these revenue farmers were assigned to the exclusive jurisdiction of the president and Council at Fort William. But Company officials continued to be worried about potential interference by district courts in matters that would have an impact on revenue collection. The whole structure of the "country courts" was altered again in 1773, when six large divisions were created, each containing districts within it and having a chief and a Provincial Council. Each Council oversaw a Court of Civil Judicature, which was to be presided over, in monthly rotation, by one of the Council members. The Council could, in addition, hear appeals from district courts or could choose to hear suits directly.[10] Superintendents of revenue (who had now replaced collectors) could not call revenue farmers without obtaining the permission of the chief and Council.

While the British were creating a special legal status for rent farmers, Indian elites were themselves quickly learning to manipulate the new legal system to further their own interests. Englishmen sent out in various capacities to the districts had little contact with Indians other than their servants and subordinates. The benefits to Indians of becoming attached to an English Company official were magnified as a result. Many officials relied on Indians for personal credit, and all relied on them for information – about local affairs, revenue matters, and, of course, the administration of justice.[11] Indians used these positions of influence astutely. A striking example is found in the wake of the Permanent Settlement Act in 1793, when flexible taxes were converted into fixed revenue payments by the English and "estates" were created where before only proprietary rights to collect revenue had been recognized. Many low-level tax collectors and clerks became wealthy through their access to land and revenue records, which brought them advance knowledge of which estates would be sold for being in arrears and allowed them even to force properties to sale.[12] British preferential treatment thus combined with the entrepreneurial actions of local elites to create groups whose status was inexactly captured by the system in place and whose maneuvers promoted both formal and informal revision.

Economic interests also blended with political pressures to create instability in the legal order. By the 1770s, tensions were mounting between Parliament and the East India Company. The extravagant fortunes being made by Company officials were helping to fuel sentiment that there was something improper about a profit-making enterprise having so much power in the East. The Company's accession in 1765 to the Diwani of Bengal, Bihar, and Orissa had also altered the role of the Company, which was now assuming governmental functions for a

---

[10] When the collectors were recalled, the district courts were presided over by Naibs.

[11] For a more detailed discussion of European dependence on Indian attendants for knowledge, credit, and translation, see Bernard Cohn, *Colonialism and Its Forms of Knowledge: The British in India*; and Bernard Cohn, "The British in Benares: A Nineteenth-Century Colonial Society."

[12] This occurred in Bengal. See Rajat Ray and Ratna Ray, "Zamindars and Jotedars: A Study of Rural Politics in Bengal."

much larger territory, and authority over a much larger Indian population. Good government seemed an impossibility given the Company's
interest in profit.

The result was the Regulating Act passed by Parliament in 1773.
Among other changes in administration, the act created the Supreme
Court of Judicature at Fort William. The court was to administer British
law to British subjects, Company employees (including Indians), and
others who wished to submit to its jurisdiction. Creation of the court was
intended to respond to pressures to rein in the Company and establish
some sovereign presence in India without, at the same time, challenging
Mughal authority. The act also established a governor-general – Warren
Hastings was named to this post – and four councillors to comprise the
Presidency of Fort William. The governor-general and Council would
issue rules and regulations that were "just and agreeable to the laws of
England."[13]

The creation of the Supreme Court made the jumble of jurisdictions still more complex. Over the next decade, participation in jurisdictional politics was obligatory. Company officials saw the presence of
the Supreme Court, which had unique authority to act independently
of the Company, as a political threat.[14] The president and Council at
Fort William had been awarded supervision over the country courts,

---

[13] The composition of this Council immediately created problems because it contained a
majority of four councillors who were not Company officials and not only had no loyalty
to the Company but were highly critical of its operation and of Hastings's leadership
in particular. The anti-Hastings majority, under the intellectual leadership of Philip
Francis, imposed policies that Hastings opposed and investigated his past actions in a
search for evidence of improprieties. The two sides were embroiled in a bitter rivalry
that colored every issue before them, including legal policy, on which Hastings and
Francis held different views, with Hastings favoring increasing British control of the
courts and Francis wishing to revert to a dual system of governance in which the Nawab
would have greater legal administrative independence. See below. For a full account
of the rivalry that is strongly pro-Hastings, see P. Moon, *Warren Hastings and British
India*. For an analysis of the intellectual differences between Hastings and Francis, see
R. Guha, *A Rule of Property for Bengal*.

[14] The rift between the court and the Council did not emerge immediately, in large part
because of Hastings's long-standing friendship with the Supreme Court's chief justice,
Elijah Impey. In fact, Hastings used the court, and Impey, to help defeat a prominent
Indian who had been helping the rival majority within the Council by providing them
with information (some of it trumped up) about improprieties of Company rule. Probably under Hastings's informal prompting, the Supreme Court accelerated consideration
of a forgery charge against Nandakumar, who was convicted and condemned to death.
The sentence, though not particularly harsh by British standards, was unusual in the
atmosphere of political intrigue and corruption, and it served as an eloquent statement
of Hastings's continuing power and the strengthened legal authority of the British.

and clashes with the Supreme Court were inevitable. Furthermore, uncertainty about the jurisdiction of the Supreme Court was present from the beginning. The court was given a mandate to rule over matters involving British subjects and Company employees. This meant that for the first time, a British court was extending jurisdiction directly, and not through the auspices of the Mughal administration, into the provinces. Yet, by not claiming full sovereignty, the charter left open the question of the court's authority over other indigenous inhabitants. It did not specifically exclude them from its jurisdiction, because it allowed that individuals who were neither British subjects nor Company employees could file suit in the court and fall within its jurisdiction if both parties to the suit were amenable. Further, the act and charter offered no clear definition of a Company employee. This vagueness was significant because in the layered system of rent farming, it was often quite difficult to determine when an individual was acting for the Company, with a portion of the revenue retained as salary, and when he was acting as an independent agent. A Supreme Court defendant who did not believe the court had jurisdiction over him had only one option: "to appear before it, and plead to its jurisdiction to secure an exemption from its jurisdiction."[15]

If the uncertainty of jurisdictional boundaries was built into the legal order, it was intensified by the actions of plaintiffs, who quickly learned legal strategies that pitted one court against the other. Even from the days of the Calcutta Mayor's Court, Indians had shown a tendency to litigate in British courts. Forum shopping was, of course, not a novel response to colonialism but a feature of the existing plural legal landscape. The possibility of obtaining less open-ended judgments may have accounted for some of the attraction. The aims of English courts were clearly different from some indigenous forums, where the return to sociability was often viewed as an outcome that was at least as important as arriving at just remedies.[16] British observers were, in turn, often puzzled or outraged by local legal proceedings that seemed to them lax and corrupt but that undoubtedly had more complex meanings.[17] For example, the common practice of qadis of charging both plaintiff and defendant for judgment

---

[15] See B.B. Misra, *The Judicial Administration of the East India Company in Bengal, 1765–82.*

[16] Rosen comments on the importance of this outcome in the operation of a qadi court in Morocco in *The Anthropology of Justice.*

[17] For an account of the Residency System that sent Company officials to the provinces, where they observed and commented on legal practices without much knowledge or understanding of Mughal institutions or local practice, see Michael Fisher, *Indirect Rule in India: Residents and the Residency System, 1764–1858.*

in a case struck the British as corrupt, but the practice may have been partly understood as a way of penalizing both sides for allowing conflict to escalate and returning both parties to the community without the aggravating stigma of "loser" attached to either side.[18] In some places, British officials were surely right that zamindars were using the courts to collect "arbitrary fines." But British motives were less than pure. One supervisor dispatched to the countryside reported in 1770 that the real problem with fines was that they acted as "a great check to industry by preventing those who had money from employing it with freedom"; he was concerned mainly that by hiding wealth Indians would also succeed in reducing the revenue arriving in British hands.[19]

Finally, there were pressures that emerged from the day-to-day functioning of the hybrid legal system. The articulation of the various courts created categories of people with "middling" roles and ambiguous status. Perhaps the best example were the vakils, or pleaders. Vakils had existed under Mughal rule, but they had acted mainly as personal agents advising and negotiating for their clients. In 1793, a formal role was established for vakils to represent clients before the court. Procedures were set up that required plaintiffs and defendants to hire vakils, who would write out complaints, defenses, and counterarguments in Persian. Oral testimony and direct pleading by participants or their allies – standard procedures in Indian courts – were greatly reduced.[20] Vakils were viewed with disdain by the British and criticized for their lack of legal training and "un-English" behavior in court (e.g., stylized forms of pleading and exaggerated deference). But by the middle of the nineteenth century vakils were seen as essential to the operation of the system and worth preserving, even strengthening, as a professional group – and they fought, too, for professional status.[21]

The ambiguous status of Muslim and Hindu legal experts was troubling to the English, too. English judges (most of whom had little

---

[18] See Rosen, *The Anthropology of Justice.*

[19] The British Library, India Office Records (IOR): G/27/1 ff. 530–550, Letter from G.C. Ducarell, 13 December 1770 (I have modernized capitalization in this quote and in others from the IOR).

[20] Formalizing the role of vakils did not transform court proceedings overnight. Misra (*Judicial Administration of the East India Company*) reports a case brought before the Provincial Council at Murshidabad and settled in 1779, in which vakils, parties to the case, and even the father of one of the participants appeared as pleaders with no apparent procedural order.

[21] For a study of the professionalization of the vakils in Madras, see John Jeya Paul, "Vakils of Madras, 1802–1928: The Rise of the Modern Legal Profession in South India."

or no legal training and even less knowledge of the local population) were charged with applying Hindu law to Hindus, and Muslim law to Muslims in the Diwani courts, and they were to rely on salaried court officials (*maulavis* for Muslim law and *pandits* for Hindu law) to instruct them. These court officers were distrusted from the start; in fact, a disproportionate effort of English legal experts in India in the late eighteenth century was devoted to translating Hindu legal texts so that judges would not have to take the word of court officials.[22] The result was reification, and rampant misinterpretation, of Hindu and Muslim law, and over time the effect was to allow English law and the common law practice of referring to precedents to alter indigenous law to make it more English. There were also more direct paths to the same end. British judges were permitted to contradict any Indian law they found to be contrary to "justice, equity, and good conscience."[23] Even when it was not exercised, this option established British law as dominant and Indian law as subordinate, a hierarchy that seemed to contradict the carefully designed separation of jurisdictions (and the initial reluctance of the British to meddle at all in criminal courts).

The "virtues" that British officials found in Indian law were also the result of misinterpretation. The British expressed admiration for Hindu and Muslim law as examples of written law, in contrast to oral legal traditions they had encountered elsewhere. But in translating Hindu texts and using them as codes, the British were distorting Hindu legal practices, which relied a good deal on oral transmission of normative judgments. The confusion stemmed also, in no small part, from British perceptions that Hindu law was "religious law" and could be separated as personal law from other forms of law. This assumption allowed the British to design a plural legal order that replicated the main features of European jurisdictional boundaries between canon and state law. But few Hindus thought of Hindu law as personal law in this way – as separable from community standards or applicable only to certain categories of actions.[24]

While in the late eighteenth century, the British thus sought to craft an administration that incorporated Mughal bureaucratic forums and

[22] For a detailed account of the efforts to codify Hindu law by translating Hindu texts for use by English judges, see Derrett, "The Ministration of Hindu Law by the British." See also Cohn, *Colonialism and Its Forms of Knowledge.*

[23] J.D.M. Derrett, "Justice, Equity, and Good Conscience."

[24] Derrett, "The Ministration of Hindu Law by the British." And for a recent, clear exposition of these assumptions, see Richard Lariviere, "Justices and *Panditas*: Some Ironies in Contemporary Readings of the Hindu Past."

officials, established procedural order and an appellate structure, and reserved sufficient authority for the Company so that revenue collection would not be affected, the order put in place to achieve these goals had, in operation, many of the features the British had criticized in Mughal law. Corruption was still widespread. A jumble of jurisdictions invited complex legal strategizing, blurred cultural boundaries, and called attention to the glaring contradictions of British claims to partial sovereignty.

Examining a single case will help to clarify just how pervasive these tensions were. The case described in the next section is instructive because, though it concerned the inheritance of one estate in a distant province, it briefly became the centerpiece of debates about colonial legal policy and the focus of tensions between the Company and the Supreme Court in the years after the court was established. To some contemporary observers, the case pointed out the inherent instability of the hybrid legal order and reinforced calls for expanding claims of British legal authority.

QADI JUSTICE

In 1776, a wealthy rent farmer of Patna, Shahbaz Beg, died without an heir.[25] The death itself was in no way remarkable; by all accounts, Shahbaz Beg's life had been long and successful, including a comfortable old age in Patna, his adopted home. He had come from Kabul, where he still had family, and he had obtained a military command under the East India Company.[26] Military service had made him wealthy. But Shahbaz

---

[25] The heading of this section, "qadi justice," echoes Weber's use of the term *kadijustiz* to refer to an ideal type of justice that is arbitrary and relatively unconstrained by rules. Case studies of the functioning of qadi courts contradict the image of adjudication that is not rule bound. In an analysis of the handling of a case from fourteenth-century Morocco, David S. Powers argues that the qadi in the case pursued reasoned justifications for his ruling and "focused on substantive legal doctrines and on the factual similarities and differences with prior cases" (David S. Powers, "*Kadijustiz* or Qadi Justice? A Paternity Dispute from Fourteenth-Century Morocco"). See also Rosen, *The Justice of Islam*. The case presented in this section reminds us that Weber's use of the term *kadijustiz* drew on a long tradition of representing Islamic justice as more arbitrary and less rational than law in the West, even though Weber intended the term as an analytical category.

[26] Some of the new Muslim elite in Bengal and the surrounding region were converts, but others were Muslims who had moved, from the earliest days of the Mughal conquest, from the northwest to settle in Bengal and surrounding territories. See Eaton, *The Rise of Islam and the Bengal Frontier*.

Beg was more than just a client of the English; he had also obtained a land grant from the Mughal emperor. He was a product of his times and of a confluence of cultures: a Muslim freelance who had found opportunity in the encounter between Mughal and European power and had succeeded in obtaining the patronage of both powers.

Shahbaz Beg had no heirs, and his death raised the question of who would be the beneficiary of his considerable wealth and who would assume the responsibilities (and profits) of revenue collection on his lands. Shahbaz Beg's nephew, Bahadur Beg, had been brought to Patna from Kabul, had married his uncle's sister-in-law, and had lived with the family in the hopes of inheriting the estate. A month or two after Shahbaz Beg died, his nephew filed a petition with the Court of the Provincial Council in Patna, to lay claim to the estate. In the petition, Bahadur Beg asserted that "Mirza Shaw Bauz Beg sent for me from Kabool, and said to me, you are my brother's son. There is no difference between my brother's son and a son; I make you the master of my house. . . . Thus is known to everybody, and the English gentleman also knew it, that he made [me] his heir, and the representative of himself."[27] The nephew complained that Shahbaz Beg's widow, Naderah Begam, was making off with goods from the house and asked that all the effects of the estate be secured and that the qadi be asked to investigate and establish Bahadur Beg's right to the estate.

The English officials in Patna seem to have known Shahbaz Beg and his nephew, hardly surprising given their standing and Shahbaz Beg's ties to the Company. The Court of the Provincial Council quickly directed the qadi and mufti (the legal scholar) of the court to make an inventory of all the property in the estate (with a representative of the widow present) and to secure it. Choosing language that was later to prove troublesome for the nephew's case, the court asked for a written report that would establish "according to ascertained facts and legal justice" who was entitled to which portions of the estate under Muslim law.[28]

From the perspective of the court, all was going as it should. A case of succession had been referred to Muslim court officials for their advice. Less than a month later, the officials presented their report, which included a *fatwa*, or a legal ruling under Muslim law. It outlined no proofs in favor of the nephew's claim, but it challenged evidence presented by

[27] IOR: P/166/82.
[28] IOR: P/166/82.

the widow. She had produced two documents, a deed of transfer and a deed of gift (both sometimes referred to as "wills" in British documents) that named her as the beneficiary. The qadi and muftis agreed with Bahadur Beg that the documents were forgeries. A few witnesses were examined – except for one, all were deposed by way of notes sent to them and oral reports brought back by couriers. The qadi and muftis concluded that the documents were drawn up and witnessed after Shahbaz Beg's death and stamped with his seal, which the widow had refused to relinquish. No evidence in support of the nephew's claim was reviewed. The report recommended awarding three-quarters of the estate to the nephew and one-quarter to the widow. A larger share for the widow could not be expected under Muslim law, they reported.

How this settlement was enforced was later to become a subject of dispute. But all parties agreed that the widow had been forced to move from room to room of the house while the inventory of goods was taken, and that she had finally left and had taken refuge in a local shrine. There the court posted sepoys to prevent her from coming and going. She still had with her Shahbaz Beg's seal and the land grant papers. The accusation of forgery was presented to the Foujdari (criminal) court, and five of the widow's closest supporters, including a nephew who had served as her vakil after a hasty appointment under pressure from the law officers, were arrested and held for the alleged forgery of the deeds.

The court's ruling, and the harsh actions taken to enforce it, would probably have gone unremarked, and maybe even uncontested, in a less complex judicial landscape. But the widow still had allies, and she still had several avenues for an appeal. Her brother-in-law smuggled out a message of appeal to the governor-general at Fort William. Not long after, the sepoys were removed, though it is not clear on whose orders. But the widow remained at the shrine, still without the inheritance she claimed was her due. Naderah Begam then filed a complaint through an English attorney in the Supreme Court (now barely three years old) against Bahadur Beg, the qadi, and the two muftis for assault and battery, false imprisonment, and personal injuries. She complained especially of the indignity of having to undergo a body search and demanded restitution in the amount of six hundred thousand rupees.

The widow's informal appeal to the governor-general had been to the authority immediately above the Patna court in the Company's judicial hierarchy. The Supreme Court was a different matter. It was independent of the rest of the court system and was charged with administering not Muslim or Hindu law, but English law. The court had already been at odds with the governor-general and Council, and the justices must have seen in the Patna case an opportunity to solidify their authority. The response to the widow's complaint was to issue a warrant for the arrest of Bahadur Beg, the qadi, and the two muftis, and to dispatch a sheriff to Patna to take them into custody.

Hastings and his four councillors at Fort William were outraged. The qadi and the muftis, they noted, were officers of the court and so salaried employees of the Company. They were being arrested for having followed the directives of the Patna court to recommend a settlement in a case where Muslim law was to be applied. For Hastings and the others, the actions of the Supreme Court threatened the very ability of the Company to maintain order, since it could not guarantee protection to salaried officials working under the direction of English superiors on matters of justice. Hastings insisted that the Council take the unusual risk of posting bail for the defendants and indemnifying them (on behalf of the Company) in the amount of four hundred thousand rupees.

Jurisdictional boundaries were at the center of the controversy. There was the narrow jurisdictional question about the scope of the Supreme Court's authority in the case. The court was supposed to have jurisdiction over English subjects and Company officials.[29] The qadi and muftis, though also Mughal officials, received salaries from the Company; even Hastings, who would have liked to have been able to argue that the Supreme Court had no jurisdiction over them, recognized that it did. Less clear was whether the same could be said for Bahadur Beg, who was in the ambiguous position of many other rent farmers in the Mughal territories now under Company rule: They were not salaried employees, but they were an integral, indispensable part of the Company's revenue-collecting system. Hastings and other Company officials feared legal policies that might expose revenue farmers as a class to litigation and so potentially disrupt collections. Further, the case called into question whether the scheme envisioned by Hastings and others – a complex

---

[29] The Company's lawyers questioned, too, whether the widow's petition should have been considered by the Supreme Court. "She is not a British subject. She never was a Servant of the Company." The court to which she was certainly amenable was the local district court at Patna. More broadly, Company lawyers argued that the statute establishing the Supreme Court made it explicitly separate from the country courts, over which it was to have no control. The arguments were developed in the Law Council and presented in a brief in 1778 (IOR: P/166/80).

intertwining of Muslim, Hindu, and British authority in a patchwork legal order – could work at all. Philip Francis, one of the members of the Council at Fort William and a vocal critic of Hastings, voiced the opinion that nothing less than a declaration of British sovereignty in the British-controlled territories (combined with the devolution of administrative rule to Mughal authorities) would solve the problems of the hybrid system.[30] Though Francis was in fact championing a model of dual rule that belonged to the days before Hastings's tenure, he was also anticipating a move toward more clearly established British hegemony that would come much later, after many more cases like the Patna cause had strained the system of multiple authorities.

Bound up with the jurisdictional dispute in the Patna case, too, were other conflicts about boundaries – real and perceived distinctions between Muslim and English legal actors. For one thing, British officials did not quite know what to make of Naderah Begam, the widow. At times, they portrayed her as a schemer who was consciously acting the part of a helpless, aggrieved woman as a matter of strategy. Evan Law, the chief of the Council at Patna, complained, "The widow's representations, of being turned out of the house, is wholly groundless: She was repeatedly told to stay there full security; but dissatisfied with the defeat her schemes had with, she . . . quitted the house *to make her condition more pitiable.*"[31] Yet British officers also found it difficult if not impossible to believe that a woman, especially a Muslim woman, would be capable of such sophisticated legal maneuvering:

> The women of this country, and particularly the Musulman women, are, from their confined situation, bred up in too much ignorance and subjection to be capable of judging or acting for themselves; they become in consequence merely tools in the hands of their vaqueels, and neither fare better or worse, which ever side succeeds in the contest. On this account there seems much reason in the custom of their being required to live under the protection of the next male heir.[32]

A further difference in the case turned on the question of whether the widow had appointed her nephew as her vakil or not. She claimed she had merely sent him to appear before the legal officers, whereupon he had been appointed vakil by the qadi, thus throwing doubt on

[30] Guha (*A Rule of Property for Bengal*) offers an extended analysis of the political differences between Hastings and Francis.
[31] Emphasis added. IOR: P/166/79.
[32] IOR: P/166/79.

whether he was in fact legally her agent. The defense countered that the appointment had taken place in close accordance with local custom, whereby women sent male relatives to court where they were formally recognized as legal representatives.

Further complicating matters was the widow's refusal to let her slave women be questioned by the law officers. Hastings felt certain that the slave women would know the truth about whether the wills were real or forged, and whether the widow had been forced out or had left her house. He wondered why the women had not simply been compelled to testify and suggested that women could be employed by the court, as they were in other regions, to search the widow and to interrogate the slave women. The British were caught simultaneously pleading the inability of Muslim women to tell the truth while arguing that the women in their testimony "would alone bring proof of the facts."[33] Hastings tried resolving this contradiction by offering unusual praise for Muslim law for holding that "the testimony of two women is only equal to that of one man."[34]

If the British were uncertain about how to regard the plaintiff and her allies, they were even more contradictory in their assessment of the qadi and muftis. Hastings and the other Company officials rose to their defense on the grounds that these men were officers of the Company and employed by the courts. Yet they did not want to suggest that these officers were the same as British officials. There was no question, for example, that their actions would not conform to the high procedural standards of British justice. On first learning about the case, Hastings acknowledged that the procedure for deposing witnesses by note was unorthodox, but, he noted, local proceedings were generally "in some degree defective in point of form and precision."[35] As it gradually became apparent that the Supreme Court case was likely to be decided on the basis of procedural irregularities, Company officials began to point out that the role that had been assigned to the qadi and muftis might be nearly impossible for them to play.

The procedural questions turned on a distinction between fact-finding and legal interpretation. In the way the plural legal order was structured, Muslim legal experts were supposed to report simply their

---

[33] IOR: P/166/79. British officials speculated that the women lied because their inexperience left them without "a *sense of religion* or a knowledge of the Laws and *a dread of the punishment* . . . against perjury" (emphasis in the original).

[34] IOR: P/166/79.

[35] IOR: P/166/79.

findings in Muslim *law*. The task of ascertaining the *facts* was to fall to British judges. Thus in the Patna case, the qadi and muftis had seemingly overstepped their duties when they had investigated the authenticity of the deeds. Rather than allowing English judges to examine witnesses in open court and determine whether their testimony was truthful, the Muslim law officers had drawn their own conclusions about the facts. The Supreme Court judges worried that the district court was placed in the role of merely confirming the qadi's findings. The arrangement suggested that "black officers" were somehow more suited than "English gentlemen conversant in the language of the country" in uncovering and establishing the facts of a case, an assertion the judges could not accept. One wrote, "I am convinced to the contrary that principles of justice are deeper rooted in the minds of my own countrymen than in the corrupt natives of this country" and especially, he added, in "such natives as are generally attendant as officers on courts of justice."[36]

As the principal architect of the plural legal order and now a defender of the Muslim law officers, Hastings was clearly troubled by this turn in the case. Could legal rulings be neatly separated from the task of fact-finding, as the rules of the plural legal order required? Hastings and other Company officials pointed out that the qadi, in addition to his duties interpreting Muslim law for the Council Court, presided over the Foujdari court on criminal matters, where he was routinely called upon to make "life and death" decisions. There he was not required to avoid fact-finding and limit himself to legal interpretation. The inconsistency in permitting him this role in one case and requiring an entirely different legal personality and function in another seemed clear. Further, Company lawyers argued, it would be simply unworkable to require the small staff of perhaps "200–300 Englishmen" to try all disputes. And would justice result? The Company argued that "it requires a knowledge of the law to try the fact, and to discover the points that are material to the cause, and upon which the law turns."[37] Yet, as the Commissioner of Laws advising Hastings pointed out, the Supreme Court justices would technically be right in finding that the qadi and muftis had usurped some of the functions of the English judges in the Patna case.

For British officials, interpreting the actions of a plaintiff who was a Muslim woman and a Muslim judge who was not permitted to judge required answering broader questions about the legal standing

[36] IOR: P/166/82.
[37] IOR: P/166/82.

of Muslims. On the one hand, British officials commenting on the Patna case argued fine points of evidence in the case and, in doing so, they emphasized familiar criteria. For example, the Commissioner of Laws noted that the widow's complaint to the Supreme Court was a *sworn* statement; it is unclear whether he found the statement believable, but he understood that the Supreme Court justices would surely be influenced by such an oath. On the other hand, the officials reminded each other again and again that the evidence and testimony of Muslim witnesses had to be weighed *differently*. Evan Law argued that, even though five witnesses had sworn to the deeds establishing Naderah Begam's claim to the estate, "the little regard that is paid to oaths in this country renders easy the proof of any deed, as far as it depends on a number of witnesses."[38] The argument might have relied on differences of the role of oaths in legal practice in the two systems of law, but it was made instead in a way that emphasized deep cultural differences. The Company reminded justices in a 1778 brief that "the credit due to an oath depends on our believing that the person who swears is impressed with a sense of religion, or a knowledge of the laws, and a dread of the punishment . . . against perjury."[39] Even the defense, then, fighting to establish the competence of Indian legal officers, agreed that Indians were fundamentally different kinds of subjects before the law.

The Patna case was unusual only in that it held the attention of Hastings and other high Company officials for so long and came to symbolize the tensions between two British courts, and between two visions of colonial law. In other cases in the provinces, British observers complained of the corruption and lax procedures of Muslim courts, clearly often misinterpreting some of what they saw and emphasizing the same virtues of British justice, in particular its procedural purity.[40] Hastings and Francis articulated two possible solutions: fine-tune the existing plural legal order to isolate indigenous legal practice, or declare all Indians in British territories to be British subjects. Oddly, the second solution ultimately emerged out of a practice designed to promote the first.

If we were to focus on this outcome, though, we might lose sight of how open-ended the process seemed to participants in the eighteenth century. In the Patna case, jurisdictional lines were hotly contested. They

---

[38] IOR: P/166/79.
[39] IOR: P/166/80.
[40] See Misra (*Judicial Administration of the East India Company*) for examples of these observations by British supervisors.

were also closely tied to changing views about cultural boundaries. Further, the debates were not forced simply by the disagreement of different factions of colonial administrators representing different interests. In this and other cases, the contradictions of legal policy were made apparent by the actions of litigants. Without the widow's complaint to the Supreme Court, and without the qadi's actions, the flaws of the plural legal order would have been much less apparent to British officials in the 1770s.

For Naderah Begam, the rewards of litigiousness were anything but abstract. The Supreme Court took ten days to try the case and decided in her favor, awarding her three hundred thousand rupees – half the damages she had claimed but still an enormous sum. Anticipating that the case would turn against the defendants and that the Company alone would be held responsible for the payment of damages if they fled, the Supreme Council under Hastings decided to seize the defendants not long after having maneuvered to get them freed. The qadi made an eloquent statement about the injustice of his imprisonment by dying on the way from Patna to Fort William for the trial. The other three defendants remained in jail until 1781, when they were freed to await an unsuccessful appeal that dragged on until 1789. The widow meanwhile continued her demonstration of legal acumen by suing the chief and two members of the Provincial Council at Patna, and securing a ruling for them to pay an additional fifteen thousand rupees to her. None of Hastings's ominous predictions about the consequences of arresting the qadi and muftis came to pass – there was no rebellion in Patna, no general breakdown in administration, no chaos – but the lessons of the case were surely not lost on those Indians who knew about it. Those lessons were not so much that British authority should be opposed, but that it was fragmented and flawed. The maze of jurisdictions and of rules governing legal roles could be seen as a dangerous web that could entrap even Indians working with and for the British, or as a map showing the weaknesses of British colonial rule.[41]

The Patna case illustrates well the ways in which the interaction of colonial policy debates and the strategies of indigenous litigants produced a strengthening of state authority that neither side precisely embraced or predicted. The Patna widow mirrored the actions of many other Indians who discovered in the fragmented and complex

---

[41] In this sense, the outcome of this case reinforced the message implied in the Nandakumar trial. See note 14 above.

architecture of colonial rule an opportunity to defeat local representatives of rule by appealing to more distant authorities. These repeated appeals to the highest representatives of imperial authority helped to solidify the place for a legal authority that was neither seated in the metropolis nor immediately dependent for its legitimacy on its standing in local politics. The paradox of pursuing anticolonial strategies that reinforced colonial rule must have been as apparent to participants as it was unavoidable. At the same time, as colonial agents disputed their relative authority, their debates highlighted procedural precision as the main distinguishing feature of imposed law. As we see in Hastings's response to the Patna case, the British claim of procedural purity effectively separated indigenous litigants and legal personnel from Europeans, who were represented as culturally conditioned to observe the sanctity of court rules.[42] Ceding legal authority to the Supreme Court was made bearable for Hastings precisely because the loss turned on a technicality, and this indicated that system rules, even if flawed, were being followed. In the confluence of political and legal maneuvering, the colonial state was slowly taking shape.

STATE HEGEMONY

The half century or so following the Patna case marked a shift toward much more aggressive claims for British legal hegemony. These claims came piecemeal, and often in response to very specific conditions, and they continued to be weighed, especially after the rebellion of 1857, against considerations of the political and economic costs of expanding judicial administration and authority. Much attention has been given by scholars to the British decision in 1829 to abolish *sati*, or Hindu widow burning, and the legalization by the British in 1856 of remarriage by Hindu widows.[43] These moves were held up after 1857 as examples of excessive intervention through the law in social regulation on a grand scale. But less symbolically charged initiatives that received less comment were perhaps more important in establishing the principle of state legal and political control. Three such trends were increasing British

---

[42] The Company's own lawyer, in advising Hastings and the Council not to pursue an appeal, blamed the confusion in the case on "the feeble, abject, and depraved state of the native mind in this country" (IOR: P/166/82).

[43] See Dagmar Engels, "Wives, Widows, and Workers: Women and the Law in Colonial India"; and Lata Mani, "The Production of Official Discourse on *Sati* in Early-Nineteenth-Century Bengal."

control over criminal law, greater direct supervision of policing, and efforts to establish tighter British rule in "frontier" areas that fell within British-controlled jurisdictions. These trends often were mutually reinforcing. For example, in the early decades of the nineteenth century, the British moved to tighten control of the mountainous regions of Bengal, Madras, and western India where hill peoples had continued to enjoy semiautonomy and somewhat volatile patron-client ties to settled groups. Now, for outward reasons that ranged from outrage at practices such as human sacrifice (among the Konds, in the northern part of the Madras Presidency) to the need to control banditry that was disrupting revenue collection (in the hills of the western Deccan), the British reacted strongly to claims of autonomy and moved to assert legal control. More broadly, the problem of rural violence – itself intensified by disruptions to the rural economy by British administration – assumed a new urgency. The British used the term *dacoity* to describe a range of forms of rural violence, including famine looting and gang raids, and even the more extreme forms that became more common in the mid-nineteenth century when whole villages were held and plundered. British efforts to suppress dacoity included the creation of a special provincial police force in 1858–59. The campaign helped to fuel sentiments among the British that some castes and communities were naturally given to crime. The 1871 Criminal Tribes Act provided for "tribes" to be registered, placed under surveillance, and resettled as needed if they were "addicted to the systematic commission of non-bailable offenses."[44] At the same time, then, that the British were extending and tightening their control, they were sharpening cultural distinctions between Indian groups viewed as docile or adapted to British rule, and who had been brought into the legal system as litigants and practitioners, and those who were "outside" the law.

This shift was clearly influenced by the rebellion of 1857, but it also predated that event and had a good deal to do with changes in the political economy of colonial India. Whereas in the late eighteenth century, the Company was focused on revenue collection and, much like the zamindars under the Mughals, used judicial authority to support revenue functions, by the mid-nineteenth century the British were beginning to view the economic value of India as residing in its potential as a market for British goods and in its production of raw materials and

---

[44] Quoted on p. 109 of Anand Yang, "Dangerous Castes and Tribes: The Criminal Tribes Act and the Magahiga Doms of Northeast India."

agricultural commodities. Judicial oversight of property transactions involving British interests rested solely in British-controlled courts. And British jurisdiction was in any case viewed as conducive of calm and therefore commerce. In fact, British trade, expanding British legal control, and Indian loyalty to the British empire were widely understood by colonial administrators as closely intertwined.[45] Establishing legal authority would make commerce possible; commerce would in turn solidify colonial rule.

In 1860, Indian law was codified and the role for Hindu and Muslim law restricted.[46] Over time, the influence of English law permeated indigenous legal forums, sources, and practices. Legal historians have consequently represented India as a case of nearly complete displacement of an indigenous legal system by a European legal order. The long historical process is described by Galanter as the "absorption" of indigenous law into "modern," British law, and by Cohn as a transition "from Indian status to British contract."[47] Though correct in its outlines, this narrative disguises the contested nature of these changes and the fragmented positions on both sides.[48] The particular form of legal pluralism that emerged in India in the late eighteenth century and into the nineteenth century was responding to a very complex mix of forces. On one side, the British used the law quite purposefully as a vehicle for the

[45] The comments of a British Commissioner during the campaign to bring the Konds under British legal authority were fairly typical. Bradstadter reports that he stressed the importance of bringing new goods to the Konds in order to gain their loyalty and ensure their dependence on the British. Edith Bradstadter, 1985, "Human Sacrifice and British Kond Relations, 1759–1862".

[46] A penal code was adopted in 1860 and a code of criminal procedure in 1861 with uniform application. These were soon followed by a code of civil procedure and the law of contracts.

[47] Marc Galanter, *Law and Society in Modern India*; Cohn, "The British in Benares"; Derrett, "The Ministration of Hindu Law by the British." For a useful overview of the approaches to the encounter of European and non-European law in India that summarizes the perspectives developed within legal history, the sociology of law, and cultural history, see Pamela G. Price, "The 'Popularity' of the Imperial Courts of Law."

[48] Support for this view of the open-endedness of legal change in India emerges in a comparison with Indonesia. Here similar forces urged the more energetic imposition of Dutch law in the nineteenth century. As in India, one response was to devise a formally plural system with a prominent role for adat law – which was, like Hindu law in India, misrepresented by Dutch legal reformers as a kind of personal religious law rather than the more complex mix of customary and Islamic legal elements. The dual system was subject to destabilizing pressures from within and also from metropolitan policy, but Dutch advocates for preserving and, ironically, codifying, adat law were able to deflect campaigns at centralization. See C. Fasseur, "Colonial Dilemma: Van Vollenhoven and the Struggle Between Adat Law and Western Law in Indonesia."

creation of the conditions they viewed as essential to Company profits and, later, capitalist enterprise – most conspicuously at first a market in land and later the territorial security that would permit the expansion of Indian production and markets. There was, however, no unity to proposals for legal reform. In pursuing reforms supportive of their interests, different British factions were also constructing (and responding to) representations of cultural difference. The law itself became associated with a presumed European cultural affinity for order, an association that was strengthened by jurisdictional complexity and the need for continual adjustments to legal procedure.

On the other side, the turns taken by legal reforms depended in large measure on existing Indian institutions and the response of Indians to British moves. Indian elites were differently situated to take advantage of the legal reforms. The new legal system both forged new elites and responded to their claims for equal treatment. The authority of the new courts was something that could not be imposed but was made, at several critical points, by Indian litigation in British-controlled forums, and by litigants' moves to exploit jurisdictional complexity to their own advantage. The strategic use of the law for short-term gains had the power to turn reforms whose results might have been fleeting into long-term institutional realities.

As a model for colonial legal policy elsewhere, the British experience in India was complex and confusing. In many ways the Indian legal order seemed idiosyncratic, the result of an unusual mix of well-developed legal traditions that shared formal recognition. The British themselves promoted a kind of "Indian exceptionalism" that exaggerated distinctions between India's written legal traditions and other non-Western legal systems, and, more generally, between the recognition of Asia's "ancient civilizations" and the assumption of backwardness elsewhere. This separation was reinforced by the structures of colonial governance that isolated the India Office from the Colonial Office.

Informal diffusion of what Cohn has called "modalities" of colonial knowledge – including and perhaps especially colonial law – did occur.[49] But the widespread move from a plural legal order toward a state-centered legal order did not result from metropolitan efforts to impose a uniform policy. We must look instead to the replay, with local variations, of a structurally similar legal politics.

[49] Cohn, *Colonialism and Its Forms of Knowledge*.

THE LEGAL LIMITS OF "ASSIMILATION"

In Africa as in Asia, Europeans were restricted for centuries in coastal enclaves and had rudimentary administrative structures and little influence on African institutions. The disease environment prolonged this situation into the second half of the nineteenth century. In the few places where enclaves encompassed large indigenous populations, as in Senegal, or where temperate climates permitted European settlement, as in the Cape, the dilemmas of rule were encountered early. Elsewhere, opportunities for exerting claims of legal jurisdiction were few. But the pattern of limited interaction began to change around the middle of the nineteenth century, then shifted rapidly in the last quarter of the century, as the competition among European powers for territorial rule propelled the extension of administrative control.

Europeans borrowed quite consciously from their prior experiences in the administration of justice in early colonies. For the English, this meant an explicit attempt to draw lessons from the experiences in India, South Africa, and the four enclaves under British control in West Africa. For the French, it meant building upon experiences in colonial Algeria and Senegal. Both powers discovered that existing models of administration had to be modified in the newly acquired African colonies. In a much-reduced span of time, we find a shift similar to the one in India: Local political conditions combined with international pressures to push toward a more clearly defined dominance of state law. Yet, in contrast to India, the explicit dominance of state law was what made legal pluralism possible as a colonial strategy. Indigenous law was recognized precisely when it was no longer considered to offer a true alternative to the power of the colonial state. Still, here as elsewhere, participants' perceptions of the open-endedness of this process and the variety of its patterns are notable. Jurisdictional politics again offered possibilities for using the complex structure of the legal order to advance group interests. And, again, the jurisdictional divides were understood not just as institutional structure but as markers of cultural and racial boundaries.

This jockeying was well under way earlier in the European footholds on the continent. Europeans in their few enclaves and settlements created courts to deal with cases involving Europeans, and they made different sets of rules depending on local conditions about whom else to include under this jurisdictional umbrella. These accommodations themselves created tensions, but they came under greater pressure to change as the territory and populations under European rule were forcefully expanded. In this process, the boundaries between colonized and colonizer, between black and white, between "traditional" and Westernized Africans – and between state-centered law and indigenous law – were redefined and sharpened.

It is commonplace to characterize British colonial policy as one of "indirect rule" and to contrast this strategy to France's "direct rule" and "assimilationist" policies. In matters of legal administration, this difference it clearly present, but its emphasis may also be misleading. The French Revolution established the expectation that culturally and racially different peoples would be worthy of French citizens' rights.[50] But in practice, citizenship status was very difficult to obtain. The vast majority of Africans and Asians in territories conquered by the French were considered mere "subjects." They administered "native" law in separate forums but were at the same time subject to the *indigénat*, or French administrative law, the demands of *corvée* labor, penal law, and other often arbitrary and harsh tools of local colonial administrators. By the first decade of the twentieth century, when French colonial officials began to study indigenous law with an eye to codifying it and regulating it more closely, the subordinate place for indigenous law in the colonial legal order was firmly established. In a broad sense, the French and British patterns of establishing state hegemony, though somewhat different in timing and certainly different in the rhetoric employed, were structurally similar.[51]

The French policy of restricting access to French courts and determining entry by "nationality" did add a distinctive dimension to legal politics and at times exacerbated the jurisdictional disorder that was symptomatic of conquest everywhere. Colonial elites militated for inclusion in the jurisdiction of French courts. French officials were often divided on jurisdictional questions, and French policy changed over time, so that there were occasional assimilationist spurts when reforms favored greater inclusiveness. Because "nationality" marked the jurisdictional divide between French and "native" courts, conflicts about where to draw the lines were directly connected to debates about cultural distinctions between Africans and the French (and whether the

---

[50] For an overview of French colonial policy in West Africa and the imprint of republican ideas, see Alice Conklin, *A Mission to Civilize: The Republican Idea of Empire in France and West Africa, 1895–1930*.

[51] Compare also the cases in this section with the discussion of shifting legal policy in the British Cape Colony in the next chapter.

differences could ever be bridged).[52] Although debates about "assimilation" versus "association" continued to characterize French colonial policy through to colonial independence, by the end of the nineteenth century these alternatives had been institutionalized in a legal order that simultaneously separated African law from French law and represented the boundary as a porous one that could be crossed in some (rare) circumstances.

Two sets of conflicts helped to shape this legal order. The first centered on the changing legal status of the *originaires*, the African inhabitants of the early French colonial enclaves of Senegal. The complexities of jurisdictional politics involving the originaires in the middle decades of the nineteenth century helped convince the French to restrict closely access to French citizenship (and thus to French courts) in the territories conquered in the last decades of the nineteenth century (and up until World War I). A second set of formative jurisdictional disputes took place in the critical years at the end of the century, when conquest brought a large territory in West Africa under French rule but a formal plan for the plural legal order had not been approved; and into the first decades of the twentieth century, when French administration was being extended and solidified in interior outposts. In this period, indigenous elites again maneuvered to advantage through the complex of jurisdictions, and French officials positioned differently in the legal order proposed opposing solutions.

Consider first the changing status of the originaires in the middle of the nineteenth century. At first, France's enclaves in Senegal were administratively much the same as other European trading posts in West Africa. Europeans in trading enclaves on the coast at first did little to influence African law. Trading companies exercised limited jurisdiction over officials and their families. Where the European presence was sustained and some settlement occurred, as in Senegambia in the eighteenth century, Europeans negotiated treaties with local rulers, often in an effort to regulate the costs of doing business by limiting the rights of African polities to levy gifts or tolls.[53] This limited legal interaction began to

---

[52] The Portuguese also restricted access to colonial courts to "civilized" Africans who could be regarded as Portuguese nationals. In contrast to the French, though, the Portuguese were quite open about closely restricted entry into this category and, in fact, assumed that most Africans would never attain it and should be subjected to summary administrative legal powers.

[53] See Curtin, *Economic Change in Precolonial Africa*; and see Chapter 2 on early European-African legal relations.

shift in the nineteenth century. In Britain's crown colonies – Freetown, Gambia, the Gold Coast, and Lagos – metropolitan legal jurisdiction was extended in various ways. In the Niger delta, courts of equity were established in the 1850s to hear property cases, with jurisdiction over not just Europeans but also Africans involved in property transactions within British-controlled territory. This and similar moves to extend jurisdiction to include some Africans were associated with the transition from slave trading to trade in other commodities, a shift that broke down former alliances and created new commercial networks. Still, most cases involving Africans continued to go before African courts, even within the crown colonies, and no formal provision was made for linking procedures in the separate court systems. The hinterland of each coastal colony was administered as a protectorate. Only Africans in the original crown colonies were considered British subjects. As British territorial claims expanded, the status of Africans in the colonies deteriorated. By 1900, Africans were essentially excluded from service as administrators in colonial government.

While the overall pattern was similar in French Senegal, legal politics here also had a special twist. France instituted a legal system based on the French system soon after the reoccupation following the Treaty of Versailles. Although the tribunals were considered courts of first instance in the French judicial system, they had an unusual structure. They were presided over by French city commandants, who were assisted by one local notable and one other senior French official. These courts operated in Gorée and Saint Louis from 1822 to 1840, when professional magistrates began to be appointed and procedures for appeal were established. The peculiarity of these courts, compared with the courts of the British crown colonies, was that in addition to adjudicating cases involving French citizens, the courts had jurisdiction over some indigenous inhabitants who were recognized as holding French civil and legal rights. These originaires, as they were called, had the status of French nationals. In 1830, they were formally granted rights of French citizens "as guaranteed by the Civil Code."[54]

This distinction created further jurisdictional complications. Some originaires were also Muslims. At first qadis were incorporated in tribunals as assessors, but Muslims pressured for a more explicit recognition of Muslim law and finally obtained it when a Muslim tribunal

---

[54] Dominique Sarr and Richard Roberts, "The Jurisdiction of Muslim Tribunals in Colonial Senegal, 1857–1932," p. 33.

was created in 1857 in Saint Louis. The tribunal was the creation of Governor-General Louis Faidherbe, whose experience in colonial Algeria had made him an advocate of policies favoring Muslim cooperation. This "Islamic" policy was explicitly opposed by French magistrates, who saw the pragmatic compromise of making the originaires simultaneously subject to French public law and religious private law as a profound contradiction of the French civil code. Over the next 75 years, originaires pushed through political channels and court actions to secure the rights of French citizens while also maintaining their special status under Muslim law, and French officials debated the merits, legality, and political implications of such an "in-between" and seemingly contradictory legal position.

The puzzle of originaire status was "resolved" by the French in the 1903 code abolishing the special status of the originaires. The code created a separate "native" legal system and assigned Muslim law to a status as one among many sources of native customary law. Rather than closing the debate, this move was met with continued pressure by originaires, other Muslims, and administrators favoring the French "Islamic" policy. In 1912, the French West Africa governor-general was pressured by the Ministry of Colonies in Paris to place all Africans under the jurisdiction of customary law. The originaires were unhappy with this shift in policy, which would allow them to keep their electoral rights but would remove their access to French courts – essentially by declaring them noncitizens who nevertheless had the right to vote. They petitioned the governor-general and were successful in retaining their special status, though, again, the result fell far short of resolving the ambiguity of their status. They were now subject to native jurisdiction outside the major towns or when they could not provide proof of their status as originaires by birth. Further, the failure to design a plural legal system with clear and fixed rules opened the way for a gradual shift in jurisdictional boundaries through cases brought to the appeals court in Dakar. Here, in the period leading up to 1932, a series of judgments had the effect of gradually restricting the jurisdiction of Muslim courts.

This trend was possible, of course, because litigants sought to exploit the ambiguities of jurisdictional boundaries as a legal strategy. For example, a 1925 case in the appeals court was brought by a woman objecting to a Muslim tribunal's decision that she should return to her husband's house. Although the couple lived in Rufisque, neither was an originaire, and the court ruled that the Muslim tribunal had no jurisdiction. In this and other similar cases, the court carved out a limited, liminal space for

Muslim courts, whose jurisdiction extended only "where it had been expressly taken from the French tribunals and not included in the jurisdiction of the native tribunals."[55]

The difficulty of defining the legal status of the originaires contributed directly to the French decision not to extend the status of nationals to the inhabitants of territories conquered in the scramble of the last decades of the nineteenth century. Instead, they recognized the authority of "chiefs" in all matters involving Africans except the most serious crimes; in practice, local legal authorities included qadis, village heads, kings, and others who presided over legal disputes. The possibility of recognition as a "civilized" African with access to French courts remained officially open. After 1887, however, French administrators had authority to dispense summary administrative justice independently of the civil and criminal courts. The result was "a patchwork of overlapping legal jurisdictions" and a period of intense jurisdictional jockeying, particularly during the period of planned reforms from 1895 to 1903, when the French formally crafted the model of a plural legal order with two systems of justice: "one for French citizens and those exercising French civil and legal rights, and the other for African subjects."[56] Even after this date, jurisdictional disputes continued to raise questions about the boundaries dividing these groups, the role of Muslim courts as a special category of native justice, and the prerogatives of French administrators to act in legal matters.

A case in the southeastern region of the Côte d'Ivoire examined by David Groff illustrates the continued jurisdictional jockeying.[57] Here, near the border with the British-controlled Gold Coast, French officials found themselves confounded by the legal maneuvering of a wealthy local. Kwame Kangah at first ingratiated himself with the French and, after 1903, took up a formal post as linguist and assessor in the colonial court. In the midst of upheaval in the region caused by the crash in rubber prices and the forced policy of cocoa production, Kangah took a leave of absence from his post and went to the Gold Coast. When he did not return, French administrators used the opportunity to strengthen

---

[55] Sarr and Roberts, "The Jurisdiction of Muslim Tribunals," p. 139; cf. Donal Cruise O'Brien, "Towards an 'Islamic Policy' in French West Africa, 1854–1914"; and Bernard Schnapper, "Les tribunaux musulmans et la politique coloniale au Sénégal (1830–1914)."

[56] Richard Roberts and Kristin Mann, "Law in Colonial Africa," p. 16.

[57] David Groff, "The Dynamics of Collaboration and the Rule of Law in French West Africa: The Case of Kwame Kangah of Assikasso (Côte d'Ivoire), 1898–1922."

their support for Kangah's rival. In a fine example of the "invention" of customary law, they arrived at the rather far-fetched ruling that both French and local customary law entitled them to declare Kangah dead and assign an heir. In 1915, they transferred Kangah's house and assets to an ally of Kangah's rival. Having learned of this from his kin remaining in the town, Kangah asked permission to return and was allowed to do so. Certainly the French administrators expected him to fight the decision, but he surprised them by refusing to challenge it in either the local or regional court (where he knew he would meet French administrators and assessors representing his rival's camp). He took his appeal instead directly to the governor-general in Dakar. He was advised by a retired French customs inspector, who probably also helped him prepare another petition, this time to the French Chamber of Deputies. Kangah had successfully exploited tensions both between central and frontier colonial administrators and between colonial and metropolitan states. He had capitalized on his own semiofficial status as an employee of the very courts he carefully avoided in his strategy for appeal. In the directives ordering an investigation of the seizure of his property, both governor-general and the French Chamber of Deputies expressed concerns about the lack of procedural fairness in the actions of the local administrators, particularly in treating a local notable once closely allied with the French. At the heart of the matter was the legitimacy of French rule and the avoidance of the appearance of arbitrary justice.

A somewhat similar example studied by Roberts in colonial French Sudan further illuminates the difficulty French officials faced in assigning a fixed legal status to Africans who owed their wealth and power to French administration.[58] In this case, Faama Mademba Sy, king of Sansading, confounded French administrators by using "customary" prerogatives to impose autocratic rule in the region and so destabilize French administration. Mademba had risen in the ranks of French colonial service and had, in the process, become a naturalized French citizen. He was praised as "un françois noir" who had adopted a French lifestyle. In 1891 he was made *faama* and installed as king in Sinsani, where there was no tradition of kingship. His authority in the legal system was carefully circumscribed: as faama, Mademba was to follow customary law in resolving disputes among subjects. He

[58] Richard Roberts, "The Case of Faama Mademba Sy and the Ambiguities of Legal Jurisdiction in Colonial French Sudan."

was not to render judgment in cases where Europeans were involved. The French military retained the right to intervene in cases of disputed judgments.

This arrangement proved almost immediately untenable. Mademba's subjects complained repeatedly that he used excessive force in responding to disturbances and disputes, profited exorbitantly by asserting rights to the local cotton trade, and misrepresented French policies as a justification for self-serving administrative acts. An inspector-general was charged with investigating Mademba's conduct and recommended in his report that Mademba be stripped of his title. In response, the governor-general of French West Africa, Jean-Baptiste Chaudie, questioned whether Mademba was "really a functionary when he exercises the authority of faama of Sansading."[59] Though he received a salary from the French, owed his title to them, and was even naturalized as a French citizen, the governor-general was eager to exempt Mademba from French law. Roberts interprets this position as a defense of local independence for French administrators in "frontier" conditions where they were a tiny minority and wanted to be able to exercise independent legal authority. In this and other cases, local administrative control emerged as strengthened from jurisdictional challenges.

Like the qadi in Patna, both Kangah and Mademba were local notables who played a formal role in the colonial legal order and whose legal authority was officially defined as emanating from both "traditional" and colonial sources. Both colonial administrators and individual notables could choose strategically to represent legal intermediaries as colonial dependents and functionaries; as freelances who were temporarily (and perhaps illegally) assuming prerogatives that the complex system made available; or as "traditional" leaders invested with more permanent authority. In French West Africa, the ambiguity of their status was further complicated by the French strategy of marking legal status by "nationality." Jurisdictional boundaries were thus intricately bound up with representations of "Frenchness." Surrounding the legal status of "acculturated" Africans continued to be a central feature of French colonial policy through most of the next century, but later disputes did not unsettle a pattern established earlier: strong, even autocratic rule by colonial officials in conquered territories outside the original colonial core, combined with formal and pragmatic support for subordinate

---

[59] Roberts, "The Case of Faama Mademba Sy," p. 192.

African legal forums. In its broadest outlines, French and British colonial legal policies had more similarities than differences.[60]

CONCLUSION

As in other colonial settings, jurisdictional politics in European colonies established over the long nineteenth century crystallized debates about difference. In India, determining the relation of English and indigenous law relied on contested interpretations about the nature of Hindu and Muslim law (and Hindus and Muslims) and about the responsibilities and motives of colonial rule. Borrowing from Mughal styles of rule and European experience with the relation of canon and secular law, the British used religious difference as an organizing principle for the plural legal order. But these boundaries were crossed and blurred repeatedly as other categories (gender, ethnicity) and groups (Company servants, religious legal experts, Westernizing elites) came into play. In French West Africa, French hegemony was shaped by the perceived need to limit the possibilities for "French" Africans to cross jurisdictional lines. The imposition of law was similar to that of earlier empires, too, in that the colonizers themselves introduced jurisdictional ambiguity into the emerging colonial legal order. In India, the tensions between Company and Parliament influenced debates about the shape of the legal order. In French West Africa, local administrators interpreted the pragmatic imperatives of rule far differently from French-trained magistrates and Parisian colonial officials. Imperial-local divides were salient in each case and were sometimes compounded by other sources of factionalism among colonial elites, particularly those derived from differences in economic interests.

Further, it is the case everywhere that indigenous actors were quick to perceive opportunity in this legal landscape. In Bengal, we find the widow of a rent farmer appealing to the Supreme Court to confound the BEIC. And in West Africa, a Muslim wife and a provincial "big man," among many others, used jurisdictional arguments and maneuvers to appeal to imperial law over the authority of "traditional" leaders and local French administrators. Factions among indigenous groups also

---

[60] For an account of jurisdictional politics in the Gold Coast, see Jarle Simensen, "Jurisdiction As Politics: The Gold Coast During the Colonial Period." For a more general account of jurisdictional shifts in the region, see Chapter 5 in Antony Allot, *Essays in African Law, with Special Reference to the Law of Ghana*.

created a wide array of interests and loyalties, and a variety of motives for legal maneuvering. But there is little doubt that the tensions within the colonial legal order were clearly perceived and exploited, and that these strategies influenced the direction of colonial legal reform.

We see, in addition, the close relation between conflicts over legal reform and struggles to redefine mechanisms for the distribution of property rights – indeed, to redefine property itself. In India, jurisdictional disputes were intertwined with legal maneuvering by both British and Indians to benefit from the reform of the revenue system and the creation of a market in land. Chanock has argued that in West and central Africa, the plural legal model of high colonialism included the invention of customary land rights residing in indigenous communities, a strategy that benefited colonizers by protecting their privileged access to courts overseeing transactions in land; this aspect of legal policy, he suggests, was central to the shift toward production of cash crops for export after the ending of the slave trade, and it is in this period, in the middle decades of the century and *before* the scramble for territory began, that the framework for hierarchical legal pluralism emerged.[61]

Legal reform changed the rules about property, but it was still possible to maneuver through those rules. Legal and cultural intermediaries were well placed to discover ways to take advantage of and sometimes challenge the new property regimes so that, once again, we would be wrong to speak simply of the imposition of Western institutional inventions. Yet, even as the opportunities for legal maneuvering continued, the authority of state law in all these examples was ultimately reinforced, and it emerged by the end of the nineteenth century as a different sort of authority than in the early stages of the colonial encounter. This assertion may seem odd given that the formal creation of a plural legal order in which indigenous forums were assigned a discrete role took place at such different times. In India, crafting such an order was a central objective of Company and government administrators in the last three decades of the eighteenth century; in Africa, legal relationships were more informal and limited in this period, and in most places it was not until the extension of territorial rule in the late nineteenth century that we find an explicit commitment to orchestrating the place for "traditional" law in the legal order. Yet, the latter exercise, as many

---

[61] Martin Chanock, "Paradigms, Policies, and Property: A Review of the Customary Law of Land Tenure."

historians have demonstrated, *assumed* the dominance of state law and
the functional subordination of "traditional" law. This relation had been
established earlier, in the enclaves and early settler colonies of Africa
and in metropolitan movements to reinvent the state as law-centered.
In French Senegal, the mid-century measures to limit the rights of the
originaires and to restrict other grants of citizenship set the stage for
continued efforts in this direction through the next century. As the next
chapter shows, a similar debate about the legal status of the Khoi in the
Cape Colony prefigured the legal treatment of African communities in
Natal. In India, the expansion of the colonial administration in policing, in criminal law, and in the control of remote territories and groups
"outside" the law in the first half of the nineteenth century prepared the
ground for claims to sovereignty after 1857.

The shift to state hegemony did not, however, put a stop to legal maneuvering, nor to jurisdictional politics as an arena for discursive struggles over difference. Participants did not regard state legal hegemony
as a foregone conclusion. Also, there was plenty of room for debates
about difference to shift to the arena of state law itself. Thus in India,
disputes about different status for British and Indian legal practitioners
intensified throughout the nineteenth century. Legal training became
almost a required entry card in the nationalist movement leadership,
and its ranks were intimately knowledgeable about the persisting formal and informal obstacles to equality for Indian litigants and legal
practitioners.[62] Rules separating British and Indian legal practitioners
were also the objects of British political fury. In 1883, the so-called Ilbert
Bill, the Bill on Criminal Jurisdiction, was proposed to make it possible for Indians in the British Judicial Service to try cases involving
Europeans, something they had been barred from doing in the past. The
move caused a storm of protest among Europeans, who secured significant changes in the bill, including a provision that Europeans would be
able to demand a jury that was at least half European in a court with a
native judge. The sharpening of racial rhetoric in this period is well documented. In debates about legal reform, tensions focused specifically on
the protection or elimination of dwindling formal distinctions between
Indians and Europeans. The existence of groups with ambiguous status

---

[62] Much has been made of Ghandi's experience as a barrister in South Africa in shaping his
ideology and political strategy. There is no doubt that the discrimination he experienced
as a legal practitioner there politicized him. See Albie Sachs, *Justice in South Africa*.

continued to be a source of tension and instability, particularly as these groups began themselves to challenge the cultural and legal boundaries that marked them as different from Europeans.

Similarly, jurisdictional jockeying continued in French and British colonies in Africa. In British West Africa, Frederick Lugard articulated the doctrine of indirect rule in an effort to systematize practices already underway throughout British colonies. In northern Nigeria, he implemented a system of rule in which "Native Chiefs" served simultaneously as authorities in local disputes and officials in the British administrative structure. Lugard also installed qadis presiding over a system of native courts and applying an amalgam of customary, Islamic, and English law. Indirect rule has been represented by Lugard and others as a judicious and pragmatic retreat from more ambitious claims to direct administrative and legal control. Yet Lugard was careful to note that native and British officials served "a single government," and he favored direct intervention to identify and install indigenous rulers who would implement British policy, regardless of whether they possessed local legitimacy.

It is often observed that Lugard's formulation of "indirect rule" lacked originality because it merely stated as a general principle a pattern of rule that had been in long use in practice. Yet, though he provided the label, Lugard envisioned a more constricted role for indigenous officials, who were to act simply as indispensable aids of the colonial administration; the emphasis was on "rule" rather than "indirect."[63] In this system, promoted throughout West, East, and southern Africa, indigenous systems of law were misrepresented and purposefully altered as part of the colonial project. While jurisdictional ambiguities continued as a feature of the system, the hierarchical ordering of the plural legal order was now fixed. "Other" legal authorities did not exist parallel to, or in a privileged relationship with, the colonial state, but as appendages of state authority.

In French West Africa, separate legal systems for French and Africans, and the subordinate place of the latter, continued, as did the formal possibility but practical difficulty of crossing these boundaries. By 1937, there were still only about two thousand West Africans subject to French law apart from the originaires. Even in Algeria, which was administered by the Ministry of Interior as a part of France, most inhabitants, as Muslims, fell under the jurisdiction of Muslim courts for personal law

---

[63] See John Flint, "Frederick Lugard: The Making of an Autocrat (1858–1943)."

and were required to renounce their status in Muslim law when choosing citizenship. By 1936, there were only about eight thousand French citizens of Muslim origin in Algeria.[64]

The "rules about rule" that had always formed the subtext of the colonial legal order were now part of the institutional structure. The repercussions of the imposition of colonial state power were often violent and ranged from the brutality of imposed criminal law, which disproportionately punished indigenous groups, to the violent suppression of claims to indigenous sovereignty, to the sanctioned brutality of installed "chiefs." Alongside this very visible evidence of state power came a more fundamental shift to establish the colonial state as the ultimate arbiter of justice, and of truth. This institutional change is often regarded as either a precondition or a consequence of colonial rule, but as we have seen, it was the object of continual debate, not just in policy circles but across colonial cultures, and in the courts themselves. Because models of legal pluralism and images of cultural hierarchy were so closely interrelated, colonizers saw their institutions' new monopoly on justice as a reflection of their special relationship to rationality and to truth. Indigenous people devised legal strategies both to blur boundaries inside the legal order, in an effort to establish their equality with colonizers, and sometimes to sharpen boundaries and protect claims to different sorts of knowledge, legal processes, and identities.

The cases surveyed in this chapter point to the special role of legal and cultural intermediaries in de-centering the carefully constructed scaffolding of the colonial legal order. In part, their challenge to the stability of the plural legal order resulted simply from the contradictions built into dual roles as insiders and outsiders. In part, it resulted from legal sophistication and efforts to exploit such ambiguities in support of their own interests. The qadi in Patna did not have to be overtly anti-British to pose a challenge to British East India Company officials; he was provocative merely by interpreting the overlapping duties of Company servant and Muslim judge in ways that usurped legal functions supposedly reserved for British judges. Similarly, in West Africa, local elites used their place in and knowledge of French administration to influence legal outcomes and manipulate the courts. Such actions showed that some colonial subjects possessed abilities and knowledge that colonial officials were busy claiming as their unique cultural property. Legal and

---

[64] See Michael Crowder, *Senegal: A Study of French Assimilation Policy*, p. 7. And see also Patricia Lorcin, *Imperial Identities*, on French legal policy in Algeria.

cultural intermediaries meanwhile produced their own contradictions, simultaneously questioning the legitimacy of colonial state law and reaffirming its legitimacy by appealing to supra-local legal authorities.

While such tensions were themselves predictable, the outcome of a strengthened colonial state legal authority was not. Real and repeated disputes drove legal change forward and gradually made a place for an entity to order the plurality of laws, forums, and personnel. This was a far-reaching legal politics. Within the legal order, it determined who could act as judges, litigants, advocates, and witnesses, and under what conditions their actions and utterances carried weight. Beyond the narrower confines of the law, it engaged such fundamental issues as the cultural ownership of procedure and the meanings of indigenous competence and performance. As state law created and protected new kinds of property, it also advanced claims about its own most important "properties" – the discovery and possession of the truth.

FIVE

Subjects and Witnesses

Cultural and Legal Hierarchies in the Cape Colony and New South Wales

While the colonial project of legal pluralism was slowly producing a space for the colonial state as a repository of rules about legal interactions, in some settings the shift to state legal hegemony took place earlier and without the creation of an elaborate system of multiple legal spheres. A tentative, "weak" pluralism that recognized the legal authority of indigenous groups without proscribing a formal plan for the interaction of colonial and indigenous law gave way within the space of several decades to more sweeping claims of legal hierarchy. This shift, still, was not uncontested, nor did it result in uniform treatment of indigenous legal subjects in colonial courts.

The legal models of jurisdictional complexity that informed Iberians' strategies and inspired the plural legal order of India were based loosely on the jurisdictional divisions between canon and secular law. But this model was not the only one available to Europeans. As Pagden has argued, Roman law was a source of multiple "discursive possibilities" for representing and legitimating overseas empire.[1] European powers drew on these rhetorical resources in various combinations to distinguish their claims from those of other colonizing powers and to legitimize conquest and colonization. This process continued a well-established tradition of using Roman texts as what Peter Stein has called a "legal supermarket."[2]

---

[1] Anthony Pagden develops this view of the multifaceted influence of Roman law as discursive resource in *Lords of All the World: Ideologies of Empire in Spain, Britain, and France c. 1500–c. 1800.*

[2] Peter Stein, *Roman Law in European History*, p. 2.

English theorists, for example, countered Spanish claims of conquest in the Americas by asserting that English settlers had not conquered New World territories but had merely occupied them. In doing so, they relied on the Roman legal principle of *terra nullius* – the idea that previously empty, "waste" lands could be settled without conquest.[3] The doctrine clashed neatly with unavoidable evidence of European encroachments on indigenous settlement nearly everywhere. One response to this contradiction was to hold that indigenous inhabitants were not in possession of the land because they did not cultivate it. Thus English "ceremonies of possession" prominently figured the planting of gardens, construction of fences, and other ways of marking the landscape as the object of agricultural improvement.[4] This geographical separation of English cultivated settlement from indigenous "waste" lands was the physical embodiment of a divide between European settlers as part of the legal community – *civitas* – and indigenous groups as permanently uncivilized, living outside the law.

It would be a mistake, however, to view either this legal theory or practices it engendered as somehow culturally or politically predetermined elements of European, or English, colonial settlement. Legal policies of English settlers, and of the metropolis, changed as they responded to the conditions and peculiar conflicts surrounding legal administration in the colonies. The embrace of terra nullius was neither immediate nor particularly simple.[5] The realities of European encounters with large

---

[3] For much of the seventeenth century, English colonial models were drawn from debate surrounding *Calvin's Case* in 1608, in which the courts were asked to rule on the status of Scottish subjects in England as a means to legitimizing James I's reign. Debates centered on two alternatives for recognizing the acquisition of territories outside England: by descent or by conquest. A third possibility – the simple occupation of land that belonged to no one (*res nullius*) was introduced on the margins of this debate by Sir Francis Bacon but did not become prominent as a justification for colonization until later. The principle was accepted by William Blackstone, whose 1767 *Commentaries on the Laws of England* would become a standard source for colonial jurists and lawyers. Blackstone also viewed the separate jurisdiction of the church as unnecessary and unworkable in the colonies. See Alex Castles, *An Australian Legal History*, Chapter 1.

[4] Seed asserts that this mode of striking claims was peculiarly English (Seed, *Ceremonies of Possession*). Pagden, however, emphasizes the rootedness of such methods in Roman law and sees their selection for emphasis on the part of the English as an answer to Spaniards' reliance on papal approval of their claims in the Americas (Pagden, *Lords of All the World*).

[5] In English North America, gestures toward inclusion of Indians in the legal community of the settlements turned sharply toward a policy of exclusion only after King Philip's War. In Australia, the doctrine was also not automatically embraced, even though England's earliest claimants had been careful to assert that it was an "empty land."

and often belligerent populations could reduce references to terra nullius to empty rhetoric, significant as a form of political discourse but legally untenable. Further, the doctrine of terra nullius did not, by itself, solve the more complex question of the legal status of indigenous inhabitants in colonial courts. In this debate, Europeans drew from a wider repertoire of legal formulae, including the idea – also derived from Roman law and carried over into canon law – that natural law extended to all people. Thus indigenous "savages" could be viewed as outside the purview of European law, but their possession of natural law qualified them for some consideration as legal subjects. The assignment of legal (and political) status to colonial subjects was particularly complex in colonies where large and increasing numbers of Europeans became settlers and found their interests in sharp conflict with those of indigenous groups.

The challenge of categorizing legal subjects was complicated, too, by parallel debates about the shifting legal status of European colonists themselves. As their identities and interests diverged from metropolitan officials and investors, they sought legal structures that would reflect these differences. At the same time, settler communities contained their own divisions, and factionalism played a part in making legal issues multisided rather than oppositional along predictable lines. Uniting settler factions was an interest in the preservation of legal distinctions marking indigenous inhabitants as politically subordinate and culturally inferior.

Non-Europeans were not merely passive observers of these controversies surrounding law. Even where their roles in colonial courts were severely restricted – their testimony rejected, their rights to litigate denied – there is evidence that indigenous actors participated in shaping the legal order. They often eagerly embraced whatever opportunities were presented for using the courts. They appeared everywhere as criminal defendants, often in cases that resulted not so much from petty or random violence but from acts that were part of a more widely "political" frontier violence. Both their presence in the courtroom and its background of conflict became essential material for the debate about the definition of colonial legal pluralism, indigenous legal status, the rights of European settlers, and the relation of colonial law to imperial authority.

In the cases examined in this chapter, colonial legal politics produced substantially different outcomes. In the British Cape Colony, establishing British hegemony over Dutch-descended settlers involved the strategic acceptance of indigenous Khoi as legal witnesses and litigants. In New South Wales, the conflict over the legal status of convict settlers encapsulated debates about the legal standing of Aborigines and reinforced their systematic exclusion as legal actors. At the same time, in larger, structural terms, the two cases contain surprising similarities. In both places, the colonial legal order began with a weak pluralism that recognized indigenous legal authority without ascribing a precisely defined "law" to native people. As frontier violence, labor relations, and internal political conflicts increasingly challenged this framework and brought more Khoi and Aborigines into the courts, the legal order was reformulated to establish wider hegemony – early formal claims of full sovereignty that would serve as the underpinnings of the colonial state. This shift took place at almost the same time, extending over the early-to-middle decades of the nineteenth century. Neither the timing of the shift, nor the particular forms that legal contests took in these settings, can be understood as the logical or necessary outcome of legal theories or sources that were developed or imposed by European administrators. Legal politics drew on a repertoire of available formulae and responded to local pressures and constraints. As occurred elsewhere, conflicts over cultural and legal boundaries were closely intertwined.

EUROPEAN LAW AND THE KHOI AS LEGAL SUBJECTS

The Cape Colony was initially a part of the Dutch trading post empire stretching to Asia, and judicial policy was similar to that in Asia. Dutch jurisdiction extended to company employees of the Dutch East India Company (VOC), free burghers, and slaves; though the legal status of each of these groups was subject to some change, they clearly fell under colonial legal authority.[6] But the Dutch claim was that of rule over persons, not over a given territory and its inhabitants. As a consequence, there was a fourth group, the indigenous Khoi, whose legal status was

---

[6] Roman-Dutch law applied to everyone in Dutch-controlled territories, except in some cases where allowances were made for the application of Islamic law to nonslave Muslims. Following a shift we traced more widely in the Atlantic world in Chapter 2, the salient legal divide between Christians and non-Christians was replaced at the end of the eighteenth century by the more prominent distinction between white master and black servant or slave. In 1792, the Church Council in Cape Town ruled that baptized persons could be slaves, effectively blocking an important avenue for manumission. See Sachs, *Justice in South Africa*, p. 28.

far more ambiguous.[7] The shift in jurisdictional claims over this group between early Dutch settlement and the first decades of British rule in the nineteenth century took place haltingly, and in response to both local tensions and international pressures. The completion of this shift to full jurisdiction of the colonial state over the Khoi marked a new kind of state legal authority and laid the groundwork for the later political strategy of recognizing indigenous law but only as subordinate to state (and imperial) law.

The Dutch initially recognized the Khoi people as legally autonomous. Khoi criminals were turned over to Khoi chiefs for punishment. In cases of murder or cattle theft, there seems to have been little divergence between Khoi and European communities about the harsh punishments such crimes deserved. Less serious cases of theft by Khoi against colonists were punished by seizing Khoi cattle – or even Khoi themselves – as hostages until restitution was made.[8] In addition to the official policy that the Khoi were a free people, colonists considered judicial restraint prudent since actions against individual Khoi might have invited reprisals on the volatile frontier. Ross cites the case of Willem Willemsz, a free burgher who killed a Khoi in 1672 and then fled to Europe. When he returned to claim his seized property with a pardon from the Prince of Orange, Willemsz was imprisoned on Robben Island while the authorities inquired if the pardon was genuine. The ruling was intended "to prevent any apprehended mischief and particularly to avoid causing any new disturbances among the native tribes, (who are a free people over whom we had no jurisdiction and who are vindictive

---

[7] I have chosen to use the term *Khoi* throughout the chapter to designate the indigenous inhabitants of the Cape Colony. This term, like its alternatives, has some problems. Dutch settlers routinely used the term *Hottentots* to refer to local inhabitants, and the term came to have such clearly negative connotations that it must be rejected by historians. A later term, *Khoisan*, is an anthropological construct that combines *Khoi*, used for the cattle-herding indigenous inhabitants of the Cape, and *San* used for indigenous inhabitants who had no cattle. The term *Khoi* seems to me better than either of these choices because it indicates that there was some early recognition of indigenous polities built upon a relatively stable political economy in the region. But, it should be noted, the settler label *Hottentots* seems to have included a wide range of ethnically and culturally situated people, including, undoubtedly, individuals who would not have identified themselves, or been identified, as *Khoi*. So long as the term *Khoi* is understood as socially contingent, it seems to do the work best of indicating the indigenous people at the Cape and their descendents who came into contact with European colonial law in the period I am examining. I would like to thank Howard Venable for urging me to be explicit about the reasons for this choice.

[8] See Richard Elphick, *Khoikhoi and the Founding of White South Africa*.

beyond all example, and will not be satisfied before they have revenged upon the offender, the death of a father, brother or relation)."[9]

Changing conditions in the colony brought changes to legal practice. In the first place, the independent status of Khoi began to be challenged as Khoi were increasingly brought into close contact with colonists and into dependent relations with them as laborers. Already in the late seventeenth century, at the same time that the court was enforcing in most cases its policy of legal separateness, exception was made in the case of a culturally assimilated Khoi woman, Sara, who was condemned posthumously for the crime of suicide. The *fiscaal*, or chief legal officer in the Cape Colony, argued for jurisdiction over Sara's crime on the basis of both territorial rule and authority over inhabitants who had adopted a Dutch way of life:

> [S]eeing that those who live under our protection, from whatever part of the world they may come and whether they be christians or heathens, may justly be called our subjects – and as this act was committed in our *territorium*, and in a free man's house under our jurisdiction; which should be purified from this foul sin, and such evil doers and enemies of their own persons and lives visited with the most rigorous punishment.[10]

Though this case was exceptional, by the middle of the eighteenth century there were other examples of jurisdiction being asserted over Khoi, particularly for crimes committed by Khoi working on farms. In 1751, for example, a young Khoi worker named Klaas was condemned to death (by torturous means) for murdering two other Khoi workers on the same farm. In such cases, cultural assimilation was less important as a basis for jurisdiction than the absence of an alternative authority, since most Khoi workers, having lost or sold cattle and having been displaced from their own communities, were no longer under the authority of Khoi chiefs. The chiefs, too, were losing authority as many came under the direct influence of Dutch authorities.[11]

---

[9] Quoted in Robert Ross, *Beyond the Pale: Essays on the History of Colonial South Africa*, p. 175.

[10] Quoted in Ross, *Beyond the Pale*, p. 170. The sentence was for her body to be dragged through the streets and hanged for public display, with her confiscated property to pay "the costs and dues of justice."

[11] Commander (later governor) Van der Stel favored greater oversight of Khoi at the end of the seventeenth century and established the right of the Dutch to install Khoi chiefs, presumably in consultation with Khoi communities.

The other consequence of the emerging cattle frontier was the increased tension between Company servants and non-Company employees. Violence on the northern frontier was followed by strife on the expanding eastern frontier. Burghers who were distant from Cape authorities and who viewed their interests as increasingly separate from those of the settled agriculturalists on the coast flaunted their independence from colonial authority. They imposed where they could their own power over Khoi workers and conducted raids against Khoi (and later Xhosa) communities. Although it would be wrong to say that the Company championed Khoi rights, it did act occasionally to curb abuses. In 1744, a farmer named Martinus Spangenberg was accused of going to a neighboring farm in search of one of his Khoi laborers, who had run away. Spangenberg had interrogated one of the Khoi workers, then beat him and finally shot him. The court would not have him hanged but instead ruled he should be banned for life. The governor appealed the decision to Batavia because the punishment seemed so light.

The actual status of Khoi before the law remained unresolved. It was not clear, for example, how Khoi testimony should be weighed. Oaths had typically not been administered to Khoi witnesses or slaves, on the grounds that they were not Christians. But as Khoi were brought into courts as defendants and, more rarely, plaintiffs, some decisions had to be made about how to consider their testimony. In one case involving the murder of a group of Khoi by burghers who had accused them of stealing cattle, the court was reluctant to act "based on the single deposition of one hottentot directed against Christians, without further evidence."[12] In another case in 1797, the *landdrost* (magistrate) and the *heemraden* (members of the local administrative board) at Stellenbosch reported that they could not agree about whether a Khoi should be allowed to complain about a white woman for payment of a debt. The landdrost said it should be permitted; the heemraden said it should not because such an action "would open a door and give the hottentots the idea that they are on a footing of equality with the burghers."[13] Further evidence of the volatility of this subject is its use as a rallying cry in the uprising of free burghers of Stellenbosch against the VOC. The leader, Etienne Barbier, listed the use of Khoi evidence against burghers as one of the group's main grievances.

[12] Ross, *Beyond the Pale*, p. 177.
[13] Ross, *Beyond the Pale*, p. 198.

In a broad sense, the imposition of British rule further complicated existing jurisdictional tension between Company or state law and the "right" of settlers to handle discipline and punishment of African workers independently from the courts. British rule coincided with the early articulation of notions of trusteeship and the moral obligation to protect indigenous inhabitants in the colonies. British legal policies in South Africa were directly influenced by parliamentary debates in the 1780s about the responsibilities of rule in India.[14] The early British administrators at the Cape determined that they would not interfere with the existing Roman-Dutch legal system, but they did want to institute reforms that would better protect the indigenous inhabitants. Specifically, they were determined to do away with torture, and they acted to abolish the Cape Court of Justice when it failed to implement ordered reforms in 1796.

This intervention was expanded in 1809 under Caledon's Hottentot Proclamation. The measure awarded the Khoi, who were routinely forced into service by Boer settlers, the right to leave service and to present complaints against employers in the courts. Debt peonage was also outlawed. But the Proclamation also made it a crime for Khoi to travel in the colony's territory without passes. Khoi could be apprehended by any European for failing to produce a pass. They could not move or change employers without approval by the fiscaal or landdrost. The Proclamation also established the right for local officials to discipline Khoi workers, including inflicting corporal punishment, without trial.[15]

The Proclamation responded to British perceptions of rampant lawlessness on the frontier, and it can be read as a first act to bring both Khoi and colonists on the frontier under the jurisdiction of the state. The 1790s, during the period of first British occupation, had been characterized by outbreaks of large-scale frontier violence. The Second Frontier War in 1793 pitted Xhosa against commandoes on the eastern frontier. Colonists in Graaf-Reinet rebelled in 1795 against the landdrost, citing among other grievances his intervention in their treatment of servants. One of the rebels' demands, too, was that they be allowed to buy and sell captives and bind them as servants for life. Then, between 1799 and 1802, a coalition of Khoi, Xhosa, and servants rebelled against the

---

[14] Accusations of misrule were sharp and explicit in the well-publicized debates in the impeachment proceedings against Warren Hastings.
[15] The proclamation was retaining measures already in place locally in Swellendam and Graaf-Reinet. See Hermann Giliomee, "The Eastern Frontier, 1770–1812," p. 452.

colonists and effectively pushed back settlers on the eastern frontier. For the British, the costs of imposing order on the frontier had to be weighed against the costs of allowing violence and instability to continue unchecked.

Following Caledon's Proclamation, and in answer to increasingly vocal missionary complaints about the treatment of African servants, the British established a circuit court, which operated between August and December of 1812, to hear complaints by Khoi servants against their masters. As with Caledon's Proclamation, the practical result for Khoi laborers was hardly noticeable. Khoi testimony was again selectively weighed, and the court was presided over by Afrikaner judges.[16] But the symbolism of the circuit was of considerable importance as British-colonist tensions mounted in the next decades. On the one side, the so-called Black Circuit was, for non-elite Afrikaner colonists, a provocative negation of their rights to local jurisdiction. To the British, on the other side, the circuit was one of a series of acts that used the issue of the legal equality of the Khoi as a vehicle for establishing its monopoly on the use of legitimate force. As Keegan puts it, "the anarchic oppression of masters was replaced by the systematic oppression of the colonial order."[17]

Measures enacted in the next decades reaffirmed this order. After South Africa became officially a colony in 1814, the British sent out Commissioners of Enquiry to review the judicial system, and they returned with recommendations for significant reforms. At the same time, missionaries stepped up their efforts to draw attention to the plight of indigenous servants.[18] A Charter of Justice for the Cape was announced in 1827, and it was followed by a second charter the next year. The charters called for the introduction of British judges and British court procedures and the gradual assimilation of Roman-Dutch law into English law. A new Supreme Court was established at the Cape in 1828. The reforms did not make racial distinctions in assigning different status to litigants, witnesses, or defendants. Further, changes were made that were explicitly

---

[16] Following Sachs (*Justice in South Africa*), I use this term to describe Dutch-descended settlers even though it did not come into use until later.

[17] Timothy Keegan, *Colonial South Africa and the Origins of the Racial Order*, p. 56.

[18] John Philip traveled to England to begin lobbying for measures to control settler abuses just before the new charters were announced. Though it is unclear precisely how much influence missionaries had on the contents of legal reform, they no doubt raised the stakes by calling public attention to conditions for indigenous peoples in South Africa. See John Comaroff and Jean Comaroff, *Of Revelation and Revolution: Christianity, Colonialism, and Consciousness*.

designed to open access to courts to free persons of color. Ordinance 50 of 1828 declared that they would be "entitled to all the rights of law to which any other of his Majesty's subjects . . . are entitled."[19] The actual conditions of servile labor for the Khoi, and for Xhosa on the eastern frontier who were also being drawn in increasing numbers into wage labor on settler farms, were little changed by these reforms. Where the reforms did have an immediate effect was in exacerbating tensions with Afrikaner settlers, who rightly perceived the charters as a definitive declaration of British authority over settled territories. Whereas objections to the Black Circuit and other challenges to British rule had hitherto pitted poorer colonists against British authorities working together with elite Afrikaners, the latter now perceived the legal reforms, which would exclude them from high office in the civil service, as directly threatening to their social status and economic prospects. The trek to the north was in this sense a flight from jurisdiction.[20]

DEFINING "CREDIBLE WITNESSES"

To get a view of the high stakes for all parties in this complex legal shift at the beginning of the nineteenth century, let us go back to early in the summer of 1807, when a burgher of the district of Swellendam, Stephanus Cloete, noticed that he was losing cattle on his property near the Gourish River. Cloete lived with his wife and four children in relative isolation, though he had family in Swellendam and seemed to be on good terms with his neighbors. He suspected that wolves were killing his livestock, but he was careful not to go out after them alone. When a Khoi laborer, Heindrik Heyn, who was in the service of another local burgher, was sent by his master on an errand to Cloete's property, Cloete asked him to go with him to hunt the wolves.[21] The two men set out together, each with a loaded rifle.

---

[19] Keegan, *Colonial South Africa*, p. 39.

[20] There were other motives, of course, including the indebtedness of many trekboers, who felt they would be permanently excluded from land ownership in the settled territories. On this and other elements of local political economy shaping the trek, see Clifton Crais, *White Supremacy and Black Resistance in Pre-Industrial South Africa: The Making of the Colonial Order in the Eastern Cape.*

[21] The court record reports his mission in various ways, stating once that he had been sent to reap some wheat, another time that he was sent to collect a beam he had hewn on Cloete's property. It is possible that Cloete felt entitled to ask for Heyn's assistance because the burgher was using resources on Cloete's property. Cloete's lawyer called his property a "Government Place" that Cloete held in "loan." Public Record Office (PRO), London: CO 48 25.

Both men agreed later that they had been walking for a short time – perhaps an hour – when they met a "Hottentot" child, a girl about thirteen years old.[22] Cloete must have been immediately suspicious of her presence on his property. The girl tried to get away, but Cloete chased and caught her, and she nervously revealed that her name was Sara and that her mother was nearby. Sara admitted that she and her mother were in the company of some other Khoi ("Hottentots" in common parlance and in court records) and that they "lived off stealing."[23] The girl showed Cloete her mother's footprints, and he followed the tracks to a small clearing, with Heyn following some distance behind.

Here the witnesses' accounts diverge. Heyn and Sara later testified that Cloete came upon Sara's mother sitting on a riverbank holding an infant on her lap. Cloete later claimed he never saw her. On one point, though, the three accounts agree: A ball from Cloete's rifle shot the mother, hitting her from close range in the jaw. The infant was unharmed, and the mother fell dead at Cloete's feet.

Cloete must have felt quite secure, in 1807, in reporting the incident. He sent for the local field commander, who came the next day to examine the body and identify it as that of "a female Hottentot named Mietze." She had "deserted" from service to another burgher, Christiaan Bester, who later testified that she had run away with her two children and with two others. Cloete must have felt completely justified in shooting her, for he filed a statement on 23 December 1807 which read: "I hereby inform you that I met a girl in the fields who had stolen sheeps, goats, and corn meal from me, and that I followed . . . 300 paces . . . upon which I shot her." His confidence that he would not be charged was no doubt buoyed by having good local connections – the last line of his statement read "I greet you your nephew."[24] But it certainly stemmed, too, from wide acceptance of settlers' disciplining their Khoi workers, with especially harsh treatment for runaways and thieves. In fact, the practice was later defended as customary by Cloete's lawyer.

It was not until four years later that Cloete found himself "unexpectedly arrested and confined" in a changed legal atmosphere and in

---

[22] The settlers used the word *Hottentot* to refer to Khoi laborers, some of whom were by now of mixed parentage and all of whom were, through contact with the settlers, culturally changed. See note 7 above.

[23] This is from Sara's own testimony. Extract for the Proceedings held by Commissioner of Circuit in Country districts, PRO: CO 48 25.

[24] PRO: CO 48 25, quoted in Exact Proceedings held by Commissioner of Circuit in Country districts.

a system now controlled by the British. Not long after Caledon's Proclamation, Cloete was arrested, in September 1811, apparently accused by Heyn of Mietze's murder. We do not know how the accusation was first brought forward, but perhaps Heyn was emboldened by the new promise to respond to Khoi accusations of brutality by colonists. In October, Cloete was formally charged with the murder and sent to prison in Cape Town. Up until then, he had probably thought the charges would not lead to serious trouble. Now he hired a lawyer. When the court ordered him banished from the colony for life, he filed an appeal, an act that created for us a written record of contrasting legal representations about the value of Khoi testimony.

Cloete's defense centered around three sets of arguments. The first rested on a rather feeble attempt to question the very strong physical evidence against him. Perhaps the gunshot wound had not caused Mietze's death, his lawyers argued; the body might have been misidentified; and another gun, Heindrik Heyn's, might have fired the fatal shot. But Cloete was undone by his own actions after the shooting; he had never contradicted the findings of the field commander and had never denied that his gun had killed Mietze. Two other sets of arguments must have seemed more promising to the defense. Both of the strategies focused on the cultural and legal roles of "Hottentots."

Cloete's conviction clearly depended on the testimony of the two Khoi witnesses, Heyn and Sara. Both testified that Cloete had shot Mietze without provocation. Heyn's testimony was especially damning. He recounted that Cloete had told *him* to shoot Mietze; when he refused, saying his gun was loaded with shot and would injure the child in her arms, Cloete ordered Heyn to take the child from her. Mietze was by now pleading for her life. As Heyn stepped forward, he heard a shot ring out and saw the woman drop to the ground. Sara testified that she came forward and took the baby from under the body of her dead mother.

Cloete's account was that he had been startled by a "wrestling in the bushes" and had shot reflexively. Sara had told him, Cloete reported, that "the gang of Hottentot deserters" had a plan to set fire to Cloete's house and kill him. In the appeal, his lawyer embellished freely: This "unexpected information terrified and confused appellant in such a degree that he almost lost his Judgement, and was for some time, as it were, out of his wits." Cloete, the lawyer said, had heard someone – "perhaps his companion Heindrik Heyn" – exclaim, "Here he is!" just as he "perceived some movement in another part of the bushes."

Terrified, and momentarily insane, he fired his rifle, only later to find that he had wounded "one of the gang members."

The difference in these accounts is between a cold-blooded execution of a woman with an infant in her arms and an accidental shooting by a terrified and outnumbered settler trying to protect his property and family. Cloete and his lawyers understood that to make the court accept his version of events they would have to discredit the testimony of the two witnesses. They would also have to argue that conditions on the frontier were such that Cloete's actions were understandable, even customary. The "Hottentots" had to be painted as dangerous and untrustworthy. Cloete had to be recast as in effect a representative of the law who was merely executing a punishment that would have been delivered anyway.

The first goal was to call into question the two witnesses' reliability; some of the objections were specific to the case, but others suggested that Khoi testimony was itself not to be trusted. Cloete's attorney pointed out that "in law it is required at least two credible witnesses" and argued that the "child as well as the accuser are not only Hottentots but also the natural enemies of the accused." Since one of the witnesses was a child, and herself a member of the gang, her testimony could not be trusted. Heindrik Heyn, for his part, was also armed and might have fired the fatal shot himself. Going further, in the appeal Cloete's lawyer noted that neither Heindrik Heyn nor Sara had taken an oath "on account of their having no religious faith whatsoever."[25]

The witnesses were, like other "Hottentots" on the frontier, a fearsome bunch. Cloete's lawyer reported that "frequently whole families are casually and inhumanly murdered by such Hottentots" and that "the honest and christian inhabitants of these distant districts" lived in "constant fear and dread." The gang members were, furthermore, runaways and criminals. Had Mietze been brought to trial for her crimes, she would have been "removed from the earth," based on both Dutch laws and customary practice in the region.[26] This argument rested on a

---

[25] Quotes are from statement by Cloete's lawyer signed 9 January 1812, and "Court of Appeals for terminal cases at the Cape of Good Hope." PRO: CO 48 25.

[26] It is interesting to find Cloete's lawyer quoting Blackstone to support this argument. He was probably aware that an appeal on the basis of Dutch law would not sway the court and that Blackstone was considered authoritative on English law. The chief justice in reply, however, chides him for quoting selectively from Blackstone (lifting a quote from a section on piracy) and brings out a quote of his own in which Blackstone condemns wanton killing.

further assertion that Mietze was, in fact, not protected under the law because she "was not a Subject of any Government or member of any community but of a gang of Vagabonds and Disturbers of the peace." Signaling that the gang belonged to a separate community, Cloete had reported that they had planned to kill him and his family, to steal all his cattle, and take them to "Cafferland." Even though the Khoi were clearly economically dependent on the settlers and had as a group undergone dramatic culture change through working and living on the settlers' farms, the view among Dutch-descended settlers on the frontier was that the Khoi must still be part of another political community, in "Cafferland." They were not, certainly, legal subjects with any standing in the world of the settlers.

The prosecution, responsive to the jurisdictional shift underway, addressed this point carefully. Though Mietze was a thief, the prosecutor responded, "the Prisoner had the said Hottentot Mietze in his power" and had "inflicted the punishment of death on a person who, according to the laws, deserved for her trifling crime, perhaps only a trifling correction, but not Death." Following the guideline that it would continue to apply Dutch law, the appeals court ruled that even according to Dutch law, killing was only justified when there was no opportunity to deliver a fugitive to the hands of justice. The court considered the cruelty of the murder, too, in its sentencing; a mother with a baby in her arms had been shot in the neck at close range, circumstances that no doubt made the case a particularly good one to justify the intervention of the circuit courts. Reporting on the failed appeal in the *Cape Town Gazette*, in October 1812, the governor decried "the willful and direct murder of a defenseless wretched Woman, holding an Infant Child in her arms at the moment of her Death," then went on to proclaim, "The Law is the same to all, the rich or poor Man, the powerful or defenseless, the Master or the Slave, the European, Colonist, or Hottentot."[27] The appeals court reaffirmed the order of banishment and continued to hold Cloete on Robben's Island until he could be sent away.

The case against Cloete was brought because of an accusation by a Khoi laborer, one corroborated by another Khoi witness. It was to be one of a series of cases in which the courts now accepted Khoi testimony and sought to curb the independent authority of settlers. For participants, the shift was simultaneously about jurisdictional lines and

[27] The *Cape Town Gazette and African Advertiser*, Saturday, October 10, 1812, Vol. VII, no. 352. PRO: CO 48 25.

cultural boundaries. The settlers' power over Khoi living in their midst was supported by an argument of cultural difference and a weak legal pluralism that suggested the Khoi were part of a still-functioning, separate polity. As outsiders, Khoi workers represented a threat that needed to be controlled; as legal actors, they had no standing. On the other side, an incipient colonial state was seeking to establish jurisdiction over all the groups and regions of the colony. This meant redefining the Khoi as legitimate legal actors, a move that was intended not to liberate the Khoi but to rein in the colonists. This move raised, in turn, a new challenge in legal policy for the British, who were certainly not eager to erase all cultural and legal distinctions between themselves and their colonial subjects.

Although it is sometimes assumed that British legal doctrines of equality before the law clashed with Roman-Dutch traditions of status distinctions in the law, and that the latter formed the basis for the apartheid state of the twentieth century, the intervening history was far more complex and, in fact, demonstrated that British legal traditions were fully compatible with the harshest of regimes for controlling the African population. The incorporation of larger numbers of Africans into the Cape Colony and the conquest of territories of majority African population in Natal prompted a growing recognition of African law and courts. The timing and context of the recognition of indigenous legal authority, however, undermined any possibility of creating a truly plural legal order. Subordination to the state was built into the relationship between indigenous and state law. At the same time, pass laws and other mechanisms for controlling Africans were legislated in the Cape Colony itself. Enforcement itself created a certain segregation in the legal order, as white litigants dominated civil proceedings and black and brown defendants proliferated in criminal courts. As one scholar summarizes the complex changes in law in the next half century, "a legal-administrative machine for the control of Africans was created which was to be imported in more rigid form into the Transvaal after conquest, and which was to return to the Cape in harsh all-Union legislation."[28]

Legal policy in Natal, and not in the Boer republics of the interior, provided part of the blueprint for a segregated legal order. In the Orange Free State, Africans were a servile population subjected to the semi-autonomous rule of white masters. African law had no standing. In Natal, in contrast, a separate structure of rule was set up that prefigured

---

[28] Keegan, *Colonial South Africa*, p. 64.

indirect rule as an articulated policy decades later. Chiefs were subsumed in the legal order as subordinate functionaries. They retained some local jurisdiction, but they occupied the bottom of a hierarchy that moved from indigenous authorities to white magistrates to the governor, who was awarded the status of supreme chief. Later native courts were established to hear all civil and criminal cases involving Africans, thus removing Africans from white courts altogether except in cases on appeal. Space in the "middle ground" was severely constricted. Exceptions granted for "civilized" Africans to transcend the boundaries of the segregated legal order were more and more difficult to obtain. Interestingly, the system was defended as a support for indigenous authority, which was of course being re-created in a more authoritarian and venal mode.

Historians of South Africa have understandably concentrated on identifying the origins of racial segregation. While a liberal version champions the British impulse to establish equality before the law and finds the seeds of apartheid in Boer racial ideology, Afrikaner nationalists promote a narrative in which the possibilities for racial harmony were forestalled by imperialist expansion. Revisionist historians falling into neither of these camps have instead emphasized the continuity of distinctions in legal status running from the imposition of Roman-Dutch law through to harsh all-Union racial legislation.[29] Yet a more nuanced view that also opposes partisan history is suggested in other revisionist works and is supported by this overview of legal change. In this perspective, the early to mid-nineteenth century stands out as a period of discontinuity in which the nature of colonial authority shifted in response to various pressures – legal and extralegal challenges to that authority, the "closing" of the frontier, and tighter integration of the colony in world markets and metropolitan affairs. Once established, the hegemony of state law, and the subordination of alternative authorities or jurisdictions, continued as conquest brought larger African populations into the polity. The shift in the nature of state authority in this period established, as Keegan puts it, the new idea "that colonial hegemony should be exercised over independent African farmers and intact African societies, rather than at the level solely of the individual colonial households or colonial enterprise."[30] This more extensive claim to

---

[29] For example, Richard Elphick and Hermann Giliomee, "The Origins and Entrenchment of European Dominance at the Cape, 1652–c. 1840"; and for a useful discussion of the historiography of the origins of race, see Keegan, *Colonial South Africa*.

[30] Keegan, *Colonial South Africa*, p. 13.

authority allowed the British to formalize racial distinctions that were already partially in place.

For our purposes, the central role in this shift of jurisdictional debates about the Khoi is enlightening. Though missionaries are often credited with bringing colonists' abusive treatment of Khoi laborers to light and advancing legal protests on their behalf, the Khoi emerge rather more as protagonists actively involved in both legal and extralegal contests.[31] Poorer colonists, too, appear in this analysis as expressing not so much Calvinist racialism as a particular sense of moral economy that viewed intervention by both colonial and metropolitan authorities in the control of labor and land as arbitrary and unjust. For elite Afrikaners, the critical break with loyalty to the emerging colonial state was over different matters and occurred when they perceived they were to be cast out of the legal order and redefined as another group among the colonized – a class of people on whom foreign law was to be imposed. The presence of European settlers in significant numbers added to the complexity of the legal order and placed debates about the legal status of the indigenous population at the center of colonial politics.

ABORIGINES AS LEGAL SUBJECTS IN NEW SOUTH WALES

A similar set of tensions, with still different results, emerged in the penal colony of New South Wales. Like the Khoi, Aborigines in New South Wales found themselves pushed out of land they had long inhabited by European settlers who were taking up pastoralism. Also like the Khoi, the Aborigines were pulled into court, in legal encounters that highlighted the ambiguity of their status before the colonial courts. But whereas the split between Afrikaner and British authorities encouraged the recognition of Khoi witnesses and litigants in Cape Colony courts, in Australia the legal conflicts among the European population exerted a different kind of pressure. New South Wales was founded as a penal colony. The main issues of legal reform in the early decades of the nineteenth century centered around the legal status of convicts and former convicts. The political faction known as *emancipists* (a term also used more narrowly to describe former convicts) led the struggle against settlers who were untainted by criminality and interested

---

[31] See Crais (*White Supremacy and Black Resistance*) and also Shula Marks, "Khoisan Resistance to the Dutch in the Seventeenth and Eighteenth Centuries." The protagonism of Khoi in legal cases regarding labor conditions is treated more specifically in Susan Newton-King, "The Labour Market of the Cape Colony, 1807–28."

in retaining the legal trappings of political and social superiority over settlers from convict backgrounds.[32] It is tempting to treat these narratives – one about the legal treatment of Aborigines, one about the legal disputes of whites – separately, as most historians have done.[33] After noting, for example, the striking degree to which politics in the early history of New South Wales "took a legal form," David Neal portrays debates about Aborigines' legal status as a sideline to the consuming battles of European factions over the rule of law. [34]

It is true that the formal redefinition of Aborigines as legal subjects in the 1830s had little practical effect on them. But it is also significant that the question was taken up precisely at the same time that the debate about the legal status of emancipists reached its climax. The redefinition of Aborigines as colonial legal subjects rather than members of a separate, indigenous community took place in the late 1830s, in a series of cases involving mainly frontier violence. Conflicts over the legal rights of convicts in the colony intensified in the 1820s and 1830s, and the transportation of convicts to New South Wales ended in 1840. Emancipists' political ambitions required legal authority to be inclusive; the realignment of the 1830s marked the formal shift from a policy of legal pluralism, with its narrow jurisdictional claims, to one of state hegemony. Aboriginal legal status could not remain unaffected by this shift. The debates formed part of a single discourse about cultural hierarchies and the law. This is not to say that the result was obvious or uncontested, or that it was favorable to Aborigines' welfare. As in the Cape Colony, the new legal regime substituted systematic oppression, and its tacit approval, for more arbitrary and disorganized forms of frontier violence.

Even more so than with the Khoi, the legal presence of Aborigines and their own participation in legal reforms is difficult to locate. Through the colony's first fifty years, Aborigines very rarely appeared as litigants in civil court; they entered the courts as criminal defendants, and then only

---

[32] Because the term is used in both ways, the label *emancipist* can be confusing. I use it largely in this chapter to refer to the political cause and stick to "former convicts" for the narrower category. Thus, for example, the attorneys Wentworth and Wardell were both free, though prominent members of the emancipist party and from convict backgrounds.

[33] An exception is the work of Bruce Kercher on the law in the colony's first twenty-five years, in which he addresses the legal treatment of convicts, women, and Aborigines as elements of a larger legal politics of inequality. See Bruce Kercher, *Debt, Seduction, and Other Disasters: The Birth of Civil Law in Convict New South Wales*.

[34] David Neal, *The Rule of Law in a Penal Colony: Law and Power in Early New South Wales*, p. 80.

in small numbers.[35] Aboriginal testimony was not accepted. Yet Aborigines were more central to the unfolding debates about the structure of the legal order than they might appear to be. Aboriginal violence had a judicial character that was implicitly acknowledged and occasionally openly recognized in colonial debates about legal pluralism. And defining cultural boundaries separating Aborigines from Europeans was at the center of discourse about legal change.

Consider first the legal arguments about the status of Aborigines and the nature of colonial legal suzerainty. These issues were aired in a series of cases heard in the Supreme Court of New South Wales between 1824, the year that the second, permanent Supreme Court was established, and 1836, the year in which the court issued its first ruling clearly placing Aborigines under the jurisdiction of the courts for crimes committed within their own communities. This period coincided with the tenure of Chief Justice Francis Forbes, who as chief justice in Newfoundland had permitted some recognition of local customs and a flexible application of English law. This "barely articulated pluralism," as Kercher dubs Forbes's approach, was quickly tested in New South Wales.[36]

Aborigines could not give sworn testimony in court because they were not Christians and could presumably not understand the sanctity of the oath or fear divine punishment for perjury. Forbes quickly learned, in a case brought before him in June 1824, that this arrangement posed special problems. The case involved an alleged murder by two whites of a third white settler. One of the defendants admitted to the shooting but claimed it was accidental. There was one witness to the shooting, an Aborigine man known to the British as Bulwaddy. Forbes had him brought into court and determined that, as the *Sydney Gazette* reported, he "appeared to know well the distinctions between truth and falsehood, and appeared to have some apprehension of an existence after death" but had no "superstitious or religious fear of a superior Being, who would punish him if he should speak falsely."[37] His testimony could

---

[35] See Kercher, *Debt, Seduction, and Other Disasters* for a description of the first case, and the only one on record prior to 1814, of a civil case involving an Aborigine litigant. Kercher reports that Governor Macquarie was eager to see the claim given careful legal consideration so that other Aborigines in contractual relationships would be protected.

[36] Bruce Kercher, "Native Title in the Shadows: The Origins of the Myth of *Terra Nullius* in Early New South Wales Courts."

[37] Macquarie University has published this case and others from the superior courts of New South Wales on a website under the direction of Bruce Kercher. This case,

not be heard, then, though the court accepted testimony from "a competent witness" to whom Bulwaddy had described the murder.[38] Forbes convicted only the defendant who had admitted to firing the shot and then forwarded the case to the colony's governor for consideration of mercy. The governor had the attorney general bring Bulwaddy before him, whereupon he again told of the murder, leading the governor to affirm the sentence of the court. The case left Forbes wondering about the wisdom of excluding Aborigine testimony. He wrote in a strong letter in August of the same year that Aborigines had no sense of divine rewards or punishments but were "governed like ourselves by that instinctive love of justice, and natural law which always leads to the expression of truth where there is no superior inducement to falsehood."[39] Describing the case, he added: "Now was it not barbarous to exclude such testimony by a mere rule of Court, which was engendered in days of superstition, and framed by men who never heard of the consequences to which it would tend. Why is not competency confined to interest, and credibility left in all cases to the jury?"[40]

As Forbes revealed here, and in later judgments about Aboriginal legal standing, he was torn between acceptance of a view of Aborigines as savages bereft of legal understanding and the assumption that they possessed customary law. Even if logic, and the pressures of pronouncing just outcomes in particular cases, threatened to lead him to the second conclusion, Forbes searched for ways of reconciling the two positions. The implications for deciding the legal status of the Aborigines were

---

R. v. Fitzpatrick and Colville, as well as the other cases from the Supreme Court cited below, appear on the site *http://www.law.mq.edu.au/scnsw*. Citations from this source henceforth appear with the document name, the name of the case, and the title of the on-line case series. This quote is from the *Sydney Gazette*, 24 June 1824, *R. v. Fitzpatrick and Colville*, "Decisions of the Superior Courts of New South Wales, 1788–1899."

[38] *Sydney Gazette*, 24 June 1824, *R. v. Fitzpatrick and Colville*, "Decisions of the Superior Courts of New South Wales, 1788–1899." Forbes later wrote, "I have felt that under the peculiar and perhaps unprecedented circumstances in which the Court was placed, that the best evidence (at least vital evidence) had not been produced." Forbes C. J. to Governor Brisbane, 24 June 1824, Chief Justice's Letter Book, Archives Office of New South Wales, 4/6651, p. 1, quoted in *R. v. Fitzpatrick and Colville*, "Decisions of the Superior Courts of New South Wales, 1788–1899."

[39] Letter to Wilmot Horton on 14 August 1824 (Catton Papers, Australian Joint Copying Project, Reel M791), quoted in notes, *R. v. Fitzpatrick and Colville*, "Decisions of the Superior Courts of New South Wales, 1788–1899."

[40] Letter to Wilmot Horton on 14 August 1824 (Catton Papers, Australian Joint Copying Project, Reel M791), quoted in notes, *R. v. Fitzpatrick and Colville*, "Decisions of the Superior Courts of New South Wales, 1788–1899."

not entirely clear. The argument that they possessed law and, therefore, a sense of right and wrong could be used to support the position that they should be accepted as legal actors in colonial courts. Yet the same argument could buttress the view that as subjects of separate polities, Aborigines were not entitled to consideration under British law.

Over the next several years, the cases brought before the court were consistent with the jurisdictional lines drawn in other European enclaves in Asia and Africa: Aborigines were tried when they were accused of acts of violence against whites, and whites were charged (though usually acquitted by juries) for acts of violence against Aborigines.[41] But this modus operandi did not rest on formal consideration of the legal status of Aborigines. As Neal puts it succinctly, for the colony's first fifty years, the legal system "had trouble deciding whether the Aborigines should be treated as subjects of the Crown or foreign enemies who could be hunted down in reprisal raids and shot."[42]

The first explicit arguments made in court about jurisdiction over Aborigines came in May 1827. Nathaniel Lowe was an army officer accused of murdering an Aborigine identified as Jackey Jackey, who was in custody at the time. The case brought the debate about Aborigine legal status into collision with another set of political struggles in the colonies. The defense attorneys were two prominent lawyers who were also political leaders of the emancipist political faction seeking expanded political and legal rights for former convicts. This pair, William Wentworth and Robert Wardell, founded the *Australian* in 1824 and used the paper to report on their pro-emancipist oratory as publicity favorable to the cause. Forbes was sympathetic to the cause, which focused on specific demands for judicial reform, most notably the right to trial by jury, as well as the broader political objective of former convicts' participation in representative government in the colony. The opposition – the exclusives – having succeeded in 1820 in prohibiting former convicts from becoming magistrates, opposed trial by jury precisely because the colony was a penal colony; the distinction between those who had come to the colony as convicts and those who had come voluntarily

---

[41] On August 6, 1824, a jury found five whites not guilty of assault on an Aborigine woman, though Forbes instructed them to reject the defense's argument that violence was justifiable as a response to recent attacks by Aborigines (*R. v. Johnston, Clarke, Nicholson, Castles, and Crear*). In *R. v. Foley*, heard just ten days later, an Aborigine was indicted for the murder of a convict at Port Macquarie. He was acquitted because the dying man declared that the defendant's father had been the one to spear him.

[42] Neal, *The Rule of Law in a Penal Colony*, p. 17.

was crucial to their own social standing. Emancipists, in turn, argued that law and legal procedure should be brought into line with the English system. But the neatness of this position was marred by the emancipist opposition to importing the English law of felony attaint, which would have erased the benefits of other legal reforms by forcing convicts and former convicts to the margins of the legal system.

Although Wentworth and Wardell never explicitly tied their arguments about jurisdiction over Aborigines to other issues of legal reform, this wider political agenda could not have been far from their minds. In fact, the political fights over the legal order had recently intensified, following an 1819 emancipist petition to the crown asking for the establishment of trial by jury and a ruling reaffirming the law of felony attaint the following year. Further, the conflict about the legal standing of former convicts was eerily analogous to the debate about Aborigines and the law. Convicts and freed convicts were being excluded from positions of power because they were seen as morally unfit to serve. They made up a large proportion of the colony's population yet had no formal standing to bring suit – though they had done so from 1788 to 1820 despite this ban.[43] It would seem logical that the emancipists, in arguing for the recognition of all settlers as full legal subjects, would also urge that sovereignty be extended to Aborigines. In fact, the reverse was more often true. In seeking to redefine themselves as the legal and political equals of other whites, emancipists sought to emphasize the cultural gulf that divided former convicts, and whites in general, from Aborigines. At the same time, though, the legal arguments had a way of becoming conflated, with perhaps unintended consequences.

The case against Lowe shows these entanglements well. Wardell opened the case by objecting that the court had no jurisdiction to try it. The argument was one of many twists and centered on the claim that since Aborigines themselves could not be subject to the jurisdiction of the court, white settlers had no other way to deal with violent acts committed by them than to punish them directly. In developing the argument that the court's jurisdiction did not extend to Aborigines, Wardell explicitly rejected the notion that the Aborigine could be defined as either "an alien enemy" or "an alien friend" because no formal agreements,

---

[43] Neal recounts that the first civil suit in the colony was filed by two convicts, the Kables, who had been transported together and on arrival had been unable to recover a trunk from the ship on which they traveled. The case, he argues, set the stage for further legal and political struggles about the legal standing of convicts. See Neal, *The Rule of Law in a Penal Colony.*

treaties, or declarations of war existed with the British monarch.[44] This view was consistent with the doctrine of terra nullius, the idea that the colony had been only sparsely inhabited by peoples who had no real claim to possession of the land. In bypassing this possible argument for a formal pluralism based on the recognition of separate and independent legal jurisdictions, Wardell was not just reaffirming accepted legal wisdom, though. Other leaders had argued for a more formal reception of Aboriginal law.[45] Endorsing terra nullius – based on a reading of the international legal writings of Vattel – narrowed the grounds on which Wardell could argue for jurisdictional limits. Since the Aborigines were clearly present on the land, he had to argue their incapacity. This approach turned into an assertion of permanent cultural difference. Aborigines could not be tried in colonial courts because they did not and could not "understand the forms of our Courts." If an Aborigine were tried, his lack of understanding would make him the legal equivalent of "a lunatic, a madman." This cultural argument was followed by a veiled political one. Wardell seized the opportunity to refer indirectly to the flaws of the New South Wales Act and its nonrecognition of civilian trial by jury:

> The New South Wales Act provides, that in all cases, trial by a jury of seven military and naval officers, shall be "the trial by jury" of this Court, in all cases – that is in all cases contemplated by the British Legislature on passing this Act. It is self evident that the Legislature never contemplated the aboriginal natives, or the trial of them, and

---

[44] *Australian*, 23 May 1827, *R. v. Lowe*, "Decisions of the Superior Courts of New South Wales, 1788–1899."

[45] Kercher comments, "The issue of legal protection of native title to land did not seem to occur to anyone in judicial office during the colony's first 25 years." Kercher, "Native Title in the Shadows," p. 3. Some colonists did, however, imagine alternatives to claiming the doctrine of terra nullius and argued that the government should negotiate treaties with the Aborigines. Governor George Arthur repeatedly urged the Colonial Office to take this approach in the 1820s. In 1836 the attorney general of New South Wales, Saxe-Bannister, argued publicly that the government should "begin, at least, to reduce the laws and usages of the aborigines to language, print them and direct our courts of justice to respect these laws in proper cases" (quoted in Henry Reynolds, *Aboriginal Sovereignty: Three Nations, One Australia?*, pp. 115–16). In 1838, the Aborigines Protection Society established a subcommittee whose report, an *Outline of a System of Legislation for Securing Protection to the Aboriginal Inhabitants of All Countries Colonized by Great Britain*, urged that Aborigines' property rights be formally recognized. As Reynolds notes, had such policies been adopted, they "would have changed the character of Australian settlement and given a more secure juridical foundation to the colonial venture" (Reynolds, *Aboriginal Sovereignty*, p. 116).

therefore they are entitled to that mode of trial provided for foreigners by the common law of England, that is, they are entitled to be tried by a jury composed half of British subjects, and half of natives, because the New South Wales Act cannot take away this right by implication, therefore the aboriginal natives cannot be tried by this Court for any offence by them committed.[46]

Wardell no doubt recognized this argument for what it was – a stretch. Since Aborigines were not permitted to give testimony in court, the chances that they would be permitted to sit on a jury were nonexistent. It is possible that the argument served Wardell as a way of pointing up the absurdity of restrictions on the legal roles assigned to convicts and freed convicts.[47] Such a connection would not have been lost on the audience in court, certainly, nor on many readers of the *Australian*.

Wardell's argument took an interesting turn as he resolutely followed its logic. If Aborigines could not be lawfully brought before the court for crimes they committed, then the defendant was acting in accordance with divine law in punishing his victim. His act was also justified under international law, which held that "any man may draw his sword" against pirates and others living outside the law. Then Wardell went still further and argued that the act of punishment was also made lawful by the fact that it conformed to local custom. Murder, in other words, as an act of retribution, was affirmed by customary law, and "surely nothing is more rational than for persons going into a strange country . . . to remain submissive to, and contented with the laws and usages, such as they are of that country, into which they come." The avenger should be regarded, Wardell argued, as both an instrument of divine justice and a "substitute for a court of Judicature." Wentworth then went on to argue for the defense that no sovereignty had been assumed over the Aborigines and that, in consequence, "they are independent families . . . possessing the free demesne of the country, without any Sovereign or laws among themselves, besides the native customs which are peculiar to their race."[48]

The court roundly dismissed these arguments and ruled that the victim was a British subject and that the New South Wales Act gave the

---

[46] *Australian*, 23 May 1827, *R. v. Lowe*, "Decisions of the Superior Courts of New South Wales, 1788–1899."

[47] See the discussion below. The intertwining of emancipist causes and Aboriginal legal issues emerged again more clearly in the trial of seven convicts for the murder of Aborigines at Myall Creek.

[48] *Australian*, 23 May 1827, *R. v. Lowe*, "Decisions of the Superior Courts of New South Wales, 1788–1899."

court "jurisdiction to try all offences."[49] This outcome might have been anticipated by Wardell and Wentworth – settlers had been tried (and acquitted) for the murder of Aborigines before. What is interesting in their arguments is the failure to embrace fully a characterization of Aborigines as living "in a state of nature." Wardell elevated Aboriginal custom to law. Wentworth, relying on Vattel's writings in international law and arguing that the colony held no right of sovereignty over the Aborigines, made a stronger statement about Aboriginal property rights than any known to be on record at the time.[50] These arguments were made, though, in support not of the protection of Aboriginal legal rights but of Aborigines' legal exclusion. Adding to this irony was that when the case was tried, the defense turned on the unreliability of oaths sworn by convict witnesses. The defense presented numerous witnesses who testified to the bad character of the main prosecution witnesses. Forbes, in his instructions to the jury, noted the lack of "[r]espectable evidence," and the jury took only five minutes to acquit Lowe.[51] No doubt the jury would have produced an acquittal anyway; as proscribed under the New South Wales Act, the jury consisted of military officers, and Lowe was one of their own. Indeed, a further irony of the case is that the pro-emancipist defense benefited from a practice – the jury as military panel – that it opposed on principle.

The same issues returned two years later in a case brought against an Aboriginal defendant, Ballard, for the murder of another Aborigine.[52] The attorney general asked the court for direction as to whether Ballard could be tried. Forbes, now joined by a less confident Justice Dowling, found that the court did not have jurisdiction in the case. Forbes explained that it had been established policy "never to interfere with

---

[49] *Australian*, 23 May 1827, *R. v. Lowe*, "Decisions of the Superior Courts of New South Wales, 1788–1899." Justice Stephen stated this more categorically; Forbes argued for jurisdiction on broader grounds and added that even if the Aboriginal victim were not considered a British subject, he would still be "entitled to *lex loci*," in this case English law as applied by the colony's courts.

[50] Kercher, in "Native Title in the Shadows," notes that these cases were effectively lost in Australian legal case history because there was no early law reporting. Decisions confirming the application of terra nullius and sovereignty over Aborigines have overshadowed earlier cases where judges are reported, in newspapers and their own letters and notes, to have endorsed some form of legal pluralism.

[51] *Australian*, 23 May 1827, *R. v. Lowe*, "Decisions of the Superior Courts of New South Wales, 1788–1899."

[52] He is Ballard in the *Australian* and referred to as Barrett in one account in the *Sydney Gazette*. See the notes by Kercher in *R. v. Ballard or Barrett*, "Decisions of the Superior Courts of New South Wales, 1788–1899."

or enter into the quarrels that have taken place between or amongst the natives themselves."[53] Acts of aggression by one group against the other did fall within the court's jurisdiction. As if predicting the future, Forbes worried, "If part of our system is to be introduced amongst them, why not the whole? Where will you draw the line: the intervention of our courts of justice, even if practicable, must lead to other interferences."[54]

Forbes's "weak pluralism" was very much intact. He seemed to ascribe no law to the Aborigenes at first, noting that the "most important distinction between the savage & civilized state of man" was that "amongst savages there are no magistrates" and all differences are decided "upon a principle of retaliation." But then Forbes, echoing Wardell, came back to a weak recognition of law among the Aborigines, who made "laws for themselves" and had "institutions" to preserve order.[55]

When the issue of jurisdiction emerged again, three years later, Justice Dowling did not hesitate in establishing the authority of the court. The defense for an Aborigine called Boatman, who was indicted for stealing two sheep, again raised the question of whether the court had jurisdiction to try a native. Dowling succinctly summarized a position which he and Forbes had struggled to define just a few years before:

> The general principle acted upon, I believe, with respect to these peoples since the foundation of this as a British Colony, is to regard them as being entirely under the protection of the law of England for offences committed against them by the white settlers & subjects of the Crown, & on the other hand to render them liable for any infraction of the British Law which may be injurious to the persons or properties of His Majesty's white subjects. We interfere not with their own habits, customs or domestic regulations, but leave them to adjust their own disputes & differences among themselves.[56]

[53] Dowling, "Proceedings of the Supreme Court, Vol. 27, Archives Office of New South Wales, 2/3205," in *R. v. Ballard or Barrett*, "Decisions of the Superior Courts of New South Wales, 1788–1899."

[54] Dowling, "Proceedings," in *R. v. Ballard or Barrett*, "Decisions of the Superior Courts of New South Wales, 1788–1899."

[55] Dowling, "Proceedings," in *R. v. Ballard or Barrett*, "Decisions of the Superior Courts of New South Wales, 1788–1899."

[56] Dowling, "Proceedings of the Supreme Court of New South Wales, Vol. 64, Archives Office of New South Wales 2/3247" in *R. v. Boatman or Jackass and Bulleye*, "Decisions of the Superior Courts of New South Wales, 1788–1899."

In this case the defense, having lost on the question of the court's jurisdiction, mounted a "cultural defense" with the aid of the Reverend Thelkeld, who had been brought up from Newcastle.[57] In addition to acting as interpreter, Threlkeld appeared as an expert witness. While he affirmed the court's already stated view that the Aborigines had "no knowledge of the laws of England," he insisted that they had a strong sense of right and wrong that regulated their own relations:

> [T]hey are exceedingly particular with regard to the rights of property amongst each other; they will not allow any thing, however trifling, to be taken by one from another; they lend to each other, and, although not over-particular in exacting the return of the thing lent, lending and giving away; they have distinct words for each in their language; they have also some idea of barter; the Newcastle tribes send up bundles of spears which they manufacture to tribes up the country, and receive, in return, a cord made of the skin of the wallobi.[58]

This testimony was crucial because, together with evidence that settlers had recently released diseased sheep into the bush nearby, it suggested that the theft of the sheep might have resulted from simple misunderstanding that the sheep constituted property. The jury found Boatman not guilty, and the solicitor-general was induced also to reverse the conviction of another Aboriginal man who had not had the benefit of this defense.

Here the court seemed to administer justice faultlessly, and in accordance with rules consistent with the "weak pluralism" that had been emerging as the court's response to the series of jurisdictional challenges. It is all the more striking, then, that the same court, in Forbes's last ruling before leaving his post, would reverse itself a mere six years later. The case that turned around the court's approach was *R. v. Murrell*, in 1836. Kercher calls this case "the founding case in Australian law for the application of the *terra nullius* doctrine."[59] Two Aborigines were indicted for the murder of two other Aborigines west of Sydney. In arguing that the court did not have jurisdiction over the case, the defense lawyer Sydney Stephen asserted a stronger legal pluralism than the court had recognized before, though his portrayal of Aborigines as a people possessing law did not appear to be anything more than a logical extension

---

[57] For a discussion of "cultural defense," see Lawrence Rosen, "The Integrity of Cultures."

[58] *Sydney Gazette*, 25 February 1832, in *R. v. Boatman or Jackass and Bulleye*, "Decisions of the Superior Courts of New South Wales, 1788–1899."

[59] Kercher, "Native Title in the Shadows," p. 10.

of the court's earlier findings. Before British occupation, he argued, the colony was populated by

> tribes of native blacks, who were regulated and governed by usages and customs of their own from time immemorial, practised and recognized amongst them, and not by the laws or statutes of Great Britain, and that ever since the occupation of the said Territory, as aforesaid, the said tribes have continued to be, and still are regulated and governed by such usages and customs as aforesaid, and not by the laws or Statutes of Great Britain.[60]

But, then, Stephen took the argument one unacceptable step further. He characterized New South Wales as an inhabited territory before British occupation. The British were intruding on Aboriginal land and should be bound by Aboriginal law. Since Aborigines did not have equal standing under British law, they could hardly be subject to it. This was too much for the justices. The newly arrived Justice Burton wrote the ruling that affirmed that the court had jurisdiction over all crimes within the territory of the colony, and he specifically rejected the argument that the Aborigines should be recognized as having possessed government and laws at the time of "settlement." The ruling marked, in other words, a rejection of pluralism, both weak and strong, and a shift toward the claim of transcendent state legal authority.

Of course, the case did not put an immediate end to debates about the legal status of Aborigines. Burton appears actually to have wished to finesse the question of whether all Aborigines were British subjects. In notes he made at the time of the ruling, he suggested that Aborigines could be aliens *or* subjects; they were entitled to become subjects but were not so by birth alone.[61] Both Dowling and Forbes were less strident in their opinions in *Murrell*, too. For some, the jurisdictional question was not yet settled. A lower court judge ruled in 1841 that Aborigines were self-governing, though he was overturned by Dowling, citing the Murrell case. As late as 1860, the debate was resurfacing in a handful of cases tried in Victoria.

Yet, there can be little doubt that the late 1830s marked a turning point. It was not just the legal rhetoric that had shifted but also the balance of

---

[60] Quoted in Kercher, "Native Title in the Shadows," p. 10.
[61] He reaffirmed, however, that there was only one law and, whether aliens or subjects, Aborigines would still enjoy the full protection of the law and would have the right to litigate. Kercher, "White Fellow Eat Bandicoots & Black Snakes Now: Aborigines, Law, and Resistance in the Supreme Court of New South Wales under Francis Forbes," p. 29.

power behind it. The court's decisive shift away from pluralism is difficult to explain as a result merely of the evolution of legal reasoning. Aboriginal legal status, and those acts that can be understood as constituting Aboriginal legal strategy, responded to, and also influenced, wider legal and political shifts.

THE "RIGHT TO STEAL WHAT THEY THOUGHT PROPER"

The debate over convicts' and ex-convicts' legal status was reaching a crescendo in these decades. Between 1788, when two convicts filed suit against the master of the ship that had carried them to Australia to recover goods they had brought with them, and 1820, the New South Wales courts recognized convicts' right to sue and accepted convict testimony. This practice diverged from the common law of England, where the law of felony attaint applied. The peculiar conditions of the penal colony seemed to require the adjustment. Convicts held property, and as the colony grew, many of them were becoming wealthy. To leave them with no recourse to the courts at all seemed unworkable. The law also developed an idiosyncratic distinction between different categories of convicts. Those assigned to serve free persons in the colony could litigate in magistrates' courts, while those who held "tickets of leave" – permission to live independently and work for themselves while still serving out their sentences – joined pardoned convicts in holding the same legal standing as free persons.

This accommodation to local conditions came under sharp attack in 1820, when two cases brought by the attorney Edward Eagar were rejected because he had been a convict.[62] Eagar's pardon was ruled invalid since it had not been endorsed in England. A year earlier, a similar ruling had been applied to actions brought by former convicts in England; now the same standard was being extended to courts in New South Wales. The decision followed a decade of Anglicization of local law under the influence of professional judges who resented, and for some years rejected altogether, the practice of law by convict and ex-convict attorneys. The shocking implications of the ruling were that the colony's convict and ex-convict residents – many of them now wealthy – were suddenly legally excluded from holding property and from giving

---

[62] My account of legal issues involving convicts in this period draws mainly from Bruce Kercher's very clear account in *An Unruly Child: A History of Law in Australia*, Chapter 2.

court testimony. The civil rights of a large proportion of the European population were abruptly swept away. Broadening the impact of this action, the legality of past transactions conducted by former convicts also came into question. Adding to the impact of these rulings, their attack on convict and ex-convict legal standing coincided with the introduction of secondary penal colonies where convicts could be retransported if they broke the law once in the colonies.

More than two decades were required for the colony to reestablish the previous local legal regime. In 1823, pardons in the colony were given full force, and previous pardons were also recognized. In 1843, the legal standing of ticket of leave holders was revised to permit them to sue and hold property (though not land). And in 1844, convict testimony was again made acceptable in the colony's courts.

The intervening decades were characterized by the adoption of a wide range of practices to extend legal rights to convicts informally. One device was for the court simply not to request a litigant's record of criminal conviction. Convict attorneys set themselves up in practice as "clerks" to free persons and continued to practice under this fiction. Convicts continued to hold accounts in the Bank of New South Wales, a practice that was sanctioned by local officials even though it was now technically illegal. Emancipists fought throughout the period to reestablish broader legal rights and to secure specific legal reforms such as trial by jury.

The influence of struggles over convict legal status on debates about Aboriginal legal standing was no doubt complex. Emancipists' resistance to the strict application of English law in rejecting the law of felony attaint seemed to parallel the argument that Aborigines should not be amenable to English law because they were so culturally distant from Europeans. This argument did not suggest any solidarity between emancipists and Aborigines; on the contrary, it reaffirmed the cultural distance of Aborigines from all whites and emphasized the shared status of convicts, former convicts, and free persons in relation to Aborigines. The political value of such a view may help to explain why arguments were made about the exclusion of Aborigines from colonial legal jurisdiction even in some cases of egregious violence. For example, commenting on the 1835 trial of two Aborigines accused of joining nine others in the brutal rape of a free servant named Margaret Hanshall, the *Australian* condemned the rape but questioned whether Aborigines were capable even of recognizing the attack as a crime. Their condition as "savages" appeared unchanged despite efforts to civilize them.

Rather than trying further to reform them, the editors recommended taking steps "to ensure their absence from our haunts."[63]

Often the connection between Aborigines' inferiority and convicts' worthiness as legal subjects was made more directly. Emancipists understood that the exclusion of convicts and former convicts – from the magistracy, and from juries – suggested that they were not just politically but also culturally close to Aborigines. The 1819 petition that proclaimed, among other causes, the establishment of trial by jury for the colony's residents, noted that the "Hindoo in India, the Hottentot in Africa and the Negro Slave in the West Indies" enjoyed trial by jury while former convicts did not.[64] And the practice of transporting Aborigines convicted of serious crimes to Van Diemen's Land (Tasmania) was an obvious parallel to the transportation that had brought convicts to Australia. In commenting on the trial of Aborigines for an attack on a house and two settlers at Brisbane Waters, the *Australian* argued that the interests of order on the frontier demanded the case be tried and the sentence of transportation to Van Diemen's Land carried through. Indeed, the commentary added, the Aborigines were receiving fairer treatment than many whites had when sentenced to transportation at home:

> We may be allowed to observe, by the way, upon the singular contrast which is exhibited between the interest that is felt for the future comfort of these men, and the barbarous indifference with which transportation in its worst shape, is seen inflicted upon those at home, whose situation strikingly resembles that of these aborigines; it is urged that these latter are ignorant and unenlightened – that they are incited by new wants, and opportunities, and that, from circumstances, they cannot have a fair trial; now take those classes of men who are transported for agrarian disturbances in England or Ireland; here you have almost equal ignorance, and a pressure of poverty which reduces the wants of the natives to absolutely nothing. [65]

---

[63] *Australian*, 6 March 1835, *R. v. Mickey and Muscle*, "Decisions of the Superior Courts of New South Wales, 1788–1899." The *Sydney Herald* also published a letter commenting on the inability of the defendants to understand the case against them or the legal procedures under which it was carried out. It contrasted "the English culprit" with "the native black" and suggested that the latter was little more than a "helpless spectator," while the former could influence the outcome of a trial through often "artful" tactics. *Sydney Herald*, 16 February 1835, *R. v. Mickey and Muscle*, "Decisions of the Superior Courts of New South Wales, 1788–1899."

[64] Quoted in Neal, *The Rule of Law in a Penal Colony*, p. 178.

[65] *Australian*, 17 February 1835, in *R. v. Monkey and Others*, "Decisions of the Superior Courts of New South Wales, 1788–1899."

The assertion of Aborigines' difference as a basis for legal separation must have reflected some anxiety, too, about the closing of cultural distance on the frontier. It was widely known that escaped convicts were in the bush, living off attacks on isolated farms, and often in contact with Aborigines.[66] In the 1835 trial of Aborigines accused of looting a house in Brisbane Water and injuring two whites there, one of the victims testified that he thought the Aborigines were "not solely to blame" and were "being led on either by bushrangers or prisoners of the crown."[67] The comment calls attention to a fact of frontier life: Whites intermingled with Aborigines and associated with them in many ways. In many cases violence resulted not from surprise encounters but "out of bitter arguments between settlers and blacks who had lived in proximity and reasonable accord for some time."[68] Witnesses described incidents during which they had recognized some of the aggressors, and even called out to them by name. In several attacks perpetrated by bands of Aborigines, the only culprits brought before the bar were those who could be identified and named by witnesses. In the 1835 prosecution of her rape, for example, Margaret Hanshall testified that there had been eleven men in the party that assaulted her, but she could recognize only the two defendants.[69] Seven Aborigines were ultimately prosecuted for

---

[66] On bushranging, see especially Paula J. Byrne, *Criminal Law and Colonial Subject: New South Wales, 1810–1830*, Chapter 5. Bushrangers sometimes blackened their faces, a practice no doubt brought from England but one that had new meaning in the context of white-Aboriginal relations. Prior to approving a campaign of violent oppression against Aborigines beyond the colony's northern limits in December 1837, Acting-Governor Kenneth Snodgrass received a report that Aborigines were being encouraged by bushrangers who were "painted like blacks." Snodgrass had also received reports that a number of attacks appeared to be in response to whites' abductions of Aborigine women. Officials were clearly aware, then, of evidence of the more complex roots of frontier violence, though they chose to ignore and even to disguise them. The force sent north by Snodgrass was responsible for the massacre of perhaps two hundred to three hundred Aborigines at Waterloo Creek in January 1835. See Roger Millis, *Waterloo Creek: The Australia Day Massacre of 1838, George Gipps, and the British Conquest of New South Wales*, p. 2.

[67] *Sydney Gazette*, 14 May 1835, R. v. Long Dick, Jack Jones, Abraham, and Gibber Paddy, "Decisions of the Superior Courts of New South Wales, 1788–1899."

[68] Henry Reynolds, *The Other Side of the Frontier: Aboriginal Resistance to the European Invasion of Australia*, p. 67.

[69] R. v. Mickey and Muscle, "Decisions of the Superior Courts of New South Wales, 1788–1899." This case is significant, too, because despite the brutality of the crime – the servant was raped by eleven men for five hours – it occasioned several public pleas that the defendants should not be tried because they could not understand the language or "legal procedure of a foreign people" (Letter to the Editor, *Sydney Herald*, 16 February 1835). Commenting on the execution of one of the culprits, the *Australian* went so far

the crimes at Brisbane Water, out of scores of attackers. Only those recognized and named by the victims were brought to trial. It was as if the legal proceedings were reaffirming that prior association of Aborigines and whites had produced cultural change, and that this change – the "recognition" of individual Aborigines by white witnesses – rather than judges' rulings on Aboriginal legal standing was producing a shift in legal status.

Being known to whites implied a degree of cultural closeness that observers seemed eager to deny. If Aborigines were transformed by contact into fit criminal defendants, was it possible they could also be changed into able witnesses and litigants? Individual Aborigines acted in ways that suggested they were in fact willing to use whatever legal opportunities they had. In *R. v. Fitzpatrick and Colville,* the case described above in which Forbes lamented the court's inability to hear testimony from an Aboriginal witness, it was the Aborigine who appears to have been responsible for the case being brought to trial. He and the defendant Fitzpatrick had been together in the hut of the victim, a shepherd named Bentley, when the murder took place. Fitzpatrick later told the others that he had been shooting at a dog. But when they arrived at Newcastle and were gathered at the house of a constable, the *Sydney Gazette* reported, "the black-man expressed vast sorrow for what had been done by Fitzpatrick, whom he, the native, then impeached with the death of 'Old John,' meaning unfortunate Bentley."[70] An inquiry immediately followed and led ultimately to charges against Fitzpatrick and Colville. The witness, whom the British called Bulwaddy, could not testify in court, but he "made certain statements to a competent witness."[71] And, as we have seen, Bulwaddy delivered a convincing and detailed account of the murder to the governor later. We might characterize these actions as those of a legal naïf, but it is equally possible that Bulwaddy was purposefully seeking justice. His actions had, in any event, a powerful effect: Colville was acquitted as an accomplice, but Fitzpatrick was hanged.

---

as to suggest that it was an extenuating circumstance that rape was customary among the Aborigines. This is an example of advocacy of legal pluralism as a vehicle for reinforcing cultural distinctions; the conclusion following this observation was that it was "hopeless to expect to inspire" Aborigines with an understanding of English views of rape "till they participate with us in the blessings of knowledge" (*Australian*, 6 March 1835).

[70] *Sydney Gazette*, 24 June 1824, *R. v. Fitzpatrick and Colville*, "Decisions of the Superior Courts of New South Wales, 1788–1899."

[71] *Sydney Gazette*, 24 June 1824, *R. v. Fitzpatrick and Colville*, "Decisions of the Superior Courts of New South Wales, 1788–1899."

In *R. v. Murrell*, too, the murder was brought to the court's attention by Aborigines. The Rev. Threlkeld sent a note to the attorney general reporting that an Aborigine had asked him to report the killing to the Supreme Court because he and his tribe wanted two Aborigines (identified by name) to be tried for murder.[72] Threlkeld might have elicited the request, but it is possible, too, that the Aborigines who came to him acted on their own. They evidently knew not to take the charges to the district constable; in the preliminary hearings, he testified that he would not have intervened in a case of violence among Aborigines. Threlkeld on one other occasion – his testimony describing Aboriginal notions of right and wrong in the sheep theft case described above – also reported that he had received "repeated complaints from the blacks of their women being taken away from them for improper purposes."[73] Though it seems that the Reverend Threlkeld had not felt compelled to report these complaints for criminal prosecution, Aborigine informants might have had precisely this outcome as their goal. In the same testimony, Threlkeld went on to offer a general assessement of the Aborigines' mental facilities, in particular their "shrewdness," and he suggested an interesting ability on their part to make distinctions in the legal status of their white victims:

> [T]hey display a remarkable cunning when they wish to accomplish any object; they make a distinction between free settlers and what they call "croppies" – that is, prisoners; if they met a free man in the bush they would not hurt him, but if they met a prisoner they would probably strip him; the reason of this is, that when Newcastle was a penal settlement, the commandants used to give them the clothes of all the runaway prisoner [*sic*] they apprehended as a reward.[74]

The possibility that Aborigines not only perceived differences in the status of convict and free settlers but adjusted their actions accordingly helps explain emancipists' support for excluding Aborigines from the social and legal order. The stigma of transportation was galling in the white world; its equation with weakness in relations with Aborigines was unacceptable.

---

[72] Kercher, "White Fellow Eat Bandicoots & Black Snakes Now," p. 25.

[73] *Sydney Gazette*, 25 February 1832, in *R. v. Boatman or Jackass and Bulleye*, "Decisions of the Superior Courts of New South Wales, 1788–1899."

[74] *Sydney Gazette*, 25 February 1832, in *R. v. Boatman or Jackass and Bulleye*, "Decisions of the Superior Courts of New South Wales, 1788–1899."

If the issues of emancipist and Aboriginal legal status were linked parts of a discourse about culture and law, they were also connected in the broader sense to shifting understandings of the relation of formal law to legal practice. For decades, the problem of convict legal standing was solved by a simple disregard for the formal requirements of the law. This "solution" recommended itself in dealing with the question of Aboriginal rights. If colonists had not fully understood this possibility before, after 1820 it became clear that whatever the law might establish regarding Aborigines as legal subjects, there would be ways of continuing a different legal regime in practice. The selective application of law for Aborigines' protection was already occurring; after the rulings in the late 1830s, the gap between formal law and practice was greater, but the disconnect was not itself new to the legal order of the colony.

In addition to the imprint of political struggles over convicts' legal rights, debates about Aborigines' legal status were inextricably tied to patterns of frontier violence and its perception. Violent clashes between whites and Aborigines had been a constant feature from the earliest days of colonial settlement. There is little doubt that frontier violence was escalating in the 1820s as the number of settlers increased dramatically and squatters pushed ranching further beyond the colony's borders. The settler population of New South Wales increased from about 31,000 in 1824 to more than 265,000 in 1850.[75] Whatever colonial administrators or the courts dictated, settlers showed, and often stated, that they considered themselves at war with Aborigines, their enemies.[76] Punitive attacks on Aborigine camps were the common response to thefts or killings committed by Aborigines against settlers. There was unofficial violence – the widespread practice of abducting and raping Aborigine women – and also the officially sanctioned violence of search parties and militia groups, whose actions were sometimes punitive but also fit an emerging policy of simple terror intended to push Aborigines away from white settlements. Reynolds has estimated that nineteenth-century frontier skirmishing resulted in at least 20,000 Aborigine deaths, figures that include the other frontiers surrounding settlements in Queensland, Tasmania, Victoria, Western Australia, as well as New South Wales.[77] Several thousand whites also died in frontier encounters.

[75] Castles, *Australian Legal History*, p. 153.
[76] Henry Reynolds, *Aboriginal Sovereignty*, p. 98. Reynolds points out that settlers' perception that they were at war with Aborigines and were invading their territory clashed with the view that the British presence was a settlement of unoccupied territory.
[77] Henry Reynolds, *Frontier: Aborigines, Settlers, and Land*, pp. 23, 53.

Not surprisingly, frontier violence made its imprint on the courts. In New South Wales, in addition to the cases already described, there were scores of other criminal cases involving violence of Aborigines against whites and, less frequently, whites against Aborigines or Aborigines against other Aborigines.[78] Leading up to *R. v. Murrell*, more and more criminal cases arising from frontier violence were arriving in court. Kercher describes a single day in February 1835, when Burton and Forbes, presiding over separate trials, between them tried 13 Aborigines for crimes ranging from rape to petty theft.[79] Other cases followed, including the trial of a small group out of an estimated 80 to 150 Aborigines who had attacked the Brisbane Waters house and the whites defending it. And the court faced not just the perpetrators of such acts but also settlers indicted for retaliatory violence – though, as we have seen, these defendants usually found sympathetic juries willing to accept claims of self-defense, insufficient evidence, or other justifications for acquittal. Whites sought a legal rationale for violence. In the trial of 5 whites accused of killing an Aboriginal woman in an area near Bathurst in 1824, witnesses described numerous armed forays to confront Aborigines in the area. The defense argued that the killing of Aborigines in the area had been legally sanctioned by a proclamation of May 1816 that prohibited Aborigines from appearing armed within a mile of any white settlement. The proclamation, published by Governor Macquarie, directed "British subjects in the interior" to drive away hostile "natives" by force and, if necessary, "to apply to a Magistrate for aid from the nearest military station."[80] One justice of the peace testified that the level of violence was such that it constituted a state of war.

As in the Cape Colony, though, European settlers in Australia would have found little support for a full-scale, openly declared war against Aborigines. So long as the legal prohibition against frontier murder did not in practice protect Aborigines from white violence, it actually offered a convenient cover for such outrages. Technically, if inquiries did not result in indictments, the crimes were not occurring; if they did, it was widely understood that whites would be convicted only rarely.

Whites also had to contend, though, with another disturbing possibility. Rather than emerging from random outbursts or simple retribution,

---

[78] For a thorough summary of such cases before Forbes's Supreme Court, see Kercher, "White Fellow Eat Bandicoots & Black Snakes Now."

[79] Kercher, "White Fellow Eat Bandicoots & Black Snakes Now," p. 21.

[80] *Sydney Gazette*, 12 August 1824, *R. v. Johnston, Clarke, Nicholson, Castles, and Crear*, "Decisions of the Superior Courts of New South Wales, 1788–1899."

Aborigine violence might have a judicial quality – a broadly punitive function.[81] Kercher glimpses this possibility in the Brisbane Water attack in October 1834.[82] A large group of Aborigines had attacked the house and had stolen what they could, also injuring one of the two men living there. One of the men testified that an Aborigine had told him that "black fellow was best fellow" and that several groups had planned the attack. The whites knew several of the attackers by name, and these four were placed on trial. One of the men in the house testified, "I asked . . . what they were destroying the house and stealing the furniture for, and they told me they had a right to steal what they thought proper."[83] One of the defendants then "held a conversation with this witness in tolerably good English, and threatened him if ever he caught him in the bush again."[84] As Kercher notes, the two men were badly outnumbered and even though they were armed with guns, the Aborigines could have killed them but did not. They were after the whites' property, to be sure, but they were also demonstrating their strength and were claiming a right to these acts.[85] One Aborigine told one of the victims that "Black fellow master now rob every body – white fellow eat bandicoots & black snakes now."[86] The only difference to these defendants between the whites and themselves was that one group had more power. Thus the Aboriginal defendant Jack Jones could stand before the bar and threaten to exact revenge if he ever encountered a white witness "in the bush."[87]

Perceptions of frontier actions fitting within a framework of Aboriginal law were as plausible as they were disturbing. European observers were vaguely aware that, while Aborigines had no strictly analogous notion of land ownership, clans claimed control over demarcated territories and punished trespassers.[88] If white incursions were initially

---

[81] The claim is not that Aboriginal violence followed any formal judicial consideration or legal pronouncements, for which I have found no evidence, but that it emerged from an Aboriginal sense of legality and illegality. See Chapter 7 for a discussion of a parallel argument about plebeian violence in the work of E.P. Thompson.

[82] Kercher, "White Fellow Eat Bandicoots & Black Snakes Now," p. 22.

[83] *Sydney Gazette*, 14 May 1835, in *R. v. Long Dick, Jack Jones, Abraham, and Gibber Paddy*, "Decisions of the Superior Courts of New South Wales, 1788–1899."

[84] *Sydney Gazette*, 14 May 1835, in *R. v. Long Dick, Jack Jones, Abraham, and Gibber Paddy*, "Decisions of the Superior Courts of New South Wales, 1788–1899."

[85] Kercher, "White Fellow Eat Bandicoots & Black Snakes Now," p. 22.

[86] Kercher, "White Fellow Eat Bandicoots & Black Snakes Now," p. 22.

[87] *Sydney Gazette*, 14 May 1835, in *R. v. Long Dick, Jack Jones, Abraham, and Gibber Paddy*, "Decisions of the Superior Courts of New South Wales, 1788–1899."

[88] Paul Carter argues that whites sought to discredit Aboriginal claims to land by denying the existence not just of Aboriginal law but also of Aboriginal language. Characterizing

overlooked, it was probably because Aborigines assumed they were only passing through. When white intentions became clear, and the numbers of settlers increased, Aborigines' resistance to their presence came quickly. As Reynolds puts it, Aborigines "never conceded the major premise of the invasion."[89] In their view, violent resistance was not only logical but also legitimate. The resistance was not explicitly in response to European claims to land ownership but to the depletion of resources caused by the pastoral economy, in particular the competition of livestock for scarce water.[90] Disparities in material wealth were also regarded, Reynolds argues, as violations of principles of reciprocity in Aborigine communities. If whites would not share their goods, they would be made to share them.[91] In many cases, then, attacks followed from the perception of settler crimes and not any generalized disposition to violence.[92] Reynolds relies on such evidence to conclude that much of the frontier violence should be interpreted as "judicial rather than martial."[93] He argues, too, however, that Aborigines' attitudes began to change in the second half of the 1820s. The escalation of conflict across the frontier reflected this shift. As one settler observed, acts of violence seemed no longer isolated but part of "a determined spirit of hostility" against blacks.[94]

It seems doubtful that we can ever sort out clearly Aborigines' motivations and how they changed. It is clear, though, that there was ample incentive for colonists to deny that acts of violence on the frontier

Aborigines' naming of geographical features as random and basely functional rather than systematic and scientific, Europeans were implying that Aborigines did not "in any recognizable sense" possess the land. Yet, with language as with law, settlers' own naming necessarily borrowed from Aborigines and mimicked a functional, particularist lexicon rather than one that was part of a comprehensive mapping project. See Paul Carter, *The Road to Botany Bay: An Exploration of Landscape and History*, p. 63 and pp. 65–67.

[89] Reynolds, *The Other Side of the Frontier*, p. 65.

[90] Reynolds, *The Other Side of the Frontier*, p. 67.

[91] Reynolds, *The Other Side of the Frontier*, p. 69. The increase in violence was not limited to raids between Aborigines and whites. Frontier tensions also fueled violence between Aboriginal clans, who sometimes blamed each other for using supernatural means to bring about specific acts of violence committed by whites.

[92] As Kercher points out, revenge killings in fact deviated from Aboriginal legal norms which sanctioned punishments for individuals guilty of crimes or, at most, reprisals against aggressors' "clans." (Kercher, "White Fellow Eat Bandicoots & Black Snakes Now.") The difficulty of determining white groupings and thus identify the "right" victims made Aboriginal violence appear more arbitrary than it probably was.

[93] Reynolds, *The Other Side of the Frontier*, p. 78.

[94] Reynolds, *The Other Side of the Frontier*, p. 81.

were judicial, or even merely punitive, in character. The justification of violence against Aborigines was that they were savages who could not be made to understand law and could therefore be controlled only through aggression. The blame for frontier violence lay neither with the Europeans nor with the systemic clash of pastoralism and Aborigines' use rights; lawlessness was ingrained in Aborigines, imprinted in their nature. When the Tasmanian Aborigines Committee examined the causes of frontier violence in the colony, it found that Aboriginal acts of aggression did not arise as reactions to "any wrongs which they conceived themselves collectively or individually to have endured" but rather from "a wanton and savage spirit inherent in them."[95]

Designing the plural legal order was, as a result of these pressures, not just legally but socially problematic. Settlers had important interests, both material and symbolic, in depriving Aborigines of legal rights. It was understood that a formal declaration of sovereignty would not simply extend the state's jurisdiction but would potentially entitle Aborigines to litigate and to recur to the courts for protection, as other indigenous peoples had shown themselves more than ready to do. As Forbes was reported to have noted in his 1829 ruling in the Ballard case, a claim of jurisdiction in criminal cases would lead to adjudication in matters of property and the need "to administer justice in all their matters."[96] Further, the status of convicts and former convicts – a large and increasingly economically powerful constituency – would be threatened by any implied equivalence with Aborigines. At the same time, pluralist representations of the legal order were to be resisted; they had the potential to bolster Aboriginal standing by awarding them implicit equality through the recognition of their status as a people with law and – by implication – property rights. In part because there was no logically consistent solution, an ad hoc legal adjustment occurred in which the dominance of state law was established, offering Aborigines no room to protect preexisting rights to property or to legitimize claims to a separate legal authority, but in which desultory enforcement of the law and continued political disenfranchisement were enshrined in practice.

This accommodation and all its contradictions were present in the celebrated criminal case surrounding the Myall Creek massacre of 1838. A group of settlers and their servants on the colony's northern frontier had

---

[95] Quoted in Henry Reynolds, *Frontier*, p. 42.
[96] *Sydney Gazette*, 16 June 1829, in *R. v. Ballard or Barrett*, "Decisions of the Superior Courts of New South Wales, 1788–1899."

brutally murdered at least twenty-eight Aborigines, including women and children. Eleven men with convict backgrounds (significantly, not their employers) were tried and acquitted of the murder of two Aboriginal men, one named and one unnamed. Seven were later charged with the murder of an unnamed Aborigine child and were found guilty. The settler community was outraged, and the case stands out mainly because the governor, in a rare act of affirmation of the rule of law, resisted tremendous pressure to commute the death sentence. Significantly, the convictions elicited the defense argument that if a grand jury had been in place, no indictment would have occurred. Emancipist politics, and the ambiguous status of convict settlers, were again closely intertwined with the issue of Aboriginal legal standing.

CONCLUSION

In both the Cape Colony and New South Wales, what appeared to be a marginal issue – the legal status of indigenous peoples – became symbolically central to conflicts over colonial rule during the middle decades of the nineteenth century.[97] The early rejection of a strong pluralist model that would give formal recognition to Khoi or Aboriginal legal authority and specify the relation of indigenous to colonial justice opened the possibility for the gradual assimilation of indigenous subjects into colonial courts. But such an adjustment implied a recognition of cultural kinship between the indigenous population and Europeans. This would have been difficult for colonial powers to accept under any circumstances. The presence of growing settler populations with divergent interests and identities made the movement toward legal sovereignty highly contested.

On one level, these histories can be recounted as narratives about the selective application of European models of legal administration. In both places, the shift we have described coincided with the professionalization of legal personnel. Judges and attorneys trained in English law arrived in larger numbers and urged, through their practice, a closer

---

[97] The broader cultural importance of representations of marginalized social groups has been recognized by Stallybrass and White, who argue that "what is *socially* peripheral is so frequently *symbolically* central" and that "despised" groups are "instrumentally constitutive of the shared imaginary repertoire of the dominant culture" (Stallybrass and White, *Politics and Poetics of Transgression*, pp. 5–6). This argument grounds Walkowitz's treatment of London prostitutes as symbolically central to the construction of gender in Victorian England. Walkowitz, *City of Dreadful Delight*, especially pp. 20–21.

resemblance of colonial to metropolitan justice. When legal personnel came from postings in other colonies, they added to administrators' knowledge about available models for colonial legal administration. Though its coordination of colonial legal policy was never very efficient, the Colonial Office symbolized the intent to make legal administration a matter of consistent imperial policy. Both legal personnel and administrators drew from a familiar repertoire of legal texts – Blackstone and Vattel, in particular, were well-worn sources – and lifted similar passages to justify and explain European dominion.

Despite these homogenizing influences, local cultural and political conflicts made legal policy anything but predictable. Colonial administrators and judges were not the only groups dipping selectively and opportunistically into a repertoire of judicial actions and arguments. European settlers did so, too. Both trekboers and emancipists had reason to search for legal formulae that would enhance their independence from imposed law. But they sought, at the same time, imperial aid and approval in extending their enterprise and authority beyond the edges of European settlement. In the Cape Colony, it was not immediately apparent that Dutch-descended settlers would fail to find a legal accommodation that would enable both autonomy and protection. In New South Wales, emancipists both advocated the importation of English legal institutions as a way of checking the power of colonial administrators and military commanders and argued that the unique character of colonial conditions warranted the selective adoption of English law – specifically, the exclusion of the law of felony attaint.

In working out these contradictions, settlers in both places saw their own political standing as dependent in no small part on legal distinctions between themselves and indigenous inhabitants. Acutely aware of the cultural and legal boundaries separating them from men in power – Dutch versus English heritage in one place, convict versus free backgrounds, in the other – settlers found the prospect of being equated with indigenous populations doubly threatening. Enhancing the legal status of local inhabitants would mark them as settlers' cultural equivalents at the same time that it would open the very real possibility of legal challenges to settlers' rights to appropriate indigenous labor and land.

This last threat should not be underestimated. In South Africa, settlers' livelihood depended closely on their continued control of indigenous land and labor. Even the hint of legal legitimacy for Khoi posed a threat to their prerogatives to discipline workers and corral unattached Khoi into service. In Australia, where Aborigines were yet to become essential as laborers in the pastoral economy, pluralism posed a danger to European material interests in a different way. There were precedents in English law for recognizing use rights that overlapped with rights to landed property. Just as the space for customary use rights was being constricted by the improving gentry in the English countryside, a similar weak pluralism was being rejected in Australia in favor of a legal regime that would clearly establish precedence for landed property over use rights.

It is important to emphasize that legal change, though, did not simply follow a European script. Both Khoi and Aborigines were present as legal actors. As the Cloete case shows us, Khoi were not timid about presenting accusations about wrongdoing by settlers once there was a chance for prosecutions to go forward and for convictions to stick. In New South Wales, even in the absence of official receptivity to Aboriginal complaints and the refusal to accept Aboriginal testimony, there is evidence that Aborigines brought crimes to the attention of authorities and occasionally even prompted prosecutions of whites. In both places, the prospect of the criminalization of routine violence against indigenous inhabitants on the frontier presented not just the threat of settler prosecutions but a challenge to settlers' local authority and control. In this sense, the Khoi and Aborigines were present as legal actors, too, in persisting in frontier theft and violence. Such acts of resistance destabilized settlers' representations of themselves as stand-ins for colonial authority and kept the issue of colonial courts' jurisdictional reach in prominent view.

For settlers, representations of indigenous culture and arguments about indigenous legal status were closely linked. Khoi and Aboriginal acts of violence were cited as evidence of their innate savagery. Cloete's defense argued that participation in frontier violence made Khoi testimony inherently unreliable. In New South Wales, cases involving crimes committed by Aborigines against other Aborigines were occasions to argue that unchecked violence was customary among them. But these strategies had their perils. The answer to Cloete's defense was condemnation of the barbarity of Cloete's own actions. And in New South Wales, discussions of Aboriginal customs brought attention to the ways in which punitive expeditions against Aborigines mirrored Aboriginal attacks, hinting that these were motivated by a sense of the injustice of Europeans' own actions.

These conflicts, and the legal cases they generated, preceded and also prompted the shift to the legal hegemony by the state. While altering the balance of power very little at first, this shift structured the legal order in ways that in turn shaped racial politics in the next century. In South Africa, the timing of the shift meant, ironically, that formal legal pluralism could be embraced as colonial control expanded into territories that were heavily populated with other groups of Africans. The formal recognition of "traditional" law was not threatening precisely because it came, as in French West Africa, after the ambiguity of the early colonial legal order had been resolved. In Australia, declaring Aborigines British legal subjects hardly solved the Aboriginal "problem." The legal fiction of inclusiveness in fact provided a more permissive environment for brutality against Aborigines, both across the moving frontier and in settlements where Aborigines were "brought in." It ended claims that Aborigines were exceptional, belonged to other, separate polities, or possessed an independent sense of justice. Indeed, the contested nature of Aboriginal status in the early years of the colony was officially forgotten, and late-twentieth-century jurists relied on the precedent set by *Murrell* rather than the debates and judicial uncertainty that had come before.

In a broader perspective, two important qualities are shared by these histories, by the parallel development of Native American law in the United States and Canada, and by the examples of colonial legal politics discussed in the previous chapter. First, there is an impressive synchronicity. Over the span of a handful of decades in the nineteenth century, or, viewed with a slightly wider lens, over the course of the long nineteenth century, formally plural legal orders were transformed into state-dominated legal orders. Second, this process involved everywhere an extended historical moment in which the question of the legal standing of the most marginal people in the colonial order became symbolically central to the development of legal culture and the broader realignment of the political order. As both strong and weak pluralism struggled with the definition of outsiders, this cultural question came to be defined through law as one of the central concerns of the new colonial states.

SIX

Constructing Sovereignty:

Extraterritoriality in the Oriental Republic of Uruguay

State making in colonial contexts always involved contests over the configuration of plural legal systems. But what occurred in places of "informal empire," where Western powers did not assert political control and did not therefore assume the task of overseeing legal administration? One might expect conflicts over the architecture of the legal order – the relation between indigenous and imposed law, or between state and nonstate legal authority – to assume a less prominent place in political and cultural discourse. The establishment of Western models of law might seem merely to follow pervasive pressures to facilitate interstate bargaining and international investment, and to flow from elite intercultural influences and Westernized education.

As in places of formal colonial control, though, debates about legal pluralism in settings of informal empire had a special place in political and cultural imagination; recurring legal conflicts, particularly jurisdictional disputes, had a tendency to keep these issues in prominent view; and legal interactions had their own transformative power. The idea and reality of a territorial sovereignty in which state law subsumed other legal authorities emerged in part in response to the dynamics of legal conflicts in complex arrangements of mixed power. In places with strikingly different legal traditions, the mid-nineteenth century saw the construction (and continual restructuring) of legal orders that simultaneously built on older forms of legal pluralism and gestured toward stronger claims of state power.

This mid-century period of political and legal maneuvering centered around shifting definitions of the legal status of citizens, foreigners, and the in-between ranks of long-term residents, naturalized citizens, foreign merchants, foreign military personnel, and new settlers. Particular legal conflicts focused attention on the meaning of nationality and the power of exclusion. Economically and militarily powerful outsiders adopted legal strategies that were inherently contradictory. They militated for legal immunity and jurisdictional protections for their subjects while at the same time basing their claims on a critique of the failings of local justice and the weaknesses of local state sovereignty. States that were not formally conquered or controlled also assigned legal pluralism an ambiguous meaning. Extraterritoriality, or the rights to legal jurisdiction over foreign subjects by foreign polities, was at times interpreted as a clear and unacceptable challenge to sovereignty. It could also, however, be strategically represented as a peculiar sign of resistance to even greater controls by foreigners since older forms of legal pluralism recognized extraterritoriality as a concession made by a powerful polity to minority groups within its realm.

The availability of such an array of arguments about the meaning of a separate legal status for foreigners made actual legal conflicts often unpredictable, and this confusion in and of itself constituted one source of pressure on legal institutions and their reform. Another pressure for change came from the instability of extraterritorial arrangements themselves. New cases continually revealed that the rules and boundaries established to assign legal identities to groups and to channel disputes to particular forums did not cover every contingency. They in fact invited new strategies to turn legal constraints into opportunities.

This chapter explores the politics of legal pluralism and its impact on state building in one Latin American case in the mid-nineteenth century. Legal authority in the early South American republics was notoriously fractured. In part, this condition was a legacy of the colonial legal order. In part, it emerged from trends following independence: the rise of caudillismo, the influx of foreigners, and the region's incorporation into new flows of international trade. The effects of postindependence conflicts were often ambiguous. Various nonstate legal authorities challenged the control of state institutions while also promoting a discourse about sovereignty that urged the turn toward state legal hegemony. This interrelation of legal politics and state making is particularly clear in legal cases and debates concerning the status of foreigners, whose efforts to preserve a special legal status required appeals to the very state authority their claims were designed to weaken. The relation between foreign subjects and the state was in especially prominent view in mid-nineteenth-century Uruguay, where widespread political disorder overlapped with the construction of national legal institutions in a new republic crowded with foreigners.

While Uruguay has some exceptional qualities that made the issue of foreigners' legal status more salient, the case should be understood as a particular version of a more widespread pattern of politics surrounding the European push to retain or expand extraterritoriality in other settings of informal empire. In the Ottoman Empire and in China in this period, extraterritoriality was also often at the center of both international and domestic politics. Placed in this broader context, the Latin American experience shows that even weak claims to extraterritoriality were discursively important to mid-nineteenth-century state making. The Latin American case, in turn, leads us to look at the classic examples of extraterritoriality and its politics in a somewhat different light, not simply as a symbol of Western dominance but as an element of state formation influenced by interactions with the West.

LAW AND SPANISH AMERICAN STATES

The distribution of legal rights in the Spanish colonial order was shaped by access to property, corporate and ethnic group membership, and ties to patronage. Such divisions coexisted with the empire's formally centralized legal bureaucracy, a key institution of colonial rule. One historian has described the resulting tension between "the aspiration to absolute domain and the reality of contingent entitlement" as the central feature of Spanish American legal culture.[1] Its other striking and consistent feature was colonial subjects' litigiousness, in particular their willingness to exploit jurisdictional tensions as part of often sophisticated legal strategies.[2] Independence unsettled colonial legal institutions, though their outlines, and many elements of colonial legal culture, continued. With only a few exceptions (Uruguay is one), national states cohered around areas that had served as seats of *audiencias*, colonial high courts.[3] Migrants crossing the new borders found few striking

---

[1] Jeremy Adelman, *Republic of Capital: Buenos Aires and the Legal Transformation of the Atlantic World*, p. 146. I make a similar argument in Chapter 3.

[2] The litigiousness of colonial Spanish America was linked to pervasive jurisdictional tensions carried over from Iberian law and exacerbated by conquest and colonization. See Chapter 3. On merchant law as a separate jurisdiction and the carryover of jurisdictional politics into the postcolonial period, see Jeremy Adelman, *Republic of Capital*, pp. 145–50.

[3] Rodriguez calls the *audiencias* "the most enduring territorial units" of Spanish America. Most of the territories became nations after independence. But the overlay was

differences in the legal practices of the infant republics. But in the new geography of independent Latin America, citizenship now mattered. Migrants, settlers, soldiers, itinerant laborers, exiles, and even caudillos often ignored this change, but there were increasingly forceful reminders.[4]

It is tempting for legal historians to move quickly from the end of the colonial period to the successful movements to consolidate the state at the end of the century, when legal reform was one of an array of important props of nation building. But as some historians have shown, the tumultuous middle decades of the nineteenth century were crucially formative.[5] Struggles over boundaries and control of the new republics featured a politically prominent discourse about the meanings of citizenship. Competing political factions championed law and order, promising a return to stability through law. Legal rhetoric was also central to emerging, contrastive images of urban and rural cultures. Even before the borders of the new republics had been fixed, political leaders embraced strong state legal institutions as a nationalist project. Litigation, no doubt fueled in part by the legacy of colonial legal culture, quickly revealed the weaknesses of legal orders that remained decentralized and fragmented. Support for codification, professionalization (and nationalization) of legal personnel, and judicial elections gathered strength slowly and in part in response to patterns of litigation and wider political conflicts.

The issue of the legal status of foreigners intersected with all these processes and was, in consequence, itself a central element of legal politics. Some foreign influences on early legal reform are obvious. Latin

---

imperfect. New Spain had two audiencias, as did the territory that was to form Peru on the eve of independence. Some smaller republics were created in areas without audiencias, as occurred in Central America outside Guatemala and in the Republic of Uruguay (Jaime E. Rodriguez, *The Independence of Spanish America*, p. 7). Law clearly constituted one of the aspects of colonial society that found surprising continuity in postindependent Latin America, despite efforts to distance the new republics from colonial institutions. For a broader treatment of the debate about continuities, see Jeremy Adelman, ed., *Colonial Legacies: The Problem of Persistence in Latin America*.

4 Legal personnel were themselves forced to contend with the new distinctions of citizenship. Law schools did not exist in every capital in the aftermath of independence. Narrow restrictions that reserved judgeships for citizens with legal training and experience were in some places desirable but impractical. Even elite groups of lawyers, especially in the smaller republics, included noncitizens.

5 See especially Adelman, *Republic of Capital*; Thomas Flory, *Judge and Jury in Imperial Brazil, 1808–1871: Social Control and Political Stability in the New State*; and Victor M. Uribe Uran, *Honorable Lives : Lawyers, Families, and Politics in Colombia, 1780–1850*.

American constitutions borrowed the rhetoric of republicanism and European models of judicial administration, including an emphasis on citizenship. Law reformers read, copied, and adapted European codes, most notably the Napoleonic Code.[6] Foreign investors and their demands for stability bolstered efforts to use legal institutions to help calm the countryside, rein in caudillos, regulate contracts, and strengthen legal protections of property.

Foreigners also had another, more indirect impact on the law that was partially hidden from view but subtly powerful. Particularly in the early decades after independence, foreigners often militated for their own immunity from the law, vilified the new national legal systems, and capitalized on jurisdictional ambiguities and tensions. Individual litigants, in maneuvering to take advantage of the smallest opportunities to exploit their foreign status, added, paradoxically, to pressures for reform by insisting on precise compliance with the law and on procedural regularity, the glaring deficiencies of the new national legal systems. Consular officials from England, France, Spain, Brazil, and other countries presented claims for limited immunity for their subjects and complained about the procedural irregularities and routine injustices of the new national legal administrations.[7] Their policies were no doubt influenced by the broader, global context of expanding European "informal empire," and the practice of seeking extraterritoriality wherever local law was held to offer European subjects inadequate protection.[8]

---

[6] See M.C. Mirow, "The Power of Codification in Latin America: Simón Bolívar and the *Code Napoléon*." Mirow details Bolívar's backing for codification in Gran Colombia and argues that it represented a (failed) strategy for political consolidation in the region.

[7] Of this array of outside agents, some mattered more than others. The increasing economic importance of English merchants, and the threat of military intervention by England and France, gave the legal pronouncements of these countries' consulates added weight. Brazil, too, represented a "foreign" influence of no small importance in the region. With the relocation of the Portuguese crown, Brazil could claim an institutional stability and a degree of international prestige that were elusive for the new Spanish republics.

[8] European struggles to erect extraterritoriality in China and Japan were contemporaneous with the construction of national legal systems in Latin America, and the rhetoric of European responses was, not surprisingly, similar. In these quite different settings, Europeans suggested that extraterritoriality was made necessary by the deficiencies of indigenous law. See Francis C. Jones, *Extraterritoriality in Japan, and the Diplomatic Relations Resulting in Its Abolition, 1853–1899*; and Wesley R. Fishel, *The End of Extraterritoriality in China*, p. 27. I do not know of a study that traces direct links among imperial legal strategies in the mid-nineteenth century, though we do know that British legal personnel circulated across different colonial and imperial postings, transporting models of legal administration across disparate parts of the empire.

Like other Latin American republics, the new, small republic of Uruguay (La República Oriental del Uruguay) began to attract increasing numbers of immigrants and foreign merchants. Like other republics, the country succumbed to a postindependence wave of internal warfare led by two dominant political factions. But the country was also unusual in some respects. Because it was sparsely populated at the time of independence, foreigners were a proportionately more important part of the population. Further, the country bordered two much larger Latin American nations and had in fact been created as a buffer state between them, with the direct intervention of Britain and France. Brazil had invaded the "Banda Oriental," as the territory on the east bank of the Uruguay River was known, in 1816, and had held it as a province of Brazil from 1820 to 1825, when the Brazilians were ousted by an Argentine-backed force. Brazilian military intervention continued to pose a threat (and, for some factions, an opportunity), and unofficial cross-border raids were still commonplace at mid-century. Political upheavals in Argentina surrounding the rise and overthrow of Rosas enveloped politics in the Banda Oriental, and Argentina and Uruguay traded prominent exiles and shared an elite political culture. Britain and France, following their direct military intervention in the region in the 1840s, were intent on maintaining their influence.[9] Under these conditions, Uruguayans considered the move to establish territorial sovereignty crucial to the country's survival. Constructing a national legal system was central to this project.

To focus on law in the middle decades of the nineteenth century is to refine the standard narrative of historical change in nineteenth-century Uruguay. In this account, the Uruguayan countryside was essentially "stateless" in the decades in the middle of the century, between independence in 1828 and the mid-1870s. Political disorder reigned, producing lawlessness. Provincial caudillos administered their own justice in rural areas under their control, and centrally imposed legal institutions could not curb their power. The central state was badly underfinanced, and rural authorities with few resources faced daunting problems, including widespread cattle theft, both by organized Brazilian raiders and by itinerant and unemployed rural laborers; land disputes, endemic because most claims to land were based on possession, not title; and violent crimes, common among a rootless population that routinely went about

---

[9] On British and French interventions in the region, see David McLean, *War, Diplomacy, and Informal Empire: Britain and the Republics of la Plata, 1836–1853.*

heavily armed. As Baretta and Markoff put it, the "cattle frontier" was a place where no one group held a "monopoly on violence."[10] Order ultimately descended on the countryside in the form of imposed controls from the capital, often as a by-product of foreign investments in production and exports. In particular, three trends – the rapid growth of sheep ranching and wool exports in the 1860s, the measures adopted by the autocratic Latorre government of the late 1870s to solidify state authority, and the widespread introduction of barbed wire fencing in the same decade – ushered in a period of national consolidation after 1875.

Legal politics in the middle decades of the nineteenth century is conspicuously absent from this narrative. But if we view lawlessness in the countryside as a variant of a more systemic condition of persisting legal pluralism, the transition to state sovereignty appears both more complex and earlier. The state faced the task of not only strengthening its institutions and asserting control but also constructing its own legitimacy while conceding elements of rule to other authorities too powerful to override. Thus foreigners used a combination of litigation strategies and consular appeals to try to preserve or create a separate legal status. While such claims were weaker here than the fully developed claims to extraterritoriality that characterized legal policy in China and the Ottoman Empire in the same period, they nevertheless posed a similarly serious challenge to Uruguay's territorial sovereignty. Such claims operated, too, against the background of caudillismo and the de facto legal autonomy of local leaders. The challenge to the state was not so much repressing "lawlessness" as controlling "other" law – the legal authority of caudillos, other states' claims to extraterritoriality, and litigants' recourse to legal strategies that placed them outside state control. Institutional change was propelled both from above and from below, as legal conflicts promoted discourse about the imperatives and complexities of state sovereignty. In this way, mid-nineteenth-century conflicts propelled a shift that was to take formal shape later in the century.

LAW AND "LAWLESSNESS" IN THE BANDA ORIENTAL

In its first decades, Uruguay did not offer an auspicious setting for institutional reform. National politics was engulfed in fighting between *Blancos* and *Colorados* over political control of the national government.

---

[10] Silvio Rogério Duncan Baretta and John Markoff, "Civilization and Barbarism: Cattle Frontiers in Latin America."

The tensions erupted into civil war in 1843, and over the next nine years governance was split between a Colorado regime installed in Montevideo – under siege for most of the war – and a Blanco government established outside the city and in control of most of the countryside. The Guerra Grande had catastrophic effects on ranching and brought ruin to the *saladeros* that produced dried meat for export to Brazil and Cuba.

Factional political fighting continued unabated in Montevideo after the war was settled, but its disruptive effects were more closely limited to the capital. In the countryside, the "prolonged period of peace" during the 1850s provided a perfect environment for continued settlement of productive land by foreigners and the purchase of large tracts of land by Montevidean speculators.[11] This "invasion" forced property values sharply higher.[12] The more active market in land took place in the context of a generalized insecurity of title to land. At the same time that landowners, and particularly new owners, sought to fix property rights by registering titles and contracts of sale, many existing estancia owners feared that the new legalism would threaten their interests. Many had staked claims through possession, while others feared that their ownership would be challenged for failure to pay taxes or because of irregularities in their titles.[13]

Despite continued political upheaval and rampant speculation, the country presented tantalizing economic opportunities. The underutilized grasslands of the Banda Oriental promised high returns quite apart from speculative profits, even if investors could not have anticipated such boons as the rise of sheep ranching and wool exports, and the introduction of barbed wire to delimit grazing lands. Montevideo, although eventually to lose its bid to eclipse Buenos Aires as a regional port, grew rapidly as the nation's center for trade and the country's

---

[11] José Pedro Barrán and Benjamin Nahum, *Historia rural del Uruguay moderno, Vol. I (1851–1885)*, p. 60.

[12] Barrán and Nahum calculate that the price per hectare increased by 248 percent between the five-year period from 1852 to 1856, and the period from 1857 to 1861, and by another 66 percent in the following five-year period. Barrán and Nahum, *Historia rural del Uruguay moderno*, p. 71.

[13] A debate over legislation in 1858 that would have temporarily halted seizures of government-owned land after its occupants were denounced by land-hungry speculators revealed fears that new, foreign-backed interests were shaking up the countryside. One delegate complained that "gangs . . . with lawyers in their inner circle" and legions of notaries and law-trained clerks "throw themselves on the countryside to disturb property, to loot property owners." Barrán and Nahum, *Historia rural del Uruguay moderno*, p. 78. My translation.

main port.[14] The result was, despite continued political instability, an influx of foreigners. The country's population doubled between 1852 and 1860, growing from 132,000 to 221,000. In 1852, 21.6 percent of the inhabitants were foreigners; by 1860, they accounted for 35 percent of the population and nearly half (48 percent) the population of Montevideo. The largest group of foreigners comprised Brazilians, followed at some distance by Spaniards, Italians, French, British, and others.[15]

The numbers do not convey the economic and social importance of these noncitizens. Two rather different, and essentially separate, contingents of foreigners stood out. In the northern districts bordering Brazil – the third or so of the country north of the Rio Negro – Brazilians dominated ranching and in many places outnumbered *Orientales*. Already in 1857, frontier districts had an estimated 428 Brazilian-owned *estancias*, ranches, together covering nearly a third of the national territory.[16] These were foreigners whose family ties and business interests extended across the border into the grasslands of Rio Grande do Sul, a relatively conservative and isolated ranching region that was itself politically marginal and economically undeveloped within Brazil.[17] The Brazilian government was very much interested in promoting stability in the Banda Oriental. Uruguay was not only a buffer between Brazil and a volatile Argentina, it also provided ranchers with cheap cattle and land, and served as an important source of trade goods for southern Brazil (some legitimate, a good deal contraband).

In contrast, a small contingent of British immigrants was fast becoming the most vocal part of a new class of immigrant ranchers and merchants in the rest of the country. Unlike the Brazilians, the British ranchers came from diverse backgrounds mainly outside of ranching. Some were small merchants, former ship captains, soldiers, or artisans who invested small savings in land and cattle. They concentrated predominantly in the southern districts alongside the Uruguay River and, in contrast to their Brazilian counterparts in the north, they maintained strong links to British merchants in Montevideo.[18] Unlike the Brazilians,

---

[14] On the rivalry between Buenos Aires and Montevideo to control the region's trade, see Philip Curtin, "Location in History: Argentina and South Africa in the Nineteenth Century."

[15] José Pedro Barrán, *Apogeo y crisis del Uruguay pastoril y caudillesco, 1838–1875*, p. 61.

[16] Barrán, *Apogeo y crisis*, p. 45.

[17] A portrait of the Rio Grandense economy and society in this period can be found in Stephen Bell, *Campanha Gaúcha: A Brazilian Ranching System, 1850–1920*.

[18] Barrán and Nahum, *Historia rural del Uruguay moderno*, pp. 320–30.

they were to be at the forefront of the movement into sheep raising and the later adoption of barbed wire fencing. But they were similar to the Brazilians in the ways that they benefited from the backing of their government. Four years after the end of the Guerra Grande, the British government successfully lobbied for consular involvement in the settlement of claims for damages by British subjects. In 1857, the Uruguayan government was pressured to establish a *Comisión Mixta* (made up of one Frenchman, one Englishman, and two Orientales) to consider claims by British and French subjects. The cases proved so contentious (and so unsatisfactory to individual claimants) that the French and British forced the Uruguayan government in 1861 to consolidate payment of the claims into a debt of four million pesos. Three years later, Brazilians would demand the same treatment, backed by military intervention, and would in turn receive their own Comisión Mixta in 1867. The British, French, and Brazilians, then, shared a special status established through diplomatic accord – a form of extraterritoriality that their consuls would seek to protect and widen in responding to citizens' complaints and particular legal cases.[19]

The volatile political and economic conditions of the country, together with continued international pressures, made strengthening the legal order a high priority for Uruguayans. It was also an elusive goal. Even the simple task of staffing the judicial posts posed a difficult challenge. In Montevideo, the highest judicial posts had to be filled by a handful of citizen lawyers who had received training in Buenos Aires or elsewhere. The higher court judgeships could be filled in this way, but the provision for a Supreme Court in the 1830 Constitution would have to wait; there were not enough law-trained Orientales.[20] In the countryside, the shortage of qualified legal personnel was drastic. The Constitution established two key district-level judges: the *juez de paz*, who would hear petty disputes and oversee required arbitration procedures called *juicios conciliatorios* or *juicios de conciliación*; and the *alcalde ordinario*, who served an appellate function for the jueces de paz of a particular *departamento*

---

[19] Barrán argues forcefully that the establishment of a separate process for adjudicating war claims by the French, English, and Brazilians constituted a form of extraterritoriality that was an abdication of sovereignty, rather than merely an administrative concession. See Barrán, *Apogeo y crisis*, p. 89.

[20] The Supreme Court was not established until 1907. Postponing the court's founding no doubt helped to keep the judiciary subordinate to political controls, but the dearth of law-trained citizens with sufficient experience was a perpetual constraint. See Nelson Nicoliello and Luis A. Vázquez Praderi, *Crónicas de la Justicia en el Uruguay*.

and presided over disputes involving significant sums.[21] Virtually all of these officials lacked legal training. They were typically men of some standing in the community, but in the more remote parts of the country the supply of candidates was especially thin.

Moreover, legal officials in the countryside found that they did not hold a monopoly on legal authority. Provincial caudillos routinely dispatched summary justice on their estancias and among their followers.[22] The caudillos disciplined ranch hands, *peones*, for minor infractions without recourse to the courts. Where their local authority was recognized by their appointment as *jefes políticos*, caudillos could also influence state-administered justice by ensuring the appointment of their followers to positions as magistrates and by directing local police to give selected fugitives free passage.[23] The election of provincial officials and centralized control over the appointment of magistrates would both become part of the agenda of national reformers attempting to consolidate national control over the countryside.

This was the context in which foreigners-as-litigants maneuvered in the middle decades of the nineteenth century. Weak legal institutions offered opportunities for positioning and protecting interests in land and livestock. They also were a potential source of instability and uncertainty. Foreigners involved in litigation knew to turn to their own governments to exert pressure on Uruguayan officials, but they also experimented with a range of other strategies that built upon their status as noncitizens. Their actions interposed a new dimension into national

---

[21] The "Reglamento Provisorio para la Administración de Justicia" passed by the Uruguayan legislature in 1829 established the areas of oversight for tenientes alcaldes, jueces de paz, and alcaldes ordinarios. The alcaldes ordinarios were to preside over disputes involving more than two hundred and less than three thousand pesos. These judges ruled in civil cases with the help of two colleagues selected randomly from a list of thirty citizens appointed by local officials. Two judicial posts were created in the capital to preside over appeals, one for criminal and one for civil cases. In civil cases involving sums greater than three thousand pesos, this civil forum would also be the court of first instance. As the volume of litigation increased and pressures for legal administrative reform also grew, the appellate structure was modified. See below.

[22] Caudillos did not simply administer a rough justice but were attentive to their need to act as patrons. Barrán describes the judicial style of the caudillo Máximo Pérez as typical: "He considered the office of police chief as part of his patrimony and acted in this role like a father, demanding but humane. Acting as judge in private matters, he solved protracted suits in brief minutes with summary rulings based on caring and coercion" (Barrán, *Apogeo y crisis*, p. 112, my translation).

[23] Fracturing caudillo power was the main purpose of reforms under the presidency of Berro in 1860 separating the appointments of military commanders and police chiefs. See Barrán, *Apogeo y crisis*, p. 75.

(and regional) legal politics. We will turn first to the development of a binational legal culture on the northern frontier, then examine Brazilian and British consular demands for special legal protections for their subjects and the response of Montevidean reformers.

LAW CROSSING BORDERS

In his wanderings in the interior of the Republic of Uruguay, Richard Lamb, the protagonist of W.H. Hudson's nineteenth-century novel *The Purple Land*, finds himself in quick sequence in the middle of two of the countryside's most common rituals: a brawl among *gauchos* and a roundup of able-bodied men to serve as government soldiers. He acquits himself ably enough in the fight, and in the encounter with army recruiters he claims exemption on the grounds that he is a foreigner. The officer decides to take him and his traveling companion to the local magistrate, and Lamb recounts:

> Seeing no help for it, we accompanied our captors at a winging gallop over a rich, undulating country, and in about an hour and a half reached Las Cuevas, a dirty, miserable-looking village, composed of a few *ranchos* built round a large plaza overgrown with weeds. On one side stood the church, on the other a square stone building with a flagstaff before it. This was the official building of the Juez de Paz, or rural magistrate; just now, however, it was closed, and with no sign of life about it except an old dead-and-alive-looking man sitting against the closed door, with his bare, mahogany-colored legs stretched out in the hot sunshine.[24]

Hudson's unflattering images of rural justice would have been familiar to the residents of Uruguay's northern provinces. There was a chronic shortage of qualified legal personnel. An 1852 letter from the town of Arredondo, on the northern edge of the frontier province of Cerro Largo, complains that the posts of juez de paz and *teniente alcalde*, the lowest positions in the judicial hierarchy, were being filled by military authorities, "in contravention of what is required in the Constitution."[25] Candidates

---

[24] W.H. Hudson, *The Purple Land*, p. 69. Hudson suggests that the relative statelessness of the Uruguayan countryside is refreshing, part of its native charm (p. 245).

[25] Letter from Nicolás Zoa Fernandes to the Juez de Paz, segunda sección, 12 April 1852, Cerro Largo, Legajo 7, Archivo General de la Nación, Sección Judicial, Montevideo (AGNJ). The teniente alcade could preside over petty cases (those involving sums less than twenty pesos) but mainly served to carry out the orders of the magistrates, for example, apprehending suspects and serving legal notices.

for the position of juez de paz moved or were ineligible. In another town, the teniente alcalde reported that he would be leaving the district soon and that there was only one eligible candidate to replace him "since the district is only made up of Brazilians, and the odd Oriental cannot read or write."[26] Filling the rural posts hardly guaranteed that the proscribed functions would be carried out. The teniente alcalde of Cañas complained that he was not able to implement any orders because he was "only one man and ... the majority of the residents do not obey orders."[27]

These were indeed tumultuous times on the northern frontier. The region had only recently been "pacified" through a bloody campaign against the remaining bands of seminomadic Charrua Indians.[28] Settlement was cut short by the outbreak of the Guerra Grande, and the vast herds of cattle that constituted the region's main resource were greatly depleted during the war. Frequent raids across the border by Brazilian ranchers accounted for a sizable portion of this loss; cattle had been slaughtered indiscriminately, too, to feed the warring armies. The population of the northern districts plummeted during the war, and communications with the capital, poor even under the best conditions, were severely strained.[29]

Despite these barriers to orderly rule, people found reason to turn to the courts. The well-documented litigiousness of colonial Spanish subjects in South America carried over into the early days of independence.[30] In Cerro Largo in 1830, civil complaints included cases about the disputed ownership of slaves; suits over land and the sale of cattle; and the indignant charge by one soldier, Justo Videla, that Leopoldo Geral had stolen his silver spurs and had shown "the most

---

[26] Letter from Eduardo Abreu to the Alcalde Ordinario, 5 September 1852, Cerro Largo, Legajo 7, AGNJ.

[27] Letter from the Teniente Alcalde Juan Lopes to the Juez de Paz de la 2a sección Eduardo Abreu, 5 September 1852, Cerro Largo, Legajo 7, AGNJ.

[28] See Part II, Chapters I–III, Volume II, Eduardo F. Acosta y Lara, *La Guerra de los Charrúas*. Because the Charruas were virtually eliminated by this campaign, there has been a tendency in some historical treatments of the north to downplay indigenous influences in this region. As Acosta y Lara points out, though, an infusion of Guaraní migrants into the region both before and after independence had a profound, if subtle, influence on local culture.

[29] The devastation of the Guerra Grande is covered extensively in Barrán, *Apogeo y crisis*.

[30] Evidence of the litigiousness of colonial subjects, including Indians, comes from a variety of sources and regions. See, for example, Steve Stern, *Peru's Indian Peoples and the Challenge of Spanish Conquest*; Cutter, *The Legal Culture of Northern New Spain*; and see note 2 above.

scandalous disregard for the Laws" in refusing a judge's order to return them.[31] Antonio Felix de Meneses was in court several times that year. He first brought suit against his own son for being too young to marry. Later in the year he was found responsible for filing false charges against Manuel Acosta; both Meneses and the juez de paz in the case were ordered to pay Acosta damages.[32]

If these litigants were not shy about using the courts, they also made it clear that they expected impartiality from the rural judges. On occasion, their expectations were met. Sorting out the facts in a case over the disputed ownership of a slave, one juez de paz heard – and credited – testimony from the slave himself, then passed the case to the alcalde ordinario for judgment.[33] In other cases, judges seem to have followed procedures of appeal closely, and litigants offered excuses for irregularities, conveying their clear sense that the law mattered. Ramón Moreno, bringing a contract for his purchase of a piece of land ten years before, explained that he had failed to register the sale and pay the land tax because of "all the political upheaval that our country has suffered."[34] He announced his intent to set the record straight, no doubt as a protection against future litigation or fines.

Even in 1850, before the official end of the civil war, rural justice operated with a certain orderliness. When officials received a report that the body of a mulatto named Miguel had been found in the countryside, they conducted a lengthy investigation to discover the murderer, taking depositions from a series of witnesses: Miguel's companion; two peones from a neighboring estancia, or ranch; the nine-year-old son of a slave from the same estancia; a Brazilian man who had seen the victim in the local provisions store, or *pulpería*; the pulpería owner; a freed slave who lived nearby; and two other laborers.[35] This was hardly the legal legwork of a "lawless" and "stateless" frontier region. Even complaints against magistrates appear in the record. In May 1850, Doña Joaquina Rodriguez presented a complaint against one juez de paz for serious procedural violations. Rodriguez claimed that on a trip to another district to trade, she had entered into a dispute with a local merchant.

---

[31] Letrados, Cerro Largo, 1830, No. 7, AGNJ.

[32] Letrados, Cerro Largo, 1830, No. 7, AGNJ.

[33] Letrados, Cerro Largo, 1830, No. 7, AGNJ. Uruguayan judges appear to have been willing on many occasions to rely on the testimony of slaves. See below for the discussion of tensions on the border regarding the treatment of, and traffic in, Brazilian slaves.

[34] Letrados, Cerro Largo, 1830, No. 7, AGNJ .

[35] "Indagación sobre la muerte del Moreno Miguel," Letrados, Cerro Largo, 1850, AGNJ.

He in turn had brought in the juez de paz, who acted "for himself and before himself, making himself both judge and party, prosecutor and court-appointed defender." Rodriquez charged that the juez de paz had "violated the law and common sense with his legal rulings" and had caused her to pay more than she owed; the case had forced her to abandon her chores and to "walk two hundred leagues to seek justice!"[36]

Given these early signs of an acceptance of the courts as a place to resolve disputes, regularize and record contracts and deeds, and pursue grievances against the authorities themselves, we should not be surprised to find that after the end of the civil war, litigation experienced a steady increase. In the northern frontier province of Tacuarembó, in the years between 1835 and 1853, an average of five civil cases a year reached the court of the alcalde ordinario. In 1854, the number shot up to fifty-six cases, and it remained at an average of thirty-seven cases a year over the next five years.[37]

Brazilian-born litigants in the northern districts were now more numerous, reflecting the change in the population. The legal order of the frontier was becoming routinely bilingual and binational. Brazilians crossed the border with an array of legal documents for which they were careful to seek recognition in local courts. The translation and recording of many such documents became a routine function of the legal system in the border districts. Brazilian ranchers holding property in Uruguay sold or rented property to Brazilians in Brazil, and these contracts were brought to Uruguayan courts with the request that they be translated and registered. Estate settlements frequently involved wills written in Portuguese and notarized in Brazil, with heirs living on both sides of the border. Brazilian litigants had powers of attorney made out in Brazil and sent with their representatives to courts on the other side of the border. Brazilian and Uruguayan policemen also exchanged information about fugitives and on occasion cooperated in their capture. The routine acceptance of Brazilian documents in the courts was such that litigants sometimes traveled across the border in search of them. Juana Fernandez Pintos found land that she had inherited from her father in Uruguay had been usurped by the

---

[36] "Da Joaquina Rodriguez en queja contra el juez de paz de la 5a sección," Letrados, Cerro Largo, 1850, AGNJ.

[37] "Inventario de las causas civiles existentes en este Juzgado Ordinario," Letrados, Tacuarembó 1855/59, AGNJ.

tenant during her long absence in Brazil, with the complicity of her brother, who controlled the titles; she petitioned the alcalde ordinario in Cerro Largo in 1867, then left for Brazil to retrieve the will and estate settlement.[38]

The border could also signify more than a minor linguistic and procedural obstacle. In Brazil, slavery remained legal; in the República Oriental it was outlawed in 1846. Antislavery sentiment in Uruguay was strong, but de facto slavery was kept alive by pressures to maintain ranching labor costs at a level competitive with Brazil and by legal loopholes that allowed slave holders entering Uruguay to sign labor "contracts" with their slaves for extended periods. The Uruguayan legislature passed a law in 1861 limiting the term to six years, and officials required that contracts be registered in Uruguayan courts in the presence of all the parties to ensure that the laborers understood that slavery was illegal in the country. Authorities on the border were often openly sympathetic to slaves' attempts to use the courts to gain their freedom. In 1846, for example, the alcalde ordinario of Tacuarembó found insufficient proof that the plaintiff Joaquín was the property of the Brazilian Celestino Dorrego, though three witnesses, including two other Brazilians, testified that they had known the slave to be in his possession for more than ten years.[39] In another case from 1869, Francisca Escoto appeared before the jefe político of Tacuarembó claiming that she was "a citizen of this Republic," born and baptized in Tacuarembó but taken at the age of six or seven in servitude to Brazil. She had traveled across the border to gain her freedom and was seeking help from the Oriental authorities in freeing her four children, who were still slaves in Brazil. Both military and judicial officials in Uruguay tried to intervene on her behalf, but the Brazilians were not cooperative. The Barón del Cerro Alegre wrote to the political chief of Tacuarembó that he could do nothing in the case "because the laws of my country don't permit the military authorities to intervene in such cases . . . only the judicial authorities."

---

[38] "Da Juana Fernandez Pintos contra Don Paulino dos Santos sobre desalojo de campos," Letrados, Cerro Largo, 1867, AGNJ.

[39] "Celestino Dorrego con el Defensor de Esclavos sobre propiedad de uno," Letrados, Tacuarembó, Legajo No. 1, 1823–55, AGNJ. In another case from 1862, a contract laborer named Francisco, learning of the new law requiring both parties to approve and register such contracts in Uruguay, ran away before his contract could be registered. His master complained to the alcalde ordinario that surely the incentive to flee was an unintended consequence of the law and that Francisco should be treated as a fugitive.

The Brazilian courts would of course not surrender jurisdiction. The municipal judge in Bagé declared that the woman should return to Brazil "to litigate in this court for her freedom, if she chooses to try, or else be returned to her master."[40]

In other cases not involving slaves, litigation had ways of stretching across the border. Cross-border cases featured two, often interrelated strategies. First was the argument, made and even successfully defended in some cases, that Brazilian legal procedures should be accepted as part of the Uruguayan legal process. This claim went further than the routine transfer and use of foreign documents, and it often contained an implicit critique of legal proceedings in the Republic. A second strategy involved the refusal of some litigants – Brazilians living either full time or part time in the Banda Oriental – to appear in court on either side of the border. This tactic appeared frequently in litigation over property, because the subsequent delays in cases gave defendants time to sell disputed land or cattle.

These two strategies related to a more general shift toward greater regularization of property transactions and titles. On the one hand, the legal system held out the promise of a more orderly protection of property rights; on the other, legal procedures could themselves contribute to instability, as in the case of notoriously arbitrary prejudgment attachments prohibiting the sale of disputed property. While Brazilian landholders who traveled back to Brazil or even lived there permanently were especially vulnerable to such legal maneuvers, they were also drawn through them into protracted litigation in Uruguayan courts, where they often triumphed by appealing for greater consistency in rulings and procedure.

Two cases from Tacuarembó a decade apart show the intersection of cross-border legal strategies and legal reform issues. The first case, from 1857, began as a dispute about payment on rented land.[41] This sort of litigation was very common; absentee landholders rented out land for extended periods and later claimed that tenants had failed to pay or had even tried to assume ownership of the rented property. In the 1857 case, the original contract on the land inside Uruguay had been signed in Brazil by the landowner, João Pedro de los Reis, and his tenant,

[40] "Simeon Fagundez de Olivera con Francisca Escolla reclamandola como esclava," Letrados, Tacruarembó, Legajo No. 12, 1869/1872, AGNJ.

[41] "Juan Pedro de los Reyes con Joaquín Manuel Teixeira cobro de pesos," 1857, R-No. 3, Letrados, Tacuarembó, Legajo No. 3 1855/59, AGNJ.

Joaquín Manuel Teixeira, in 1849.[42] In 1855, Reis filed a complaint with a judge in Pelotas, in Brazil, saying that Teixeira was not paying him. Since Teixeira would not appear in court in Pelotas, Reis petitioned the alcalde ordinario in Tacuarembó with the same charge two years later. Reis now feared that his tenant had been selling the cattle on his estancia and had left the country "for an unknown place."

Reis was in effect asking the judge to substitute the Brazilian legal proceeding for a lower-court judgment in the República Oriental. Legal procedure in Uruguay required litigants to submit to an arbitration hearing – a juicio conciliatorio – before a juez de paz prior to bringing a case before the alcalde ordinario.[43] Reis was arguing that the Pelotas procedure should serve as the hearing. At first, this approach worked surprisingly well. Citing Teixeira's failure to appear before the court in Pelotas, the alcalde ordinario prohibited Teixeira's sale of his land and cattle. But the strategy was destined for trouble. When local officials went to inform Teixeira, they found his son in residence on the estancia; even without legal counsel, he pointed out that the property had been attached without a hearing, "as required by Law." Reis's lawyer argued that there had been no alternative to holding the conciliación in Brazil "because the parties both lived there."

The alcalde ordinario either felt he lacked the legal expertise to rule on this jurisdictional matter, or he wished to avoid taking responsibility for the decision. As these judges were entitled to do, he appointed a legal advisor to the court to help him rule on the jurisdictional issue. The court advisor, a local lawyer named Antonio Segui, reported that banning the sale of Teixeira's property had indeed been illegal. No trial had taken place. Segui recommended that the magistrate sign an order to remove the restraint under the condition that Teixeira appear within twenty days. Reis's lawyer pleaded for the case to move forward, since his client lived in Brazil and "any delay can only prejudice my side and in no way the other." Nevertheless, the magistrate followed Segui's advice, also fining Reis for holding a contract written on paper without the proper seal.

---

[42] Two years later, Reis appeared with witnesses before a juez de paz inside Uruguay to register the contract, which had been written on "plain paper" and without the required seals.

[43] This was also a requirement in the revised Brazilian court system. See Flory, *Judge and Jury in Imperial Brazil.*

If Reis had difficulties as a foreign litigant, Teixeira soon sought advantage in his own foreign status. Within months of writing his advisory ruling, Antonio Segui had contracted to represent both Teixeira and a third man, Julian Grane, and Segui reported to the court that Teixeira was now in Corrientes, in Argentina, where he had legally sold his share of the property he held with Reis to Grane. It was not necessary, Segui argued, to enter into a discussion of whether Teixeira owed Reis any money, but only to show "that the purchase of the land made by my client was valid." As an aside, Segui noted that it was well-known that Teixeira owned valuable properties in Rio Grande in Brazil. He was perhaps hinting that the debt could be claimed in Brazilian courts and that its fulfillment did not depend on what happened in the República Oriental. No doubt Segui, who had recently advised the alcalde ordinario on points of law in the case, held some sway with the judge, who approved the sale in December of 1857. With this move, Teixeira had effectively won the case.

Reis did not give up, however. After a lengthy stay in Montevideo, his lawyer returned in April of 1858 to inquire about the progress of the case. When he discovered what had happened, he pointed out to the alcalde ordinario that he had ruled back in May of 1857 that Teixeira could not sell his lands unless he appeared. Bending once again, the judge reverted to his previous order. A court-appointed representative for the absent Teixeira was named so that the case could continue without him. In 1859, the case remained in limbo.[44] Finally, in August, the two parties, with Teixeira represented by a court-appointed lawyer, held the juicio conciliatorio. The hearing was a formality. With no effective advocate, Teixeira's side folded. It is unclear from the record whether Reis was ever successful in receiving any remedy from Teixeira, who had sold his land in the interim.

This case shows two Brazilians in litigation over property rights within Uruguay. The plaintiff's claim that by living in Brazil he was disadvantaged in actively pursuing the case appears to hold some truth. But his first strategy was to try to use his foreign residence in arguing that the conciliación carried out in Brazil should substitute for one conducted in the República Oriental. The defendant was also adept at using

44 A new alcalde ordinario took over. In March of 1859, a teniente alcalde was ordered to carry out the formality of notifying Teixeira's son of the order to appear in court. It is interesting to note that this rural official's report was written half in Portuguese; this subaltern official could not even manage to produce formal Spanish for court correspondence.

border crossings to his advantage. While not appearing or even sending a representative to respond to the litigation, he found a lawyer close to the case to arrange the sale of his property, registered in the consulate outside the country. The case also demonstrates the weaknesses of judicial administration in the countryside. In this and in many other cases, judges responded to whatever arguments were put before them. The records show us a growing number of cases in which judges enjoined the sale of property without much deliberation, and with little consistency. No doubt in some of these cases, magistrates were motivated by patronage ties or even self-interest. But in others, they simply sought summary judgments to troublesome issues. The fact that so many litigants were Brazilian, some living in Brazil, also recommended such a strategy. Litigants from Brazil could not always forcefully present their cases, sometimes did not show, and might have recourse to other legal remedies in Brazil. At the same time, though, the Brazilians learned the rhetoric and the procedures needed to defend their interests in the Republic. The rhetoric required quoting the constitutional right to protection under the laws of the state. As for procedure, it was possible to make an appearance at any time in the course of a case and argue that procedural requirements had not been met. It was a fair bet that in most cases they had not been. Brazilian litigants could thus claim residence outside the country as long as it was convenient, but they also argued strategically that the state of judicial administration in the country prevented them from receiving justice.

A second case a decade later helps us to view these strategies in somewhat different combination. It was brought by a Brazilian lawyer, Joachín Pacheco da Silva, against another Brazilian, Doña Ana Joaquina de Azambuya, in 1867, in Tacuarembó.[45] Pacheco claimed he had represented Azambuya in settling her husband's estate in the República Oriental, where Pacheco had been forced to go as her representative, abandoning his business in Brazil. He asked the alcalde ordinario to request that the municipal judge of Bagé, where the widow lived, summon her to the Tacuarembó court. The alcalde ordinario complied, signing an order for Azambuya to appear in July. In September, Pacheco's representative was in court again asking for a second, then a third notice. The defendant was trying, Pacheco's advocate argued, to avoid a trial, "saying that she has nothing in this country, whereas this is untrue and

---

[45] "Juan Pacheco da Silva con Ana Joaquina de Azambuya cobro de honorarios," 1867, P No. 11, Letrados, Tacuarembó, Legajo No. 10, 1866/67, AGNJ.

she is trying to sell her properties" to escape the claims made against her. In early 1868, notices appeared in both the Tacuarembó and Bagé newspapers ordering Azambuya to appear in court. In March, Pacheco's side successfully argued that the case should go forward without the defendant.

The case appeared to be leaning Pacheco's way. He outlined the basis for his claim that Azambuya owed him six thousand pesos. Nearly half that amount, he claimed, consisted of losses he had incurred by abandoning his business in Bagé; the rest were costs for handling the widow's case, and his own honorarium. The court-appointed defender conceded that Pacheco had indeed worked for Azambuya and had not been paid. Only the amount remained in dispute. The alcalde ordinario appointed two assessors, who agreed in May of 1867 that Pacheco had done a valuable service; the widow's rights to the inheritance had been contested since she was living in Brazil and separated from her husband, a colonel in the army of the República, and Pacheco had secured her share of the estate. The assessors nevertheless recommended reducing the amount owed to four thousand pesos. Pacheco lamented the decrease in his award but agreed to it, and the court-appointed defender for Azambuya also raised no objection to the settlement.

But rather than settling, the case now entered a new phase. Pacheco's representative was back in June, claiming that Azambuya had sold all her property in the República except one piece of land in Tacuarembó. He warned, too, that she had contracted a representative locally, a man named José de Mora. The court had to act, he pleaded, to prevent either Mora or Azambuya from selling the remaining land. The court's approval of this course of action, though, did little to help Pacheco's cause. José de Mora, through his own representative, reported back that he had legally bought the land from Azambuya back in January, so that the restraint on the property could not be valid.

Pacheco saw his chances slipping away. His lawyer argued that the sale was fraudulent. It had been made before a notary "in a foreign country," and the title had been presented for registry the day after the court had barred the sale of the property. "The laws of this country are very explicit regarding sales made in foreign countries," Pacheco's side argued. There were tax-reporting procedures that had been violated. The sale must be nullified.

Once again, the court decided to name a legal advisor. A Montevideo lawyer, Ramón Lagastizabal, was chosen this time. His advisory report had the ring of an appellate ruling. He found that Pacheco's claims to the debt by Azambuya were unsubstantiated. Pacheco had not supplied receipts for his work, he had not presented evidence of the losses he had incurred in Brazil, and the court-appointed lawyer for Azambuya had presented no defense. The advisor went further, arguing that "absentee or captive" parties to a suit must be given the same rights as minors, and he cited an article from the new Civil Code protecting minors from arbitration or awards committed on their behalf. What was more, Lagastizabal argued, the contract of sale presented by Mora, though executed in Brazil, had to be considered authentic, "having been legalized by the Vice-Consul of the República" in Brazil. Pacheco might object to the contract only if he could show that it had not been drawn up in accordance with the laws of Brazil. A separate document recommended assessing Pacheco court costs, including the fee for paying the court-appointed lawyer for the other side. Without comment, the alcalde ordinario affirmed the opinion in June as the final sentence in the case.

Pacheco must have been distraught at this outcome, having seen the case close to settlement in his favor. His lawyer appealed in July. Pacheco now had to find representation in Montevideo. After numerous delays, the case was changed by the sudden presentation in August 1869 of a power of attorney signed in Bagé by the absent Doña Azambuya. This was her first appearance in the case. She named as her representatives a firm of well-connected lawyers in Montevideo, one of whom was Ramón Lagastizabal, the former legal advisor in the case.

In the first six months of 1870, the appellate judge received briefs from the three litigants, Pacheco, Azambuya, and Mora. Pacheco's side reiterated his claims and presented new documents supporting his work for the widow. More gently, he criticized the *asesor* for advising on the facts of the case rather than on the narrow question of the legality of the prohibition on the sale of Azambuya's property. He stopped short of accusing Lagastizabal of complicity but did point out that "he had already served as judge in the case" and was now an advocate.

For the defense, the lawyers for Azambuya and Mora introduced a new argument. The rural court had never enjoyed jurisdiction over the case, Azambuya's attorneys wrote. Not only was the demand too large to be considered by even an alcalde ordinario, but the Señora "was *known* to have her residence in Brazil, and so had the right not to be cited anywhere but there." Her absence, too, made it impossible for the court to be assured that she had received three notices to appear. The court defender had been "illegally appointed." Mora's lawyer concurred. "Any Judge is incompetent and commits an abuse of power when he goes beyond the limits of his jurisdiction and exercises judicial functions over persons not within his purview or in causes that belong to another judge . . . [and] no one is permitted to exceed the jurisdictional limits that the law has established." The appellate judge reaffirmed the lower-court ruling, and the court appended a new list of costs, presumably also for payment by Pacheco.

The lack of commentary by the appellate judge does not let us determine which set of arguments swayed him. In Montevideo's small legal community, the reputation of Azambuya's representatives might have been enough to win the case. It is certainly clear, however, that jurisdictional issues were central to the defendants' case. In arguing for a strict limit on jurisdiction over Brazilians, the Montevidean lawyers were, oddly, reaffirming an immunity for foreigners that they often railed against as a matter of policy.[46] They were also, though, advocating a vision of the functioning of the courts that was quite different from practice on the frontier, where cases between two Brazilian litigants, and summonses sent to Bagé or Yaguarón, were familiar and even routine. Once again, a foreign litigant was simultaneously arguing for greater procedural rigor in the courts and for an exemption from their purview.

A "COUNTRY CLAIMING TO BE CIVILIZED"

This seeming contradiction – claiming immunity while exclaiming the legal equality of residents and citizens – was the hallmark of another steady source of judicial commentary and controversy, the communications from foreign legations in Montevideo in and around the same period. A steady stream of letters from the Brazilian and British legations, and somewhat less voluminous communications from Argentine, Italian, French, and Spanish officials, from the 1850s through the 1870s, addressed the twin concerns of the treatment of foreign criminal defendants and the search for justice in cases where foreigners were victims. Added to these issues was the Brazilian preoccupation with actions taken by the República Oriental that threatened the property rights of Brazilian slaveholders. Both Brazil and Britain were concerned, too, with

---

[46] If this argument seemed acceptable here, it was perhaps because it was coupled with a critique of the handling of the case in the rural courts. Both Lagastirábel's earlier brief and the defense lawyers' arguments to the appellate judge also imply disdain for the lower-court proceeding. See below for a discussion of legal policy movements in the capital.

deserters who either crossed the border or jumped ship, and with the Oriental habit of pressing foreigners into military service.

These communications were part of the standard flow of consular correspondence. But the claims for various degrees and forms of ex-traterritoriality are of more than minor significance, for several reasons. One is that these complaints were a forum for commentary by foreign-ers on the deplorable state of judicial administration in the República Oriental – and, parenthetically, on the advanced state of the law in their own countries. Second, the complaints were routinely passed along from the Ministry of Foreign Affairs directly to the *Tribunal Superior*, the high-est court then in operation. Even though, as we shall see, the response was often no response at all, the legation communiqués persisted over decades, and acted as a constant buzzing in the ear of highly placed le-gal officials in Montevideo about the deficiencies of the administration of justice. The officials reacted in part by hardening their position that control over the country's legal institutions was the linchpin of state sovereignty. It cannot be regarded as coincidence, though, that many of the same officials were meanwhile advocating legal reforms that would ultimately address the concerns raised by the foreign legations. Third, both Brazil and Britain entered these discussions with the background of treaties giving their subjects special legal status. These limited claims to immunity formed a crack in the state's sovereignty that Uruguayans feared might widen – and that under special circumstances foreign lega-tions would, indeed, seek to widen. Finally, the stream of complaints about judicial practice helps to remind us that law was not viewed sim-ply as instrumental to trade; indeed, British and Brazilian officials often spent far more time on judicial matters than in advocacy of trade pol-icy or protection of individual investors. There is no doubt that internal order was considered as essential to expanding investments on the part of the British in the region, and that British victims of crime were them-selves sometimes investors or landholders of some importance. But the passion with which the legation pursued perceived injustices was only indirectly connected to economic interests. Fixed ideas about how jus-tice should be administered, and to whom, were central to the decision of Britain to cut off diplomatic ties with the Uruguayan state in the 1870s; the issue of justice was seen as related to, but not less important than, the narrower concern of Uruguay's defaulted debt (itself the result of adjudication over claims of war damages by British subjects).

For Brazilian officials, the Treaty of 1851 gave them a basis for various complaints against judicial proceedings in the República Oriental. One clause of the agreement protected Brazilians from serving in the army. Another pledged that runaway slaves and deserters crossing the border would be returned to Brazil. Desultory enforcement of these clauses generated numerous complaints. We have already noted, for example, that the Uruguayan courts tended to look favorably on slaves claiming their freedom. Within just two years of signing the treaty, the government released a circular to all provincial jefes políticos that created a stir because it implied that slaves entering the national territory after the treaty was signed need not be returned. The Brazilians had their own narrow interpretation of the treaty when questions emerged about the surrender of Uruguayan deserters who crossed the border into Brazil. Though the exchange of deserters was explicit in the treaty, Brazilians reported that they were under no obligation to return fugitives wanted for political crimes, a distinction that allowed them to harbor renegades of all stripes and infuriated the Montevidean government.[47] Such issues were a recurring focus of tensions and drew legal wrangling squarely into the realm of international politics.

Consider the interesting case of the Brazilian soldier Manoel Bernardino da Pacheco. Authorities in Cerro Largo had asked the police in the Brazilian city of Yaguarão (Yaguarón in Spanish) to arrest him for trial in Uruguay. To the dismay of national Brazilian officials, the local police had promptly complied, depriving him, the legation argued, of rights conferred by his nationality and residence, and affirmed in the treaty, "as it is in almost all international conventions of this kind." Going further, the legation argued that even if Bernardino *had* committed a crime in the República, he had done so while there with the Brazilian army in 1851. His status as a soldier placed him outside normal criminal jurisdiction. "Neither the Authorities of Cerro Largo nor those of Yaguarão had jurisdiction over this act." Instead, they argued, the matter needed to be resolved "Government to Government."[48]

The appeal for special status for Brazilians was balanced, though, by the claim that they were entitled to the rights of citizens under the law. Similar cases at either end of this formative period illustrate the ways in which Brazilians used the complaints as a forum for a critique of Uruguayan justice. In 1852, the legation registered a complaint about the treatment of the Brazilian subject Adriano Monix Fagundes, who

[47] Restos Antiguos, Ministerio de Relaciones Exteriores (MRE), Legación de Brasil, Caja 1, Carpeta 2, Archivo de Relaciones Exteriores, Montevideo (ARE).

[48] Legación de Brasil, Carpeta 60, Archivo General de la Nación, Montevideo (AGN).

had purchased cattle in Paysandú with a partner. He was then cited to appear before the jefe político, and a short time later the court enjoined the sale of all his property. He spent two months in the provincial capital trying to petition the jefe político and the alcalde ordinario, but his case was never heard. His only recourse, he decided, was to complain to his own government, writing that the facts of the case "recall the calamitous era this State has passed through." The complaint to the Foreign Ministry was followed up with an inquiry to the jefe político in Paysandú, who replied that Fagundes was involved in a criminal case that was being referred to the provincial court and then on to the criminal appeals court in Montevideo. The prosecutor in Montevideo responded curtly to inquiries about the case, saying that he could find "no substantial procedural defect" in the case and that it should be returned to the court, "so that the laws and justice of the nation continue their course."[49]

Two decades later, the rhetoric was much the same in a case from Paysandú reported by the Brazilian legation. The legation passed on a complaint by the Brazilian Hipolito Ribeiro, who had left his estancia in Paysandú to fight in the war with Paraguay, leaving his sheep in a herd mixed with animals belonging to the Oriental José Prates. According to the complaint, Prates convinced four recently arrived Italians to swear before the local juez de paz, in an act that took place in Prates's house, that Ribeiro had been slaughtering his sheep. The juez de paz ordered 663 sheep and 17 cows to be selected from Ribeiro's flock and given to Prates. Ribeiro's lawyer made three separate appeals to the alcalde ordinario but "no action was taken in order to guarantee the property of the absent foreigner." The complaint contrasted this "horrifying" act with the legal order in Brazil, where citizens were "so accustomed to seeing the sacred right of property respected."[50]

Like the Brazilians, the British claimed special status for their citizens under some circumstances and they also dwelled on the necessity of improving Uruguayan justice so that British subjects would have proper protection under the law. Already in the late 1850s and early 1860s, the British legation in Montevideo showed unusually detailed attention to legal cases involving British citizens as defendants or victims.[51] The

---

[49] Legación de Brasil, Carpeta 35, AGN.

[50] Restos Antiguos, MRE, Legación de Brasil, Caja 1, Carpeta 2, ARE.

[51] Perhaps the inclination to pursue these cases is explained in part by the arrival in 1856 of James St. John Munro as vice consul; in this post and later, as chargé d'affaires, Munro displayed a great passion on the subject of the law.

complaints insisted especially on the failures of the justice system in the countryside, where murders of British citizens routinely went unsolved. In 1862, the legation forwarded the complaint of judicial misconduct by a rural magistrate acting against a British citizen. In 1865, we find the first reference to the murder of an entire British family, the Campbells, and other complaints about violence against British citizens. Disorder in the countryside became a central preoccupation of the legation after 1870 during the so-called Revolt of the Lances led by the caudillo Venancio Flores.

The increasingly strident complaints of the British, most of them authored by the vice consul, James St. John Munro, show the British to be not merely registering their objections to the handling of various legal cases but following the details of each case and, in some instances, independently gathering evidence and even taking depositions – acting, in essence, as a shadow legal authority. Following up on the trial of the man accused of the Campbell family murders, for example, Munro complained that the verdict "declared Damasio Escobar to be guilty of the robbery which was committed at the time of the murders, but declares the crime of his having committed the murders to be 'not proven.' How the Jury came to pronounce such a verdict in the face of the fact of the bloody knife which is known to have belonged to Damasio Escobar having been found on the scene of the murders I am at a loss to comprehend."[52] Munro's call for a new trial gave way quickly to another concern when Escobar escaped from prison; Munro learned not from the authorities but from "several English gentlemen" that Escobar was living openly in the place where the crime had been committed.

When in July of 1868, a British subject from Gibraltar was killed by a policeman for comments he made about a street brawl, Munro took a sworn statement by a witness in his office and passed it on to the minister of foreign affairs, together with this remark:

Upon the 24th of last month Your Excellency was pleased in conversation with me to express an opinion that the taking away of life so lamentably common in this Republic and which Your Excellency described as a disgrace to a country claiming to be civilized, called for the practice of decided measures, and Your Excellency then announced a

---

[52] Restos Antiguos, MRE, Legación de Gran Bretaña, Caja 1, Carpeta 2, ARE.

determination, as a Minister of the State, that in all such cases in the future the law should be strictly vindicated.[53]

The minister referred to was Manuel Herrera y Obes, one of the country's leading law-trained politicians, and though his comments had no doubt been intended to placate Munro, he probably also shared his disdain for the shoddy and interest-laden legal practices of the local courts. But the response from Uruguayan officials was purposefully slow. The judiciary reported back that Munro's witness had never given a statement to the criminal court. Subsequent complaints by the British went unanswered for months, and at least one letter was mislaid. This is not to say that the British appeals made no impression. The Tribunal Superior was asked for a report on the case in July of 1869, and a month later, the foreign affairs minister stated that the president had personally approved a payment of three hundred pesos in compensation to the victim's widow.

Munro wrote during the same year to urge, in similarly detailed letters, the prosecution of the murderers of three other British subjects, all on estancias. In 1869, there were three more murder cases. Munro's tone grew more strident in his letters, and he continued to offer himself in the role of investigator. In reporting on the murder of Stephen Tucker in Soriano in December of 1868, Munro noted that in March he had taken sworn depositions from witnesses in the case. But because the government's response to his inquiries in other cases had been so slow, he had delayed writing about the Tucker case "until I might be able, if possible, to discover through my own efforts the actual place of residence of the assassin." He now reported that the suspected murderer had been sighted "at a place called the Tres Arboles on the north side of the Rio Negro" and offered a reward of fifty pounds for further information on his whereabouts.[54]

In 1870, reports of thefts against British subjects in the countryside became more common as government forces – in some cases subaltern officials acting on their own – seized property, ostensibly to support the campaign against the revolt. Munro dutifully recorded his outrage at these incidents. In the same year an incident occurred that was to provide a focus for British frustrations. In July of 1870, an English captain aboard the English ship "Bobecito" was murdered by three English sailors at

---

53 Restos Antiguos, MRE, Legación de Gran Bretaña, Caja 1, Carpeta 4, ARE.
54 Restos Antiguos, MRE, Legación de Gran Bretaña, Caja 1, Carpeta 8, ARE.

Fray Bentos.[55] Munro did not limit himself to the role of investigator this time – he sought English jurisdiction in the case, "as every detail in this affair was English, the scene of the crime an English ship, the murderers English, though in Uruguayan waters." He seemed to be aware that there was no legal basis for making this claim but argued that the Uruguayan state had, through its own disorganization and past inability to provide justice, forfeited its right to try the case.[56] In response, the president asserted that the sovereignty of the state was at stake. In refusing to deliver the English sailors, the president reportedly told Munro "that such a proceeding would be considered a lowering of the dignity of the state" and cited "its right to try the man before its own tribunals."[57] When it came to the notice of British officials that two of the suspects had been permitted to volunteer for military service, while a third was in prison but had not been tried, Munro lodged another vigorous protest.

There were, to be sure, now other sources of friction between the two governments. The Uruguayan government, in perpetual financial difficulties, had defaulted on the payment of British debt. The government had also temporarily shut down the services of an English telegraph company and arrested its English director for transmitting messages sent by rebel forces. There was trouble about a promised railroad concession for a British subject that was assigned instead to local political insiders without any compensation being paid. But in the long explanatory letter from the legation in November 1871, listing reasons for the decision to break off diplomatic relations, the problems of the judiciary – in particular, the many unsolved crimes committed against British subjects – received the most extensive comment. The handling of the "Bobecito" incident was particularly galling to the British, who accused the Tribunal Superior of itself acting "in contravention of the law" in its treatment of the suspects, "whether because of ignorance

---

[55] The Uruguayans almost always referred to the British as *ingleses*, and the British legation also often used the term *English* when referring to British subjects, even though many, if not most, British residents in Uruguay were from outside England. I have preserved the term *English* in describing this incident because both sides argued specifically over the validity of claims to "English jurisdiction."

[56] Restos Antiguos, MRE, Legación de Gran Bretaña, Caja 1, Carpeta 15, ARE. Munro argued that "under the unfortunate circumstances of the Civil War prevailing in the Republic and disorganizing the whole machinery of the state, there was no chance of the course of justice with regard to these men being properly carried through in this country."

[57] This is Munro paraphrasing the president. Restos Antiguos, MRE, Legación de Gran Bretaña, Caja 1, Carpeta 15, ARE.

of the law in such cases or because of an intentional wish to deprive Her Majesty's Consul of his right to claim these captives and send them to be tried in England." In refusing England's jurisdiction in the case, the president had "assumed a duty that he could not discharge."[58] In general, the letter went on, any statement by the government that cases involving the interests of foreigners could be solved according to the laws of the country was "the equivalent of a predetermined decision to deny" foreign claims.[59] Finally, in an argument that echoed British claims for extraterritoriality in China, the consul accused the government of a nearly complete ignorance and avoidance of the conventions of international diplomacy.

LEGAL REFORMS

Quite apart from the larger question of the Uruguayan government's view of the diplomatic break with England, how did the (fractured) political elite respond to these strident critiques of the state's administration of justice? Even before the end of the Guerra Grande, a legal reform movement was taking shape in Montevideo. The Uruguayan historian Pivel Devoto calls the period between 1851 and 1867 one of an "extraordinary flowering of juridical literature."[60] A handful of prominent political leaders with legal training pressed for reforms of the legal system as part of the solution to the disruptive politics of caudillismo. The legal status of foreigners was a recurring theme for these law reformers as well as an influence on the direction of reform.

The lawyer Eduardo Acevedo founded the newspaper *La Constitución* and wrote passionately in it about the need to unify the country and defend the "strict observance of the Constitution."[61] He favored an aggressive campaign to naturalize foreigners and objected to the extension of even limited political rights to foreigners who chose not to accept citizenship.[62] Advocating a stricter implementation of election

---

[58] My translation from the Spanish version of the letter. Restos Antiguos, MRE, Legación de Gran Bretaña, Caja 1, Carpeta 6, ARE.

[59] Restos Antiguos, MRE, Legación de Gran Bretaña, Caja 1, Carpeta 6, ARE.

[60] Juan E. Pivel Devoto and Alcira Ranieri de Pivel Devoto, *Uruguay a fines del siglo XIX*, p. 29.

[61] Eduardo Acevedo, *Eduardo Acevedo, años 1815–1863: Su obra como codificador, ministro, legislador y periodista*, p. 114.

[62] For example, Acevedo argued against allowing foreigners to vote for judges: "It is clear that if foreigners are given the right to vote in the elections for Judges, it would not be possible to deny them the right to vote for representatives" (Acevedo, *Eduardo Acevedo*, p. 173).

laws requiring registration of eligible voters, for example, Acevedo complained that under the current conditions, anyone "was authorized to call himself a citizen today, and tomorrow a foreigner, with nothing to serve as a way of fixing nationality."[63] When Acevedo became the minister of government and foreign affairs between March 1860 and June 1861, he aggressively defended the rule of law as the basis for the sovereignty of the state.[64] In response to repeated Brazilian complaints about the victimization of Brazilians in the Uruguayan countryside, Acevedo was unapologetic. He noted in a memorandum in March 1861 that although it was unfortunate that some Brazilians had been victims of crime, the danger was a common condition of those living far from home and in a newly forming society. He suggested that Orientales living in Brazil were in much the same position and that Brazilian courts had not done better in tracking down Brazilian aggressors. In fact, he wrote, it was surprising that more violence was not being reported against Brazilians.[65] On another occasion, Acevedo specifically attacked consular interventions in legal cases as an infringement of state sovereignty. Writing in May 1860 in response to a note from the representatives of Portugal, France, Spain, Great Britain, and Brazil protesting the legal actions being brought by one Uruguayan, Francisco de la Serna, against their subjects on the left bank of the Solís Grande, Acevedo wrote that there was nothing he could do to interfere with the courts. He accused the legations of violating "the doctrine of international law that teaches that diplomatic intervention can only take place when ordinary means have been exhausted and justice has been denied by the incumbent administrative authority."[66]

It was hardly a coincidence that Acevedo was also the author of an early draft of the country's first civil code.[67] The code was first presented

---

[63] Acevedo, *Eduardo Acevedo*, p. 172.

[64] His administration pursued measures to contain the power of jefes políticos in the countryside, and, in 1861, forced the church to change its policy when it prohibited burial of a German mason in a public cemetery.

[65] Juan E. Pivel Devoto and Alcira Ranieri de Pivel Devoto, *Intentos de consolidación nacional, 1860–1875*, pp. 6–7. In another note to the Brazilians, Acevedo was quite clear about his opposition to any form of extraterritoriality. He argued that "when an individual sets foot in the territory of a foreign nation, he contracts the obligation of being subject to the laws and as a consequence to the established rules for the administration of justice." Those rules required following appellate procedures rather than recurring to the consulate after an undesirable result in a lower court. See Acevedo, *Eduardo Acevedo*, p. 315.

[66] Acevedo, *Eduardo Acevedo*, pp. 316–17.

[67] During six years of political exile in Buenos Aires, Acevedo also played a key role in writing the Argentine commercial code.

to the Parliament in May of 1853, but it was not adopted until January of 1868, in revised form (with Tristan Narvaja as the main author). Acevedo saw in the code an opportunity for a formal break with Spanish law and its layered and anachronistic sources. Codification gathered steam in the next decades; the late 1870s saw approval of the criminal code, a code of civil procedure, and the rural code. This last was a document written by and for wealthy ranchers. It detailed the terms of rural labor and proscribed severe penalties for vagrancy. Certainly adoption of the rural code was intended to mark the end of an era of fractured loyalties and controls in the countryside. It redefined the unattached and itinerant peones who subsisted on the margins of large estates as vagrants or, worse, as bandits.[68] While this shift to centralized control has tended to be the focus of narratives about legal reform in this period, it cannot be understood except in the broader context of reformers' concerns with the strengthening of state institutions as a way to offset foreign political interventions and their threat.[69]

Acevedo's views were echoed by other influential statesmen. Andrés Lamas, the law-trained diplomat who was instrumental in writing the controversial treaty with Brazil in 1851, combined a pragmatic view of the need to compromise with foreign powers with a marked defensiveness against any claims to special legal status for foreigners. A widely circulated manifesto published by Lamas in 1855 laid out an agenda for state reforms that would aid in controlling caudillismo, including the strengthening of judicial institutions. Later critiquing concessions made to the Brazilians in the 1851 treaty, he decried the "mutilation" of the country by the "occupation" of the territory north of the Río Negro by Brazilians. This occupation had led to the exclusion from the territory of "all the elements that constitute effective nationality," so that "we are left only with high jurisdiction . . . [that] encounters difficulties in even its most uncontestable applications."[70]

---

[68] On the repressive nature of the rural code in Uruguay and also in Argentina, see Bell, *Campanha Gaúcha*.

[69] The connection emerged clearly in a hemispheric conference hosted by Uruguay in 1888 and 1889 on international private law. Delegates from Uruguay, Argentina, Paraguay, Brazil, Chile, Peru, and Bolivia signed treaties establishing, among other provisions, "a foundation for international relations [through] . . . the application of the principle of territoriality and the exclusion of foreign laws applying to persons and goods." The treaties explicitly sought to end extraterritoriality in the region. Pivel Devoto and Ranieri de Pivel Devoto, *Uruguay a fines del siglo XIX*, pp. 33–34.

[70] Pivel Devoto and Ranieri de Pivel Devoto, *Intentos de consolidación nacional*, pp. 57–58. It is interesting to go back further and find Lamas, serving early in his career as a

While insisting that exclusive control of the administration of justice in the country was a condition of sovereignty, these and other Montevidean reformers were also painfully aware of the failings of the courts, particularly in rural areas under the control of caudillos. A series of reforms enacted in the 1850s sought to introduce a greater professionalism into the court system by curtailing the responsibilities of the alcaldes ordinarios. In 1861, the new procedures for rural magistrates and judges were published and circulated, with detailed instructions on record keeping and the taking of sworn testimony. Although judicial posts were made elective, the reform in practice had little effect in insulating the judiciary from local politics, as reformers had hoped.[71]

Information about the problems in the administration of justice came not just through the steady stream of complaints by foreign consulates but through the judiciary itself. The appellate system was notoriously spotty in its functioning. In the 1860s, a series of changes in reporting requirements by lower courts established for the first time an official source of information about the functioning of justice in the countryside. The new reporting structures were designed to introduce accountability in provincial legal institutions.[72]

The combination of legal and political disorder, challenges from foreign powers, and chronic instability in the definition and legal protection of property rights produced, finally, a resolute strengthening of central political power in the 1870s. Under the dictatorship of General Latorre,

magistrate dealing mainly with the settlement of intestate cases, reacting with special vehemence to the death of a Spanish captain and the potential for jurisdictional claims by the Spanish government. The issue merited a strident four-page letter by Lamas to the Superior Tribunal in 1846 arguing that the practice of ceding such cases to the authority or intervention of foreign consulates contradicted the authority of the state over all residents. Even in this borderline case, in which legal residence had not been established, it was important, Lamas argued, to defend the state's jurisdiction. Catálogo del Ex Archivo y Museo Histórico Nacional, Caja 120, Carpeta 2, AGN.

[71] In fact, the politicization of these elections was made painfully clear in 1875, when a protest focusing on the election of judges in the capital turned violent and sparked the collapse of the democratically elected government.

[72] They also revealed that rural magistrates with little or no legal training were presiding over a surge of litigation. The report from Salto, for example, from the beginning of 1862, listed approximately eighty-seven civil and criminal cases, and fifty-four cases still under review in the first half of February. "Tribunal de Apelaciones 2a Sección, Despacho Tomo 10, 1862," AGNJ. It is important to note that the activities of the appeals courts of this period, including the Tribunal Superior de Justicia, have been little studied, in part no doubt because documentation for the higher courts in this period has not been catalogued and is mostly inaccessible to researchers. It lies in the Archivo General de la Nación, Sección Judicial, but is under the control of officials of the Supreme Court, a situation giving rise to its own jurisdictional tensions.

between 1876 and 1880, a series of state centralization measures included comprehensive legal reforms: codification, professionalization of the judiciary, and the regularization of judicial procedure. The reforms took place both at the level of the state and as internal policy measures within the legal administration directed by the Tribunal Superior, which held both judicial and administrative authority in the absence of a Supreme Court. The legal changes went hand in hand with other centralizing Latorre policies, particularly the extension of free, secular public education throughout the country, and with the decade's most significant economic change, the mass introduction of barbed wire fencing in the countryside. The new ability to mark off grazing lands and enclose cattle and sheep depended on, and also reinforced, recourse to more secure legal titles and contracts. Further reforms followed during what is often regarded as the key period of liberal state building between 1880 and 1910.

The jurisdictional ambiguities of this period did not disappear abruptly. Border hopping as a form of forum shopping was still a familiar strategy to caudillos and their dependants along the Brazilian border, as Chasteen has shown in his portrait of the Saravia family in the last decades of the century.[73] Jurisdictional tensions continued to figure into the politics of rebellion. The important difference was that if the reality of state authority was still in question, the principle of territorial sovereignty was not. Rebels could be relabeled as bandits, and eluding the law could be redefined as lawlessness, rather than as the challenge of parallel or subordinate legal authorities.

It is important, though, to separate this late-century labeling of rural upheaval as lawlessness from earlier perceptions of the countryside as unruly because its control was fragmented. Without this distinction, we will confuse earlier struggles around the legitimacy of claims to territorial sovereignty with later conflicts over its implementation. In mid-century, legal actors interpreted property disputes and criminal prosecutions as defining events shaping their relation to the new nation. Frontier litigation involving foreigners and consular legal interventions were as much about citizenship and sovereignty as they were about property rights and protection. The oddity is that in seeking a special legal status, foreigners implicitly recognized the state's unique place in assigning political identity.

---

[73] John Charles Chasteen, *Heroes on Horseback: A Life and Times of the Last Gaucho Caudillos.*

INFORMAL EMPIRE AND EXTRATERRITORIALITY
IN A GLOBAL CONTEXT

Viewed broadly, the close timing in the move toward codification and the consolidation of state legal institutions across Latin America has tended to reinforce the idea that these changes resulted from a contagious borrowing of foreign institutions – followed by the corruption of their liberal-democratic intent. Foreign influences are decidedly different if we instead view the process of legal institutional formation as one that involved foreigners as interested parties and that simultaneously undercut and reinforced aspects of state sovereignty. The ambiguous imprint on state institutions of merchants is one piece of this puzzle, as they sought both to strengthen state guarantees on domestic transactions while maintaining their own controls over international trade.[74] The example of Uruguay points to another dimension of legal-institutional change and shows that, while maneuvering to retain exceptions to state control and proclaiming the need for order, foreigners were indirectly promoting discourse about sovereignty and the realignment of alternative law to a subordinate position vis-à-vis state law.

If relatively weak claims to extraterritoriality in Latin America had this complex impact on state making, we can expect to see similarly ambiguous effects in the Ottoman Empire and China in the same period. In both cases, extraterritoriality was central to a legal politics that was, in turn, the focus of both imperialist and domestic reform agendas. Extraterritoriality built upon earlier traditions of concessions made by imperial powers, and the legal status of foreigners took on new meaning as extraterritoriality became not a concession but an imposition. Both the case for extraterritoriality and its rejection involved arguments about the nature of sovereignty.

Let us consider first the Ottoman *Tanzimat* reforms between 1839 and 1876. These reforms featured the widespread adoption of Western codes, including French commercial and criminal codes. The move responded in part to Western calls for the more equitable judicial treatment of foreigners. More generally, shifting patterns of production and trade required adjudication of new types of property transactions and debt involving foreigners. One of the results was the institutionalization

---

[74] Adelman, for example, sees merchants at mid-century as making a discursive shift to a new kind of "property talk" well before state institutions were in place that could support a new regime of private property. See Adelman, *Republic of Capital*.

of mixed courts. This development, together with the creation of new forums, increasingly relegated shari'a law to the realm of family and religious matters. Yet, reformers usually attempted to place the changes within the framework of a broadly Islamic legal tradition recognizing the right of the ruler to supplement shari'a law with public and administrative law.[75]

The history of the Ottoman Capitulations created an institutional starting place for the politics of foreign legal influence. The early Ottoman concessions to foreign jurisdiction had been granted in the fifteenth and early sixteenth centuries from a position of relative strength and were understood as voluntary. Considerable strains arose in the nineteenth century as the new conditions of international power turned extraterritoriality into "a ruthlessly enforced and bitterly resented extraterritorial privilege" that was being imposed by the West.[76] The recognition of extraterritoriality as an attack on state sovereignty presupposed, however, the embrace of state sovereignty as a political goal above others. In this regard, the politics of legal reform in the nineteenth-century Ottoman sphere was complicated in many of the same ways observed in Latin America. Institutional reform involved not merely Westernization but also considerable conflict among elite factions; the recasting, sometimes by violent means, of the political status of non-Muslim Ottoman subjects; and the ambiguous pressures of foreign investors eager both to promote institutional stability through law and retain their own exceptional status within the legal order.

One of the most interesting elements of this complex political maneuvering involved the alliances between Western powers and non-Muslim Ottoman subjects. France claimed a special relationship with Roman Catholics within the empire, and Russia with the much more numerous Orthodox Christians. Britain experimented with sponsorship and protection of Ottoman Jews, even viewing favorably the settlement of Jews in Palestine.[77] The interventions encompassed support for political revolts (of the Serbs and Greeks, for example) and pressures on the courts in individual legal cases.[78] Such cases were added to a growing

---

[75] Coulson, *A History of Islamic Law*, p. 161.

[76] Lewis, *Islam and the West*, p. 48.

[77] Bernard Lewis, *The Jews of Islam*, pp. 159–61.

[78] The legal intervention was not always for the protection of non-Muslims. Lewis discusses the impact of European, in particular French, anti-Semitism on the rise of blood libel cases against Jews and outlines the celebrated case of blood libel charges against

pattern of Western protection for non-Muslims who were serving foreign powers directly. The legal interventions were viewed by Ottoman
officials as an attempt to abrogate religious minorities' *dhimma* status
and, thus, as a direct attack on Ottoman political power and legitimacy. The Morocco sultan, for example, felt compelled to lecture the
French consul in a letter of 1841: "If in your country [the Jews] are your
equals in all matters, if they are assimilated to you, this is all well and
good for your land, but not for Ours."[79] On the other side, European
powers explicitly linked advocacy of non-Muslims' legal rights to the
agenda of expanding the capitulatory regime to protect the activities
of foreign merchants by relating both causes to the liberal vision of
the state as a guarantor of individual rights. Thus the new Ottoman
sultan, Abdulmecid, was invited to London in 1840 "to absorb lessons
supposedly learned by countries that had passed from a situation of
arbitrary governmental authority to a commitment to ordered rule by
law."[80]

Foreign support for Tanzimat reforms had, in addition, significance
for political control across the empire, as Cannon notes in his study
of legal politics in nineteenth-century Egypt. Pressures by foreign merchants, and by elites linked to their interests, urged Egyptian legal innovations ahead of Ottoman reforms.[81] Later, widespread "capitulatory
malaise" (featuring the habitual extrajudicial interventions of consuls in
legal disputes) indirectly promoted the idea that institutional stability
depended on the loosening of imperial controls and the contrivance of
legal solutions peculiar to Egypt. The mixed court system that made
international legal influence "quasi-permanent" in the latter part of the
century retained ambiguous political symbolism. Embraced as a necessary element of modernization by one generation, it was the subject of increasing skepticism by both nationalists and traditionalists in
the next.

The question of extraterritoriality had a similarly central and ambiguous significance in China in the long nineteenth century. Most accounts

---

Jewish leaders in Damascus in 1840, who were accused of murdering a Capuchin
monk and his servant. The French consul directly encouraged the Jews' prosecution. A
delegation from Britain succeeded in having the surviving Jewish prisoners freed. See
Lewis, *The Jews of Islam*, pp. 156–58.

[79] Letter from the Moroccan Sultan, Mulay Abd al-Rahman, to the French consulate at
Tangiers, reproduced in Ye'or, *The Dhimmis*, p. 304.
[80] Byron Cannon, *Politics of Law and the Courts in Nineteenth-Century Egypt*, p. 18.
[81] Cannon, *Politics of Law and the Courts in Nineteenth-Century Egypt*.

of the tensions leading up to both the first and second Opium Wars emphasize Western reactions to several prominent criminal cases involving Westerners.[82] This standard narrative places special emphasis on an incident in 1784, when the gunner on the British ship *Lady Hughes* fired a salute from the boat while it was lying off Whampoa. One of three Chinese in a nearby boat died the next day, and a second died days later. The Chinese demanded the surrender of the gunner and imprisoned the ship's supercargo while also threatening to suspend trade. The gunner was turned over for trial and, after the *Lady Hughes* had left Chinese waters, he was executed by strangling. The case marked a turning point in British attitudes toward extraterritoriality in China. Thereafter Chinese jurisdiction was energetically opposed in cases involving British subjects, leading up to the formalization of extraterritoriality in the Treaty of Nanking. Later, disputes contributing to the outbreak of the Arrow War included the Chinese seizure of the Chinese crew of a ship sailing under a British flag and the judicially sanctioned murder of a French missionary. Both incidents were regarded by Westerners as evidence of the need for strengthened and expanded foreign legal rights by treaty.

This narrative is not wholly misleading and at least points to legal issues as inextricably tied to mounting tensions over the control of trade. But these particular conflicts were part of a broader pattern of conflict over extraterritoriality that showed more continuity than discontinuity over the span of several centuries of Western-Chinese interactions. The difference in the mid-nineteenth century was mainly that the arrangement of extraterritoriality by treaty plainly involved national entities rather than merchant communities, though the Chinese continued to portray Western maritime trade as falling under Chinese suzerainty. In the early decades of the twentieth century, continuing conflict over extraterritoriality was also central to the formation of Chinese nationalism and demands for full state sovereignty.

In the early centuries of contact, Chinese authorities were at great pains to characterize British and other seagoing merchants as mere marauders rather than representatives of potentially powerful polities. It helped that it was possible to accommodate most early claims for European and American jurisdiction over their subjects within familiar Chinese patterns of granting limited extraterritoriality. In most cases involving foreigners only, European authorities retained jurisdiction, while Chinese authorities energetically claimed jurisdiction over cases

---

[82] For example, see Peter Ward Fay, *The Opium War, 1840–1842*, p. 37.

of homicide involving Chinese victims.[83] The Chinese resisted making treaties, but this was not because of a systemic or cultural disapproval; China and Russia had agreed as early as 1689 to formal recognition of bilateral extraterritoriality.[84] The difference was that Russia was a land empire – expected still to recognize Chinese superiority but nevertheless recognized as an imperial polity on its own, whereas the Chinese did not consider maritime powers to hold the status of "empires" until at least the end of the first Opium War.

Nevertheless, negotiating extraterritorial arrangements even on an ad hoc basis rested on certain shared understandings across the various legal orders. Most important was the widespread acceptance of capital punishment.[85] Increasingly, though – and this was brought out most clearly in the *Lady Hughes* case and accounts in part for its notoriety – Europeans and the Americans complained that Chinese law did not recognize intent as a differentiating feature of crime or an influence on punishment. In addition to exacting punishment for accidental murder, Chinese magistrates also assigned responsibility collectively and were willing to impose punishments on surrogates if they could not try actual suspects. Torture was also recognized (and feared) as a common element of Chinese justice. Foreigners perceived Chinese justice as consisting almost exclusively of criminal law.[86] In practice, the British learned that they could sometimes pay to escape Chinese

---

[83] The resolution of individual cases responded, though, to particular strategies adopted by both sides. In a case involving the Portuguese at Macao in 1826, for example, the Portuguese tried and sentenced to death a Timor slave for murdering a Chinese. The Chinese residents at Macao rioted in response to this usurpation of local jurisdiction, but higher authorities refrained from backing them up. The Portuguese had asserted jurisdiction in other cases less successfully. In 1773 they tried Francis Scott, an Englishman, and acquitted him for killing a Chinese man at Macao. He was later tried, found guilty, and executed by Chinese authorities. George Williams Keeton, *The Development of Extraterritoriality in China*, Vol. I, p. 37.

[84] As Keeton points out, practices and pressures lacked uniformity before the nineteenth century. "With Russia bilateral extraterritoriality existed. The Europeans at Canton enjoyed a limited unilateral extraterritoriality, whilst from Burma the Chinese claimed either the surrender of Burmese for the murder of Chinese subjects in Burma, or, more frequently, the application of Chinese law, by the Burmese courts, to such cases – another form of extraterritoriality" (Keeton, *Development of Extraterritoriality in China*, p. 74).

[85] Thus in the Macao case described in note 83 above, the Portuguese could rightly point out that the result of their seizing jurisdiction gave the same outcome as would have occurred under Chinese law.

[86] There is still scholarly debate about this point, and about the nature of Chinese law in general. Philip Huang argues persuasively that Chinese litigants used civil courts for a wide range of disputes and that civil law had a significant presence in Chinese life (Philip Huang, *Civil Justice in China: Representation and Practice in the Qing*). In

jurisdiction.[87] But the combination of uncertainty, danger of prosecution, and perceived injustices led to the increasingly frequent portrayal of Chinese justice as "arbitrarily and corruptly administered ... [and] in many respects incompatible with European ideas of equity or Justice."[88] From the perspective of Western merchants, the demand for formal extraterritoriality grew organically out of a belief that the Chinese system, and the Chinese understanding of justice, were deeply different and flawed.

From the perspective of the Chinese authorities, in contrast, extraterritoriality had its origins (as it did for the Ottomans) in concessions made to subordinate, "guest" communities. From the earliest recorded cases involving Western merchants, Chinese authorities tied jurisdictional demands to control of trade. Failure to produce suspects or to cooperate with Chinese authorities brought threats of suspension of trade. Not surprisingly, then, Chinese concerns about jurisdictional prerogatives intensified when two trends coincided. The first was the escalation of the opium trade. Efforts to tighten controls on foreigners and rein in provincial authorities and Chinese merchants profiting from the trade clearly linked domestic illegality with foreign prerogatives. The second trend was the perceived imperfect authority of foreign trade organizations or governments over increasingly numerous foreign merchants. As Keeton puts it succinctly, the Chinese "could scarcely be expected to

a monograph about the Shanghai Mixed Court, in contrast, Thomas Stephens asserts that Chinese justice should not be characterized as "law" but as a disciplinary order (Thomas B. Stephens, *Order and Discipline in China: The Shanghai Mixed Court 1911–1927*). Huang concedes that Chinese law was a system of domination but demonstrates that "the Qing legal system routinely protected the legitimate claims of common litigants to property, contracts, inheritance, and old-age support (Huang, *Civil Justice in China*, p. 235).

[87] In 1807, several sailors from the *Neptune* were involved in a brawl in which one Chinese was killed. The affair, by agreement, was investigated by a mixed forum involving both Chinese magistrates and Company officials. The English recounted that there was little evidence to identify the culprit but that some action had to be taken, and they agreed to a fine, approved with the intercession (and probably the financial help) of a Chinese merchant. George Staunton, a Company official, complained that the case showed both sides in the worst possible light: "In this case, all the proceedings were founded on a story fabricated for the purpose; a story in which the Europeans did not concur, though asserted to have done so; which, in fact, the Chinese magistrates themselves, or the merchants under their influence, invented, which the witnesses, knowing to be false, adopted; and which, lastly, the sovereign himself appears to have acquiesced in without examination" (quoted in Keeton, *Development of Extraterritoriality in China*, p. 52).

[88] Morse, *China Diary*, ii, p. 69; quoted in Keeton, *Development of Extraterritoriality in China*, p. 50.

approve of a situation in which a mass of foreigners, British, American, and European, refused to submit to Chinese jurisdiction in homicide cases, and at the same time were not amenable to the command of the heads of their respective companies or of the appropriate consular officer."[89]

The opposed views and interests led to the formal imposition of extraterritoriality after the first Opium War. First the British, in the Treaty of the Bogue in 1843, followed in quick succession by the Americans and the French in 1844, and later by other powers, established jurisdiction over nationals residing in treaty ports.[90] But rather than resolving earlier tensions, the treaty rights became the subject of continuing disputes, with Chinese officials (often led by local officials with stronger antiforeign sentiments than those at court) pushing to limit foreign jurisdiction on one side, and consular officials, responding to a series of cases involving foreigners that were not clearly covered in the treaties, pushing to extend extraterritoriality on the other. Such tensions, as I have already noted, contributed to the outbreak of a second war in 1856. They produced a further clarification of extraterritoriality in 1876, under the Chefoo Convention. But no period of settled plural administration of justice followed. Each of the powers set up multiple consular courts and an appellate system and in Shanghai administered a Mixed Court to apply Chinese law to Chinese subjects living in foreign-controlled areas.[91] The resulting multiplicity of forums and jurisdictions, as Fishel notes, was never "accepted graciously by the Chinese" and "never functioned to the entire satisfaction of foreigners."[92]

Two aspects of the politics of extraterritoriality are especially relevant to the concerns of this chapter. First, extraterritoriality was tied to, and helped to inform, Western perceptions of China; second, it became central to Chinese discourse about law and sovereignty in the first decades

---

[89] Keeton, *Development of Extraterritoriality in China*, p. 70.

[90] The Americans secured the Treaty of Wanghia in 1844, in which they not only established jurisdiction over Americans involved in criminal proceedings but also a "most favored nation" clause guaranteeing them privileges that might later be awarded to other nationalities. The French negotiated the Treaty of Whampoa later in 1844.

[91] Fishel, *End of Extraterritoriality in China*, p. 27. The Mixed Court of the International Settlement operated from 1869 until 1911 under rules devised by the British and Americans and agreed to by the Chinese, and it continued under the aegis of the foreign powers from 1911 to 1927. Though the original rules established narrow guidelines for actual foreign intervention in the court, these were increasingly infringed upon. See Fishel, *End of Extraterritoriality in China*, pp. 23–25, and Stephens, *Order and Discipline in China*.

[92] Fishel, *End of Extraterritoriality in China*, p. 27.

of the twentieth century. In both regards, extraterritoriality came to mean more than a jurisdictional arrangement; it came to stand for a panoply of practices establishing and protecting foreigners' prerogatives in China.

The establishment of extraterritoriality for Europeans and Americans involved (and in a sense required) harsh public judgments about the deficiencies of Chinese justice. As Chinese opposition to extraterritoriality, together with the difficulties emerging out of repeated examples of cases that did not fit easily within the rules of jurisdictional boundaries, continued after the treaties, foreigners increasingly adopted the view that the deficiencies of Chinese law might one day be rectified. The Mackay Treaty of 1902 thus included an article stating that Britain would "be prepared to relinquish her extraterritorial rights when she is satisfied that the state of the Chinese laws, the arrangement for their administration, and other conditions warrant her in so doing."[93] Such rhetoric, repeated by observers and consular officials, signaled the impermanence of extraterritorial arrangements, despite accompanying warnings that Chinese justice was still very far from acceptable standards.

The Chinese undertook a program of legal reform over the next several decades. They pressed for an end to extraterritoriality at the Versailles Conference and opportunistically shut down extraterritoriality for Germans and Austrians after World War I and for Russians following the Revolution of 1917. Growing antiforeign sentiment culminated in 1925 with widespread antiforeign demonstrations and riots, and outrage triggered by the foreign violence in response. Though another two decades would pass before complete abolition of the "unequal treaties" would take place, the strong links between abolition of extraterritoriality and Chinese nationalism made it impossible for challenges to the treaties – and to extraterritoriality as a particularly visible symbol of the abrogation of Chinese sovereignty – to disappear.

The formal nature of extraterritoriality and its longer history (and later demise) in the Ottoman Empire and China may suggest that it was an altogether different phenomenon from the informal influences in Latin America and the collective legal strategies of foreigners there. But placing these phenomena together is both analytically useful and empirically defensible on several grounds. In all these cases, the legal status of foreigners became central to political discourse in the nineteenth century and posed similar opportunities and problems of state making. As in the plural colonial legal orders discussed in Chapter 4, the

---

[93] Quoted in Fishel, *End of Extraterritoriality in China*, p. 27.

rules guiding the functioning of extraterritoriality could not contain the production of legal cases and strategies challenging those rules. Ongoing tensions and patterns of litigation continued to thrust the (re)definition of foreigners' legal status into prominent view. At the same time, arguments used to support extraterritoriality in all its forms involved rhetoric about the shortcomings of local states and urged both legal reform and claims about territorial sovereignty in response. We need not deny that extraterritoriality was imposed by force in order to see that it was also used strategically by local elite factions in representing and shaping state institutions. At times, the history of extraterritoriality as a concession made by strong host communities to subordinate part-polities provided a way to turn apparent weakness into a symbol of political authority. Treaty making itself (and even consular diplomacy) implied, after all, the existence of an interstate order that all sides were coming to recognize as an important objective of legal reformulations.

Seen in this light, the politics of extraterritoriality forms part of a wide array of prominent debates shaping the nineteenth-century legal order. Past chapters have explored two sets of contests: struggles over the definition of the legal status of culturally different part-subjects and conflicts over the relation of imposed and indigenous forums and legal personnel. The construction of sovereignty formed part of this wide and varied political field. To isolate the study of extraterritoriality from these parallel processes would prevent us from understanding its formative influence on state making and lead us instead to relegate its analysis to the more narrowly defined field of diplomatic relations. But as the case studies of this chapter show, external images of the state and its internal representations were inextricably tied. Foreigners by definition crossed borders, defining those boundaries in the process. Territorial and hegemonic state legal authority in this sense was made out of the politics of defining exceptions to sovereignty.

SEVEN

Culture and the Rule(s) of Law

This book has argued that the colonial state was in no small part the product of the politics of legal ordering. Early, multicentric legal orders promoted a pattern of jurisdictional complexity whose continuity across regions itself formed an element of international order. Colonial rule magnified jurisdictional tensions and gave greater urgency and symbolic importance to the task of defining the interactions of various legal forums, sources, and personnel. As we saw in the cases of Spanish America, the Ottoman Empire, and British India, territorial colonial expansion prompted a turn to legal pluralism as a colonial project – the formal mapping of interrelations of imposed and indigenous law. This project, aimed at the creation of order, introduced new rules as objects of conflict.

The new hybrid orders struggled especially with the challenge posed by cultural others and intermediaries whose legal roles were difficult to fix and who themselves exploited and attacked ambiguities in the law. The political and symbolic importance of defining the legal status of indigenous subjects stretched across the colonial world. In the cases we examined in the Cape Colony and New South Wales, the legal status of seemingly marginal actors in the legal order became symbolically central to multisided struggles over the structure and scope of new colonial bureaucracies. Throughout the colonial and postcolonial world, as the case study of jurisdictional politics in Uruguay illustrates, the ambiguous status of foreigners in local courts unified external and internal political and legal maneuvering, simultaneously urging a more explicit state claim to territorial sovereignty.

These historical findings depend upon and support a particular approach to the politics of legal pluralism. The architecture of the plural legal order had simultaneously a discursive importance – it was, we have shown, the object of continual struggle over definitions and markers of cultural difference – and a structural dimension that acted to shape and constrain political and economic interactions. Further, this double-sided quality of conflicts over the relation of multiple legal authorities reproduced knowledge about power that carried across both internal and external borders. The knowledge that permitted the mutual recognition of one polity by another in part derived from, and in turn reinforced, the political engagement of legal authorities, forums, and sources of law *within* emerging polities. This echoing effect both linked internal and external politics and fused international ordering to cultural conflicts. Such connections show that the classic image of stacked levels of law within the plural legal order was itself a cultural representation and a product of conflict.

Both these findings and the conceptual framework they support comment on prominent debates about the rule of law and the divergent character of the colonial state. Interventions in these debates tend to circle and return to E.P. Thompson's deservedly famous epilogue to *Whigs and Hunters*. In this essay, Thompson seeks to explain the rise of the rule of law in England. He ruminates on the paradox of plebeian loyalty to a legal order that was most of the time blatantly tipped in favor of the interests of the ruling class and all too willing to bring immoderate force to bear in controlling commoners. Much of the body of the book tells a familiar Thompson narrative; it is a story of the "grid" of capitalist relations and state's law descending with a crash upon the "grid" of customary law. Here, as in his other works, Thompson wants to convince us of the logic of plebeian responses to capitalist incursions, even those rituals that seem either unplanned and chaotic – the ubiquitous food riots – or acts that appear peculiar, like blackening faces and ceremoniously poaching game in royal forests.

Then Thompson's account takes a turn that has infuriated some of his most enthusiastic followers. He writes that the rise of the rule of law was a "universal good," a historic move that must be recognized as generally positive in its outcome, even if in so many individual cases the courts' work was repression. The fury that has greeted this single remark is not surprising, but its intensity perhaps is. Writing about the formation of the colonial state, Guha goes out of his way to criticize E.P. Thompson for his complicity in an ultra-Orientalist vision of "other" histories as pale approximations of a Western model. Conceding that there was a definable moment of establishment of state hegemony in the West and that the rule of law was central to this shift, Guha derides the notion that the rule of law ever came to exist in colonial settings. Here, instead, the state developed "dominance without hegemony," a form of power that relied much more heavily on coercion than persuasion.

More broadly still, in a critique of not just Thompson but of social history in general, Guha attacks revisionist attempts to respond to the earlier tendency of colonial history to chronicle empire's "administrative career." This revisionist strategy portrayed colonial institutions as emerging out of the interaction of "imperial stimulus and native response."[1] Guha firmly rejects even the possibility of choice for subjugated peoples and denies their influence on shaping the colonial state in India: "The colonial state in India did not originate from the activity of Indian society itself. No moment of that society's internal dynamics was involved in the imposition of the alien authority structure which provided the process of state formation both with its primary impulse and the means of its actualization."[2]

Since I have argued throughout this book that the colonial state emerged in part out of a legal politics engaging both colonizers and the colonized, I must defend what Guha rejects as a revisionist half measure, the replacement of an elite colonial history with an interactional one. I can do so best, I think, by returning to E.P. Thompson's discussion of the rule of law. Of particular interest are parts of the epilogue to *Whigs and Hunters* that Guha tosses out together with, or because of, Thompson's provocative remarks about the universal value of the rule of law.[3] In particular, the approach that Thompson uses to explain plebeians' willingness to appeal to the courts at all, given their notorious reputation for bias and excessive force, is directly relevant to an understanding of the production of state legal hegemony in colonial settings.

---

[1] Ranajit Guha, *Dominance Without Hegemony: History and Power in Colonial India*, p. 85. And for his critique of E.P. Thompson, see pp. 66–67.

[2] Guha, *Dominance Without Hegemony*, p. 64.

[3] I do not plan to enter this part of the debate, but it is worth noting that Thompson qualifies this statement more than Guha allows us to see. He chides Thompson for calling the rule of law "a cultural achievement of universal significance" (Guha, *Dominance Without Hegemony*, p. 67). But Thompson goes on in the very next sentences to state, "I do not lay any claim as to the abstract, extra-historical impartiality of these rules," and he suggests that in conditions of even greater inequality, the law was more nearly (though never, still, completely) an instrument of repression. Thompson, *Whigs and Hunters*, p. 266.

Thompson's argument about the rule of law in eighteenth-century England turns on his assertion that the law's legitimacy depended on the ways in which it distinguished itself from arbitrary force. The *appearance* of impartiality was essential, and creating that appearance meant crafting a kind of formalism that in turn generated occasional just outcomes, results that either frustrated ruling class objectives or protected commoners' interests in particular cases. These exceptions made the law "a great deal more than sham."[4] Most criminal defendants and litigants with meager resources understood perfectly that the system was effectively stacked against them. But the possibility of justice, however remote, had great force. Even powerful Whigs, in rare instances, suffered defeats in the courts or had to alter their behavior in anticipation that they might do so. Thompson's problem as a historian is to try to explain why the leap from this glimmer of hope to a generalized acceptance of the rule of law was the product neither of false consciousness nor of simple miscalculation.

Thompson has some difficulty in explaining this central paradox. Part of his answer is to rely on an explication of the qualities of custom. Translated into the terms employed in this book, Thompson's vision is one of a weak legal pluralism. The plebeian world had its own, separate "law" situated in custom and enforced by social pressures and the actions of the crowd. Thus the foresters Thompson describes in *Whigs and Hunters* reacted to the incursions of improving gentry on the commons with a form of poaching that was at times purely punitive: They killed protected deer and, instead of carrying off the venison, left the bodies in prominent view on the estates. Ironically, it is this strong, but separate, vision of justice that Thompson suggests explains the significance given to the perception of the law's ability to produce occasional justice. In the terms we have been using in this book, the plural legal order contained within it the power of mutual recognition. State power, and state law, may have been new historical forces, but as forms of power and sanctioned violence, they were neither new nor foreign to legal actors situated in different spheres of the legal order.

Thompson's failure to go no further in his critique of "structural reductionism," the idea that law can be reduced merely to an instrument of oppression, is to my mind much larger as a shortcoming than his quip about the universal goodness of the rule of law. Thompson expends so much effort, in this work and in many others, establishing the existence

---

[4] Thompson, *Whigs and Hunters*, p. 265.

of a separate moral economy for the plebeian class, that he is left over-simplifying the process by which the two "grids" become one. In this sense, it is ironic that Guha, a founding voice of subaltern studies and someone who has insisted on the autonomy of colonial subjects, repudiates Thompson, whose narrative is organized so clearly around an implicit schema of a *separate* customary realm. Guha holds fast to the autonomy of the subaltern; for him, the intricacies of colonial administration and indigenous bourgeois conciliation are reduced to historical epiphenomena, a pair of "failed" agendas, precisely because the subaltern stands outside this relation, a not-very-attentive bystander to all the fuss. Thompson does not go this far, surely; his foresters poach, after all, in reaction to Whig policies. But one gets little sense that the two realms, the two grids, are truly interpenetrating. The foresters are as monolithic in this sense as their counterparts, each side's interests homogeneous, rarely overlapping, even at the margins. The parallels result instead from the reproduction of the logic of the law across essentially separate levels. The gentry built on legal traditions emerging out of the struggle against royal absolutism, and petty property holders found that the ideology of law as a defense for property could extend to their own customary use-rights.

Unlike Guha, though, I am reluctant to abandon Thompson's reflections on the law as a helpful guide to colonial legal politics, even if substituting a more sympathetic critique. Since *Whigs and Hunters* was published, several turns in social theory have appeared to urge Thompson's insights further. Given his insistence, with some qualifications, on the structural relation of spheres of law, the most helpful contribution in this regard is Bourdieu's critique of structuralism.[5] The influence of Foucault in the study of the modalities of colonial control is another important aid, though we must prevent "discourse" from merely floating above unexamined structures of power.[6]

Bourdieu would tell us that the conceptual leap from recognizing the mere possibility of justice in state's law to the consent implied in becoming legal actors in state's courts is not a leap at all. It is commonplace, he argues, for social actors to participate in routines about which they simultaneously hold contrasting understandings. These interpretive differences do not easily fall into categories that are objective (for example, the understanding that legal outcomes mainly favor elites)

---

[5] Philippe Bourdieu, *Outline of a Theory of Practice.*
[6] See Cohn, *Colonialism and Its Forms of Knowledge,* on colonial modalities.

or subjective (the hope that they might yield benefit in individual cases) but involve a third kind of understanding produced out of practice: a "studied ignorance" of the objective qualities of these relations. As in relationships of gift exchange, where the possibility of every sort of outcome, from minor gaffes to the rupture of relations, shapes the pace and content of normative exchanges with only small observable irregularities, legal actors interpret the repressive qualities of legal institutions against the background of both the possibilities of occasional just outcomes and the existence of other arenas and sources of law. In the colonial world, indigenous legal actors are not necessarily collaborators if they take actions that affirm the legitimacy of colonial courts. The knowledge of the harm inflicted by legal institutions coexists with the knowledge that they are a part of a larger spectrum of behaviors and beliefs that constitute law. It is possible simultaneously to use imposed law (thereby reaffirming it) and to seek to undermine its authority.

Up to this point, we have gotten, through Bourdieu, only a little farther than with E.P. Thompson toward an understanding of the production of legal legitimacy through legal conflict. But the difference is not trivial. Following the poststructuralist formulation, representations of alternative law and discourse about the qualities of colonial state law are never produced independently from one another, thence to come into contact and conflict like Thompson's two grids. The very definitions of separate legal authorities are produced through an interactive cultural praxis. This is not an attempt to rescue a mechanistic model of colonial imposition and indigenous response, as Guha's critique would have it. The autonomy that he ascribes to a realm of culture standing outside the colonial relation is illusory in the sense that it is, itself, a discursive product of colonial politics. Indigenous litigants at times assert and define their legal standing in the course of maneuvering through colonial legal institutions in ways that reinforce their authority. And the autonomy of indigenous legal authorities is a claim sometimes extended by colonial authorities themselves.

Returning to Guha's assertion that the colonial state is characterized by "dominance without hegemony," it is easy enough to see where this approach goes wrong (and, also, in what ways it is partially right). Guha recognizes only one discursive shift in colonialism: the moment of conquest. Once conquest has occurred (or any disguised version of conquest, as with English claims to be engaged in mere settlement in New South Wales), a relation of dominance and subordination is established. It remains to be seen, according to Guha, merely which combination of persuasion and coercion (inevitably, colonial states will be heavy on coercion) and collaboration and resistance (much of both) particular colonial histories then produce. Guha entirely misses, however, a second discursive shift, the one this book is concerned with. Colonial states did not in an important sense exist *as* states in the early centuries of colonialism. They did not claim or produce a monopoly on legal authority or on the assignment of political and legal identity. Indeed, colonial conditions often intensified the fluidity of the legal order and enhanced the strategic importance of personal law by multiplying claims made by, and on behalf of, cultural and religious communities to their own legal authorities. There was dominance, undeniably, but both colonizing factions and colonized groups were not irrational or deluded when they sought advantage in the fractured qualities of rule.

In the later discursive shift that Guha misses, his ideas about the colonial state become more relevant, but not in the way that he predicts. This shift, as the chapters on mid-nineteenth-century legal politics show, involved the halting emergence of representations of the state as legally dominant. Recognizing the existence of this shift is not the same, however, as arguing that colonial politics produced "the rule of law" or that the institutional change was the product of its universal appeal. Rather, the very politics that emerged out of the fractured international legal regime of the earlier period had the tendency to generate a juridical space for the state that was historically novel. Debates about the ordering of plural legal orders reinforced the notion of state oversight of this ordering, a role that itself signaled state legal hegemony. The close association of cultural and legal boundaries meant, too, that representations of group characteristics had implications (some intended, some not) for legal ordering, and vice versa. To take an example not from this study, Lorcin shows that the French representation of Kabyles as culturally superior to Arabs in colonial Algeria emerged partly out of perceived differences in legal practices and, in turn, generated significantly different legal policies toward these groups. The French preoccupation with such distinctions then itself became a defining rationale for French colonial rule; here as elsewhere, a substantive shift in the middle to late nineteenth century collapsed these distinctions as the colonial state became a state.[7]

Guha is no doubt right to emphasize that nineteenth-century state making was not the product of consensus (in fairness, he should note

[7] Patricia Lorcin, *Imperial Identities: Stereotyping, Prejudice, and Race in Colonial Algeria.*

that neither Thompson nor Hay, in uncovering the function of theater in establishing legitimacy for the courts, confuses this potent technique with "persuasion").[8] But the forms of dominance taken, and the timing of this second institutional shift, were fashioned out of an interactive politics and not simply the logical extension of conquest. In many places, the decisive shift toward a state monopoly of law provided an interesting twist to E.P. Thompson's formulation. In establishing supremacy over a plural legal order, the *improbability* of justice could actually serve as a support for legitimacy for emerging states. The state-centered quality of the legal order was itself new, and the state asserted its centrality by demonstrating its authority to administer law with any degree of consistency or standards of justice. Thus in Uruguay the state could assert power by institutionalizing the ruthlessness of caudillos, or by imitating the indifference of larger, more powerful states. Legitimacy through impartiality was less important than the mere assertion of dominance over "other" types of law in the plural legal hierarchy. Yet there was more to this shift than the mere assertion of power. The distinctiveness of state's law resided partially in its control of violence but also in its special relationship to rule setting. Procedure trumped justice; institutions outlived bandits.

In a narrow sense, the colonial state was not, in fact, built on hegemony, if the term is narrowly defined to imply either persuasion or consent. But if we define hegemony instead, with the Comaroffs, as "constructs and conventions that have come to be shared and naturalized throughout a political community," then the shift we have identified in legal politics as occurring over the span of the long nineteenth century is indeed one that establishes the hegemony of state law.[9] Just as, across the early modern world, coterminous and fluid legal jurisdictions were naturalized features of the political landscape, by the end of the nineteenth century the subordinate status of nonstate law to state law no longer required a formal ideological defense. It became possible to fight over the control of the state rather than over its location. The process that moved polities from one legal regime to another involved not persuasion and consent (or even starkly divided collaboration and resistance)

---

[8] Douglas Hay Peter Linebaugh, John E. Rule, E.P. Thompson, and Cal Winslow, eds., *Albion's Fatal Tree: Crime and Society in Eighteenth-Century England.*

[9] For this quote and for what is in general a more nuanced discussion of hegemony in colonial settings than the one provided by Guha, see Comaroff and Comaroff, *Of Revelation and Revolution*, p. 24.

but a series of contests over the structure of the legal order that shaped a juridical space for the state and brought participants into a single discourse about the law.

There is something so striking about the synchronicity of this shift that one is tempted to look further for pressures shared across these cases. One obvious contender – the shared influence of European legal sources and ideas – cannot completely account for the patterns we observe. Certainly legal policies crossed geographically disparate parts of empire, and legal ideas traveled with law-trained administrators and even, as in New South Wales, with felons. But in general, colonial governors, settlers, and even political leaders in the metropole treated European legal traditions as a useful collection from which they might draw selectively in crafting colonial legal systems.

More compelling than the influence of shared sources of law is the unifying function of structural frameworks for defining "other" legal authorities. In this sense, the familiar fluidity of legal orders in the early modern world provided institutional continuity that itself gave legal politics a certain similarity across widely disparate legal systems. The territories for which this condition of jurisdictional fluidity was true are so vast and diverse that they can be described as encompassing a *global legal regime*.[10] The structural similarities – in particular, the treatment of minority legal communities that is illustrated by the comparative analysis of the law of the "other" in Iberian and Islamic empires – provided a baseline for legal politics. They formed, too, a basis for analogy building among litigants who were therefore able to adjust quickly to the particular demands of legal strategy under colonial rule.

Another unifying force was the pressure to frame new types of property holding and transactions. As the cases we have examined suggest, jurisdictional disputes accumulated and intensified at critical conjunctures, often marking a shift to new property regimes: the imposition of a market in land in India; the demarcation of landholdings and the recruitment of labor in pastoral economies from South Africa, Australia, and South America; and the eclipse of ethnic trade diasporas by merchants and their agents in global trade generally. These shifts in productive

---

[10] I have not concentrated in this study on determining the extent or borders of this legal regime. Surely, though, if Wallerstein can dub interlinking areas of production and trade spanning the Americas and Europe but excluding Africa and Asia as a "world system," I am justified in calling the vast area of institutional continuity from the Americas to Africa, Europe, and the Indian Ocean (and perhaps beyond) a "global legal regime."

relations had a necessary legal dimension. As E.P. Thompson notes, they were in part "only meaningful in terms of their definitions at law."[11] Yet, the cases I have examined caution against turning this observation into a simple formulation about the unifying forces of global capitalism. Such forces – and they did exist – became immediately translated into local idioms of order, exchange, and legal sanction. Institutional developments did not simply "respond" to economic pressure; the two processes were blended into one matrix and subject to a host of conflicts that might objectively be seen as marginal to either kind of change. When fights about definitions of property seemed to blend into struggles over cultural boundaries, it was not because the participants could not "see" the underlying material interests, or were attempting purposefully to disguise them. Legal norms encoded both culture and property, and neither could change without the other.

This brings us again to culture. In this account of colonial legal politics, culture becomes a globalizing force itself, though in a way that is rarely recognized in discussions of the coming "global culture." I do not mean that culture was in this process a homogenizing force. Rather, routines for organizing cultural difference took institutional forms, and these structures, in replication, became themselves an element of international continuity. Such a view moves beyond tentative efforts to seek the origins of international law in custom.[12] It was not the *content* of custom that stretched across boundaries (though sometimes this was also the case) but rather the legal and political *space* for custom that reproduced itself and, in the process, created new possibilities for colonial governance and cross-regional capitalist economies. The globalizing *imaginaire*, in other words, was quintessentially cultural in its emphasis on difference, but profoundly legal and political, and had an enduring, if changeable, institutional dimension.[13]

---

[11] Thompson, *Whigs and Hunters*, p. 267.

[12] In this regard, my argument does not belong to the project of international legal theorists analyzing the customary sources of international law. See Beyers, *Custom, Power, and the Power of Rules*; and D'Amato, *The Concept of Culture in International Law*.

[13] In all the settings I have written about in this book, contemporary legal actors would not have used the term "culture" to categorize themselves or others. Whether describing themselves or others according to religious affiliation, by degree of civilization or barbarism, or in reference to other social categories, their discourse was, however, uniformly about difference. My view of culture thus meshes with that of Appadurai, who defines culture as "a pervasive dimension of human discourse that exploits difference to generate diverse conceptions of group identity" (Arjun Appadurai, *Modernity at*

It is as if the internal relation between cultural practice and institutions that we glimpse, following Bourdieu, were mirrored at the global level. Internally, the cultural conflicts surrounding the definition of legal boundaries create through their own repetition an institutional landscape, an increasingly routine and naturalized ordering of legal authorities. Similarly, a global institutional structure takes shape out of the replication of the politics of legal and cultural reordering. In this sense, culture does not cohere at the local level and structure reveal itself as a map of international connections. Legal and cultural contests simultaneously produce institutional patterns and expectations about cultural and legal ordering elsewhere. To borrow and revise a phrase from Geertz, the global institutional order has its origins in the stories that people tell themselves about others.

In the earlier period, this was a story about law's belonging to bounded communities. Later, conflicts over the shape of the legal order urged a function and a place for state law that had not existed before. Jurisdictional disputes, struggles over the legal status of cultural and legal intermediaries, and conflicts over the definition and control of property connected to this historical turn.[14] As the case studies have shown, there is no single protagonist of this narrative – and certainly not a Western model of governance or its proponents. The instability of colonial legal politics, the appeals of litigants to a still-forming state legal authority, the cultural uncertainties of boundary crossing, the independent interests of colonial settlers and outside investors – these processes combined to shape a place for the colonial state as a state, in many cases decades before imperial powers were ready either to concede or consciously to propel such a shift, and before colonial elites were motivated or prepared to advocate it.[15]

Large: Cultural Dimensions of Globalization, p. 13). Yet my approach differs in two ways, first by identifying "cultural dimensions of globalization" further back in time and second by emphasizing the homology between cultural and institutional dimensions of globalization.

[14] Christopher Bayly traces other multicentric global processes through a similar chronology, in which "archaic globalisation" of the seventeenth and early eighteenth centuries created spaces for a hybrid globalism of the period from 1760 to 1830 and then continued to shape the emerging international order of the nineteenth century. Bayly, "From Archaic Globalisation to International Networks, c. 1600–2000."

[15] Benedict Anderson concedes that he initially misrepresented colonial nationalism as having been modeled on European nationalism and argues that its origins instead must lie in "the imaginings of the colonial state" (Anderson, *Imagined Communities,*

The picture of the politics of legal pluralism that emerges from this view differs in important respects from Thompson's image of the descent of the grid of capitalist relations and its legal matrix on the grid of custom, with indigenous legal culture standing in for the plebeian moral economy of eighteenth-century England. In colonial settings and also within Europe, familiarity with a complex legal order involving multiple legal authorities and the borrowing of procedures, legal rules, sources, and rhetoric conditioned (and helped to propel) the shift toward state and capitalist hegemony. This constant referencing of other legal authorities and forums intensified in colonial settings, and this intensification itself helped to produce a shift toward a hierarchical understanding of the plural legal order and a recognition of the dominance of state law. The imagery of separate legal levels was itself partly a product of this shift, rather than an accurate representation of the architecture of the legal order. This picture could not have been drawn by colonizers alone, an observation that pretends no apology for the brutality of colonial rule but places indigenous institutions and cultural practice on an equal footing with the institutions and discourse of colonizers by recognizing their internal logic, inventiveness, and ability to change. In this sense, we should label legal transformations in the long nineteenth century not as the rise of the rule of law but as an iterative cultural politics centering on rules about law.

I began this book by commenting on the possibility of drawing connections to the legal politics of the colonial past and the political conflicts of the postcolonial world. Many of the legal issues discussed in these pages are still with us: debates about the legal status of Aborigines, indigenous Canadians, American Indians, Mexican Indians, South African Zulus, Indonesian Chinese, Egyptian Copts, and many other groups call forth competing theories about legal pluralism and the relative authority of the state. Added to such cases are the challenges of governance of new forms of transnational association. The shift toward state legal hegemony has not foreclosed possibilities for the emergence of alternative legal authorities centered in ethnic subpolities or cross-border communities. Nor does the institutional continuity provided by jurisdictional fluidity in the early modern period offer a model for a future of diminished states. If anything, the knowledge that pluralist visions of the law

p. 163). The case studies of this book have examined precisely the important contribution of complex legal politics in producing a space for the colonial state and the nonmodular nature of global reproduction of that politics.

contributed to state making should suggest that state *un*making (or re-making) would involve another historical shift matching widespread legal and cultural reordering. Struggles surrounding such a shift would invoke many of the old routines for organizing difference, with some groups claiming that these patterns are immutable products of one or another legal tradition. We should beware of such claims. And we should look to seemingly small struggles over cultural boundaries in the law as having a potentially profound impact on new structures of power everywhere.

Bibliography

PRINCIPAL ARCHIVAL COLLECTIONS

India Office Records (IOR), British Library, London.

Records of the Colonial Office (CO), Public Record Office (PRO), London.

France V. Scholes Collection, Center for Southwest Research, University of New Mexico, Albuquerque.

Archivo General de la Nación (AGN), Montevideo.

Archivo General de la Nación, Sección Judicial (AGNJ), Montevideo.

Archivo de Relaciones Exteriores (ARE), Montevideo.

SECONDARY AND PUBLISHED PRIMARY SOURCES

Abou-El-Haj, Rifaʿat ʿAli. 1991. *Formation of the Modern State: The Ottoman Empire, Sixteenth to Eighteenth Centuries.* Albany: State University of New York Press.

Abu-Lughod, Janet. 1989. *Before European Hegemony: The World System, A.D. 1250–1350.* New York: Oxford University Press.

Acevedo, Eduardo. 1908. *Eduardo Acevedo, años 1815–1863: Su obra como codificador, ministro, legislador y periodista.* Montevideo: Imprenta el Siglo Ilustrado.

Acosta y Lara, Eduardo F. 1998. *La Guerra de los Charrúas.* Montevideo: Talleres de Loreto Editores.

Adelman, Jeremy. 1999. *Republic of Capital: Buenos Aires and the Legal Transformation of the Atlantic World.* Stanford, CA: Stanford University Press.

ed. 1999. *Colonial Legacies: The Problem of Persistence in Latin America.* New York and London: Routledge.

Alden, Dauril. 1996. *The Making of an Enterprise: The Society of Jesus in Portugal, Its Empire, and Beyond 1540–1750.* Stanford, CA: Stanford University Press.

Allot, Antony. 1960. *Essays in African Law, with Special Reference to the Law of Ghana.* London: Butterworths.

Anderson, Benedict. 2000 [1983]. *Imagined Communities: Reflections on the Origin and Spread of Nationalism.* London and New York: Verso.

Anderson, Michael R. 1993. "Islamic Law and the Colonial Encounter in British India." In *Institutions and Ideologies,* edited by David Arnold and Peter Robb, pp. 165–85. Trawbridge, Wiltshire: Redwood Books.

Appadurai, Arjun. 1998 [1996]. *Modernity at Large: Cultural Dimensions of Globalization.* Minneapolis and London: University of Minnesota Press.

Arnold, David. 1985. "Crime and Crime Control in Madras, 1858–1947." In *Crime and Criminality in British India,* edited by Anand Yang, pp. 62–88. Tucson, AZ: University of Arizona Press.

Baepler, Paul, ed. 1999. *White Slaves, African Masters: An Anthology of American Barbary Captivity Narratives.* Chicago: University of Chicago Press.

Baepler, Paul. 1999. Introduction. In *White Slaves, African Masters: An Anthology of American Barbary Captivity Narratives,* edited by Paul Baepler, pp. 1–58. Chicago: University of Chicago Press.

Baretta, Silvio Rogério Duncan, and John Markoff. 1978. "Civilization and Barbarism: Cattle Frontiers in Latin America." *Comparative Studies in Society and History* 20: 587–620.

Barkey, Karen. 1996. "In Different Times: Scheduling and Social Control in the Ottoman Empire, 1550–1650." *Comparative Studies in Society and History* 38 (3): 460–83.

Barrán, José Pedro. 1974. *Apogeo y crisis del Uruguay pastoril y caudillesco, 1838–1875,* Montevideo: Ediciones de la Banda Oriental.

Barrán, José Pedro, and Benjamin Nahum. 1967. *Historia rural del Uruguay moderno, Volume I (1851–1885).* Montevideo: Ediciones de la Banda Oriental.

Bayly, Christopher. 2001. "From Archaic Globalisation to International Networks, c. 1600–2000." Keynote address delivered at the conference "Interactions: Regional Studies, Global Processes, and Historical Analysis," March 2–4, 2001, Washington, DC.

Bell, Stephen. 1998. *Campanha Gaúcha: A Brazilian Ranching System, 1850–1920.* Stanford, CA: Stanford University Press.

Benton, Lauren. 1996. "From the World Systems Perspective to Institutional World History: Culture and Economy in Global Theory." *Journal of World History* 7 (2): 261–95.

   1994. "Beyond Legal Pluralism: Towards a New Approach to Law in the Informal Sector." *Social and Legal Studies* 3: 223–42.

Berman, Harold. 1983. *Law and Revolution: The Formation of the Western Legal Tradition.* Cambridge, MA: Harvard University Press.

Beyers, Michael. 1999. *Custom, Power, and the Power of Rules: International Relations and Customary International Law.* Cambridge: Cambridge University Press.

Bhabba, Homi. 1997. "Of Mimicry and Man: The Ambivalence of Colonial Discourse." In *Tensions of Empire,* edited by Frederick Cooper and Ann Laura Stoler, pp. 152–62. Berkeley: University of California Press.

Blaut, J.M. 1993. *The Colonizer's Model of the World: Geographical Diffusionism and Eurocentric History.* New York: Guilford Press.

Borah, Woodrow. 1983. *Justice by Insurance: The General Indian Court of Colonial Mexico and the Legal Aides of the Half-Real*. Berkeley: University of California Press.

Bourdieu, Philippe. 1977. *Outline of a Theory of Practice*. Cambridge: Cambridge University Press.

Boxer, C.R. 1969. *The Portuguese Seaborne Empire, 1415–1825*. New York: A.A. Knopf.

Bradstadter, Edith. 1985. "Human Sacrifice and British Kond Relations, 1759–1862." In *Crime and Criminality in British India*, edited by Anand Yang, pp. 89–127. Tucson, AZ: University of Arizona Press.

Braude, Benjamin. 1982. "Foundation Myths of the *Millet* System." In *Christians and Jews in the Ottoman Empire: The Functioning of a Plural Society, Vol. I*, edited by Benjamin Braude and Bernard Lewis, pp. 69–88. New York and London: Holmes & Meier.

Braude, Benjamin, and Bernard Lewis. 1982. "Introduction." In *Christians and Jews in the Ottoman Empire: The Functioning of a Plural Society, Vol. I*, edited by Benjamin Braude and Bernard Lewis, pp. 1–34. New York and London: Holmes & Meier.

Brodman, James William. 1986. *Ransoming Captives in Crusader Spain: The Order of Merced on the Christian-Islamic Frontier*. Philadelphia: University of Pennsylvania Press.

Brundage, James. 1995. *Medieval Canon Law*. New York: Longman.

Burman, Sandra, and Barbara E. Harrell-Bond, eds. 1979. *The Imposition of Law*. New York: Academic Press.

Burns, Robert. 1973. *Islam Under the Crusaders: Colonial Survival in the Thirteenth-Century Kingdom of Valencia*. Princeton, NJ: Princeton University Press.

Byrne, Paula J. 1993. *Criminal Law and Colonial Subject: New South Wales, 1810–1830*. Cambridge: Cambridge University Press.

Calloway, Colin G. 1992. *North Country Captives: Selected Narratives of Indian Captivity from Vermont and New Hampshire*. Hanover and London: University Press of New England.

Cannon, Byron. 1988. *Politics of Law and the Courts in Nineteenth-Century Egypt*. Salt Lake City: University of Utah Press.

Carrol, Patrick. 1977. "Mandinga: The Evolution of a Mexican Runaway Slave Community, 1735–1827." *Comparative Studies in Society and History* 19: 488–505.

Carter, Paul. 1987. *The Road to Botany Bay: An Exploration of Landscape and History*. Chicago: University of Chicago Press.

Castañeda Delgado, Paulino, and Pilar Hernández Aparicio. 1989. *La Inquisición de Lima, Vol. 1*. Madrid: Demos.

Castells, Manuel. 1997. *The Power of Identity: The Information Age – Economy, Society, and Culture, Vol. 2*. New York: Blackwell.

Castles, Alex. 1982. *An Australian Legal History*. Sydney: The Law Book Company Limited.

Cathcart, James Leander. 1999 [1899]. "The Captives, Eleven Years a Prisoner in Algiers." In *White Slaves, African Masters*, edited by Baepler, pp. 105–46. Chicago: University of Chicago Press.

Chanock, Martin. 1991. "Paradigms, Policies, and Property: A Review of the Customary Law of Land Tenure." In *Law in Colonial Africa*, edited by Kristin Mann and Richard Roberts, pp. 61–84. Portsmouth, NH: Heinemann.

1985. *Law, Custom, and Social Order: The Colonial Experience in Malawi and Zambia*. Cambridge: Cambridge University Press.

Chasteen, John Charles. 1995. *Heroes on Horseback: A Life and Times of the Last Gaucho Caudillos*. Albuquerque: University of New Mexico Press.

Chaterjee, Partha. 1993. *The Nation and Its Fragments: Colonial and Postcolonial Histories*. Princeton, NJ: Princeton University Press.

Clendinnen, Inga. 1987. *Ambivalent Conquests: Maya and Spaniard in Yucatan, 1517–1570*. Cambridge and New York: Cambridge University Press.

Cohen, Ammon. 1984. *Jewish Life Under Islam: Jerusalem in the Sixteenth Century*. Cambridge, MA: Harvard University Press.

Cohn, Bernard. 1996. *Colonialism and Its Forms of Knowledge: The British in India*. Princeton, NJ: Princeton University Press.

1961. "From Indian Status to British Contract." *Journal of Economic History* 21 (4): 613–28.

1961. "The British in Benares: A Nineteenth-Century Colonial Society." *Comparative Studies in Society and History* 4: 169–99.

Comaroff, John, and Jean Comaroff. 1991. *Of Revelation and Revolution: Christianity, Colonialism, and Consciousness*. Chicago: University of Chicago Press.

Conklin, Alice. 1997. *A Mission to Civilize: The Republican Idea of Empire in France and West Africa, 1895–1930*. Stanford, CA: Stanford University Press.

Conrad, Joseph. 1996. *Nostromo*. New York: Wordsworth Editions Limited.

Conrad, Robert Edgar. 1984. *Children of God's Fire: A Documentary History of Black Slavery in Brazil*. University Park, PA: Pennsylvania State University Press.

Cope, R. Douglas. 1994. *The Limits of Racial Domination: Plebeian Society in Colonial Mexico City, 1660–1720*. Madison, WI: University of Wisconsin Press.

Coulson, N.J. 1964. *A History of Islamic Law*. Edinburgh: Edinburgh University Press.

Crais, Clifton. 1992. *White Supremacy and Black Resistance in Pre-Industrial South Africa: The Making of the Colonial Order in the Eastern Cape*. Cambridge: Cambridge University Press.

Craton, Michael. 1997. *Empire, Enslavement, and Freedom in the Caribbean*. Kingston: I. Randle Publishers; Princeton, NJ: Marcus Wiener Publishers.

1982. *Testing the Chains: Resistance to Slavery in the British West Indies*. Ithaca: Cornell University Press.

Crowder, Michael. 1967. *Senegal: A Study of French Assimilation Policy*. London: Methuen.

Cruise O'Brien, Donal. 1967. "Towards an 'Islamic Policy' in French West Africa, 1854–1914." *Journal of African History* 8 (2): 303–16.

Cuoq, Joseph M., ed. and trans. 1975. *Recueil des sources Arabes concernant l'Afrique occidentale du VIIIe au XVIe siècle (Bilad Al-Sudan)*. Paris: Éditions du Centre National de la Recherche Scientifique.

Curtin, Philip. 1999. "Location in History: Argentina and South Africa in the Nineteenth Century." *Journal of World History* 10 (1): 41–92.

1984. *Cross-Cultural Trade in World History*. Cambridge and New York: Cambridge University Press.

1975. *Economic Change in Precolonial Africa: Senegambia in the Era of the Slave Trade*. Madison, WI: University of Wisconsin Press.

Cutter, Charles. 1995. *The Legal Culture of Northern New Spain, 1700–1810*. Albuquerque: University of New Mexico Press.

1994. "Community and the Law in Northern New Spain." *The Americas* 4: 467–80.

1986. *The Protector de Indios in Colonial New Mexico, 1659–1821*. Albuquerque: University of New Mexico Press, 1986.

D'Amato, Anthony. 1971. *The Concept of Culture in International Law*. Ithaca and London: Cornell University Press.

Delgado, Richard. 1995. *Critical Race Theory: The Cutting Edge*. Philadelphia: Temple University Press.

Derrett, J. Duncan M. 1963. "Justice, Equity, and Good Conscience." In *Changing Law in Developing Countries*, edited by J.N.D. Anderson, pp. 113–53. London: George Allen & Unwin.

1961–62. "The Ministration of Hindu Law by the British." *Comparative Studies of Society and History* 4: 10–52.

Dhavan, Rajeev. 1989. Introduction. In *Law and Society in Modern India*, by Marc Galanter, pp. xiii-c. Delhi: Oxford University Press.

Dillard, Heath. 1984. *Daughters of the Reconquest: Women in Castilian Town Society, 1100–1300*. Cambridge: Cambridge University Press.

Eaton, Richard M. 1993. *The Rise of Islam and the Bengal Frontier, 1204–1760*. Berkeley: University of California Press.

Ellickson, Robert. 1990. *Order Without Law: How Neighbors Settle Disputes*. Cambridge: Cambridge University Press.

Elliott, Mark. 1999. "Race, Color-Blindness, and the Democratic Public." Paper presented at the Legal History Colloquium, New York University Law School, January 20.

Elphick, Richard. 1985. *Khoikhoi and the Founding of White South Africa*. Johannesburg: Raven Press.

Elphick, Richard, and Hermann Giliomee. 1988 [1979]. "The Origins and Entrenchment of European Dominance at the Cape, 1652–c. 1840." In *The Shaping of South African Society, 1652–1820*, edited by Richard Elphick and Hermann Giliomee, pp. 521–66. Middletown, CT: Wesleyan University Press.

Elphick, Richard, and V.C. Malherbe. 1988 [1979]. "The Khoisan to 1828." In *The Shaping of South African Society, 1652–1820*, edited by Richard Elphick and Hermann Giliomee, pp. 3–65. Middletown, CT: Wesleyan University Press.

Engels, Dagmar. 1992. "Wives, Widows, and Workers: Women and the Law in Colonial India." In *European Expansion and Law*, edited by W.J. Mommsen and J.A. de Moor, pp. 159–200. New York: Berg.

Equiano, Olaudah, Mary Rowlandson, and Others. 2000. *American Captivity Narratives*, edited by Gordon M. Sayre. Boston and New York: Houghton Mifflin.

Ewing, K.I., ed. 1988. *Shariʿat and Ambiguity in South Asian Islam.* Berkeley: University of California Press.

Faroque, Suraiya, and Cornell Fleischer. 1991. Preface. In *Formation of the Modern State: The Ottoman Empire, Sixteenth to Eighteenth Centuries*, by Rifaʿat ʿAli Abou-El-Haj, pp. ix–xvii. Albany: State University of New York Press.

Farriss, Nancy. 1968. *Crown and Clergy in Colonial Mexico, 1759–1821: The Crisis of Ecclesiastical Privilege.* London: Athlone.

Fasseur, C. 1992. "Colonial Dilemma: Van Vollenhoven and the Struggle Between Adat Law and Western Law in Indonesia." In *European Expansion and Law*, edited by W.J. Mommsen and J.A. de Moor, pp. 237–256. New York: Berg.

Fawcett, Sir Charles. 1934. *The First Century of British Justice in India.* Oxford University Press.

Fay, Peter Ward. 1997 [1975]. *The Opium War, 1840–1842.* Chapel Hill: University of North Carolina Press.

Fishel, Wesley R. 1952. *The End of Extraterritoriality in China.* Berkeley: University of California Press.

Fisher, Allan G. B., and Humphrey J. Fisher. 1970. *Slavery and Muslim Society in Africa: The Institution in Saharan and Sudanic Africa and the Trans-Sahrara Trade.* London: C. Hurst.

Fisher, Michael. 1991. *Indirect Rule in India: Residents and the Residency System, 1764–1858.* London and New York: Oxford University Press.

Fitzpatrick, Peter. 1983. "Law, Plurality, and Underdevelopment." In *Legality, Ideology, and the State*, edited by David Sugarman, pp. 159–82. London and New York: Academic Press.

Flint, John. 1978. "Frederick Lugard: The Making of an Autocrat (1858–1943)." In *African Proconsuls: European Governors in Africa*, edited by L.H. Gann and Peter Duigman, pp. 290–312. New York: The Free Press.

Flory, Thomas. 1981. *Judge and Jury in Imperial Brazil, 1808–1871: Social Control and Political Stability in the New State.* Austin and London: University of Texas Press.

Foss, John. 1999. "A Journal of the Captivity and Sufferings of John Foss." In *White Slaves, African Masters*, edited by Paul Baepler, pp. 73–102. Chicago: University of Chicago Press.

Forster, E. M. 1958 [1924]. *A Passage to India.* New York and London: Harcourt Brace.

Frank, Andre Gunder. 1998. *ReOrient: Global Economy in the Asian Age.* Berkeley: University of California Press.

——— 1991. "A Plea for World System History." *Journal of World History* 2 (1): 1–28.

Frederick, Bonnie. 1993. "Fatal Journeys, Fatal Legends: The Journey of the Captive Woman in Argentina and Uruguay." In *Women and the Journey: The Female Travel Experience*, edited by Bonnie Frederick and Susan H. McLeod, pp. 85–99. Pullman, WA: Washington State University Press.

Frederick, Bonnie, and Susan H. McLeod, eds. 1993. *Women and the Journey: The Female Travel Experience.* Pullman, WA: Washington State University Press.

Friedman, Ellen G. 1983. *Spanish Captives in North Africa in the Early Modern Age.* Madison, WI: University of Wisconsin Press.

Friedman, Jonathan. 1994. *Cultural Identity and Global Process*. New York: Sage.

Galanter, Marc. 1989. *Law and Society in Modern India*. Delhi: Oxford University Press.

Gerber, Haim. 1994. *State, Society, and Law in Islam: Ottoman Law in Comparative Perspective*. Albany: State University of New York Press.

Gibb, Sir Hamilton, and Harold Bowen. 1960 [1950]. *Islamic Society and the West: A Study of the Impact of Western Civilization on Moslem Culture in the Near East*. London and New York: Oxford University Press.

Giliomee, Hermann. 1988 [1979]. "The Burgher Rebellions in the Eastern Frontier, 1795–1815." In *The Shaping of South African Society, 1652–1820*, edited by Richard Elphick and Hermann Giliomee, pp. 338–56. Middletown, CT: Wesleyan University Press.

—— 1988 [1979]. "The Eastern Frontier, 1770–1812." In *The Shaping of South African Society, 1652–1820*, edited by Richard Elphick and Hermann Giliomee, pp. 421–71. Middletown, CT: Wesleyan University Press.

Goodblatt, Morris S. 1952. *Jewish Life in Turkey in the XVIth Century As Reflected in the Legal Writings of Samuel de Medina*. New York: Maurice Jacoby.

Granovetter, Mark. 1985. "Economic Action and Social Structure: The Problem of Social Embeddedness." *American Journal of Sociology* 91: 481–510.

Greenblatt, Stephen. 1991. *Marvelous Possessions: The Wonder of the New World*. Chicago: University of Chicago Press.

Greenleaf, Richard. 1990. "Historiography of the Spanish Inquisition: Evolution of Interpretations and Methodologies." In *Cultural Encounters: The Impact of the Inquisition in Spain and the New World*, edited by Mary Elizabeth Perry and Anne J. Cruz, pp. 248–76. Berkeley: University of California Press.

—— 1965. "The Inquisition and the Indians of New Spain: A Study in Jurisdictional Confusion." *The Americas* 22: 138–66.

Griffiths, J. 1986. "What Is Legal Pluralism?" *Journal of Legal Pluralism* 24 (1): 1–55.

Groff, David. 1991. "The Dynamics of Collaboration and the Rule of Law in French West Africa: The Case of Kwame Kangah of Assikasso (Côte d'Ivoire), 1898–1922." In *Law in Colonial Africa*, edited by Kristin Mann and Richard Roberts, pp. 146–66. Portsmouth, NH : Heinemann.

Guha, Ranajit. 1997. *Dominance Without Hegemony: History and Power in Colonial India*. Cambridge, MA: Harvard University Press.

—— 1996 (1963). *A Rule of Property for Bengal*. Durham, NC: Duke University Press.

Gutierrez, Ramon. 1991. *When Jesus Came, the Corn Mothers Went Away: Marriage, Sexuality, and Power in New Mexico, 1500–1846*. Stanford, CA: Stanford University Press.

Hackett, Charles Wilson, ed. 1937. *Historical Documents Relating to New Mexico, Nueva Vizcaya, and Approaches Thereto, Vol. III*. New York: Carnegie Institution.

Hallaq, Wael. 1984. "Was the Gate of Ijtihad Closed?" *International Journal of Middle East Studies* 16 (1): 3–41.

Hann, C.M., ed. 1998. *Property Relations: Renewing the Anthropological Tradition*. Cambridge: Cambridge University Press.

1998. "Introduction: The Embeddedness of Property." In *Property Relations: Renewing the Anthropological Tradition,* edited by C.M. Hann, pp. 1–47. Cambridge: Cambridge University Press.

Hasenclever, Andreas, Peter Mayer, and Volker Rittberger. 1996. "Interests, Power, Knowledge: The Study of International Regimes." *Mershon International Studies Review* 40: 177–228.

Richard Hart. 1985. *Slaves Who Abolished Slavery, Vol. 2: Blacks in Rebellion.* Kingston, Jamaica: Institute of Social and Economic Research, University of the West Indies.

Harvey, L.P. 1990. *Islamic Spain: 1250–1500.* Chicago: University of Chicago Press.

Hay, Douglas, Peter Linebaugh, John G. Rule, E.P. Thompson, and Cal Winslow, eds. 1975. *Albion's Fatal Tree: Crime and Society in Eighteenth-Century England.* New York: Pantheon Books.

Hay, Douglas, and Paul Craven. 1994. "The Criminalization of 'Free' Labor: Master and Servant Law in Comparative Perspective." *Slavery and Abolition* 15 (2): 71–92.

Hebb, David Delison. 1994. *Piracy and the English Government, 1616–1642.* Aldershot, England: Scolar Press.

Hilton, Anne. 1985. *The Kingdom of Kongo.* Oxford and New York: Clarendon Press; Oxford University Press.

Hobsbawm, E.J. 1968. *Industry and Empire.* London: Penguin Books.

Hodgson, Marshall G.S. 1993. *Rethinking World History: Essays on Europe, Islam, and World History.* Cambridge: Cambridge University Press.

Hooker, M.B. 1975. *Legal Pluralism: An Introduction to Colonial and Neo-Colonial Laws.* Oxford: Clarendon Press.

Huang, Philip. 1996. *Civil Justice in China: Representation and Practice in the Qing.* Stanford, CA: Stanford University Press.

Hudson, W.H. 1904. *The Purple Land: Being the Narrative of One Richard Lamb's Adventures in the Banda Oriental, in South America, As Told by Himself.* New York: Three Sirens Press.

Hull, Richard W. 1976. *African Cities and Towns Before the European Conquest.* New York: Norton.

Inalcik, Halil. 1989 [1973]. *The Ottoman Empire: The Classical Age 1300–1600.* New Rochelle, NY: Orpheus Publishing.

1978. *The Ottoman Empire: Conquest, Organization, and Economy.* London: Variorum.

Jenkins, Myra Ellen. 1966. "Taos Pueblo and Her Neighbors." *New Mexico Historical Review* 41 (2) 85–114.

Jennings, Ronald C. 1993. *Christians and Muslims in Ottoman Cyprus and the Mediterranean World, 1571–1640,* New York and London: New York University Press.

Johansen, Baber. 1999. *Contingency in a Sacred Law: Legal and Ethical Norms in the Muslim Fiqh.* Leiden: Brill (Studies in Islamic Law and Society).

Jones, Francis C. 1931. *Extraterritoriality in Japan, and the Diplomatic Relations Resulting in Its Abolition, 1853–1899.* New York: AMS Press.

Kagan, Richard. 1981. *Lawsuits and Litigants in Castile, 1500–1700.* Chapel Hill, NC: University of North Carolina Press.

Karpat, Kemal H. 1982. "*Millets* and Nationality: The Roots of the Incongruity of Nation and State in the Post-Ottoman Era." In *Christians and Jews in the Ottoman Empire: The Functioning of a Plural Society, Vol. I,* edited by Benjamin Braude and Bernard Lewis, pp. 141–69. New York and London: Holmes & Meier.

Kasaba, Resat. 1994. "A Time and a Place for the Nonstate: Social Changes in the Ottoman Empire During the Long Nineteenth Century." In *State Power and Social Forces: Domination and Transformation in the Third World,* edited by Joel Migdal, Anil Kohli, and Vivienne Shue, pp. 207–30. Cambridge: Cambridge University Press.

Keegan, Timothy. 1996. *Colonial South Africa and the Origins of the Racial Order.* Charlottesville, VA: University of Virginia Press.

Keeton, George Williams. 1928. *The Development of Extraterritoriality in China, Vol. I.* New York: Longmans.

Kellogg, Susan. 1995. *Law and the Transformation of Aztec Culture.* Norman, OK: University of Oklahoma Press.

Kent, R.K. 1965. "Palmares: An African State in Brazil." *Journal of African History* 6 (2): 161–75.

Kercher, Bruce. 1999. "White Fellow Eat Bandicoots & Black Snakes Now: Aborigines, Law, and Resistance in the Supreme Court of New South Wales under Francis Forbes." Paper presented at the meetings of the American Society for Legal History, Toronto.

1999. "Native Title in the Shadows: The Origins of the Myth of *Terra Nullius* in Early New South Wales Courts." Paper presented at the World History Association meetings, Victoria, Canada.

1996. *Debt, Seduction, and Other Disasters: The Birth of Civil Law in Convict New South Wales.* Sydney: Federation Press.

1995. *An Unruly Child: A History of Law in Australia.* St. Leonards, NSW, Australia: Allen & Unwin.

Klor de Alva, Jorge. 1990. "Colonizing Souls: The Failure of the Indian Inquisition and the Rise of Penitential Discipline." In *Cultural Encounters: The Impact of the Inquisition in Spain and the New World,* edited by Mary Elizabeth Perry and Anne J. Cruz, pp. 3–22. Berkeley: University of California Press.

Krasner, Stephen. 1985. *Structural Conflict: The Third World Against Global Liberalism.* Berkeley: University of California Press.

1984. "Approaches to the State: Alternative Conceptions and Historical Dynamics." *Comparative Politics* 16 (2): 223–46.

1983. "Structural Causes and Regime Consequences: Regimes As International Variables." In *International Regimes,* edited by Stephen Krasner, pp. 1–21. Ithaca: Cornell University Press.

Kratochwil, Frederich V. 1989. *Rules, Norms, and Decisions on the Conditions of Practical and Legal Reasoning in International Relations and Domestic Affairs.* Cambridge: Cambridge University Press.

Kubálková, Vendulka, Nicholas Onuf, and Paul Kowert, eds. 1998. *International Relations in a Constructed World.* Armonk, NY: M.E. Sharpe.

Lapid, Yosef, and Friedrich Kratochwil, eds. 1996. *The Return of Culture and Identity in IR Theory.* Boulder, CO: Lynne Rienner.

Lariviere, Richard. 1989. "Justices and *Panditas*: Some Ironies in Contemporary Readings of the Hindu Past." *Journal of Asian Studies* 48: 757–69.

Léry, Jean de. 1992. *A History of a Voyage to the Land of Brazil,* translation and introduction by Janet Whatley. Berkeley: University of California Press.

Leue, J. J. 1992. "Legal Expansion in the Age of the Companies: Aspects of the Administration of Justice in the English and Dutch Settlements of Maritime Asia, c. 1600–1750." In *European Expansion and Law,* edited by W. J. Mommsen and J.A. de Moor, pp. 129–58. New York: Berg.

Lewis, Bernard. 1993. *Islam and the West.* New York: Oxford University Press.
    1984. *The Jews of Islam.* Princeton, N J: Princeton University Press.

Lockhart, James. 1992. *The Nahuas After the Conquest.* Stanford, CA: Stanford University Press.

Lorcin, Patricia. 1999. *Imperial Identities: Stereotyping, Prejudice, and Race in Colonial Algeria.* London and New York: IB Taurus.

Lovejoy, Paul. 1983. *Transformations in Slavery: A History of Slavery in Africa.* Cambridge: Cambridge University Press.

Lynch, John. 1992. "The Institutional Framework of Colonial Spanish America." *Journal of Latin American Studies* 24: 69–81.

MacCaulay, Stuart. 1963. "Non-Contractual Relations in Business." *American Sociological Review* 28: 55–66.

MacLachlan, Colin M. 1988. *Spain's Empire in the New World: The Role of Ideas in Institutional and Social Change.* Berkeley: University of California Press.

Mani, Lata. 1985. "The Production of Official Discourse on *Sati* in Early-Nineteenth-Century Bengal." In *Europe and Its Others Vol. I, Proceedings of the Essex Conference on the Sociology of Literature, July 1984,* edited by Francis Barker, Peter Hulme, Margaret Iversen, and Diana Loxley, pp. 107–27. Colchester: University of Essex.

Mann, Kristin, and Richard Roberts. 1991. *Law in Colonial Africa.* Portsmouth, NH: Heinemann.

Manning, Patrick. 1990. *Slavery and African Life: Occidental, Oriental, and African Slave Trades.* Cambridge: Cambridge University Press.

Marks, Shula. 1972. "Khoisan Resistance to the Dutch in the Seventeenth and Eighteenth Centuries." *Journal of African History* 20: 55–80.

Marques, A.H. de Oliveira. 1976. *History of Portugal, Vol. I.* New York: Columbia University Press.

Martin, Maria. 1999 [1807]. "History of the Captivity and Sufferings of Mrs. Maria Martin." In *White Slaves, African Masters,* edited by Paul Baepler, pp. 149–57. Chicago: University of Chicago Press.

Masud, Muhammad Khalid, Brinkley Messick, and David S. Powers, eds. 1996. *Islamic Legal Interpretation: Muftis and Their Fatwas.* Cambridge, MA: Harvard University Press.

Matar, Nabil. 1999. *Turks, Moors, and Englishmen in the Age of Discovery.* New York: Columbia University Press.

Mather, Cotton. 2000 [1702]. "A Notable Exploit; Wherein, Dux Faemina Facti." In *American Captivity Narratives,* edited by Gordon M. Sayre, pp. 183–85. Boston and New York: Houghton Mifflin.

1999 [1703]. "The Glory of Goodness." In *White Slaves, African Masters: An Anthology of American Barbary Captivity Narratives*, edited by Paul Baepler, pp. 61–69. Chicago: University of Chicago Press.

McLean, David. 1995. *War, Diplomacy, and Informal Empire: Britain and the Republics of la Plata, 1836–1853*. London and New York: British Academic Press.

McNeill, William. 1993. "Preface." In *The World System: Five Hundred Years or Five Thousand*, edited by Andre Gunder Frank and Barry Gills, pp. xv–xxii. London: Routledge.

Mecham, J. Lloyd. 1966 [1934]. *Church and State in Latin America: A History of Politico-Ecclesiastical Relations*. Chapel Hill: University of North Carolina Press.

Merry, Sally Engle. 2000. *Colonizing Hawai'i: The Cultural Power of Law*. Princeton, NJ: Princeton University Press.

1988. "Legal Pluralism." *Law and Society Review* 22(5): 869–96.

Miers, Suzanne, and Igor Kopytoff. 1977. "Introduction." In *Slavery in Africa: Historical and Anthropological Perspectives*, edited by Suzanne Miers and Igor Kopytoff, pp. 3–81. Madison, WI: University of Wisconsin Press.

Millis, Roger. 1992. *Waterloo Creek: The Australia Day Massacre of 1838, George Gipps, and the British Conquest of New South Wales*. Ringwood, Victoria: Penguin.

Mills, Kenneth. 1997. *Idolatry and Its Enemies: Colonial Andean Religion and Extirpation, 1640–1750*. Princeton, NJ: Princeton University Press.

Mintz, Sidney. 1977. "The So-Called World System: Local Initiative and Local Response." *Dialectical Anthropology* 2 (4): 253–70.

Mirow, M.C. 2000. "The Power of Codification in Latin America: Simón Bolívar and the *Code Napoléon*." *Tulane Journal of International and Comparative Law* 8: 83–116.

Misra, B.B. 1961. *The Judicial Administration of the East India Company in Bengal, 1765–82*. Delhi: Motilal Banarsidass.

Mitchell, Timothy. 1991. *Colonising Egypt*. Berkeley: University of California Press.

Mokhiber, James. 1990. "Forms of Authority and the Ordering of Empire: The Native Justice System in Colonial Senegal, 1903–1912." B.A. honors thesis, Department of History, Stanford University.

Moon, Penderel. 1949. *Warren Hastings and British India*. New York: Macmillan Company.

Moore, Sally Falk. 1986. *Social Facts and Fabrications: "Customary" Law on Kilimanjaro, 1880–1980*. Cambridge and New York: Cambridge University Press.

Moreno de los Arcos, Roberto. 1990. "New Spain's Inquisition for Indians from the Sixteenth to the Nineteenth Century." In *Cultural Encounters: The Impact of the Inquisition in Spain and the New World*, edited by Mary Elizabeth Perry and Anne J. Cruz, pp. 23–36. Berkeley: University of California Press.

Mota, A. Teixeira da, and P.E.H. Hair. 1988. *East of Mina: Afro-European Relations on the Gold Coast in the 1550s and 1560s: An Essay with Supporting Documents*. Madison, WI: African Studies Program, University of Wisconsin-Madison.

Muldoon, James. 1979. *Popes, Lawyers, and Infidels: The Church and the Non-Christian World, 1250–1550.* Philadelphia: University of Pennsylvania Press.
  1975. "The Indian As Irishman." *Essex Institute Historical Collections III* 4: 267–289.
Neal, David. 1991. *The Rule of Law in a Penal Colony: Law and Power in Early New South Wales.* Cambridge: Cambridge University Press.
Newton-King, Susan. 1980. "The Labour Market of the Cape Colony, 1807–28." In *Economy and Society in Pre-Industrial South Africa,* edited by Shula Marks and Anthony Atmore, pp. 171–207. London: Longman.
Nicoliello, Nelson, and Luis A. Vázquez Praderi. 1997. *Crónicas de la Justicia en el Uruguay.* Montevideo: Suprema Corte de Justicia.
North, Douglass. 1990. *Institutions, Institutional Change, and Economic Performance.* Cambridge: Cambridge University Press.
Obeyesekere, Gananath. 1992. *The Apotheosis of Captain Cook: European Mythmaking in the Pacific.* Princeton, NJ: Princeton University Press.
Odell, John. 1982. *U.S. International Monetary Policy: Markets, Power, and Ideas As Sources of Change.* Princeton, NJ: Princeton University Press.
Orucu, Esin. 1992. "The Impact of European Law on the Ottoman Empire and Turkey." In *European Expansion and Law,* edited by W. J. Mommsen and J.A. de Moor, pp. 39–58. New York: Berg.
Pagden, Anthony. 1995. *Lords of All the World: Ideologies of Empire in Spain, Britain, and France c. 1500–c. 1800.* New Haven and London: Yale University Press.
Parry, J.H. 1948. *The Audiencia of New Galicia in the Sixteenth Century: A Study in Spanish Colonial Government.* Cambridge: Cambridge University Press.
Paul, John Jeya. 1986. "Vakils of Madras, 1802–1928: The Rise of the Modern Legal Profession in South India." Ph.D. diss., University of Wisconsin, Madison.
Pearson, M.N. 1987. *The Portuguese in India, The New Cambridge History of India, I.* Cambridge: Cambridge University Press.
Pereira, Carlos Renato Gonçalves. 1964. *Historia da administraçao da justiça no Estado da Índia, século XVI, Vol I.* Lisbon: Agência-Geral do Ultramar.
Phelan, John Leddy. 1960. "Authority and Flexibility in the Spanish Imperial Bureaucracy." *Administrative Science Quarterly* 5: 47–65
Pivel Devoto, Juan E., and Alcira Ranieri de Pivel Devoto. 1973. *Uruguay a fines del siglo XIX.* Montevideo: Editorial Medina.
  1973. *Intentos de consolidación nacional, 1860–1875.* Montevideo: Editorial Medina.
Pospisil, Leopold. 1971. *Anthropology of Law.* London: Harper and Row.
Powers, David S. 1996. "*Kadijustiz* or Qadi Justice? A Paternity Dispute from Fourteenth-Century Morocco." In *Law, Morality, and Religion: Global Perspectives,* edited by Alan Watson, pp. 123–64. Berkeley: University of California Press.
  1992. "On Judicial Review in Islamic Law." *Law and Society Review* 6: 315–41.
Prakash, Gyan. 1994. "Subaltern Studies As Postcolonial Criticism." *American Historical Review* 99 (5) 1475–1490.
Price, Pamela. 1992. "The 'Popularity' of the Imperial Courts of Law: Three Views of the Anglo-Indian Encounter." In *European Expansion and Law,*

edited by W. J. Mommsen and J.A. de Moor, pp. 179–200. New York: Berg.

Price, Richard. 1996. "Palmares come poderia ter sido." In *Liberdade por um fio: História dos quilombos no Brasil*, edited by João José Reis and Flávio dos Santos Gomes, pp. 52–9. São Paulo: Companhia das Letras.

——— 1990. *Alabi's World*. Baltimore, MD: Johns Hopkins University Press.

——— 1983. *First Time: The Historical Vision of an Afro-American People*. Baltimore, MD: Johns Hopkins University Press.

——— 1979. *Maroon Societies: Rebel Slave Communities in the Americas*. Baltimore, MD: Johns Hopkins University Press.

Priolkar, A.K. 1961. *The Goa Inquisition*. Bombay: Bombay University Press.

Ray, Rajat, and Ratna Ray. 1975. "Zamindars and Jotedars: A Study of Rural Politics in Bengal." *Modern Asian Studies* 9 (1) 81–102.

Reis, João José, and Flávio dos Santos Gomes, eds. 1996. *Liberdade por um fio: História dos quilombos no Brasil*. São Paulo: Companhia das Letras.

Reis, João José, and Flávio dos Santos Gomes. 1996. "Introdução – Uma história da liberdade." In *Liberdade por um fio: História dos quilombos no Brasil*, edited by João José Reis and Flávio dos Santos Gomes, pp. 9–25. São Paulo: Companhia das Letras.

Renteln, Alison Dundes, and Alan Dundes, eds. 1994. *Folk Law: Essays in the Theory and Practice of Lex Non Scripta, Vols. I and II*. Madison, WI: University of Wisconsin Press.

Reyes, A.F.T. 1986. "English and French Approaches to Personal Laws in South India, 1700–1850." Thesis submitted for the degree of doctor of philosophy in law, St. John's College, Cambridge, University Library, Cambridge.

Reynolds, Henry. 1996. *Aboriginal Sovereignty: Three Nations, One Australia?* Sydney: Allen & Unwin.

——— 1995 [1981]. *The Other Side of the Frontier: Aboriginal Resistance to the European Invasion of Australia*. Ringwood, Victoria: Penguin Books Australia.

——— 1987. *Frontier: Aborigines, Settlers, and Land*. Sydney: Allen & Unwin.

Roberts, Andrew. 1990. "The Imperial Mind." In *The Colonial Moment in Africa: Essays on the Movement of Minds and Materials, 1900–1940*, edited by Andrew Roberts, pp. 24–76. Cambridge: Cambridge University Press.

Roberts, Richard. 1991. "The Case of Faama Mademba Sy and the Ambiguities of Legal Jurisdiction in Colonial French Sudan." In *Law in Colonial Africa*, edited by Kristin Mann and Richard Roberts, pp. 185–203. Portsmouth, NH: Heinemann.

Roberts, Richard, and Kristin Mann. 1991. "Law in Colonial Africa." In *Law in Colonial Africa*, edited by Kristin Mann and Richard Roberts, pp. 3–58 . Portsmouth, NH: Heinemann.

Robinson, David. 1988. "French 'Islamic Policy' and Practice in Late-Nineteenth-Century Senegal." *Journal of African History* 29 (3): 415–36.

Robinson, F. Bruce. 1985. "Bandits and Rebellion in Nineteenth-Century Western India." In *Crime and Criminality in British India*, edited by Anand Yang, pp. 48–61. Tucson, AZ: University of Arizona Press.

Rodriguez, Jaime E. 1996. *The Independence of Spanish America*. Cambridge: Cambridge University Press.

Rosen, Lawrence. 2000. *The Justice of Islam: Comparative Perspectives on Islamic Law and Society.* London: Oxford University Press.

——— ed. 1995. *Other Intentions: Cultural Contexts and the Attribution of Inner States.* Santa Fe, NM: School of American Research Press.

——— 1991. "The Integrity of Cultures." *American Behavioral Scientist* 34 (4): 594–617.

——— 1989. *The Anthropology of Justice : Law As Culture in Islamic Society.* Cambridge: Cambridge University Press.

Rosenau, James N. 1997. *Along the Domestic-Foreign Frontier: Exploring Governance in a Turbulent World.* Cambridge: Cambridge University Press.

Ross, Robert. 1993. *Beyond the Pale: Essays on the History of Colonial South Africa.* Hanover and London: Wesleyan University Press.

Rowlandson, Mary. 2000 [1682]. "The Sovereignty and Goodness of God." In *American Captivity Narratives,* edited by Gordon M. Sayre, pp. 132–76. Boston and New York: Houghton Mifflin.

Russell-Wood, A.J.R. 1992. *A World on the Move: The Portuguese in Africa, Asia, and America, 1415–1808.* New York: St. Martin's Press.

Sachs, Albie. 1973. *Justice in South Africa.* London: Sussex University Press.

Sahlins, Marshall. 1995. *How "Natives" Think: About Captain Cook, for Example.* Chicago: University of Chicago Press.

Saladino, Gaspare. 1999. "Review of Peter Charles Hoffer, *Law and Peoples in Colonial America, Revised Edition.*" H-Law, H-Net Reviews, January 1999.

Sarr, Dominique, and Richard Roberts. 1991. "The Jurisdiction of Muslim Tribunals in Colonial Senegal, 1857–1932." In *Law in Colonial Africa,* edited by Kristin Mann and Richard Roberts, pp. 131–45. Portsmouth, NH: Heinemann.

Schacht, Joseph. 1964. *An Introduction to Islamic Law.* Oxford: Clarendon Press.

Schnapper, Bernard. 1961. "Les tribunaux musulmans et la politique coloniale au Sénégal (1830–1914)." *Revue historique de droit français et étranger* 39:90–128.

Scholes, France. 1942. *Troublous Times in New Mexico.* Albuquerque: University of New Mexico Press.

——— 1937. *Church and State in New Mexico, 1610–1650.* Albuquerque: University of New Mexico Press.

Schwartz, Stuart B. 1973. *Sovereignty and Society in Colonial Brazil: The High Court of Bahia and Its Judges, 1609–1751.* Berkeley: University of California Press.

Seed, Patricia. 1995. *Ceremonies of Possession in Europe's Conquest of the New World, 1492–1640.* Cambridge: Cambridge University Press.

Serulnikov, Sergio. 1996. "Disputed Images of Colonialism: Spanish Rule and Indian Subversion in Northern Potosí, 1777–1780." *Hispanic American Historical Review* 76 (2): 189–227.

Shapiro, Barbara J. 1991. *Beyond Reasonable Doubt and Probable Cause: Historical Perspectives on the Anglo-American Law of Evidence.* Berkeley: University of California Press.

Shirodkar, P. P. 1997. "Socio-Cultural Life in Goa During the 16th Century." In *Goa and Portugal: Their Cultural Links,* edited by Charles J. Borges and Helmut Feldman, pp. 23–40. New Delhi: Concept Publishing.

Simensen, Jarle. 1992. "Jurisdiction As Politics: The Gold Coast During the Colonial Period." In *European Expansion and Law*, edited by W.J. Mommsen and J.A. de Moor, pp. 257–77. New York: Berg.

Singha, Radhika. 1993. "Providential Circumstances: The Thugee Campaign of the 1830s and Legal Innovation." *Modern Asian Studies* 25 (1): 83–102.

Sinha, Mrinalini. 1992. "Chathams, Pitts, and Gladstones in Petticoats: The Politics of Gender and Race in the Ilbert Bill Controversy, 1883–84." In *Western Women and Imperialism: Complicity and Resistance*, edited by Nupur Chaudhuri and Margaret Strobel, pp. 98–116. Bloomington, IN: Indiana University Press.

Smith, Robert S. 1976. *Warfare and Diplomacy in Pre-Colonial West Africa*. Madison, WI: University of Wisconsin Press.

Staden, Hans. 2000 [1557]. "The True History of His Captivity." In *American Captivity Narratives*, edited by Gordon M. Sayre, pp. 21–58. Boston and New York: Houghton Mifflin.

Stallybrass, Peter, and Allan White. 1986. *The Politics and Poetics of Transgression*. Ithaca, NY: Cornell University Press.

Starr, June, and Jane F. Collier, eds. 1989. *History and Power in the Study of Law: New Directions in Legal Anthropology*. Ithaca, NY: Cornell University Press.

Stein, Peter. 1999. *Roman Law in European History*. Cambridge: Cambridge University Press.

Stephens, Thomas B. 1992. *Order and Discipline in China: The Shanghai Mixed Court 1911–1927*. Seattle and London: University of Washington Press.

Stern, Steve. 1982. *Peru's Indian Peoples and the Challenge of Spanish Conquest: Huamanga to 1640*. Madison, WI: University of Wisconsin Press.

Subrahmanyam, Sanjay. 1993. *The Portuguese Empire in Asia, 1500–1700: A Political and Economic History*. London and New York: Longman.

Thomas, Nicholas. 1994. *Colonialism's Culture: Anthropology, Travel, and Government*. Princeton, NJ: Princeton University Press.

Thompson, E.P. 1975. *Whigs and Hunters: The Origins of the Black Act*. New York: Pantheon Books.

———. 1971. "The Moral Economy of the English Crown in the Eighteenth Century." *Past and Present* 50: 76–136.

Thompson, Janice E. 1994. *Mercenaries, Pirates, and Sovereigns: State Building and Extraterritorial Violence in Early Modern Europe*. Princeton, NJ: Princeton University Press.

Thornton, John. 1992. *Africa and Africans in the Making of the Atlantic World, 1400–1680*. Cambridge: Cambridge University Press.

Tracy, James D., and Douglass North, eds. 1991. *The Political Economy of Merchant Empires*. Cambridge: Cambridge University Press.

Unger, Roberto Mangabeira. 1976. *Knowledge and Politics*. New York: Free Press.

Uribe Uran, Victor M. 2000. *Honorable Lives : Lawyers, Families, and Politics in Colombia, 1780–1850*. Pittsburgh: University of Pittsburgh Press.

Vogt, John. 1979. *Portuguese Rule on the Gold Coast, 1469–1682*. Athens, GA: University of Georgia Press.

Voll, John. 1994. "Islam As a Special World-System." *Journal of World History* 5: 213–26.

Walkowitz, Judith. 1992. *City of Dreadful Delight: Narratives of Sexual Danger in Late-Victorian London*. Chicago: University of Chicago Press.

Wasserstrom, Steve. 1995. *Between Muslim and Jew: The Problem of Symbiosis Under Early Islam*. Princeton, NJ: Princeton University Press.

Watson, Alan. 1989. *Slave Law in the Americas*. Athens, GA: University of Georgia Press.

White, Richard. 1991. *The Middle Ground: Indians, Empires, and Republics in the Great Lakes Region, 1650–1815*. Cambridge: Cambridge University Press.

Williams, Robert A. 1990. *The American Indian in Western Legal Thought: The Discourses of Conquest*. New York: Oxford University Press.

Wolf, Eric. 1999. *Envisioning Power: Ideologies of Dominance and Crisis*. Berkeley: University of California Press.

1982. *Europe and the People Without History*. Berkeley: University of California Press.

Yang, Anand. 1985. "Dangerous Castes and Tribes: The Criminal Tribes Act and the Magahiga Doms of Northeast India." In *Crime and Criminality in British India*, edited by Arnand Yang, pp. 108–27. Tucson, AZ: University of Arizona Press.

Ye'or, Bat. 1985. *The Dhimmis: Jews and Christians Under Islam*. London and Toronto: Associated University Press.

Young, Crawford. 1994. *The African Colonial State in Comparative Perspective*. New Haven and London: Yale University Press.

Yusuf, K.M. 1965. "The Judiciary in India Under the Sultans of Delhi and the Mughal Emperors." *Indo-Iranica* 18 (4): 1–12.

Index